CONRAD IN THE NINETEENTH CENTURY

By the same Author

THE RISE OF THE NOVEL

CONRAD
IN THE NINETEENTH CENTURY

IAN WATT

1980

CHATTO & WINDUS

LONDON

Published by
Chatto & Windus Ltd
40 William IV Street
London WC2N 4DF

*

Clarke, Irwin & Co. Ltd
Toronto

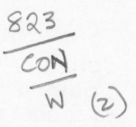

823
CON
W (2)

*British Library Cataloguing
in Publication Data*
Watt, Ian
  Conrad in the nineteenth century.
  1. Conrad, Joseph - Criticism and interpretation
  I. Title
  823'.9'12   PR6005.04Z/
  ISBN 0-7011-2431-8

© 1980 by The Regents of the University of California

Printed in Great Britain by
REDWOOD BURN LIMITED
Trowbridge & Esher

To George and Josephine

Contents

Preface

This attempt to provide a comprehensive account of Conrad's literary career has three main aspects: biographical, historical, and interpretative.

The study is not a critical biography, but it presents in a relatively summary fashion the markedly different picture of Conrad's life which has begun to emerge from the works of many scholars in the last twenty years—notably those of Zdzisław Najder and Jocelyn Baines. There is an introductory chapter on the early years; after that, each chapter concentrates on one particular novel, but begins with a section about Conrad's life during the period of composition. The difficulties and dangers of biographical criticism are well known; the justification for its use in the present case is that although Conrad was not a directly autobiographical writer, his fictional world is an intensely personal one whose nature is illuminated by an understanding of the inordinate difficulty of his life, and of the close but complicated relationship in his works between their sources in personal experience and their fictional embodiment.

The biographical perspective is closely connected with the historical. Partly, perhaps, because the critics of the last few decades have not been very interested in literary and intellectual history, these aspects of Conrad's work have not received much attention. Conrad certainly raises especially difficult, and in part insoluble, problems for the literary historian; but the difficulties arise not because Conrad was anomalously immune to the historical process, but because his inheritances from the past were so rich and diverse. For this reason the early chapters place Conrad in his literary context at considerable length, taking up such matters as Conrad's relationship to his Polish past, to the romantic movement, to the popular and highbrow traditions in the novel, to the impressionist and symbolist traditions, and to the treatment of time in narrative. This placing of Conrad in his historical perspective also involves some account of how his works stand in relation both to the multifarious literary currents of the late nineteenth century, and to what we are still calling the "modern" movement in literature. These historical considerations help us to understand the nature and the originality of Conrad's narrative methods more clearly; and these methods, in turn, are directly related to Conrad's sensitiveness to the fundamental social and intellectual conflicts of his period. The ideological sections of the chapters on *The Nigger of the "Narcissus"* and *Heart of Darkness* suggest that although Conrad was not exactly a philosophical novelist, his basic intellectual assumptions were very similar to those of the most original and influential thinkers of the last decades of the nineteenth century.

But the main emphasis of this study is, in a broad sense, exegetic. The complete diversity—or disarray—of contemporary opinion about what literature and its criticism is or should be, has meant that we are further than ever from anything like a consensus in our views of the basic character of Conrad's literary achievement; and this disagreement may justify an attempt to see whether a measure of critical consensus may not be promoted by a fairly detailed and literal interpretation of Conrad's main works. This attempt imposes a special kind of critical approach: there must be enough quotation to enable the reader to see the evidence in the text for the interpretation given; and the primary commitment must be to what may be called the literal imagination—the analytic commentary restricts itself to what the imagination can discover through a literal reading of the work.

These aims and methods largely account for the unexpected length of this study: it seemed better to be explicit, even at the risk of seeming obvious, than to leave unclear the relation of the argument to the text, or to omit reference to significant contrary evidence. One regrettable result of the length imposed by these objectives is that a good many of Conrad's works are relatively neglected. This neglect is certainly not meant to countenance the notion that Conrad does not have to be read entire—variety and magnitude are an essential part of his achievement; but to give a reasonably full account of Conrad's development as a novelist, and of a dozen or so of his major works, is already a very large enterprise.

The problem of scale is particularly evident in this first volume, which deals with Conrad's career up to 1900, and concentrates on only four works, *Almayer's Folly, The Nigger of the "Narcissus", Heart of Darkness,* and *Lord Jim.* The second volume, although of much the same length, will contain ten chapters, dealing with the short stories, the autobiographical writings, the last years, and seven of the novels: *Typhoon, Nostromo, The Secret Agent, Under Western Eyes, Chance, Victory,* and *The Shadow-Line.*

Acknowledgments

My debts are too numerous, and stretch too far back, to acknowledge fully. When I began research in 1955, I received much generous help from people who had known Conrad, and especially from his sons John and Borys Conrad, and his friends Richard Curle, Joseph Retinger, David Garnett and Dame Rebecca West. Since then I have accumulated many further debts: to such notable Conrad scholars as Jocelyn Baines, Albert Guerard, Larry Graver, Thomas Moser, Zdzisław Najder, and Norman Sherry, who was long ago my guide along Captain Whalley's walk in Singapore; to many students at the universities of Hawaii, East Anglia, California at Berkeley, and Stanford, of whom at least three, Douglas Dey, Lowell Cohn and Hunt Hawkins, must be singled out; to those who read earlier versions of this book, Brian Barry, Andrzej Busza, Donald Davie, John Foster, Michael Levenson, Thomas Moser, Przemysław Mroczkowski, Zdzisław Najder, Ruth Watt, and Cedric Watts; and to those who kindly supplied me with copies of unpublished letters or other material on Conrad, including Edmund A. Bojarski, Mario Curreli, Bill Daleski, Eloise Knapp Hay, Frederick Karl, Ugo Mursia, Ray Stevens, Wit Tarnawski, David Thorburn, Tzvetan Todorov, Hans van Marle and Ivo Vidan. I am also deeply indebted to those who materially assisted the completion of this book; to my research assistants at different times and places, John Halverson, John W. Carr, Christine Peutsche, Suzanne Doyle, and especially to Bob Beitcher, Jack Prostko, and Ken Whiting whose devoted help in the later stages of copyediting, proofreading and indexing saved me from innumerable errors of fact or expression; to those with whom I have talked or corresponded about Conrad, who include, in addition to many of those above, Fred Crews, Leon Edel, Avrom Fleishman, Samuel Hynes, David R. Smith and Tony Tanner; to those who have helped me solve particular problems, notably Gabriele Davis, Joseph Harris, Georges Poulet, John Powers, and Edward Said; to Joan Warmbrunn, Kay Jenks and Josephine Guttadauro, who rose nobly to the occasion when time grew short; to Dorothy Brothers, for her two years of dedication and cryptographic skill; to Patricia Hodgart, Thomas Moser, John Gladstone and Mark Wollaeger who were more than up to proof; and lastly to Virginia Shrader, whose help with the final version and the index has been invaluable.

This study, to say nothing of my life, would have been impossible without the facilities of the British Museum, of the university libraries of Cambridge, Norwich, Berkeley, and Stanford. I am much indebted to them, to the London Library, which supplied me with books when I began the first draft of this volume in Spain in 1971, and to Margaret Amara and Christine Hoth, at the library of the Center for Advanced Study in the Behavioral Sciences, for their special efforts on my behalf. To the British Museum, the Houghton Library at Harvard, the Beinecke Library at Yale, the Manuscript Division of the New York Public Library, the Morgan Library, the Academic Center Library at the University of Texas, the Philip H. and A. S. W. Rosenbach Foundation, and to Doubleday and Company Inc., and Withers (Richard Underwood), acting on behalf of the Trustees of the Joseph Conrad Estate, I gratefully acknowledge permission to reprint copyright materials.

I am indebted to the generosity of the John Simon Guggenheim Memorial Foundation for making possible a half-year of research in 1959, and a whole year in 1972–1973; to the American Council of Learned Societies for a fellowship in 1966–1967; to the authorities at Berkeley and Stanford for sabbatical leaves; to the Neophilological Committee of the Polish Academy of Sciences for inviting me to Poland in September 1972, where I was memorably initiated into some of the Polish aspects of Conrad; to the National Endowment for the Humanities for a fellowship for independent study and research in 1976–1977; to the Center for Advanced Study in the Behavioral Sciences for a fellowship in 1966–1967, and another in 1976–1977 during which the basic drafts of this volume were completed; and finally to my colleagues at Stanford, Bliss Carnochan, Dean of Graduate Studies, and Halsey Royden, Dean of Humanities and Sciences, whose provision of research and secretarial assistance did much to mitigate the rigours of the last stages of composition.

Portions of the present text have earlier appeared in various journals: "Conrad Criticism and *The Nigger of the 'Narcissus'*," in *Nineteenth-Century Fiction*, 12 (1958), 257–83; "Joseph Conrad: Alienation and Commitment," in *The English Mind: Studies in the English Moralists Presented to Basil Willey*, ed. H. S. Davies and George Watson (Cambridge, 1964); "Conrad's Preface to *The Nigger of the 'Narcissus'*," in *Novel*, 7 (1974), 101–15; "*Almayer's Folly*: Memories and Models," in *Mosaic*, 8 (1974), 163–82; "Pink Toads and Yellow Curs: An Impressionist Narrative Device in *Lord Jim*," in *Joseph Conrad Colloquy in Poland, 5–12 September 1972* (Warsaw, 1975); "Impressionism and Symbolism in *Heart of Darkness*," in *The Southern Review*, 13 (1977), 96–113; "*Heart of Darkness* and Nineteenth-Century Thought," in *Partisan Re-*

view, 45 (1978), 108–19; "From Joseph Conrad," in *The Missouri Review,* 1 (1978), 79–87; "Marlow, Henry James, and 'Heart of Darkness,' "in *Nineteenth-Century Fiction,* 33 (1978), 159–74; and "The Ending of *Lord Jim,*" in *Conradiana,* 11 (1979), 3–21. To the editors and publishers of these, for permission to reprint, I render, as is customary, thanks.

Annotation and Abbreviations

I have tried to identify all but the briefest or most incidental quotations, to acknowledge my main sources of information and ideas, and occasionally to indicate further sources and contrary opinions. On the other hand, I have not attempted to substantiate information which is widely available in the main works on Conrad, or to provide a full conspectus of Conrad scholarship and criticism on the matters being discussed. Considerations of space have constrained me to some rather unaesthetic abbreviated forms of documentation. Thus nearly all page references for quotations from Conrad are given in the body of the text as a simple numeral (e.g., in a discussion of *Almayer's Folly* the parenthetic reference (13) gives the page number in the most complete available text, *Dent's Collected Edition of the Works of Joseph Conrad* [London: J. M. Dent, 1946–1955]). Where there are several successive quotations from Conrad which come from the same or immediately adjoining pages, a page reference is normally given only for the passage first quoted; if no page references are given for the succeeding quotations, they will be found either on the same page, or on the page immediately before or after. In the case of Conrad's shorter works—stories or essays—I have given the abbreviated form of the volume title, followed by the page number, as a parenthesis in the text; thus (*T U*, 93) is the reference to the page in "An Outpost of Progress," from the Dent volume entitled *Tales of Unrest.* The abbreviations used for Conrad's works and other much-quoted sources are listed below.

Unless otherwise indicated in the reference, the translations are my own.

Abbreviated Titles

A B   Andrzej Busza, "Conrad's Polish Literary Background and Some Illustrations of the Influence of Polish Literature on his Work," *Antemurale* 10 (Rome and London, 1966): 109–255.

B   William Blackburn, ed., *Joseph Conrad: Letters to William Blackwood and David S. Meldrum* (Durham, N. C.: Duke University Press, 1958).

B C M   Bernard C. Meyer, *Joseph Conrad: A Psychoanalytic Biography* (Princeton: Princeton University Press, 1967).

C   *Conradiana: A Journal of Joseph Conrad,* 1968–. Now published by The Textual Studies Institute, Texas Tech University, Lubbock, Texas.

C G   C. T. Watts, ed., *Joseph Conrad's Letters to R. B. Cunninghame Graham* (Cambridge: Cambridge University Press, 1969).

E G   Edward Garnett, ed., *Letters from Conrad, 1895 to 1924* (London: Nonesuch Press, 1928).

E K H   Eloise Knapp Hay, *The Political Novels of Joseph Conrad* (Chicago: University of Chicago Press, 1963).

F M F   Ford Madox Ford [Hueffer], *Joseph Conrad: A Personal Remembrance* (London: Duckworth, 1924).

G   Albert J. Guerard, *Conrad the Novelist* (Cambridge, Mass.: Harvard University Press, 1958).

H D N   *Heart of Darkness,* ed. Robert Kimbrough, A Norton Critical Edition (New York: W. W. Norton, 1971).

J A   Jerry Allen, *The Sea Years of Joseph Conrad* (New York: Doubleday, 1965).

J B   Jocelyn Baines, *Joseph Conrad: A Critical Biography* (London: Weidenfeld and Nicholson, 1960).

J C C   Jessie Conrad, *Joseph Conrad and his Circle* (London: Jarrold's, 1935).

J D G   John Dozier Gordan, *Joseph Conrad: The Making of a Novelist* (Cambridge, Mass.: Harvard University Press, 1940).

L F   G. Jean-Aubry, *Joseph Conrad: Lettres françaises* (Paris: Gallimard, 1929).

L G   Lawrence Graver, *Conrad's Short Fiction* (Berkeley and Los Angeles: University of California Press, 1969).

L J N   *Lord Jim,* ed. Thomas Moser, A Norton Critical Edition (New York: W. W. Norton, 1968).

L L   G. Jean-Aubry, *Joseph Conrad: Life and Letters,* 2 vols. (London: Heinemann, 1927).

M   Thomas Moser, *Joseph Conrad: Achievement and Decline* (Cambridge, Mass.: Harvard University Press, 1958).

N   Zdzisław Najder, ed., *Conrad's Polish Background: Letters to and from Polish Friends,* tr. Halina Carroll (London: Oxford University Press, 1964).

N N D   *The Nigger of the "Narcissus"* (Garden City, N.Y.: Doubleday, 1914).

O E D   *Oxford English Dictionary*

P   John A. Gee and Paul J. Sturm, tr. and ed., *Letters of Joseph Conrad to Marguerite Poradowska, 1890–1920* (New Haven: Yale University Press, 1940).

R C   Richard Curle, ed., *Conrad to a Friend: 150 Selected Letters from*

Joseph Conrad to Richard Curle (London: Sampson Low, Marston, 1928).

R R   René Rapin, ed., *Lettres de Joseph Conrad à Marguerite Poradowska* (Geneva: Droz, 1966).

S C H   Norman Sherry, ed., *Conrad: The Critical Heritage* (London: Routledge and Kegan Paul, 1973).

S E W   Norman Sherry, *Conrad's Eastern World* (Cambridge: Cambridge University Press, 1966).

S W W   Norman Sherry, *Conrad's Western World* (Cambridge: Cambridge University Press, 1971).

T S   *The Sisters: An Unfinished Story,* by Joseph Conrad, With an Introduction by Ford Madox Ford, ed. Ugo Mursia (1928; rpt. Milan: U. Mursia, 1968).

The main abbreviations used for Conrad's works (in the Dent Collected Edition) are:

L E   *Last Essays*
M S   *The Mirror of the Sea*
N L L   *Notes on Life and Letters*
P R   *A Personal Record*
T   *Typhoon and Other Stories*
T H   *Tales of Hearsay*
T U   *Tales of Unrest*
W T T   *Within the Tides*
Y   *Youth—A Narrative; and Two Other Stories*

CHAPTER I

The Earlier Life: 1857–1894

i. 1857–1874: Poland

The exiled bard of Mickiewicz's *Pan Tadeusz* begins Poland's national epic with a patriotic apostrophe on the theme: No one can prize his health fully until he has lost it; and thus it is with one's native land. The burden of this and other losses weighed so deeply on Conrad all through his life that anyone beginning to write about it must wonder how far the triviality of his own deprivations may have disabled him for the task.

Poland can claim a much older continuous national tradition than England or France, not to mention its more recently consolidated neighbours Russia and Germany. It emerged as a nation within something like its present frontiers under the reign of Mieszko I towards the end of the tenth century; and in the fifteenth and sixteenth centuries Poland was one of the largest, most powerful, and most civilized of the European powers. In the eighteenth century, however, foreign wars and internal political dissensions made Poland an easy prey to stronger neighbours, and it was eventually partitioned piecemeal by Austria, Prussia, and Russia in 1772, 1793, and finally in 1795. So it was in a great country, which for two generations already had ceased to exist as an independent state, that Józef Teodor Konrad Korzeniowski was born, on 3 December 1857.

His father, Apollo Korzeniowski, came from a family whose ancestral lands had been confiscated in 1831 for their part in the last great national rising against Russian rule. Apollo was then attempting to farm a leased estate near Berdichev, a town in Podolia, one of the borderland provinces of Poland, and now part of the Soviet Ukraine. Both Apollo and Conrad's mother, Ewa (or Evelina) Bobrowska, came from the *szlachta*, or Polish nobility. Conrad himself later preferred to describe them as "land-tilling gentry," to disassociate his ancient but relatively unassuming stock from any suggestion of wealth or social exclusiveness: the Korzeniowskis and Bobrowskis certainly had little in common with the European aristocracy, or with such rich and powerful Polish magnates as the Radziwiłls, Potockis and Czartoryskis. But although the *szlachta* were numerically a very large group, and often of modest means and occupations, they were nevertheless a nobility in the sense that they had the right to bear arms, and had constituted the hereditary ruling class of Poland since feudal times. Conrad was always to retain much of their traditional chivalric code, and many of their general social attitudes and expectations. Though he never farmed, his dress and life style in England approximated, as far as means permitted, to that of the country gentleman—shotguns, dogs, horses, a groom; to his Polish friend J.H. Retinger, "he seemed," even as late as 1909, "a typical Polish landowner from the Ukraine."[1]

Poland's triple bondage after the partitions had driven many of her nobility into exile—among them Tadeusz Kościuszko; many more had left in the "Great Emigration" which followed the defeat of the 1830 insurrection. These "knights of liberty," as they were called, settled in their thousands throughout Western Europe, and there kept alive Polish hopes of independence both through their direct political activities and through their writings. One of the main forms taken by the patriotic feeling of the Poles was that expressed by their great Romantic poets, Mickiewicz, Słowacki and Krasiński; they developed a national Messianic myth, according to which the sufferings of Poland, which had arisen from its historic role of defending Europe against the barbarians and infidels of the East, were eventually destined, like those of Christ, to redeem the world. In practical political terms, however, and especially for the Poles who remained at home, the outlook seemed hopeless, and the long series of disastrous past failures led many to renounce any active resistance to Russia and to concentrate on internal economic and educational progress, combined with attempts to induce the Tzar to relax his tyranny. Still, to many Poles at home and abroad, anything seemed better than enslavement; there were several desperate local revolts; and in 1861, after two savagely repressed demonstrations in Warsaw, various groups began to prepare what was to prove the last and, at least in immediate terms, the most catastrophic, of Polish attempts to throw off the Russian yoke by force of arms.[2]

Conrad's father was prominently involved. After the failure of his

1. *Conrad and his Contemporaries* (London, 1941), pp. 54–55. According to Ford Madox Ford, Conrad was "frequently taken for a horse fancier," and liked it (*Joseph Conrad: A Personal Remembrance* [London, 1924], pp. 56–57; hereafter cited as F M F). The most authoritative account in English of Conrad's Polish aspect is that of Zdzisław Najder, whose *Conrad's Polish Background: Letters to and from Polish Friends*, trans. Halina Carroll (London, 1964) was a major landmark in Conradian studies; hereafter cited as N.

2. On the political background see Aleksander Gieysztor et al., *History of Poland* (Warsaw, 1968), pp. 508–31; W.F. Reddaway et al., *The Cambridge History of Poland, 1697–1935* (Cambridge, 1941), pp. 374–88; Piotr S. Wandycz, *The Lands of Partitioned Poland, 1795–1918* (Seattle, 1974); and Eloise Knapp Hay, *The Political Novels of Joseph Conrad: A Critical Study* (Chicago, 1963), pp. 31–80, hereafter cited as E K H.

attempt at farming he had moved to nearby Żytomierz, and later to
Warsaw, so that he could devote himself wholly to underground political organisation. In Warsaw he became the leader of a movement to
unite various secret insurrectionary and progressive groups who were
known as the "Reds," as opposed to the more gradualist "Whites." It
was the Reds who formed the underground National Central Committee which was eventually to proclaim the insurrection, on 22 January 1863; but long before then Apollo Korzeniowski had been arrested and imprisoned by the Russian authorities.

Conrad's earliest surviving autograph recalls this period. Written
on the back of his photograph, it is addressed "To my beloved
Grandma who helped me send cakes to my poor Daddy in prison—
grandson, Pole, Catholic, nobleman—6 July 1863—Konrad" (N, 8).
The inscription was written in Conrad's first exile. After seven months
in prison, Apollo, along with his wife, had been tried and sentenced to
deportation to a remote Russian province. On 8 May 1862, they and
their son, then four years old, had left Warsaw under police escort. At
Vologda, a cold and marshy city to the northeast of Moscow, both
mother and son soon became seriously ill, and the family was eventually allowed to go south to the warmer climate of Chernikov, not far
from Kiev. On 11 April 1865, Ewa died of tuberculosis. Conrad was
only seven years old, and he spent the next four years of his life
mainly with his father, whose health gradually worsened until in 1867
he was allowed to return to Poland, where he died, also of tuberculosis, at Cracow on 23 May 1869. His eleven-year-old son walked
alone behind the hearse at the head of the funeral procession, which
had been converted into a great patriotic manifestation. The Poles,
Conrad recalled in 1915,

> had not come to honour a great achievement, or even some
> splendid failure. The dead and they were victims alike of an
> unrelenting destiny which cut them off from every path of
> merit and glory. They had come only to render homage to the
> ardent fidelity of the man whose life had been a fearless con-
> fession in word and deed of a creed which the simplest heart
> in that crowd could feel and understand.[3]

Both Conrad's parents had exceptional qualities of mind and heart,
and they had been intensely devoted to their only child. But even if
they had not often been absent or ill they could hardly have compen-
sated for a childhood spent on the move and under terrible duress.
One of Conrad's earliest memories was of his mother "dressed in the

3. "Poland Revisited," 1915, in *Notes on Life and Letters* (London, 1949), p. 169;
hereafter cited as *N L L*.

black of the national mourning worn in defiance of ferocious police regulations";[4] he came to fuller consciousness among the bitter insecurities of exile—prisoner number twenty-three in a small society of dispirited and disease-ridden victims of oppression;[5] then he watched his mother, and later his father, slowly die; and this last blow, he recalled, "stripped off me some of my simple trust in the government of the universe" (*N L L,* 168).

Not surprisingly Conrad's health as a child was very poor; there were long periods of bad migraines, and he was also subject to nervous fits, perhaps a form of epilepsy, which he later outgrew (*N,* 9–10). Conrad also moved about too much in his first eleven years to have friends of his own age, or any sense of belonging to a stable home: only the world of books offered a refuge from loneliness and despair. "I don't know what would have become of me," he later wrote, "if I had not been a reading boy" (*N L L,* 168). From the age of five Conrad had been a voracious reader—mainly of history, travels, and novels; he was especially fond of Fenimore Cooper, Captain Marryat, and Dickens, all of them read in Polish or French translation. Conrad's precocious literary interest had been stimulated by his father, himself a considerable poet and playwright, who did a great deal of translation from English, French and German, especially in his last years.[6] Conrad particularly recalled reading the manuscript of his father's translation of *Two Gentlemen of Verona,* and the proofs of Victor Hugo's *Les Travailleurs de la Mer* (*P R,* 71–72).

Even while his parents were alive, Conrad spent a good deal of time with his mother's family; and on Apollo's death, Ewa's oldest surviving brother, Tadeusz Bobrowski, gradually assumed responsibility for Conrad. Both sides of the family, and especially, of course, the men, had suffered heavily in the insurrection and the pitiless reprisals which followed: three died, others were imprisoned or exiled, and Tadeusz's brother, Stefan, the head of the underground National Government, was killed in a duel which arose out of the intense political disagreements which dogged the revolt. So it fell to cautious Uncle Tadeusz, who had remained sceptically aloof, to pick up the pieces; and as he was soon to lose his wife and only child as well, there was room, even need, in his heart, for Conrad, the only, and now orphaned, child of his much loved sister.

4. *A Personal Record: Some Reminiscences,* 1912 (London, 1946), p. x; hereafter cited as *P R.*

5. Leo Gurko, *Joseph Conrad: Giant in Exile* (New York, 1962), p. 9.

6. The fullest account in English of the work of Apollo Korzeniowski is given by Andrzej Busza, "Conrad's Polish Literary Background and Some Illustrations of the Influence of Polish Literature on his Work," *Antemurale* 10 (Rome and London, 1966): 109–255; hereafter cited as *A B.*

No one, perhaps, could have done very much to heal the wounds of
Conrad's first eleven years; but Bobrowski, though in many ways enlightened and humane, was very much the prudent, conservative and
practical lawyer. His seventy-one surviving letters to Conrad, together
with a few other letters and documents, and his own posthumously
published memoirs, are by far the most important source of information about Conrad's early life.[7] Bobrowski's rather reserved, sarcastic,
and occasionally supercilious character, and his complacent
platitudinising about social and fiscal responsibility, may well have
concealed from his young nephew the depth of his love, and done
more to exacerbate than to control the exceptional waywardness of
Conrad's adolescence.

Conrad could not live with Bobrowski because his estate was at
Nowofastów, near Kiev, in Russian-occupied Poland. Conditions there
were much more repressive than under Austrian rule, so for the next
four years Conrad lived in Austrian-occupied Poland, and was brought
up mainly by his maternal grandmother, Teofila Bobrowska, a figure
of heroic devotion. Conrad's education continued to be irregular,
partly under private tutors and partly in schools in Cracow and Lvov.
There he briefly experienced the pleasures of schoolboy friendship,
and later, apparently, the pangs of adolescent love. But Conrad, precocious in some ways and backward in others, was impatient with school
and remained lonely, unhappy and restive.

By the age of fourteen he had formed the wish to go to sea. In his *A
Personal Record*, which beautifully records "the feelings and sensations
connected with the writing of my first book and with my first contact
with the sea" (*P R*, xxi), Conrad speaks of "the mysteriousness of his
impulses to himself" at this time: there was "no precedent" for "a boy
of my nationality and antecedents taking a, so to speak, standing jump
out of his racial surroundings and associations" (*P R*, 121). Conrad's
reading had certainly played a part in shaping his wish; but if youthful dreams of exploration and romantic adventure gave their particular shape to the impulse, its roots were surely in even more irresistible
compulsions; in the need, above all, to bid a resounding farewell to
everything he knew in a homeland which was heavy with memories of
irreparable national and personal loss.

For some two years Bobrowski tried to dissuade him, but was eventually constrained to yield. It would have taken several years for Conrad to complete his studies at school, where his progress had been

7. Bobrowski's letters, and his "The Document for the Information of my Beloved
Nephew Konrad Korzeniowski," which gives a meticulous financial and legal account-
ing of his unofficial wardship of Conrad down to 1890, are reprinted by Najder. There
is an interesting and fairly full account of Bobrowski's memoirs in Busza (*A B*, 147–61).

slow and very uneven; in any case there was no likely career open to
him anywhere in Poland. As a Russian subject and the son of a de-
ported political convict, Conrad was liable to no less than twenty-five
years' military service with the Russian army, to be served in the
ranks. Conrad had to get out, and France was the obvious choice: it
had a considerable merchant navy, its language was no problem for
Conrad, since French was the second language of all educated Poles;
and France was traditionally the country most favoured by Polish
exiles. So on 15 October 1874,[8] well before his seventeenth birthday,
Conrad left Cracow on his way to Marseilles.

Conrad was leaving a nightmare; as he put it in a letter to Galsworthy, he "got into a train . . . on my way to the sea, as a man might get
into a dream" (L L, II, 157). The metaphor evokes something of the
unreal, mysterious, and yet in retrospect imperative, nature of his act;
nor do the implications of the metaphor stop there, for Conrad was
entering an unknown world in which, as each occurrence filled out
the dreamlike blankness of the future, it also disclosed the obstinate
contours of the past.

Many of the dominant themes and attitudes that separate Conrad's
novels from those of his English, French, or Russian contemporaries,
for instance, are characteristic of the history, the society, and the
literature, of his native country.

Doomed resistance and heroic defeat constitute the sadly recurrent
burden of Poland's history. The last two hundred years have done
little but enact betrayal by foreign allies or through internal divisions;
and this habituation has engendered a corresponding admiration for
individual loyalty and group cohesion. These themes dominate Conrad's fiction; fidelity is the supreme value in Conrad's ethic, but it is
always menaced and often defeated or betrayed. Conrad once insisted
to Edward Garnett that he must be understood not as a Slav, but as a
Pole, and specifically as a member of a nation which, for the last
hundred years, had "been used to go to battle without illusions."[9]

There is a literary reflection of this inheritance in his name. Jósef
and Teodor were the given names of his paternal and maternal
grandfathers respectively; but as a child he was called Konrad (or
Konradek), and the associations of that name were wholly literary and
patriotic. "For a Pole," Czesław Miłosz writes, "the name Konrad sym-

8. This is the date given in the standard biography, Jocelyn Baines's *Joseph Conrad:
A Critical Biography* (London, 1960), p. 30; hereafter cited as *J B*. G. Jean-Aubry, in the
other main biographical source, his authorised *Joseph Conrad: Life and Letters*, 2 vols.
(London, 1927), I, p. 27, hereafter cited as *L L*, gives a date one day earlier.

9. Edward Garnett, *Letters from Conrad, 1895–1924* (London, 1928), p. 216; hereafter cited as *E G*.

bolizes the anti-Russian fighter and resister."[10] This is largely because of Adam Mickiewicz's long narrative poem, *Konrad Wallenrod* (1828). Its hero is a Lithuanian brought up by the Teutonic Knights; he eventually becomes the grand master of the order, and their commander in chief. One day, however, he hears an old Lithuanian minstrel whose lays bring back to him the long sufferings of his native country at the hands of the conquering foreign invaders; Konrad then deliberately leads the army of the Teutonic oppressors into a disastrous defeat, and kills himself to avoid being executed. The medieval setting of the poem, as Polish readers well knew, was a necessary historical disguise for portraying the current situation of Poland and Russia. In that context Konrad Wallenrod was an emblematic figure; the idea of suicidal treachery for patriotic reasons is a perfect expression of the deepest imaginative needs of a subjugated people; it is the most plausible form of heroism possible under an irresistible, ubiquitous and mindless tyranny.

Najder has stressed the equal importance of another symbolic Konrad in Mickiewicz—the protagonist of his visionary poetic drama *The Forefathers' Eve* (N, 4–5). Gustaw is a typical romantic hero—egocentric, moody, sentimental, imaginative; but in a Czarist prison he finally renounces his former self-indulgent life, takes on the name of Konrad, and identifies himself with the sufferings of humanity, and more specifically of the Polish nation.

In both *Konrad Wallenrod* and *The Forefathers' Eve*, Byronic individualism is corrected through an identification with national suffering; and this transformation from a narrow self-concern to a larger loyalty is a characteristic theme not only of Mickiewicz but of Słowacki, the other Polish romantic poet whom Conrad most admired.[11] Conrad's protagonists often undergo a similar conflict, and he himself remained deeply devoted to the idea of national sentiment; unlike the other great figures of modern literature, Conrad was not the critic but the nostalgic celebrant of the civilization of his homeland; and the steady insistence on the patriotic values of courage, tenacity, honour, responsibility and abnegation gives Conrad's fiction a heroic note very rare in twentieth-century literature.

In other respects Conrad's early heritage accustomed him to some of the main social and historical attitudes of modern literature. There

10. "Joseph Conrad in Polish Eyes," *Atlantic Monthly* (1957), reprinted in *The Art of Joseph Conrad: A Critical Symposium*, ed. R. W. Stallman (East Lansing, Mich., 1960), p. 36. The general Polish literary background is illuminatingly presented in Milosz's *The History of Polish Literature* (London, 1969).

11. N, 15–17, and A B, 205–8, contain good accounts of the influence of Polish literature on Conrad's writing.

is, for example, the scornful rejection of bourgeois values. The Polish *szlachta*, who had always stayed aloof from industry and commerce, were contemptuous of the concern for economic and material growth which dominated Polish life after the 1863 uprising; and so Conrad did not need the twentieth century to teach him to be sceptical about the much-touted civilising effects of economic progress. As to political progress, Conrad did not have to wait until 1914 for a brutal disillusionment. The Poles, he wrote in "The Crime of Partition" (1919), had long known "Oppression, not merely political, but affecting social relations, family life, the deepest affections of human nature, and the very fount of natural emotions" (*N L L*, 130). Conrad was in Poland when the news of the 1914 war arrived, and what he said of his country's position then was also true of his own situation fifty years before: "all the past was gone, and there was no future, whatever happened; no road which did not seem to lead to moral annihilation."[12]

This pessimistic perspective, both deeply historical and intimately personal, pervades Conrad's fictional world, which is mainly concerned with how to manoeuvre among intolerable and yet intractable realities. If we attend to it, we must surely see this inheritance to be of more enduring importance than any specific influence of his native literature. Here there are incontestable debts, especially to the Polish romantic poets, but they mainly concern style, mood, and descriptive methods.[13] Conrad's basic literary and intellectual outlook was European; his moral and social character remained largely Polish.

Still one need not assume that because Conrad retained so deep an imprint of his native country, and yet found his separation from it a source of irremediable pain, he must therefore have felt guilty as a deserter from Poland, and given hidden expression to this in his fiction, notably in *Lord Jim*.[14]

There is no doubt that, at least until the rebirth of Poland after 1918, Conrad tended to be very touchy and reticent about everything connected with Poland; but the cause need not have been guilt at leaving it. There had, after all, been the many earlier emigrations, and they were to become even more massive in scale during Conrad's lifetime.[15] Of course, in dealing with Poles who had stayed at home, Conrad must always have been aware that they might see his depar-

12. "First News," *N L L*, 178.
13. See especially *N*, 28–31, and *AB*, 203–38.
14. Gustav Morf was the first to give an allegorical interpretation, according to which Jim represents Conrad jumping off a doomed *Patna* (read *Polska*), in *The Polish Heritage of Joseph Conrad* (London, 1930). Several Polish critics have given a similar but more general view of the pervading presence in Conrad's works of his guilt at leaving Poland, notably Józef Ujejski, Wit Tarnawski and Ludwik Krzyżanowski.
15. Two and a half million Poles emigrated to the New World between 1870 and 1914, and half a million to Western Europe (Gieysztor, *History of Poland*, pp. 584–86).

ture as a betrayal of his country, as some had apparently seen it in 1874. Writing in 1909, Conrad declared in *A Personal Record:* "I catch myself in hours of solitude and retrospect meeting arguments and charges made thirty-five years ago by voices now for ever still; finding things to say that an assailed boy could not have found" (*P R,* 121). The primary motive here seems not guilt but shame and anger at what other people think—the typical adolescent impatience at the impossibility of making anyone understand him on his own terms.

The complex resentments Conrad felt in 1874 were renewed and exacerbated in 1899, when his novels began to be translated and discussed in Poland. An acrimonious controversy about the "Emigration of the Talents" developed in which a well-known Polish novelist, Eliza Orzeszkowa, attacked Conrad as a "camp-follower or huckster" who had prostituted himself for richer gains abroad.[16] Conrad was deeply and permanently angered (*J B,* 353). But of course his anger would have been just as great if he had felt the charges to be wholly false, especially as defence or explanation were equally unacceptable to Conrad's pride.

This psychological deadlock took a different, but equally insoluble, form as far as Conrad's dealings with people in England were concerned; no one there could have the knowledge or the experience needed to understand the complexities of Conrad's Polish past. If the issue of his nationality was raised, the stock response would be inadvertent Podsnappery—as when his mother-in-law to be, confronting her first Pole, exclaimed: "Oh dear; one could never take him for an Englishman, and he doesn't look French, either."[17] As for those English who were more cosmopolitan in their sympathies, H. G. Wells and Edward Garnett for instance, they would tend to call his politeness Oriental, and his soul Slav, and thus in either case mortify Conrad by outraging the Western allegiance which is at the heart of the Polish sense of national identity. But for Conrad to explain this to the uninitiated meant traversing endless tracts of national, family, and personal history, all of them too painful to contemplate and too complicated to share. It was better to keep quiet.

There must always be pain, then, but guilt is not a necessary hypothesis to explain Conrad's later attitude to leaving his native land. We must also remember that Conrad's essential moral and psychological burdens would have been no lighter if he had remained at home. On this Najder quotes Conrad's moving tribute to Poland in "Prince Roman": "that country which demands to be loved as no other coun-

16. The fullest account in English seems to be *A B,* 189–99.
17. Jessie Conrad, *Joseph Conrad and his Circle* (London, 1935), p. 14; hereafter cited as *J C C.*

try has ever been loved, with the mournful affection one bears to the unforgotten dead and with the unextinguishable fire of a hopeless passion."[18] Najder then finely comments: "Hopeless fidelity was the essence of Conrad's feeling for Poland, but that made him not closer to but, on the contrary, more estranged from other Poles" (*N*, 26).

So, all things considered, and until a firmer basis for the psychological understanding and moral judgment of others becomes available, we should surely take Conrad at his own eloquent word in *A Personal Record:*

> No charge of faithlessness ought to be lightly uttered. The appearances of this perishable life are deceptive like everything that falls under the judgment of our imperfect senses. The inner voice may remain true enough in its secret counsel. The fidelity to a special tradition may last through the events of an unrelated existence, following faithfully, too, the traced way of an inexplicable impulse.

It would take too long to explain the intimate alliance of contradictions in human nature which makes love itself wear at times the desperate shape of betrayal (*P R*, 35–36).

ii. 1874–1878: France

Conrad was to spend less than four years in France, but they were the crucial formative years between seventeen and twenty-one. He arrived fairly well prepared. For one thing, he was assured of a sufficient yearly allowance of 2000 francs, partly from his uncle's own pocket, but mainly from funds Bobrowski managed out of various small gifts and legacies given Conrad by many relatives and friends of the family; for another, Conrad bore two letters of introduction, and he also had some sort of contact with a small firm of shipowners, Delestang. It was on their sailing ship, the *Mont Blanc*, that Conrad began his sea career.[1] On it he made two long voyages to the West Indies, officially registered first as passenger and then as apprentice. Conrad next spent some six months ashore at Marseilles before making a third long voyage to the Caribbean on another Delestang sailing ship, the *Saint Antoine*, this time as a steward with a nominal salary. On his return early in 1877 Conrad was apparently prevented from making a further voyage by an anal abscess, and a longer period ashore ensued, which ended disastrously.

18. *Tales of Hearsay* (London, 1955), p. 51; hereafter cited as *T H*.
1. The fullest account of Conrad's sea career, in which much remains obscure, is that of Jerry Allen, *The Sea Years of Joseph Conrad* (New York, 1965); hereafter cited as *J A*.

Marseilles was a very lively place, and Conrad had enough means to take some part, not only in the life of the port, but also in the social and cultural activities of the city—the theatre, the opera, the bohemian cafés, and the legitimist salon of the Delestangs. But he soon began to overspend his allowance; Bobrowski's letters harped constantly on his extravagance and general fecklessness, and finally Conrad was warned that no further advances would be forthcoming under any circumstances. Very soon, however, they had to be.

What happened must be pieced out mainly from what Bobrowski wrote on 24 March 1879 to Stefan Buszczyński, who had been Apollo's closest friend. In October 1877, Bobrowski explained, he had been prevailed on to send a large sum of money out of Conrad's capital to equip him for a very lengthy projected voyage round the world. Hearing no more, he was quite sure that Conrad was "somewhere in the Antipodes"; but early in March 1878 Bobrowski received a telegram from Marseilles reading: "Conrad blessé envoyez argent—arrivez" (N, 175–79). When Bobrowski arrived he found that Conrad had been unable to sail—official regulations, which had previously been evaded, forbade his serving on a French vessel without a permit from the country in which he was liable to military service—in Conrad's case Russia. In addition, Bobrowski wrote,

> another catastrophe—this time financial—befell him. While still in possession of the 3,000 francs sent to him for the voyage, he met his former Captain . . . who persuaded him to participate in some enterprise on the coasts of Spain—some kind of contraband! He invested 1,000 francs in it and made over 400 which pleased them greatly so that on the second occasion he put in all he had—and lost the lot.

The reference is probably to the gunrunning adventures on the *Tremolino*, of which Conrad gives colourful but somewhat different and eventually implausible accounts in *The Mirror of the Sea* and *The Arrow of Gold*. According to Bobrowski, however, what had actually happened was that the vessel's captain absconded to Buenos Aires, leaving Conrad penniless and heavily in debt . . .

> for while speculating he had lived on credit, had ordered the things necessary for his voyage, and so forth. Faced with this situation, he borrows 800 francs from his friend Mr. Fecht and sets off for Villa Franca where an American squadron was anchored, with the intention of joining the American service. He achieves nothing there and, wishing to improve his finances, tries his luck in Monte Carlo and loses the 800 fr. he had borrowed. Having managed his affairs so excellently he returns to Marseilles and one fine evening invites his

friend the creditor to tea, and before his arrival attempts to take his life with a revolver. (Let this detail remain between us, as I have been telling everyone that he was wounded in a duel. From you I neither wish to nor should keep it a secret.) The bullet goes durch und durch near his heart without damaging any vital organ. Luckily, all his addresses were left on top of his things so that this worthy Mr. Fecht could instantly let me know . . .

There is no later record that Conrad ever mentioned an attempt at suicide to anyone. On the contrary, over the years, and apparently as early as 1893,[2] he gave his family and friends to understand that the visible scars to the left of his heart were the result of a duel. Towards the end of his life, Conrad's account got more circumstantial, notably in his novel *The Arrow of Gold,* of which he wrote that "all the persons are authentic and the facts are as stated" (*J B,* 50). The novel is narrated by a M[onsieur] Georges (a name by which Conrad was known in Marseilles); he fights a duel over a woman, Rita, with an American adventurer called Blunt, and is shot in the left breast.

Are we to believe Conrad's account of many decades later, or Bobrowski's version, written just over a year after the shooting had occurred towards the end of February 1878? Conrad must certainly be convicted of lying, either to Bobrowski at the time of his visit, or to many others later. Anyone who has honestly attended to his own behavior, however, may find it fairly easy to absolve Conrad of any very serious offence. Surely not many people, especially when young, have got into a spectacular mess and then told the whole truth about it to anyone; it is much easier to confess folly in the abstract than to spell it out in all its foolish details; and it would have been especially difficult with Bobrowski, who had long been loud in his warnings against the very weaknesses—imprudence, extravagance, self-delusion—which caused the catastrophe.

If in fact Conrad did fight a duel about a woman, he might originally have spread the suicide story mainly to shield her reputation and to keep the affair from his uncle; but whereas Conrad's own later accounts of the duel, as well as of the *Tremolino* and Rita, are mutually inconsistent,[3] Bobrowski's is not, and he twice referred to it elsewhere, notably in a letter to Conrad soon after his return from Marseilles—"You deliberately shot yourself" (8 July 1878; *N,* 54).[4] In any case,

2. According to Edwin Pugh, quoted in Witold Chwalewik, "Conrad in the Light of a New Record," *Kwartalnik Neofilologiczny* 18 (1971): 51–55.
3. See, for instance, Baines (*J B,* 46–57), and Bernard C. Meyer's *Joseph Conrad: A Psychoanalytic Biography* (Princeton, N.J., 1967); hereafter cited as *B C M.*
4. The attempted suicide, which had already been briefly mentioned as early as

Bobrowski's account of the whole matter has the ring of authenticity. Conrad makes desperate efforts to break out of a hopeless tangle by a frenzied snatching at a succession of improbable stratagems that seem hatched from the clichés of popular novels: first, sailing off to America; next, staking everything on a dramatic recouping of his fortunes through trying his beginner's luck at the gambling table; and when this, too, fails, it seems easier to end it all with a revolver rather than have to face Fecht, and later Bobrowski, with all his humiliating confessions. But an unconscious voice imposes another devious strategy: Conrad leaves the address of the trusted guardian conveniently available for his expected visitor, and thus makes what is in effect an oblique but harrowing appeal to Bobrowski: "Now you see how bad things are with me. Please take over."

Bobrowski certainly believed the suicide version, and his reasons for giving out the duel story are very obvious: in Roman Catholic theology suicide is a mortal sin. This may have also been Conrad's motive; the autobiographical hero of his unfinished novel *The Sisters* regards it as "the unpardonable crime."[5] Duelling, on the other hand, was widely regarded as honorable both in Poland and France. Bobrowski's brother, Stefan, had died in a duel; one of Conrad's friends at Marseilles, Clovis Hugues, had very recently killed a political rival in a duel (*J B,* 35); and Conrad himself apparently approved of duelling (*F M F,* 79–80, *E G,* xv).

Much later, after Conrad had married and had children, going along with the duel story must have seemed much better than confessing the suicide attempt: to have tried to kill himself would be a troubling example to give his two sons; to have failed only added a note of ineptitude; and confessing the truth would also call for deeply humiliating explanations of the sufferings of a distant past which nobody else would ever really understand anyway. What remains very puzzling is that over the course of forty years Conrad seems to have come to believe in the invented version. But this would only be an extreme example of Conrad's general tendency in his later years to reconstruct his past in a flattering and romantic way; and in any case there is one essential psychological similarity between the two versions.[6] Suicide is like duelling in one respect; both are drastic impo-

1937 in a Polish paper (*Kurjer Warszawski*), first received widespread attention in September 1957, when Zdzisław Najder published Bobrowski's two letters in the Cracow journal *Literary Life* (*Życie Literackie*) 40 (1957): 298.

5. *The Sisters: An Unfinished Story by Joseph Conrad,* with an Introduction by Ford Madox Ford, ed. Ugo Mursia (1928, rpt. Milan, 1968), p. 53; hereafter cited as *T S.*

6. It should be added that Conrad seemed to regard the facts of his own life as his own business and nobody else's. Jessie Conrad reports that once, during a discussion of

sitions of the individual's will over the conflicts and confusions of his existence, reckless and dramatic projections of the subjective picture of the self upon a public stage. That, surely, was the primary impulse behind Conrad's act at Marseilles. Very few sensitive and imaginative people can have struggled to adulthood without fantasies of ceasing to battle with the peremptory denials of reality; even fewer can have had more personal cause for this than Conrad; and fewer still can have grown up with their lives so totally and continuously at their own disposal.

We know much too little to be able to gauge the psychological significance of Conrad's attempted suicide for his later life; but the role of suicide in Conrad's fiction is certainly of exceptional importance—it occurs at least seventeen times (*B C M*, 274); and there are also a number of rather indeterminate willed cessations, such as that of Almayer. Conrad's treatment often suggests an unconscious wish to exculpate or justify suicide, though the issue is never faced very directly. It is, for instance, never presented from the inside, even in the case of characters who, like Decoud and Heyst, are very close to Conrad, and from whose point of view much of the earlier narrative has been told. On the other hand, Conrad often seems to suggest either that suicide is a positive moral act, or that it is the outcome of unbearable human loneliness. Thus suicide often has a strong element of heroic self-sacrifice for the good of others, as with Captain Whalley in *The End of the Tether* or Peyrol in *The Rover;* there is certainly a note of honourable expiation in the more ambiguous case of Lord Jim; and, most revealingly, Decoud and Winnie Verloc drown themselves, and Heyst is burned to death, because they can find no internal strength with which to resist the isolation caused by the breaking of their only significant human ties.

Bobrowski stayed a fortnight at Marseilles, and he was in the main relieved by what his investigative eye could discover. Conrad was "handsome" and "quite robust"; his manners were "very good, as if he had never left drawing-rooms"; socially he was "very popular with his captains and also with the sailors," although he had not picked up any of their typical "bad habits"; "in his ideas" he was "ardent and original"; above all he was "a man who knows his profession"—in the two weeks of Bobrowski's stay Conrad was "twice called for to bring vessels into the port." Of course Conrad was still "extremely sensitive, conceited, reserved, and in addition excitable"; nevertheless, Bobrowski's

---

whether "The Black Mate" or *Almayer's Folly* was his first work, Conrad "burst out: 'If I like to say 'The Black Mate' was my first work, I shall say so!' " (R. L. Mégroz, *Joseph Conrad's Mind and Method,* [London, 1931], p. 88).

scrutiny had "not deprived [him] of the hope that a real man might still be made of him" (*N*, 177–78).

But where? Quite apart from the pressure to leave the scene of his humiliation, there were imperative practical reasons for Conrad to leave France. He could not get a berth there again until he was naturalised, and that would involve military service—either for six months to a year, or for five years, according to a lottery.[7] In any case—to Bobrowski's expressed gratification—Conrad did "not like [the French] at all" (*N*, 51, 178). Various other possibilities, some of which had already been mooted, were discussed, including the plan that Conrad go back to Austrian Poland, "get naturalised, and look for a career there"; but Conrad, Bobrowski wrote, steadily demurred, "maintaining that he loves his profession, does not want to and will not change it."

Conrad later wrote that even in Poland he had formulated "the determined resolve, that 'if a seaman, then an English seaman' " (*P R*, 122). But what evidence is available makes it virtually certain that Conrad was never decisively committed either to a sea career, or to England, and that in fact it was circumstance which eventually made the decision for him. Looking back on our lives it seems inconceivable that things could possibly have been otherwise, or that they should actually have been mainly determined by accident or momentary convenience; and yet such is often, perhaps usually, the case, as it was in 1878. Conrad had to get out of France; and his only training—intermittent and irresolute as it had been—was that of a sailor. Britain had no conscription; it had the largest merchant fleet in the world, with an extensive Mediterranean commerce; and, most important of all, virtually no official formalities were required for signing on alien seamen. Those factors alone might have been decisive; but Britain also had a long tradition of freedom for political exiles, and it had a literature which, in translation, had already been an important element in Conrad's life. The overwhelming odds were that when Conrad next signed on as a seaman, it would be under the red ensign. And so it was.

iii. 1878–1894: England

On 24 April 1878 a small British steamer, the *Mavis*, left Marseilles for Constantinople with a cargo of coal, and Conrad was aboard as an ordinary seaman; on its home voyage the *Mavis* docked at Lowestoft,

7. R. D. Challener, *The French Theory of the Nation in Arms: 1866–1939* (New York, 1955), p. 38.

and it was in that ancient Suffolk port, on 18 June 1878, that Conrad first set foot on English soil.

He spent the next few months on coastal voyages from Lowestoft to Newcastle "perfecting his English," which, according to Bobrowski, was "rather weak" (*N*, 178). In September 1879 Conrad went to London, paid a considerable premium to an agent who could arrange a kind of three-year term as an unofficial apprentice, and went on two long voyages to Australia and the Orient, beginning as an ordinary seaman at a shilling a month. On the *Duke of Sutherland* and the *Loch Etive*, both full-rigged ships, Conrad received an intense initiation into the world of sail, which had reached its apogee with the great tea and wool clippers of the last half of the nineteenth century. In 1880 Conrad passed his second mate's examination; that for first mate in 1884; and on 10 November 1886, only eight years after his arrival in England, he received his certificate of master in the British merchant service.

It was an astonishing performance. Conrad began, it is true, with some knowledge of seamanship learned in France; but at first he knew virtually no English; the endless physical hardships of life aboard a sailing vessel, especially on long voyages as an ordinary seaman or even as a third mate, taxed his health very severely; and since Conrad did not start out with introductions, as he had in Marseilles, and in any case spent much less time ashore, he was often desperately lonely.

Conrad wrote much about his sea career, and in a prevailingly buoyant or nostalgic, in any case strongly affirmative, tone. But the legend he created concealed a good deal. For one thing, his irascible temper continued to get him into trouble—he quarrelled with at least three of his captains, those of the *Mavis*, the *Europa*, and the *Riversdale*; and for another, he remained erratic about money and very accident-prone. There also continued to be some periods of ill-health and paralysing inertia, and it now appears that at the first attempt Conrad failed some parts of his examinations both for first mate and for master.[1] Much more important, and wholly coercive, was the fact that, for reasons quite beyond his control, it gradually became evident that a career at sea could not provide a permanent and satisfactory basis for Conrad's life.

1. In 1884 for "the Day's Work" (meaning, roughly, routine navigation and recording it in the ship's logbook), and in 1886 both for that and for arithmetic. See Hans van Marle, "Plucked and Passed on Tower Hill: Conrad's Examinations Ordeals," *Conradiana* 8 (1976): 99–109; hereafter cited as *C*. Van Marle shows that Conrad misrepresented his length of service and other matters on various official forms to a fraudulent degree; and he documents how Conrad's sea career presents a much more chequered picture than he gave later in his reminiscent writings.

The blame must finally rest on the industrial revolution. It was through its capacity to develop ships built of iron and later of steel, to power them by steam, and to stoke them by coal, that Britain was able to keep pace with its rivals in the growing world competition for freight; but in that process the sailing ship was bound to become a casualty. By 1883 the registered total tonnage of British steamships for the first time exceeded that of sail,[2] and by 1894, the year Conrad's career as a seaman ended, sail accounted for barely one-third of the tonnage of the merchant fleet. Even more disastrous for Conrad's chances was the rapid increase in the average size of ships, and the consequent decrease in the number of vessels—and therefore of commands. At the beginning of Conrad's sea-going career, in 1875, Britain's merchant marine numbered 25,461 vessels; at its end, in 1894, the number had declined to 21,206, although the total tonnage of shipping had risen from 6,153,000 to 8,956,000. The decline was even more dramatic for sailing ships—the number was almost halved, from a total of 21,291 registered in 1875 to 12,943 in 1894. One expert, Edward Blackmore, estimated that over this period "an average of 260 [masters] must have lost employment every year."[3]

Another result of the fierce competition with steam was that sailing ships increasingly carried too few men and too much canvas—often to a dangerous degree; and this was in addition to a general deterioration of conditions under sail and steam alike, in which safety precautions, nautical training, and rates of pay all suffered. During Conrad's years in the British merchant service, the hardships and perils of the seaman's life were getting worse,[4] and the increasing public concern with the numbers of lives lost at sea led to two royal commissions of enquiry, which reported in 1874 and 1887.[5] It is probably not a wholly exceptional fact that of the first seven British vessels on which Conrad sailed, no less than five were lost in a period of four years, although only in the case of the last of them, the *Palestine,* was Conrad on board (*J A,* 317–20).

Despite all these difficulties Conrad continued to follow the sea, and to disregard the warning of his examiner for the master's certificate: "Everybody goes into steam" (*P R,* 117). All Conrad's main berths were on sailing ships; and these got more and more difficult to obtain

2. B. R. Mitchell and Phyllis Deane, *Abstract of British Historical Statistics* (Cambridge, 1962), pp. 217–24.

3. Edward Blackmore, *The British Mercantile Marine: A Short Historical Review* (London, 1897), pp. 132–35.

4. See Robert Dana Foulke, "Life in the Dying World of Sail, 1870-1910," *Journal of British Studies* 3 (1963): 105–36; R. J. Cornewall-Jones, *The British Merchant Service . . .* (London, 1898), pp. 262–72, 281–82.

5. See Blackmore, *British Mercantile Marine,* pp. 104–27.

as the years passed. The only real command Conrad ever got, that of the *Otago,* came about through the accident of its former captain's death in the Gulf of Siam when Conrad happened to be available as a replacement at Singapore; in any case the *Otago* was a small barque, with a total complement of ten.

Conrad was her captain from January 1888 to March 1889, when he resigned, so that he could see his aging uncle again; his naturalisation as a British subject in 1886, and his final formal release from Russian citizenship in 1889, had at last made it possible for him, after fifteen years, to revisit Poland. On his return, finding it impossible to get work in England, he was forced to seek employment on the Congo, and under the Belgian flag. There the promised command of a small river steamer failed to materialise; and after again waiting vainly for a berth as captain on a British ship, Conrad was forced, in November 1891, to accept an appointment as first mate of the clipper *Torrens,* on which he made two long voyages to Australia. There followed another very long period of unemployment ashore, until finally Conrad was forced to accept an even lower position; so it was as the second mate of the iron steamer *Adowa,* in the winter of 1893, and tied up in the port of Rouen waiting for emigrant passengers who never arrived, that Conrad ended his first professional career. Following the family tradition, he had backed another lost cause.

Even if Conrad had been able to get regular commands, however, it is very unlikely that he would have spent the rest of his life at sea. Except on a few of the largest vessels, the pay would not have been enough to enable him to live like a gentleman; throughout his years at sea Conrad had continued to be subsidised by Bobrowski, and his annual allowance of about a hundred pounds in the early years was more than his monthly pay of eight pounds as mate on the *Torrens,* and not much less than the fourteen pounds he received as captain of the *Otago.*[6] It is not surprising that in 1885 Conrad should have told Bobrowski that he felt "sick and tired of sailing about for little money and less consideration" (*L L,* I, 83), or that he was continually searching for alternatives. In the letter just quoted, Conrad was thinking about going into whaling on his own. It was one of the more serious of his many projects for becoming financially secure; and in 1884 Bobrowski had already given him £350 to buy a partnership in a small firm of shipping agents, Barr, Moering and Co. (*N,* 94).

Conrad, then, can never have felt any confidence that life as a seaman could offer him a reliable future; and in any case the social

---

6. See *N,* 198–201, and *J A,* 320–24. Conrad's allowance was reduced to fifty pounds in 1881 and to thirty in 1884, but he received various occasional supplements.

and intellectual disparities between himself and the average ship's officer must also have become increasingly evident. One can hardly imagine a greater contrast between Conrad and the traditional old salt with tar in his fingernails and filth on his tongue. The earliest description available is by Paul Langlois, his French charterer in Mauritius, who saw Conrad often in 1888, when he was commanding the *Otago*. He recalled later that "Captain Korzeniowski was always dressed like a fop [*petit maître*] . . . in a dark jacket, usually a light-coloured waistcoat, and a fancy pair of trousers, all of these well made and of great elegance; he wore a black or grey bowler hat slightly to one side, always had gloves on and carried a gold-headed Malacca cane" (*J B,* 96). Langlois adds that Conrad's "relations with . . . the other captains were of purely formal politeness," and that "he was not very popular among his colleagues who called him, ironically, 'the Russian count.' "

Conrad's fiction portrays many ship's officers very favorably, but there are none with whom one can imagine him having much intellectual or inward rapport; the only exceptions are characters who are in part self-portraits, notably Marlow. It is also significant that the only close friends Conrad made during his sea years were not seamen,[7] and that the first person to whom he is known to have showed his writing was a Cambridge graduate, Jacques, who happened to be a passenger on the *Torrens* (*P R,* 15–18).

Conrad usually wrote as though he had become a sailor by lifelong design and an author wholly by accident. There are probably many reasons for this. Most obvious, perhaps, was the fact that stressing his vocation as a seaman countered the charge of deserting Poland— after all he could have become a novelist, but hardly a seaman, at home. In any case, Conrad had genuinely loved his first profession; he continued to seek berths long after he had become a published author; and when he wrote about his years at sea, he was also looking back at his youth.

Actually, being a ship's officer must in many ways have suited Conrad very well. For one thing, he knew that the psychological pressure of a ready-made daily routine and a set pattern of conduct was good for him; a ship, Conrad once wrote, "is a creature which we have brought into the world, as it were on purpose to keep us up to the

---

7. Of these four, to all of whom he dedicated books, E. L. Sanderson, John Galsworthy, Adolph Krieger, and G. W. F. Hope, only the last had been a sailor, and he had become a company director by the time they met (see especially Norman Sherry's important *Conrad's Western World* [Cambridge, 1971], pp. 122–24, 326–34; hereafter cited as *S W W*). Cornewall-Jones comments that "on all hands it appears to be conceded that Merchant Service officers are considerably behindhand in educational attainments" (*The British Merchant Service,* p. 281).

mark";[8] and Conrad came to believe that his frequent bouts of "black melancholy" were the "result of idleness."[9] Secondly, he felt less of an exile, for on shipboard he belonged, automatically but intensely and incontrovertibly, to a society—to a society, moreover, that was composed of people from many countries, and where neither his past nor his future was an issue. Thirdly, Conrad must have discovered an unexpected congruence between his life as a ship's officer and some of his inherited expectations as a member of the *szlachta*. His pay and his life ashore might be dismal and humiliating, but on board the officers' mess and the attentions of the steward provided a framework of privileged status for his daily life. His role as officer also involved the exercise of independent authority whose goal was not economic advantage but collective survival. As a ship's officer, in short, Conrad was still an important and needed member of a community rather than someone who merely worked for a living; and the moral essence of his life remained the discharge of traditional responsibilities within a defined hierarchy.

There were also deeper and more intimate satisfactions. By the first relatively free decision of his life, Conrad had become a merchant seaman, and against everyone's advice. As Bobrowski had written in 1878: "You wanted it—you did it—you voluntarily chose it. Submit to the results of your decision" (*N*, 55). Not without hesitations and backslidings, Conrad had submitted; and the moral rewards had proved to be of unexpected magnitude. "I had elected," Conrad wrote much later, "to be one of them very deliberately, very completely, without any looking back or looking elsewhere. The circumstances were such as to give me the feeling of complete identification, a very vivid comprehension that if I wasn't one of them I was nothing at all" (*N L L*, 183).

Conrad's sea career both restored the exile to a community and enabled him to develop and exercise the plenitude of his powers as an individual. Something of this comes out in the first account we have of Conrad on board ship. John Galsworthy, who was a passenger on the clipper *Torrens* in 1893, remembered that Conrad "was a good seaman, watchful of the weather, quick in handling the ship; considerate with the apprentices—we had a long, unhappy Belgian youth among them, who took unhandily to the sea and dreaded going aloft; Conrad compassionately spared him all he could. With the crew he was popular; they were individuals to him, not a mere gang. . . . He

---

8. *The Mirror of the Sea*, 1906, p. 28; hereafter cited as *M S*.
9. *Letters of Joseph Conrad to Marguerite Poradowska, 1890–1920*, ed. and trans. John A. Gee and Paul A. Sturm (New Haven, 1940), p. 54; hereafter cited as *P*.

was friendly with the young second mate . . . and respectful, if faintly ironic, with his whiskered, stout old English captain."[10]

Against all odds, then, it was in the British merchant service that the feckless Polish orphan had justified himself to the world, and found a large, though never an unalloyed or an uninterrupted, measure of personal fulfillment. But although it was this experience which laid the basis for his becoming an English novelist, Conrad must not be seen as a seaman who wrote fiction, and he was right to resent this view of his achievement as a novelist.

If there was one thing that infuriated Conrad more than being treated as a spinner of yarns about the ocean deep, it was the idea that he had hesitated about whether to write novels in English or French (*J B*, 152–53). The supposition was natural enough; there is surely no other case of someone becoming a great writer in his third, possibly his fourth, language. A good many have written in two languages, like Rilke, Julian Green, and Samuel Beckett; and a few, such as Nabokov, have made their greatest reputation in a language not their own; but Conrad's case is unique.[11]

It was not a question of exceptional linguistic skill. Although Conrad's spoken and written Polish remained perfectly fluent, his writing was apparently somewhat formal and not impeccable as regards orthography (*A B*, 181–84). As to French, Conrad spoke idiomatically; his written French, however, though easy and effective, was somewhat stiff, and with a good many incidental errors of idiom and spelling.[12] Conrad had learned English much later in life, and his pronunciation retained a marked foreign accent, especially with "th" sounds, and what should be mute final "e"s;[13] throughout the forty-six years of his life with the English, Conrad's speech immediately identified him as a foreigner. Nor did Conrad's written English ever wholly free itself

10. "Reminiscences of Conrad," in *Castles in Spain and Other Screeds* (New York, 1927), p. 102.

11. This view is maintained by Věreboj Vildomec, who treats Conrad as quadrilingual, in his *Multilingualism* (Leyden, 1963), pp. 56–58. In addition to Polish, French and English, Conrad also learned some German at his schools in Austrian Poland, and he apparently retained some fluency in conversation (Borys Conrad, *My Father: Joseph Conrad* [London, 1970], p. 97). Conrad also picked up a smattering of Russian in his early years (*N*, 170).

12. This is the only aspect of Conrad's language which has been thoroughly studied, in René Rapin's analysis of "Le Français de Joseph Conrad," prefixed to his *Lettres de Joseph Conrad à Marguerite Poradowska* (Geneva, 1966), hereafter cited as *R R*. Rapin nicely remarks of Conrad's handling of written French that he treated it with "une négligence de grand seigneur": this no doubt also applies to many of his lapses in written Polish and English.

13. H. G. Wells writes that Conrad "would say, '*Wat* shall we do with *thesa* things?' " (*Experiment in Autobiography* [New York, 1934], p. 525).

from Polish (*N*, 29–30) and French influences[14] in vocabulary, syntax, and rhetorical style; while his manuscripts show that although his spelling improved, it never became perfect, especially in the more unphonetic vagaries of English orthography—the word "length," for example, Conrad "usually though not invariably spelled *lenght*."[15]

As regards linguistic knowledge and skill, then, Conrad had three more or less equal possibilities open to him when he began to write fiction: Polish might initially have been easiest to write, but the public was not very large; French would have the advantage of giving him a European audience, including many more readers than would English in his native country.[16] Yet Conrad steadfastly maintained that the idea of "choice had never entered my head," and that, far from his having adopted English, "it was I who was adopted by the genius of the language, which directly I came out of the stammering stage made me its own so completely that its very idioms I truly believe had a direct action on my temperament." Conrad even made the ringing affirmation that he had "the right to be believed when I say that if I had not written in English I would not have written at all" (*P R*, v–vi).

Conrad confessed that his possession by the English language was "too mysterious to explain"; but that in fact he never hesitated in his literary choice is confirmed by what little we know: he used English, for instance, in the private diary he kept during his voyage to the Congo in 1890. Polish remained the language of Conrad's childhood memories and of unconscious instinct—he spoke Polish, for instance, when he was delirious from fever (*J C C*, 26); French remained his ideal language for literary and intellectual analysis, cosmopolitan politeness and rhetorical elegance; but English became the necessary language of Conrad's mature self, of the self he had achieved in the British merchant service. As he wrote to Hugh Walpole, "When I wrote the first words of *Almayer's Folly*, I had been already for years and years *thinking* in English" (*L L*, II, 206). The fact that the language was difficult, that even in 1907 Conrad could write "English is . . . still a foreign language to me, requiring an immense effort to handle" (*P*, 109), was probably part of its appeal. English had been his language in the years when he had escaped from being "nothing at all"; it was, Conrad said, "the speech of my secret choice" (*P R*, 136), the symbol of the man he had become, of the person he had painfully managed to construct out of chaos and misery; and it was a

14. See, for example, J. I. M. Stewart, *Joseph Conrad* (London, 1968), pp. 20–22.

15. William Blackburn, ed., *Joseph Conrad: Letters to William Blackwood and David S. Meldrum* (Durham, N. C., 1958), p. xxxv; hereafter cited as *B*.

16. *N*, 106; Bobrowski thought that "here English is likely to be known only to a few women," though he no doubt exaggerated somewhat.

natural—perhaps necessary—continuation of this process of self-creation that he should become an author in English.

Conrad's England, however, was primarily the England of the merchant navy, and of a great literature; what Conrad really thought of the English people—among whom he spent his shore leaves and subsequently settled for the last thirty years of his life—is very difficult to know. The English may not exactly be xenophobes, but they do not take quickly and warmly to foreigners. Bobrowski's letters certainly do not suggest that his nephew took to his adopted countrymen easily or enthusiastically; and although what Conrad later said about them was almost unexceptionally laudatory, we must remember what politeness exacts from the guest, and how gratitude exaggerates benefits. In private Conrad was certainly critical of the complacency, insularity, and philistinism of English bourgeois society; Ford, for instance, related that one evening at the Empire music hall, "during applause by the audience of some *too* middle-class joke one of us leaned over towards the other and said: 'Doesn't one feel lonely in this beastly country!' "[17]

Still, there was much in England that Conrad loved and admired: especially, perhaps, the residues of the past, of the sailing ship, and of the age of Palmerston and the *Pax Britannica*. He found a society which combined the lingering social and political dominance of a landed class with a considerable degree of national cohesion and individual freedom, much as the Polish state had once done; there was also the surprising capacity of its people—exemplified in sea captains like MacWhirr—to do very well without being clever; and, above all, there was what his compatriot Retinger noted of the English—"the silent, the discreet, but passionate loyalty."[18]

Yet Conrad was not at home. He no doubt believed what he wrote in 1905 from Capri to Edmund Gosse, that "I . . . find that I need the moral support, the sustaining influence of English atmosphere even from day to day" (*L L*, II, 15); but his residence in England remained faintly provisional; even when he could have afforded it Conrad never bought a house; and to the end it was Poland which involved his deepest, his most private, and his most conflicting, feelings. Conrad's abiding sense of personal loneliness is suggested in his story "Amy Foster," which tells how an emigrant who seems to come from Poland is shipwrecked and cast up on the Kentish coast, marries a local girl,

17. *F M F*, 240. Ford says much about Conrad's attitude to England, and his is perhaps the best testimony we have although, as here, one can never be quite sure how much is actually Conrad and how much Ford. See also *F M F*, 20, 47–48, 241.

18. J. H. Retinger, *Conrad and his Contemporaries*, p. 43.

and is eventually driven to madness and death because the barriers of language and custom prove insurmountable.

There was no final solution; to be pleasantly surprised at what we have become does not efface the imprint of what was not to be. Answering the enquiry of a fellow Polish expatriate in 1903, Conrad once attempted to articulate the nature of his divided allegiance: "Both at sea and on land my point of view is English, from which the conclusion should not be drawn that I have become an Englishman. That is not the case. Homo duplex has in my case more than one meaning. You will understand me. I shall not dwell upon that subject" (N, 240). Conrad's lapse into the silent complicity of compatriots in exile is eloquent testimony to how settling in England had merely compounded those inward duplicities which had been involved in leaving Poland, and which continued to make "love itself wear at times the desperate shape of betrayal."

iv. The Past as Prologue

In appearance Conrad was of middle height, not much above five foot six according to most accounts, though his wife said he was over five foot eight (J A, 2), and his "Application to be Examined" in 1886 gives it as five foot nine and a half inches. His photographs[1] show a large, somewhat receding forehead, high cheekbones, and a strong nose; as he grew older the sensitive upper lip and rather weak chin of his childhood were covered by a dark-brown moustache and beard. Conrad's body was square and sturdy; his powerful shoulders were slightly rounded and hunched, but the upturned carriage of his head gave an impression of redoubtable vigilance. That his appearance was striking, and in later years strikingly handsome, was mainly due to his hazel brown eyes "over which the lids were deeply folded";[2] Langlois remembered them as melancholy, dreamy, and gentle (J B, 96); but even in the earliest photographs, taken when he was a child of four, five, and seven, Conrad's gaze has a penetrating concentration on the world before it which is compounded of reserve, apprehension, and scornful challenge.

In manhood Conrad largely outgrew his early sickliness, but he remained very highly strung. On his nervous days, according to Langlois, "he had a tick of the shoulder and of the eyes, and the most

1. See Norman Sherry, *Conrad and his World* (London, 1972), for reproductions of most of the extant photographs of Conrad, and a remarkable collection of other pictorial Conradiana. I am indebted to Norman Sherry for a copy of Conrad's official application.

2. John Galsworthy, *Castles in Spain*, p. 101.

minor unexpected occurrence—something falling on the floor or a door slamming—would make him jump. He was what we would call a neurasthenic."[3] That was in 1888, and in 1890 Conrad's Congo voyage seriously worsened his physical and nervous health. From then on he was intermittently immobilised by severe attacks of malaria, rheumatism, and especially gout, as well as by periods of prostrating psychological depression.

It is very difficult to know how to assess the ultimate importance of Conrad's recurrent ill-health and nervous instability. Some biographies, of which that by his wife, Jessie Conrad, was the first, and that by Bernard Meyer is the fullest, make this side of Conrad's personality dominant; and although one certainly cannot blame them for not explaining Conrad's genius—who could?—one is left wondering how the psychologically crippled valetudinarian they present could have managed to survive past the age of sixty-six, and produce some twenty volumes of fiction that are marked by gloom, certainly, but also by a moral strength and sanity that remains unrivalled in the literature of our century.

A marked disparity between personal character and creative achievement is not uncommon among writers. The parallel with Samuel Johnson is particularly illuminating. Neither Johnson nor Conrad wrote directly about their inner lives, and in each case it is only our subliminal sense of great energies at play to keep turbulent and destructive personal feelings under conscious control which makes us feel that we are in touch with one of the great heroes of the wars of the mind.

In some ways it is more difficult with Conrad than with Johnson to understand the man. One reason is the nature of the evidence. Very few of Conrad's own letters from the first half of his life have survived; and although his autobiographical writings, notably *A Personal Record* and *The Mirror of the Sea*, are both illuminating and of supreme literary quality, they are highly selective. Conrad scorned the confessional genre as "a form of literary activity discredited by Jean-Jacques Rousseau on account of the extreme thoroughness he brought to the work of justifying his own existence" (*P R*, 95); and Conrad was the last man either to provide raw biographical data for public consumption, or to disclose anything which might prove in the slightest embarrassing to himself or to others.

Nor do the numerous descriptions of Conrad by those who knew him well help as much as might be expected. Conrad's personality tended to elicit intense reactions, but they varied widely according to

3. *J B*, 97. Conrad applied the term to himself ("The *Torrens:* A Personal Tribute," 1923, in *Last Essays* 1926 [London, 1955], p. 24; hereafter cited as *L E*).

the person. For instance, although Bertrand Russell ended his eloquent portrait by wishing that he could make Conrad's "intense and passionate nobility . . . shine for others as it shone for me,"[4] it utterly fails to shine through the pages devoted to him by H.G. Wells.[5] This divergence was partly the result of Conrad's mercurial temperament, which emerges very clearly from his letters. Everyone is different with different people, but with Conrad the variation of personality was extreme. He had an intuitive awareness of where he could find a responsive chord in others that would reciprocate some part of the unappeased complexity of his inner life; and he also had a masked but inexhaustible need to be accepted, reassured, admired, and loved. In both these traits we can surely trace the residual effects of his early life.

As a boy Conrad once broke in on the conversation of two grown-ups with the question: "And what do you think of me?" To which the ancients predictably responded: "You're a young fool who interrupts when his elders are talking" (*J B*, 22–23). The lonely self-preoccupation which prompted the question could hardly be more lacerating; and the answer vouchsafed must have taught young Conrad to be more cautious later about exposing his vulnerability to rebuff. One imagines Conrad paying even more continuous and desperate attention than most children to the problem of what behaviour was likely to win adult approval; he had no other approval to fall back on. Many people later remarked on Conrad's ingratiating manner and his tendency to fulsome compliment; one also notices that in his letters to literary friends he always praises, or is at least critically very kind, about their work. It is the special kindness of those who have often missed it, and a measure of the insecurity with which, from the beginning and of necessity, Conrad approached most personal relations.

Conrad's early life had not supplied him with any of the normal foundations of psychological stability; and when he was thirty years old he wrote in an *Album de confidences* that the natural gift he would most have liked was "self-confidence" (*J B*, 98). He wrote later, in "An Outpost of Progress," that most people's character is really "only the expression of their belief in the safety of their surroundings."[6] The posthumous resonance of the fictional world Conrad created no doubt partly derives from the fact that he had never shared that confidence.

There are many other, and more tangible, residues of his early

4. *The Autobiography of Bertrand Russell, 1872–1914* (Boston, 1967), p. 324.
5. *Experiment in Autobiography*, pp. 525–35.
6. *Tales of Unrest*, 1898 (London, 1947), p. 89; hereafter cited as *T U*.

circumstances both in Conrad's life and in his work. As Bernard Meyer has noted (*B C M*, 114), Conrad's fiction is virtually devoid of sons with mothers, although many of his women are idealised mother-figures, such as the childless Mrs. Gould. On the other hand, no doubt partly because his father lived longer than his mother, so that Conrad knew him much better, Conrad's fiction is very rich in father-son relationships, either literal, as with Heyst in *Victory*, or, much more commonly, symbolic, as with Marlow and Jim. The prevalence of surrogate father-figures in Conrad's fiction must also have been increased by the special difficulties Conrad later encountered in initiating himself into his adult and vocational roles; and these stresses no doubt played their part in making Conrad's fiction so deeply concerned with the problem of authority, and especially of youth's assumption of responsibility within a system of command.[7]

In Conrad's personal case the most important of these paternal figures, apart from his father, was his uncle, Bobrowski, to whom, as he later wrote, he stood "more in the relation of a son than of a nephew" (*E G*, 166). The richly opposite characters of these two men embody many of the discrepancies within Conrad's own character, and in the typical conflicts of value in his works.

In 1900 Conrad responded to a request from Edward Garnett for biographical information. In it he wrote of his father: "A man of great sensibilities; of exalted and dreamy temperament; with a terrible gift of irony and of gloomy disposition; withal of strong religious feeling degenerating after the loss of his wife into mysticism touched with despair. His aspect was distinguished; his conversation very fascinating; his face in repose sombre, lighted all over when he smiled" (*E G*, 168). Conrad's account of Bobrowski is briefer: "a man of powerful intelligence and great force of character and possessed an enormous influence in the Three Provinces (Ukraine, Volhynia and Podolia). A most distinguished man" (*E G*, 166).

The contrast between the two descriptions is revealing. Conrad's attitude towards his father is detached, if not critical, but it immediately establishes him as a very real and vital person. Actually Conrad resembled his father a good deal, not only in appearance and build, to judge from early photographs, but in temperament—there is nothing in Conrad's remarks about his father which does not apply equally well to himself, except for the religious mysticism. On the other hand, Conrad's characterisation of Bobrowski is rather formal and lifeless, although its unqualified praise echoes his earlier tribute that despite having seen his uncle only on four brief visits during the

7. See Robert M. Armstrong, "Joseph Conrad: The Conflict of Command," *The Psychoanalytic Study of the Child* 26 (1971): 485–534.

twenty years between his leaving Poland and Bobrowski's death, "I attribute to his devotion, care, and influence, whatever good qualities I may possess" (*N*, 239).

Conrad, we may say, was torn between the qualities of the man he naturally was, his father's son, and those he had later acquired as Bobrowski's ward. Conrad must have become aware of the conflict between these two paternal presences very early, because Bobrowski was never tired of warning Conrad against whatever he considered a reflection of his father's side of the family. "You always . . . made me impatient," Bobrowski wrote to Conrad in 1876, "by your disorder and the easy way you take things—in which you remind me of the Korzeniowski family—spoiling and wasting everything" (*N*,37). In 1891, when Conrad was in a state of physical and mental collapse after his return from the Congo, he wrote to Bobrowski: "It is better to die young as in any case one is bound to die sometime" (*N*, 150). He had previously asked his uncle to "indicate those shortcomings" of his character which he had observed. In his reply Bobrowski harped on how Conrad "lacked endurance and perseverance in decisions," and asserted that this was "a trait of character inherited from your Grandfather—your paternal Uncle—and even your Father: in short the Nałęczs"—Nałęcz was the name of Apollo's coat of arms. Bobrowski found another of their "shortcomings" in Conrad's basic temperament: "You let your imagination run away with you—you become an optimist; but when you encounter disappointments you fall easily into pessimism—and as you have a lot of pride, you suffer more as the result" (*N*, 147–48).

The other side of the family inheritance only began to appear after the nadir of Marseilles. Once Conrad had settled down in the British merchant service, Bobrowski saw "with pleasure that the 'Nałęcz' in you has been modified under the influence of the Bobroszczaki," that is, of the maternal family strain (*N*, 66). Being a seaman both required and developed the energy, responsibility, discipline, and stoicism which Bobrowski had possessed, and, much against the evidence, attributed to his family in general. "Work and perseverance are the only values that never fail," Bobrowski preached (*N*, 63); and he warned Conrad against the Polish tendency to grandiose self-delusions: "Nobody has the right to withdraw from" the life of ordinary duties just "because of his conviction that he is not part of the team" (*N*, 154). Bobrowski consistently inculcated the practical or Positivist set of values which had come to the fore in Poland since the 1863 uprising. He argued that: "If both Individuals and Nations were to make 'duty' their aim, instead of the ideal of greatness, the world would certainly be a better place than it is! . . . The devotion to duty interpreted more widely or narrowly, according to circumstances and time—this constitutes my practical creed [which] may be of some use to you."

It was. It became the Conradian ethic. But although the Bobrowski values were indispensable as ballast to keep Conrad on an even keel, they were hardly likely to provide much creative momentum; for Conrad's career as a writer his other inheritance was essential; and, as Bobrowski acutely saw, these paternal attitudes were in conflict with Conrad's life as a seaman: "Both in you as an individual and in what you have inherited from your parents I detect the dreamer—in spite of your very practical profession—or perhaps because of it?"

The tension in Conrad between the practical ethic on the one hand, and the disillusioned pessimism of the Romantic visionary on the other, pervades the whole of his creative world. One aspect of it was most memorably described by E.M. Forster when he asked whether "the secret casket of [Conrad's] genius" does not contain "a vapour rather than a jewel." The vapour, Forster wrote, may have its source in what he saw as "the central chasm of his tremendous genius," the chasm which divided Conrad the seaman from Conrad the seer.[8] Forster contrasted the no-nonsense quarterdeck manner with which Conrad the seaman asserted or defended his "loyalties and prejudices and personal scruples," with the other side of Conrad, which "holds another ideal, a universal, the love of Truth." "There are," Forster argued, "constant discrepancies between his nearer and his further vision, and here would seem to be the cause of his central obscurity. If he lived only in his experiences, never lifting his eyes to what lies beyond them: or if, having seen what lies beyond, he would subordinate his experiences to it—then in either case he would be easier to read."

Forster seems not to allow for what had been made abundantly clear in Conrad's life—that he could hardly have had his experiences if he had tried to subordinate them to what he saw beyond them; any action would have been paralysed or at least undermined by the darkness, despair, and boredom of his further vision. Conrad had no doubt that it was the private individual consciousness which must be the supreme reality for the writer; he wrote in 1903 that "a work of imagination" should express "that inner life (which is the soul of human activity)" (N, 240). In his own case, however, Conrad's inner life brought little strength or comfort as far as practical existence was concerned. We are condemned, he wrote in 1894 to his relative and intimate friend, the writer Marguerite Poradowska, to "drag the ball

8. In his 1921 review in *The Nation and Athenaeum* of Conrad's *Notes on Life and Letters*. Originally entitled "The Pride of Mr. Conrad," it was reprinted, somewhat shortened, in *Abinger Harvest* (London, 1946), pp. 134–38.

and chain of one's selfhood [*individualité*] right to the end. That's what one pays for the devilish and divine privilege of Thought;—so that in this life it is only the Elect who are convicts—the glorious company of those who understand and groan, but who tread the earth amidst a multitude of phantoms with the gestures of maniacs [and] the grimaces of idiots."[9]

But if the familiar romantic dichotomy between the sensitive individual and the crass mob could not be reconciled philosophically, it could be overcome in practice, at least partially and some of the time. When Conrad became a sailor his further vision was mastered by a foreground of the most direct physical, social and moral commitments; and closer view must surely have revealed that the ordinary seamen he worked with were neither maniacs nor idiots. Bobrowski, it seemed, had been right. There was a "basic truth of life" available to "those who do not work on the basis of a philosophical system but who in their existence abide by simple rules and who apply them in judging both themselves and their fellow men" (*N*, 152–53). Only action could make the conflict between this moral orientation and the despairing indifference and corrosive scepticism of Conrad's further vision, seem less absolute; and so in his nearer vision Conrad followed the words which the greatest of British empiricists gave Sir Andrew Aguecheek in *Twelfth Night:* "I have no exquisite reason for't, but I have reason good enough." Wherever the immediate problems of life were concerned, whether in his own world or in that of his fiction, Conrad tended to impose a sort of moratorium on the endless war between his further and his nearer vision; it was only a provisional arrangement, but since no prospect either of peace or a victory could be discerned on the horizon of possibility, the moratorium had reason good enough.

The conflict certainly explains much of the discrepancy between the man and the work. Conrad's public voice is predominantly that of the seaman and Bobrowski's ward, and therefore involves an implicit rejection of the paternal temperament as he saw it. That this was a premeditated and conscious choice is made clear in one of the more confessional moments in Conrad's "Familiar Preface" to *A Personal Record,* where he wrote: "It may be my sea training acting upon a natural disposition to keep good hold on the one thing really mine, but the fact is that I have a positive horror of losing even for one moving moment that full possession of myself which is the first condition of good service. And I have carried my notion of good service from my earlier into my later existence" (*P R*, xvii).

9. *P*, 72. I have modified the translation somewhat, and follow Rapin's amended reading at one point (*R R*, 36, n. 2).

The tensions in Conrad's character sometimes proved too violent to be controlled—there is a suggestion of this in the puzzling way he here makes it part of his "natural disposition" to have "a positive horror" of losing his self-possession. The conflict, however, took a more creative form in Conrad's fiction, and we can find it in almost every area of his achievement, from his general historical and moral perspective to the characteristics of his prose style. This is not to say that the elements in the conflict are always aligned symmetrically, as will later appear; and a more detailed analysis would no doubt reveal that the basic pattern of moral conflict in Conrad is multiple rather than dual; nevertheless Forster's polarity illuminates a great deal.

One can see the conflict, for instance, both in the weaknesses and in the strengths of Conrad's prose. At times the seaman's style is a little too obvious, and we can discover something of Bobrowski's tedious practicality in Conrad's remorseless preoccupation with bulwarks and bollards. In this mood Conrad's writing is as forced and hollow as when, in the opposite mood, its gloomy magniloquence genuflects to the melancholy romantic shade of Apollo Korzeniowski. On the other hand, it is surely the presence of the same quality in a less extreme form which gives Conrad's writing at its best a special strength, an alliance of quotidian concreteness and timeless implication which impels us to experience both the world and the self, the object and the idea, as equally and insistently real.

Conrad's prose also enacts the difficulty of establishing any stable relationship between the two. T. E. Lawrence once wrote that Conrad's style is "not built on the rhythm of ordinary prose, but on something existing only in his head, and as he can never say what it is he wants to say, all his things end in a kind of hunger."[10] The hunger, no doubt, arises from one's sense that Conrad is often moving towards, but not attaining, the resolution of pressing emotional and intellectual contradictions; what we get, most commonly, is a vast natural or historical perspective which in theory should undermine the heroism, and indeed the validity, of any human effort, but in practice gives it a deeper and more touching reality; in the novels, as in the life, Conrad's purpose was to oppose all the forces that dwarf human effort; and this involved asserting the moral imperatives of the nearer vision, to which Conrad sometimes gave the name of "solidarity."

The theme of solidarity or commitment is most directly and positively treated in the works dealing with the sea, and especially in the three masterpieces: The Nigger of the "Narcissus," Typhoon, and The Shadow-Line. On board ship it is relatively easy to connect daily life

10. The Letters of T. E. Lawrence, ed. David Garnett (London, 1938), p. 302.

and a larger moral order; for there, as Conrad wrote, "a wrestle with wind and weather has a moral value like the primitive acts of faith on which may be built a doctrine of salvation and a rule of life" (*B*, 133). But the primacy of the values of the nearer vision is also strongly present in many other of Conrad's greatest works, which are not primarily concerned with the sea but which centre on the movement of the protagonist towards another person or group. The movement is often incomplete, as in *Heart of Darkness, Lord Jim,* or *Chance;* sometimes it comes too late, as in *Nostromo, Under Western Eyes,* and *Victory;* but the reader's attention is nonetheless focused on following the movement of an alienated character outwards from the self. This movement helps us to understand why, much more than his Victorian contemporaries, Conrad belongs to modern literature, and yet points beyond it.

Alienation and exile were central to the lives and the art of Joyce and Lawrence, Pound and Eliot; they were not much less so to the later generation of Hemingway, Beckett and Auden. Conrad's case, though, was special, and in two ways. For one thing, Conrad did not choose his exile—the fate of his family and his country forced it on him; and for another, Conrad's exile was much more absolute—with very minor exceptions he did not write about his own country, and he wrote nothing for publication in his native tongue. The very absoluteness of his exile, however, set the course of Conrad's thought in a different direction from that of his peers. They tend to equate individuality with alienation: the poetry of Eliot and Pound, for instance, typically leads us away in critical revulsion from all contemporary actuality, while the novels of Lawrence and Joyce present the breaking of ties with family, home, class, country, and traditional beliefs as necessary stages in the achievement of spiritual and intellectual freedom: both the poets and the novelists incite us to a sharper sense of separateness. They see very much the same world as Conrad's further vision disclosed: a panorama of chaos and futility, of cruelty, folly, vulgarity, and waste; but, being less sceptical, perhaps, about the powers of their own minds, they then invite us to share the larger transcendental or private systems of order and value which they have adopted or invented. Conrad was much less sanguine; the son of Apollo, the defeated orphan, the would-be suicide, the inheritor of the Polish past, the initiate of all the destructive legacies of nineteenth-century thought, had walked the Waste Land from childhood on; the terrors which history held in ambush for the generations of Henry James or of T. S. Eliot had been his birthright. But Bobrowski's ward sailed with a different compass; he was always, as Edward Said has written, "the restless seeker after normative vision," and his "solutions always had one end in view—the achievement of character."[11] Today this makes him both more contemporary and more old-fashioned than his modern peers.

Old-fashioned because Conrad's movement towards the ageless solidarities of human experience was much commoner among the Romantics and Victorians. But the first half of his life had forced Conrad to see that his problematic dependence on others was a necessary condition for the very existence of the individual self; and so during the second half of his life his imagination was impelled, in many different ways, to confront a more contemporary question, and one which was not to be of any particular concern to the other great figures of modern literature: "Alienation, of course; but how do we get out of it?"

11. Edward W. Said, *Joseph Conrad and the Fiction of Autobiography* (Cambridge, Mass., 1966), pp. 15; 13.

CHAPTER 2

Almayer's Folly

i. Memories: Composition and Sources

One fine autumn morning in 1889, ashore in London after leaving the *Otago,* Conrad did not dawdle after breakfast as usual but summoned the landlady's daughter to clear the table. In *A Personal Record,* written in 1908, he stresses the obscurity of his sudden impulse: "I was not at all certain that I wanted to write, or that I meant to write, or that I had anything to write about . . . . It seems to me that I thought of nothing whatever, but this is an impression which is hardly to be believed at this distance of years. What I am certain of is, that I was very far from thinking of writing a story, though it is possible and even likely that I was thinking of the man Almayer" (*P R,* 70, 74).

Conrad had met "the man Almayer" some two years earlier (Conrad says four) during his third, longest, and last, stint of duty in Eastern seas. In the summer of 1887 a back injury had forced him to leave his ship and go into hospital at Singapore; on recovering, he signed on as chief mate of the *Vidar,* a small steamship which traded in local products with Borneo and the Celebes. On one of the *Vidar's* routine stops at an isolated settlement some thirty miles up the Berau river in Eastern Borneo, Conrad had dealings with a half-caste trader from Java called Charles Olmeijer. In *A Personal Record* Conrad gives a diverting account of their first meeting: alongside the little wharf on the edge of the jungle, Almayer emerges through the mist clad "in flapping pyjamas of cretonne pattern (enormous flowers with yellow petals on a disagreeable blue ground)" (74), to take delivery, oddly enough, of a riding pony, which knocks him flat on his back as soon as it is landed. After relating his impressions during their subsequent encounters—which actually cannot have numbered more than four visits of a few days each—Conrad makes the surprising assertion that "if I had not got to know Almayer pretty well it is almost certain there would never have been a line of mine in print" (*P R,* 87).

The offhandedly preposterous exaggeration is characteristic of Conrad: partly because he often attributed the initial impetus for a novel to a passing glimpse of someone or to a casual encounter; but especially because he liked to maintain that he had become an author by pure accident. Actually, it seems probable that some three years before, in 1886, Conrad had already written a short story, "The Black

Mate"; he said later that it was "for a prize competition, started, I think, by *Tit-Bits*" *(L L,* II, 264). The story, which now exists only in the presumably much-rewritten form of its eventual publication in 1908, is amusing but trivial; it only faintly qualifies Conrad's assertion that *"Almayer's Folly* may keep its place as my first serious work."

Almayer's Folly, Conrad wrote, was "begun in idleness—a holiday task" *(P R,* 68), but it was continued with the utmost seriousness; during the five years of its writing, he said, "there was not a day I did not think of it"*(L L,* I, 158, n. 2). The manuscript, most of which survives, was nearly lost in the Congo when Conrad's boat capsized, and again when it was left behind in a Berlin railway station; but the novel grew "line by line, rather than page by page" *(P R,* 19), until, after many other vicissitudes, the first draft was finally completed in April 1894. This was during the long period of unemployment after the end of Conrad's brief connection with the *Adowa;* there followed a process of intensive revision, including one, and probably two, typed versions; and then, on 4 July 1894, Conrad finally sent a boy messenger to deliver the typescript by hand to a publisher, Fisher Unwin.[1]

Unbearable silence followed. After much fretting about the possible loss of his only copy of the final version, Conrad wrote one, perhaps two, letters of enquiry: but, by what must now seem a miracle of publishing expedition, a letter arrived early in October offering him twenty pounds for the copyright. The novel came out on 29 April 1895, under the name Joseph Conrad.

Conrad had originally submitted *Almayer's Folly* for Unwin's "Pseudonym Library," and had given as pen name "Kamudi," the Malay word for rudder; but the novel proved too long for the series, and so it appeared under what is, strictly speaking, another pen name. For Conrad's real surname, of course, was Korzeniowski; he always regarded it as such, and so signed himself on official occasions. However, years of exasperation at the way his Polish surname was continually mispronounced and misspelled, had gradually led him to use his two easiest given names, Józef Konrad, for most purposes; and when he became an English author it was natural that he should use these names in their anglicised form, and eventually become known, even in Poland, as Joseph Conrad.

Conrad is characteristically uncommunicative about why an obscure Dutch trader should have precipitated him into authorship and fame, but something can be surmised. The Almayer who emerges from *A Personal Record* is an extraordinary blend of dreamer and defeatist.

1. See John Dozier Gordan, *Joseph Conrad: The Making of a Novelist* (Cambridge, Mass., 1940), pp. 112–29; hereafter cited as *J D G.* Conrad may have sent the typescript earlier to Edmund Gosse, who edited a series for Heinemann's (*J B*, 135).

"What he wanted with a pony," Conrad comments, "goodness only knows, since I am perfectly certain he could not ride it; but here you have the man, ambitious, aiming at the grandiose" (*P R*, 76). At the same time, when Almayer asked, "I suppose you haven't got such a thing as a pony on board?", he spoke "hardly audibly . . . in the accents of a man accustomed to the buffets of evil fortune"; and Conrad comments that his "pathetic mistrust in the favourable issue of any sort of affair touched me deeply." There was a similar lack of conviction about Almayer's attitude of his business enterprises: " 'The worst of this country,' " he mumbles to Conrad, " 'is that one is not able to realise . . . it's impossible to realise . . .' His voice sank into a languid mutter. 'And when one has very large interests . . . very important interests . . .' he finished faintly . . . 'up the river' " (*P R*, 86).

Almayer's baseless claims to be regarded as an exceptional person had made him a man "whose name apparently could not be uttered anywhere in the Malay Archipelago without a smile" (*P R*, 84); but Conrad says that he himself found "nothing amusing whatever" in Almayer. He had presumably recognised behind Almayer's ludicrous public aspect an extreme version of his own personal alternations between grandiose romantic dreams and a tired inurement to defeat; it was surely because Conrad himself had often felt that "nothing was ever quite worthy of you" that he admired Almayer for holding "this lofty theory with some force of conviction" (*P R*, 88). Conrad's own tendency to take a dark view of the future must have led him to recognise a kindred spirit when, having solicitously wondered if Almayer wouldn't catch "pneumonia or bronchitis or something, walking about in a singlet in such a wet fog," he had received the "sinister" answer: " 'No fear,' as much as to say that even that way of escape from inclement fortune was closed to him" (*P R*, 78).

Almayer's situation had probably raised another personal question of absorbing interest for Conrad. How had this particular lonely derelict come to be stranded at Berau? *A Personal Record* gives no answer; but *Almayer's Folly* does, and keeps fairly close to the historical facts. In the novel, Kaspar Almayer is the son of a minor official in Java, and leaves home to work as a clerk at the port of Macassar in the Celebes. There he meets a famous English trader, called Tom Lingard, who proposes that Almayer marry his ward, a native girl who will inherit Lingard's fortune. Though he has no feeling for the girl, and is ashamed to be marrying a Malay, Almayer agrees because he believes that he will then be able to realize the "earthly paradise of his dreams"—make a huge fortune and live in a "big mansion in Amsterdam."[2] Almayer then goes out to manage a small river settlement,

2. *Almayer's Folly* (London, 1947), p. 10; hereafter cited by page number only.

called Sambir in the novel, where Lingard has a trading monopoly.

The main action of *Almayer's Folly* occurs some twenty years after the marriage. Lingard has disappeared, trying to raise further capital somewhere in Europe; the trading post is derelict because Lingard's secret channel for navigating the Pantai river has been betrayed to rival Arab traders; the splendid new house on which Almayer has wasted his last resources in the vain hope that the British Borneo Company, not the Dutch, would take over Sambir, and that his trade would flourish again, has been dubbed "Almayer's Folly" by his mocking compatriots. It now stands unfinished, untenanted, and already much decayed; while its universally despised master is suffered to live on by the Malay and Arab leaders merely because they believe that only Almayer can tell them the secret of Lingard's rumoured mountain of gold further inland.

Recent research has confirmed much of Conrad's account of "Sambir."[3] Even the layout of the fictional setting corresponds very closely to the actual settlements of Gunung Tabur and Tanjong Redeb astride the Berau river. Olmeijer had indeed been settled there for some seventeen years; he was, in fact, the representative of an actual Captain Lingard, though one called not Tom but William; and this William Lingard really was a famous trader and adventurer, widely known as the *Rajah Laut*—Malay for "King of the Sea"—whose fortunes had in effect begun to decline soon after Olmeijer's arrival. In the plot of *Almayer's Folly*, Conrad also seems to have followed the historical facts in a good many minor details—for instance, William Lingard and Olmeijer apparently did prospect for gold further upriver, and did deal in contraband arms and gunpowder with the Dyak tribesmen of the interior.

Conrad also omitted and changed a great deal. The reasons for most of the omissions are very evident. For instance, it is surely to emphasize Almayer's isolation that there is no mention of the three other whites who were residing at Berau at the time of Conrad's visits, and that, instead of the four children then alive out of the eleven Olmeijer fathered, Almayer has only one child, his daughter Nina. As to Conrad's changes, two are particularly important. In the novel, Almayer is not a half-caste; this has the effect of dramatising the conflict in Nina's loyalties between her European father and her Malayan mother. Secondly, Conrad alters the likely cause of Almayer's failure; for while there is no evidence that any secret channel

3. See especially Norman Sherry, *Conrad's Eastern World* (Cambridge, 1966), pp. 89–138; hereafter cited as *S E W*. Jerry Allen (*J A*, 192–96; 220–24) gives an account of the researches made in 1951 by R. Haverschmidt, manager of a coal mine six miles upriver from Berau. He found the graves of two of the Olmeijer children, and talked to sundry local ancients who remembered the place in Olmeijer's day.

was betrayed to the Arabs, there is another less romantic explanation of the decline of Lingard's fortunes: steam.

Conrad's own visits to Berau were made on a steamer which belonged to a wealthy Arab in Singapore, whose eldest son, Syed Abdulla, like his namesake in the novel, had become the chief trader at Berau (*S E W*, 108–10; 117–18). William Lingard's monopoly had, in fact, ended with the coming of steamships, which made river navigation much easier, and fostered the development of regular coastal trade routes.

The dreams of Almayer had really been foreclosed, not by a betrayed secret, but by history. The Malay archipelago had seen two generations of heroic individual achievement: that of Sir Stamford Raffles (1781–1826), founder of Singapore; then that of Sir James Brooke (1803–1868), who became the rajah of Sarawak. Later, some of their merchant-adventurer successors in the fifties and sixties, such as William Lingard, had at least become figures of legend; but as Western penetration developed, individual opportunities declined, and the merchants and sailors of the seventies and eighties, the generation of Olmeijer, were a much more humdrum group. Even Borneo, one of the last areas to be taken over by the colonial powers, had now been largely consolidated; the long series of Dutch local wars ended in 1886; and in 1888 Sarawak officially became a British protectorate.

During his first voyage to the East in 1879 Conrad had written to Bobrowski from Australia "with the greatest enthusiasm," about the "beauty and wealth" of the area, and had even talked of taking up a position there which he said he had been offered by a famous captain and shipowner whom he had met at Sydney (*N*, 180). Nothing came of the project, and when, in 1883, 1885, and especially in 1887, Conrad actually saw Southeast Asia (which he had not when he wrote to Bobrowski), the exposure of his romantic youthful fantasies must have been brutal. Conrad had come East too late; too late to share the dreams of William Lingard or even those of his foolish protégé Olmeijer.

That Olmeijer was ultimately a doomed victim of the accidents of history may have been part of his initial appeal. But Conrad did not take this fictional direction, with its personal applications to his own case, very far—perhaps because his knowledge of Olmeijer's past was too sketchy to supply the action for a whole novel. At all events, during some relatively late stage of composition, Conrad was constrained to add to the story of Almayer what, for the rest of his career as a novelist, was to remain his closest approach to an invented romantic intrigue.[4]

4. The early pages of the manuscript suggest that when he began writing Conrad

This addition is based on Almayer's daughter, Nina, who has become the only sustaining force in his life: he has wholly absorbed her into his old dream of European splendour. The plot begins with Almayer awaiting the arrival of a dashing Balinese prince, Dain Maroola, who is to supply the ship and the men to secure the gold. But actually the Dutch have just intercepted Dain's brig for its contraband arms, and so he arrives a hunted man with only two followers. Abetted by Mrs. Almayer, Dain eventually carries off Nina, who is now the sole reason for his interest in Sambir; and when Almayer discovers that he has been robbed both of his last hope of wealth and of his last human connection, he determines to force himself to forget. But forgetting proves impossible; and when, a year or so later, he hears that Nina has given birth to a son, Almayer takes to opium and dies.

There is no reason to believe that any part of this intrigue is based on fact; but Conrad used a number of names belonging to real local people, although he attached them to quite different characters.[5] This use of real names is characteristic of Conrad in general; *Almayer's Folly* is an extreme case only in using the name of someone still alive for its protagonist. When the novel came out Olmeijer could well have read it, since he only died in 1900, in Java (*J B*, 89); and as early as 1896 a reviewer in a Singapore paper wrote that Lingard's friends considered Conrad's portrayal "a libel on his memory," adding that "the portrait of the 'Raja Laut' is not the only one which has been drawn from real life."[6] Conrad's alterations were so minor—from Olmeijer to the anglicised spelling of its sound, Almayer, and from William to Tom Lingard—that one is driven to wonder why, if he was changing the names at all, Conrad changed them so very little? What caused these stubborn and apparently pointless mnemonic adhesions, which are found throughout Conrad's writings?

In *A Personal Record* Conrad wrote that once he had begun *Almayer's Folly,* he would "hold animated receptions of Malays, Arabs and half-castes" in his imagination (9–10). "They came," he continues, "with silent and irresistible appeal," which in retrospect "seems now to have had a moral character, for why should the memory of these beings . . . demand to express itself in the shape of a novel, except on the ground of that mysterious fellowship which unites in a community of hopes

---

had not made up his mind about Dain's relation to Almayer or Nina, or Almayer's love for his daughter. See *J D G*, 125–126, and Marion Cicero Michael, "Joseph Conrad: A Textual and Literary Study of Four Stories" (Dissertation, University of Georgia, Athens, Ga., 1963; Ann Arbor, Mich.: University Microfilms, 1967), pp. 19–28.

5. For instance, three of the main Malay characters, Lakamba, Babalatchi, and Maroola, are named after real traders in the area (*S E W*, 162–70).

6. *Straits Budget*, 19 May 1896, reviewing *An Outcast of the Islands* (*S E W*, 118).

and fears all the dwellers on this earth?" Conrad goes on to affirm that
this sense of mysterious fellowship lay behind all his output: "After all
these years . . . I can honestly say that it is a sentiment akin to piety
which prompted me to render in words assembled with conscientious
care the memory of things far distant and of men who had lived."

No other novelist talks like that about his work; it seems closer to
more archaic notions of art as a ceremonial invocation of the tribal
gods and heroes; and the attitude of sacred homage to the people of
his past life is dominant in much else that Conrad said about his
approach to fiction. For instance, he once wrote that "a man who puts
forth the secret of his imagination to the world accomplishes, as it
were, a religious rite" (*L L*, II, 89). This seems puzzling if we consider
how often Conrad's attitude to his characters is ironic and irreverent,
as it is with Almayer; but there is no question that Conrad's recorded
statements about writing novels persistently disdain both fictional invention and "the famous need of self-expression" (*P R*, 68), and in
their place affirm the spirit of retrospective piety. Why that abiding
reverence for people in his past merely because they had left traces in
his memory?

One possible biographical clue is given in *A Personal Record* when
Conrad quotes Novalis: "It is certain my conviction gains infinitely the
moment another soul will believe in it," and then comments: "And
what is a novel if not a conviction of our fellow-men's existence strong
enough to take upon itself a form of imagined life clearer than reality . . ." (15). Two very different preoccupations are involved. That of
Novalis is general and philosophical: he is merely saying that our
intellectual opinions[7] are strengthened when someone else agrees
with them. The "fellow men" that Conrad speaks of, however, are not
hypothetical readers or listeners but actual people on whom he bases
the characters of his novels; and Conrad seems to be asserting that it is
the strength of his own conviction of their reality which enables them
to be given "a form of imagined existence" in fiction. If we seek any
analogy with Novalis's argument, we must perhaps assume that Conrad's "conviction" is one which concerns not his opinions but his

7. The word in the original German is not conviction but opinion (*Meinung*). The
quotation comes from the beginning of fragment 153 of *Das Allgemeine Brouillon*, where
Novalis is actually explaining the persuasive power of indirect quotation (*Novalis Schriften*, ed. Richard Samuel [Darmstadt, 1968], III, p. 269). Conrad's version, which he also
used as the epigraph for *Lord Jim*, was probably based on L. Tieck's edition (*Novalis
Schriften* [Berlin, 1837], II, p. 139), possibly through an English translation (*Hymns and
Thoughts on Religion by Novalis*, trans. and ed. W. Hastie [Edinburgh, 1888], p. 86), but
much more probably from Carlyle's quotation of it in *On Heroes, Hero-Worship, and the
Heroic in History*, 1841 (ed. H. D. Gray, London, 1906, p. 56); Conrad follows this
version verbatim. I am indebted to Richard Samuel for tracking down the Novalis
original, and to Edward Said for pointing out the Carlyle source.

memories; in that case *Almayer's Folly* would, in effect, serve to authenticate the truth of Conrad's own "memory of things far distant and men who have lived," and, by extension, the present repository of those memories.

David Hume had long before located the "source of personal identity" in the individual memory which "alone acquaints us with the continuance" of our images of past perceptions;[8] and Conrad's attitude seems particularly close to that of his contemporary, Unamuno. Unamuno writes: "We live in memory and by memory, and our spiritual life is at bottom simply the effort of our memory to persist"; and he concludes that memory is really "the effort of our past to transform itself into our future."[9] For Conrad it was through memory that the past of the sailor was to become the future of the writer; the names enshrined in Conrad's memory were the most objective bridge between his past and his present, and therefore the symbolic tokens of the continuing identity of the man who had carried them in his mind.

Proper names, Jean Starobinski has written, are "situated symbolically at the confluence of existence 'for oneself' and of existence 'for others' "; they are the "common denominators" between the inner ["être profond"] and the social being.[10] This may help to explain why it was in Conrad's first novel that the most extreme correspondence between the name of a fictional and a real character should have occurred. If it was indeed the memory of Olmeijer which set off the unconscious process by which Conrad interlocked both the outer and the inner world of his past self with his present existence, and projected them into future life through his novel, it becomes somewhat easier to understand why Conrad should have asserted that if he had not "got to know Almayer . . . there would never have been a line of mine in print."

ii. Models: Exotic Romance, Naturalism, and Flaubert

For a first novel by an unknown author, *Almayer's Folly* received a surprisingly large number of reviews both in England and America. They were preponderantly favourable, and one influential critic, T. P. O'Connor, even proclaimed in a leading article that "a new great writer," a "genius," had "entered into our literature" (*JB*, 158). Other critics mentioned various great names in Conrad's connection— Balzac, Turgenev, Zola; but the dominant note concerned the novel's

8. *A Treatise of Human Nature*, Bk. 1, Part IV, section 6 (Selby-Bigge ed., p. 261).

9. Miguel de Unamuno, *The Tragic Sense of Life*, trans. J. E. Crawford Flitch (London, 1921), p. 9.

10. Jean Starobinski, "Stendhal Pseudonyme," *L'Oeil vivant* (Paris, 1961), p. 198.

exotic background. One reviewer, indeed, was so full of resentment against all the "tiresome fiction supposed to be descriptive of outlandish places" that he concluded ironically of the particular example before him: "Borneo is a fine field for the study of monkeys, not of men" (*J D G*, 272). On the other hand, the *Spectator's* reviewer was so enthusiastic about the novel's exotic aspect that he ventured to hope that Conrad "might become the Kipling of the Malay Archipelago."

Some later critics also have thought very highly of *Almayer's Folly*. Its most extravagant panegyrist was H. L. Mencken: "I challenge . . . Christendom to point to another Opus 1 as magnificently planned and turned out . . . If it is not a work of genius then no work of genius exists on this earth."[1] We can at least agree that for a first novel *Almayer's Folly* is indeed an extraordinarily professional piece of writing. It also reveals the contradictory tendencies of the various literary models which shaped Conrad's initial approach to writing fiction.

In a sense, Conrad is the least derivative of writers; he wrote very little that could possibly be mistaken for the work of anyone else; and he consciously avoided following the doctrines of any particular literary school. But he did read very widely; and as is usual in an author's first significant work, the main residues of his reading are more clearly present in *Almayer's Folly* than elsewhere.

In 1895 the days of the great Victorian novelists had long been over. Among their successors, Stevenson had died the previous year, while Thomas Hardy was about to close his career as a novelist with *Jude the Obscure* (1896). The aesthetic movement had been the main new literary force in the eighties and nineties, but its decline was now being heralded by the sentencing of Oscar Wilde. *The Yellow Book* had begun in 1894 and was much talked about, but the greatest new power on the literary scene was the "yellow press."[2] The conjunction of these last two phenomena symbolizes the growing polarisation of tastes between "highbrow" and "lowbrow"[3] which was to be such a marked feature of the reading public in the twentieth century, and which was to have profound effects upon Conrad's writing career.

There were both literary and economic reasons why the fragmentation of the audience for fiction raised particular difficulties for Conrad. Personally, he wanted to write for readers as dissimilar as the

1. H. L. Mencken, *A Mencken Chrestomathy* (New York, 1949), p. 522. The original version, in *Smart Set* (1919), was even more laudatory.

2. See *Oxford English Dictionary.* The term supposedly originated with a 1894 comic-strip character called the Yellow Kid in Pulitzer's New York *World;* the nearest English equivalent was Alfred Harmsworth's *Daily Mail,* founded in 1896.

3. "Highbrow" and "lowbrow" as nouns are recorded in 1902–3 for the United States (Wentworth and Flexner, *Dictionary of American Slang*), and in 1911–13 for England (*O E D*).

seamen he had known and the people of advanced and cosmopolitan tastes who admired the same writers that he did; but Conrad's main concern—obsession would hardly be an exaggeration—was to attract a large enough share of the reading public to enable him to become financially secure. His first two pieces of fiction were clearly intended to appeal to a very wide audience: Conrad's first story, "The Black Mate," had been written for *Tit-Bits*, George Newnes's cheap weekly, which was the precursor of later developments in exploiting the mass public;[4] and *Almayer's Folly* had been submitted for publication in the *Pseudonym Library*, which was Fisher Unwin's paperback series for short popular fiction.

As the reviews of *Almayer's Folly* make clear, Conrad was in part following current market formulae. *Almayer's Folly* could after all be regarded as a romance in the most popular sense, since it contained a love story with a happy ending; and it also fitted in with contemporary interest in exotic adventure. Following the fashion set earlier by Chateaubriand and Byron, the exotic became a major mode of later nineteenth-century literature. In the eighties, the novel about foreign lands had become an established and popular genre in France with the immensely successful Pierre Loti, and in England with Stevenson and Kipling; at a lower literary level the genre had attracted many best-selling novelists, notably Rider Haggard and such prolific but now almost forgotten writers as the Australians Louis Becke (1855–1913) and Carlton Dawes (1865–1935). Conrad was early compared with the first four of these, and he certainly knew their work. He found Rider Haggard "too horrible for words" (*E G*, xiii), but seems to have had some admiration for Becke, Stevenson, and Kipling.[5]

The English works which have been most plausibly suggested as possible direct sources for Conrad stories are by Kipling and Stevenson. But the undeniable similarities of plot both between Kipling's "The Man Who Would Be King" (1888) and Conrad's "An Outpost of Progress,"[6] and between Stevenson's "The Beach of Falesá" (1893, in *The Island Night's Entertainments)* and *Heart of Darkness,*[7] are hardly close enough to be convincing evidence of significant influence; and there is no reason to suppose that Conrad was particularly indebted either to Stevenson or Kipling beyond their part in creating an audience for exotic narrative.

4. See R. C. K. Ensor. *England 1870–1914* (Oxford, 1936), pp. 145, 310–16.

5. A. Grove Day, *Louis Becke* (New York, 1966), p. 146; *L L*, II, 223; *C G*, 47.

6. See Lawrence Graver, *Conrad's Short Fiction* (Berkeley, 1969), pp. 10–15; hereafter cited as *L G*.

7. See Albert J. Guerard, *Conrad the Novelist* (Cambridge, Mass., 1958), p. 43 n; hereafter cited as *G*.

In any case, the exotic novel could hardly have provided a permanent direction for Conrad, if only because he had been ashore much too briefly to have anything but the most superficial understanding of Malay life, as Hugh Clifford pointed out in an otherwise favourable early article on Conrad (*S E W*, 139–40). But in *Almayer's Folly* the genre at least afforded Conrad an opportunity of developing one of his characteristic strengths as a writer, his power to describe the outside world. The power is of a special kind: Conrad is not in the ordinary sense a nature writer; his memory and imagination distil and recreate the characteristic Malayan landscapes with vividness and truth, but his primary interest is both wider and more subjective. Conrad looks at the visible universe with the eye of one who believes that only by deciphering its features can the individual hope to find clues to life's meaning or lack of it. Thus in *Almayer's Folly* there is a steady pressure on the reader to experience the essence of what one sees and feels when living in Sambir; and out of his careful attention to its topography and daily routines, his evocation of the changing moods of the river and the sky, and his scenes displaying the public yet mysteriously oppressive nature of its social life, Conrad builds up an atmosphere of doomed and stagnant enclosure from which, like Almayer and Nina, we want out.

The conventional glamour of the East is present in *Almayer's Folly* only superficially. For instance, in the most often cited scene in the novel, where the lovers, Dain and Nina, are parting in their separate canoes after a secret tryst, the passage begins like an Oriental travelogue, but soon modulates into something quite different:

> ... the two little nutshells with their occupants floated quietly side by side, reflected by the black water in the dim light struggling through a high canopy of dense foliage; while above, away up in the broad day, flamed immense red blossoms sending down on their heads a shower of great dew-sparkling petals that descended rotating slowly in a continuous and perfumed stream; and over them, under them, in the sleeping water; all around them in a ring of luxuriant vegetation bathed in the warm air charged with strong and harsh perfumes, the intense work of tropical nature went on: plants shooting upward, entwined, interlaced in inextricable confusion, climbing madly and brutally over each other in the terrible silence of a desperate struggle towards the life-giving sunshine above—as if struck with sudden horror at the seething mass of corruption below, at the death and decay from which they sprang (71).

The passage is typical of Conrad in presenting a picture, not of a static landscape but of nature in motion: and the kind of movement involved here violently subverts the conventional assumptions of popular romance. The lush tropical aubade, with the jungle showering the happy lovers with nuptial petals, is soon disclosed as an ephemeral moment in a larger and grimmer process; nature's cycle begins in death and decay, and though some spectacular flowers may manage to thrust themselves up into the sunshine, they soon fade, die, and sink back into the corruption where they began.

The inexorable struggle for survival in the natural order is presented in Darwinian terms, and human aspirations can plainly be deciphered among its fated victims. One early reviewer of *Almayer's Folly* actually used this passage as evidence of Conrad's having "studied Zola to some purpose",[8] and, in a way that cannot but surprise anyone accustomed to the later triumphs of literary modernity, Conrad was often seen by contemporary critics as a representative of the sordid brutality and heartless pessimism ascribed to the Naturalists. Conrad certainly knew the work of Zola, and George Moore's naturalist *Evelyn Innes,* but he was far from being a disciple; indeed, to judge by a remark made in 1899, he thought the movement "very old-fashioned" (*N*, 228). Still, there is undoubtedly more than a trace of biological determinism in *Almayer's Folly.* For instance, in accord with the generally accepted beliefs of his time, Conrad makes the effects of inherited racial characteristics an important element in the novel: Mrs. Almayer quickly rejects the European veneer derived from her convent training and relapses into the morose ferocity of her Sulu pirate forebears; and then her daughter, Nina, in turn rejects the white inheritance of her father and the values of the Protestant household where she was brought up, in favour of Dain and the Malay part of her heredity. Conrad also follows the naturalist perspective by supplementing the determining force of biological heredity on the Almayers with that of the physical and social environment. However, he does not fully share all the naturalist assumptions; in *Almayer's Folly* both heredity and environment are merely contingent circumstances through which a more universal view of human life works itself out; in the last analysis, Conrad is really closer to Hardy than to Zola in the way he presents the territorial imperative: the physical and social environment is not so much a collective conditioning force as the fated eternal antagonist of individual aspiration.

In any case, the determinist perspectives either of the Naturalists or of Hardy are in direct contradiction to the basic assumptions of popu-

8. Norman Sherry, ed., *Conrad: The Critical Heritage* (London, 1973), p. 52; hereafter cited as *S C H.*

lar romance, whose heroes and heroines require a world which offers that unconditional freedom which is the essence of individual wish-fulfillment. In themselves Nina and Dain are perfect romantic lovers—they have ideal beauty, grace, courage, mutual devotion; and their destiny—the wandering son of a great rajah arrives from beyond the sea and bears away the granddaughter of another—is equally romantic. Yet, as we have seen, the environment denies the primary absolute of romantic love—that it is eternal; and in a later scene Conrad subverts another convention of romance—the notion that woman is the sublimely passive creature of Victorian convention. When the assignation reaches its climax Conrad writes of Nina: "She drew back her head and fastened her eyes on his in one of those long looks that are a woman's most terrible weapon; a look that is more stirring than the closest touch, and more dangerous than the thrust of a dagger, because it also whips the soul out of the body, but leaves the body alive and helpless, to be swayed here and there by the capricious tempests of passion and desire" (171). Conrad plies his rhetoric along these lines until the time is ripe for giving the look its label: "Men that had felt in their breasts the awful exultation such a look awakens become mere things of to-day—which is paradise; forget yesterday—which was suffering; care not for to-morrow—which may be perdition. They wish to live under that look for ever. It is the look of a woman's surrender."

The general inflation of language and attitude would have been quite at home in the popular romances of the period, but the particular view of sexual relations certainly would not. It may be that, as Thomas Moser argues,[9] the passage reveals Conrad's unconscious fear that woman's "surrender" really means man's defeat, although what Conrad probably intended to communicate was only the over-mastering excitement provoked in the man by the woman's silent yes. In either case the psychological implications in the passage run counter to the essential presuppositions of romance, even in its notoriously carnal tropical variety.

As regards plot, Conrad again seems to follow, but actually under-mines, the prescriptions of popular romance. *Almayer's Folly*, like much of Conrad's later fiction, embodies many standard adventure-story motifs: Lingard's secret channel up the river; his notebook with its vague clues to the treasure; pirates and gun-running and mysterious political intrigues; and, above all, the hunted hero, Dain. At different times Dain's life is threatened by the Dutch, the Arabs, the

9. Thomas Moser, *Joseph Conrad: Achievement and Decline* (Cambridge, Mass., 1957), pp. 52–54; hereafter cited as *M*.

Malay chief Lakamba, even Almayer; and he is saved by two of the most implausible but time-hallowed devices of fiction: first, that of mistaken identity—the false clue of Dain's ring on the drowned corpse; and second, that of the heroine's dauntless self-sacrifice—the scene where Nina interposes herself between her lover and her irate father's drawn revolver. Despite these standard melodramatic elements, however, the novel never reads like a romance or an adventure story for very long: by the accepted convention such intrigues and dangers are clever, exciting, larger than life; but in *Almayer's Folly* they come to seem foolish and irrelevant because they are overpowered by the dominant presences of the novel—the changeless torpor of Sambir and its symbolic representative, Almayer.

In its most general terms, the discrepancy involves the kind of relationship which Conrad establishes between his fictional form and real life. The conventions both of the adventure story and of the popular romance obviously require the absence of many important components of the real world, and the presence of many others which are contrary to ordinary experience. The basic reason is presumably that the devotees of popular fiction read in order to be taken out of the realities of the ordinary world and their own selves; all the characters, actions, and situations must be quite different—in some sense extreme, unusual, or ideal; there must be no carry-over of quotidian norms into the fictional world of romance. Most devotees of serious or highbrow literature, on the other hand, tend to scorn the pleasures of romance, fantasy, adventure, even of entertainment, in favour of fiction whose characters and actions illuminate the real world and its daily life; the presumption is that the essence of a good novel should be a view of reality which is somehow transferable; only the carry-over of social criticism or moral insight into the reader's understanding can justify the fictional vehicle.

In Conrad's first novel there is a total contradiction between these two kinds of fictional allegiance. The worlds of adventure and romance in general ask us for an uncritical acceptance of fantasy; but in *Almayer's Folly*, the fantasies which are mocked in Almayer are used uncritically in the treatment of Nina; Conrad's presentation of his heroine asks us to luxuriate in that very immunity from reality which is the defining essence of her father's folly.

Almayer is an example of what we have come to call an anti-hero, and belongs to a variant of that tradition which is typical of the later nineteenth century. Conrad was characteristically unhelpful about what literary models may have influenced *Almayer's Folly*, and wrote only that it was "very likely" that "on the evening before I began to write myself" he had read "one of Anthony Trollope's novels" (*PR*, 71). But it was surely not Trollope, any more than Scott, Marryat, Dickens, or Thackeray, who had provided Conrad with the antecedents for the character of Almayer, or shaped his idea of the novel.

At the time that he was writing *Almayer's Folly,* Conrad would probably have accepted Henry James's disparaging, and at best one-sided, judgment in "The Art of Fiction" (1884), that "only a short time ago it might have been supposed that the English novel was not what the French call *discutable.* It had no air of having a theory, a conviction, a consciousness of itself behind it—of being the expression of an artistic faith, the result of choice and comparison."[10] The nearest Conrad ever came to a public expression of a similar critical attitude was in an essay, "A Glance at Two Books." It was written in 1904 but, discreetly enough, only published in 1925, after Conrad's death. The essay begins very revealingly: "The national English novelist seldom regards his work—the exercise of his Art—as an achievement of active life by which he will produce certain definite effects upon the emotions of his readers, but simply as an instinctive, often unreasoned, outpouring of his own emotions. He does not go about building up his book with a precise intention and a steady mind. It never occurs to him that a book is a deed, that the writing of it is an enterprise as much as the conquest of a colony. He has no such clear conception of his craft" (*L E*, 132).

Neither the intrinsic justness of Conrad's generalisation, nor the psychological interest of his colonial metaphor, may detain us here, but only the passage's support for the generally accepted view that Conrad's basic conception of the novel was not of English origin. Nor was it derived from Polish sources, if only because the novel developed rather late in Poland, compared to poetry and drama. For Conrad the exemplary novelists were French, and, in particular, Flaubert and Maupassant.

There was also Alphonse Daudet. He is no longer the great name he was, but Conrad confessed to a "youthful enthusiasm" for him, and even thought of sending Daudet a copy of *Almayer's Folly*: "You know my worship of Daudet," he wrote Marguerite Poradowska, "Do you think it would be ridiculous on my part to send him my book—I who have read all his books under every sky?" (*P*, 91). Lawrence Graver has pointed out that Conrad's first story, "The Black Mate," is like Daudet in many ways—an expansion of a wry anecdote, told from an ironic and yet sympathetic point of view, and largely dependent for its interest on a deft attention to scene and atmosphere.[11] Conrad must

10. *The Future of the Novel,* ed. Leon Edel (New York, 1956), p. 3.
11. "Conrad's First Story," *Studies in Short Fiction* 2 (1965): 164–69.

have admired and envied Daudet as a popular writer able to convey rather stereotyped interests with consummate literary skill. Thus in an obituary tribute, Conrad wrote that Daudet "is glad of the joys of the commonplace people in a commonplace way," and added ironically: "He never makes a secret of all this. No, the man was not an artist."[12] Here Conrad's sardonic paradox against the critical elite's view of the artist as superior to the interests of ordinary mankind reminds us that Conrad was not a committed highbrow. On the other hand his powers of critical judgment were formidable when he cared to mobilize them, as he casually went on to do in his verdict on Daudet's characters: "Their fate is poignant, it is intensely interesting, and of not the slightest consequence."

At the outset of his career, it was probably Guy de Maupassant who influenced Conrad most directly and powerfully. He would feel personal affinities with another aristocrat, sceptic, orphan, depressive, even would-be suicide; and as a writer no one had a clearer conception of his craft than Maupassant, or worked at it more assiduously. When Conrad took up writing, he studied both Maupassant's theory and practice intensively. "I am afraid I am too much under the influence of Maupassant," he wrote to Marguerite Poradowska in 1894; "I have studied *Pierre et Jean*—thought, method, and everything—with the deepest despair. It looks like nothing at all, but as a mechanism it is so complicated that it makes me tear my hair out" (*R R*, 146–47). Conrad's admiration for Maupassant's narrative method comes out in many other comments; in 1898, for instance, Conrad found *Bel-Ami* an "amazing masterpiece," and said of its technique, "it is simply enchanting to see how it's done" (*E G*, 130).

It is no doubt because Conrad was, as he later wrote, "saturated" in Maupassant (*L E*, 52) that there is much more evidence in his works of indebtedness to Maupassant than to anyone else: there is influence, imitation, even borrowing. Maupassant's detached and reductive irony of style and structure is most apparent in Conrad's two earliest published short stories, "The Idiots" and "An Outpost of Progress," both written in 1896. Conrad himself confessed that the first of them was "an obviously derivative piece of work."[13] Many verbal borrowings from Maupassant, some of them convincing and even disturbing, have also been pointed out in several of Conrad's novels and short stories, especially in *The Nigger of the "Narcissus"* (from *Bel-Ami*), "A Smile of Fortune" (from "Les Sœurs Rondoli"), and *Victory* (from *Fort comme la Mort*).[14] Paul Kirschner has further suggested that Conrad

12. "Alphonse Daudet" (1898), in *N L L*, 23.
13. "Author's Note," *Tales of Unrest*, p. vii.
14. See Paul Kirschner, *Conrad: The Psychologist as Artist* (Edinburgh, 1968), pp.

had recourse to Maupassant for many details in his treatment of particular episodes, especially for the sexual psychology in *Victory*, and for the description of James Wait's death in *The Nigger of the "Narcissus"*. There are certainly good grounds for the charge of verbal plagiarism in half a dozen brief passages. The gravity of the charge, however, is somewhat qualified if we consider the circumstances. Arthur Symons wrote that Conrad always had a volume of Maupassant open on his worktable,[15] and Ford that Conrad could recite a great deal of Maupassant by heart.[16] This continual immersion may help to explain the verbal, and some of the other, borrowings, most of which seem more curious than important; they look like unconscious residues of Conrad's remarkable but erratic memory: he probably forgot that he was remembering.

In any case, although Conrad was perhaps too proud to own up to what he owed, he was also too proud to owe very much to anyone; and as regards influence in the wider sense, apart from the two early stories, Conrad is never very like Maupassant. The economy of Maupassant's style, the rapidity of the narrative development, and the cool distant clarity of his moral analysis, were not Conrad's way; and in a 1904 essay on Maupassant he made it clear that his admiration was not without serious reservations. Conrad wrote: "If our feelings (which are tender) happen to be hurt because his talent is not exercised for the praise and consolation of mankind, our intelligence (which is great) should let us see that he is a very splendid sinner, like all those who in this valley of compromises err by over-devotion to the truth that is in them. His determinism, barren of praise, blame and consolation, has all the merit of his conscientious art" (*N L L*, 26). Conrad, then, found the determinism of the naturalist perspective too narrow as a view of life; it was primarily the "conscientious art" of Maupassant which won and retained his enthusiasm.

In the last half of the nineteenth century the supreme figure of the novelist as artist was unquestionably Maupassant's master, Gustave Flaubert.

In 1915, Hugh Walpole wrote of the "unmistakable" influence of the style of "the author of *Madame Bovary*" on Conrad's.[17] Conrad at once wrote Walpole a letter strongly denying that he had "been under the formative influence of *Madame Bovary*," and claiming that he had

---

191–229. Not all the particular borrowings, much less the claims made for their importance, seem justified to me.

15. *A Conrad Memorial Library, The Collection of George T. Keating* (Garden City, N.Y., 1929), p. 180.

16. At least by 1898 (*F M F*, 36).

17. Hugh Walpole, *Joseph Conrad* (London, 1915), p. 77. Conrad's annoyance arose

"read it only after finishing *Almayer's Folly*" (*L L*, II, 206). The chronological argument is certainly wrong, for a letter of 1892 survives in which Conrad writes that he has "just reread" *Madame Bovary* "with an admiration full of respect" (*R R*, 101). More generally, it seems clear that although Conrad mentions Flaubert less often than Maupassant, and never talks of conscious imitation or detailed analysis, there is no question of his early and detailed familiarity.[18] This is actually quite consistent with the rather equivocal concession with which Conrad ended his rebuttal of Walpole: "I don't think I learned anything from him. What he did for me was to open my eyes and arouse my emulation. One can learn something from Balzac, but what could one learn from Flaubert? He compels admiration,—about the greatest service one artist can render to another" (*L L*, II, 206).

What Conrad had specifically denied to Walpole was the formative influence of one particular work, *Madame Bovary*. Somewhat earlier, when Richard Curle had written that "the influence of Flaubert is the strongest in Conrad,"[19] Conrad had given tacit approval; but he usually maintained, as in his letter to Walpole, that his subjects and methods were closer to other works by Flaubert—notably *L'Education sentimentale* and *La Tentation de Saint Antoine*—than to *Madame Bovary*. This is probably true in general, but *Almayer's Folly* surely suggests not only Conrad's admiration for the art of Flaubert in general, but the thematic influence of *Madame Bovary* in particular.

Almayer is a Borneo Bovary. Like Emma, he devotes his entire life to one obsessive fantasy—though not of great love but of great wealth. Both Almayer and Emma begin by making a loveless marriage merely as a step towards realising their fantasies; and then, refusing to abandon their early dreams and come to terms with the ordinariness of their own selves and of the lives offered by Sambir or Yonville, they are steadily driven into a deepening tangle of circumstances from which death is the only way out.

There are, of course, important differences: above all, that *Madame Bovary* is a larger, richer, and more vital book. Emma's disillusionment

---

partly because Walpole had connected the "French inflection" of Conrad's style with the old legend that Conrad had "hesitated . . . as to whether he would write in French or English." As to Flaubert's influence, in his own copy of Walpole's book Conrad apparently marked the passage on the Flaubertian qualities of his style "Very acute" (Józef Ujejski, *Joseph Conrad*, trans. Pierre Duméril [Paris, 1939], p. 191).

18. See also Kirschner, *The Psychologist as Artist*, pp. 184–91.

19. Richard Curle, *Joseph Conrad: A Study* (New York, 1914), p. 188. Conrad made detailed comments on the manuscripts and proofs of Curle's book (*Conrad To a Friend: 150 Selected Letters from Joseph Conrad to Richard Curle* [London, 1928], pp. 8–22), which says a good deal about the similarities in thought, method, and style between Flaubert and Conrad; hereafter cited as *R C*.

is bravely, even heroically won, whereas Almayer has done very little about his dream except not give it up.

Albert Beguin said of *Madame Bovary* that it is the book "of the impossible escape, the heavy-hearted poem of eternal ennui":[20] *Almayer's Folly* represents a different and later variant of Emma Bovary's attempt to escape the boredom of ordinary life. Since the brave days of the Romantics, the idea of existence as essentially an attempt by the individual to realise his private dream had been widely diffused and progressively debased both in literature and in life. Emma's wish to travel abroad with a rich lover, and Almayer's to become a millionaire, are both very petty-bourgeois versions of romantic aspiration compared to those of Goethe, Chateaubriand, or Byron; and in his turn Conrad portrays a markedly later stage of the vulgarisation of the theme than Flaubert; the will and the poetry which inspire Emma Bovary have dwindled into Almayer's dream of enviable consumer status.

In the decades after *Madame Bovary* the diffusion and internationalisation of Romantic individualism had proceeded in highbrow as well as in popular literature; and Almayer's *ennui* can be seen as a distant demotic variant of that flaunted by the decadent heroes of J.K. Huysmans's *A Rebours* (1884) and Villiers de l'Isle Adam's *Axël* (1890). The world-weary isolation of Des Esseintes and Axël is obtained and solaced through great wealth; and these two might perhaps have recognised, as Emma certainly would not, a remote kinship to their contemporary Almayer, whose sense of selfhood is expressed by his unique pony and flock of geese, his flowered pyjamas, his pet monkey, even his final recourse to opium in the architectural extravagance of his folly.

If Almayer in some measure belongs both to the petty-bourgeois and the Decadent stages in the history of *Bovarysme*, the narrative methods by which he is presented are much more direct developments from Flaubert. Conrad's obtrusive detachment as narrator, for instance, follows from Flaubert's conception of the novelist as God, felt everywhere but never seen: "l'artiste doit être dans son œuvre comme Dieu dans la création, invisible et tout-puissant."[21] Flaubert further assumed, without disclosing his evidence, that God was a tireless and dedicated craftsman; and it followed that every element in the novel should manifest the hidden artist at work. One could hardly make the highest claims for the technique of *Almayer's Folly* in this respect; but we are at least continually aware, as in Con-

20. In "En relisant *Madame Bovary*" (1950), cited from *Madame Bovary*, ed. Paul de Man, Norton Critical Edition (New York, 1965), p. 297.
21. *Correspondance* (Paris, 1926–1933), vol. 4, p. 164.

rad's work generally, that every compositional unit, from the basic structure to the cadence of each phrase, has been carefully and consciously fashioned. There is, for instance, no trace in *Almayer* of the multiple plot of the Victorian three-decker novel; the main action is highly unified, and, as in *Madame Bovary,* everything remorselessly forecloses the hopes of the protagonist and contributes to the ordained catastrophe.

Conrad departed from the Victorian tradition of the intrusive author in favour of Flaubert's attitude of narrative impersonality and emotional *impassibilité* towards his creation; and he also adopted Flaubert's ideal of artistic completeness in the rendering of a single unified theme. The most specific aspect of his likeness to Flaubert can be seen in the way that, both in *Almayer's Folly* and his later fiction, Conrad proceeds through an exhaustive and primarily visual presentation of each aspect of the central subject. Conrad's letter to Walpole had singled out Flaubert's skill in "the rendering of concrete things and visual impressions. I thought him marvellous in that respect." This admiration is implicit from the first pages of *Almayer's Folly,* where we are introduced to Almayer through the impressions evoked in him by the river; and the method dominates the whole narrative, where every important aspect of the action has patently been conceived so that it can be rendered in concrete and predominantly visual terms. Such is the passage which T. P. O'Connor singled out as being one which "only a writer of genius . . . could write." When Nina's prau finally drops from his sight, the mortal wound to Almayer's hopes is enacted visually: "Now she was gone his business was to forget, and he had a strange notion that it should be done systematically and in order. To Ali's great dismay he fell on his hands and knees, and, creeping along the sand, erased carefully with his hand all traces of Nina's footsteps. He piled up small heaps of sand, leaving behind him a line of miniature graves right down to the water" (195).

Here Conrad no doubt obtrudes himself considerably more than Flaubert would have done when he supplies the explanatory metonymy of "graves" for Almayer's piles of sand; and the symbolic action itself is rather more unlikely than anything in Flaubert. But the passage can be seen as an extension of the way Flaubert presented thought as well as action in terms of sensory images; and Conrad uses the method to show psychological moods and tensions objectively in many other scenes. For instance, there is the high comedy between the rajah, Lakamba, and his adviser, Babalatchi. Afraid that Almayer may be forced to reveal the secret of the gold to the Dutch, Lakamba decides that Babalatchi must poison him first; and then, exhausted by his unwonted attention to the cares of state, Lakamba asks for music. Thereupon Babalatchi

> ... went reluctantly behind the curtain and soon reappeared carrying in his arms a small hand-organ, which he put down on the table with an air of deep dejection. Lakamba settled himself comfortably in his arm-chair.
>
> "Turn, Babalatchi, turn," he murmured, with closed eyes.
>
> Babalatchi's hand grasped the handle with the energy of despair, and as he turned, the deep gloom on his countenance changed into an expression of hopeless resignation. Through the open shutter the notes of Verdi's music floated out on the great silence over the river and forest. Lakamba listened with closed eyes and a delighted smile; Babalatchi turned, at times dozing off and swaying over, then catching himself up in a great fright with a few quick turns of the handle. Nature slept in an exhausted repose after the fierce turmoil, while under the unsteady hand of the statesman of Sambir the Trovatore fitfully wept, wailed, and bade good-bye to his Leonore [sic] again and again in a mournful round of tearful and endless iteration (88–89).

The tone of the passage is very different from anything in Flaubert or Maupassant; indeed its facetious comedy, with Babalatchi wanting only to sleep while his master hides the pleasures of tyranny under the affectation of deep aesthetic sensibility, is one passage out of several which explains why Ford thought that *Almayer* was "written too much in the style of Alphonse Daudet" (*F M F*, 16). On the other hand, as Albert Guerard has pointed out, the function of the episode recalls Flaubert's use of the blind man's song in *Madame Bovary*, "that brilliant forestatement of Emma's squalid destiny."[22] The words of the Trovatore's song are not quoted; compared to Flaubert their application is less clear and their irony much less savage; still, although it is not by Babalatchi's poison, Almayer is going to die, and to die without the Trovatore's consolation that his love Leonora will join him in heaven. It is difficult not to see the scene as a specific, though not necessarily conscious, recollection of the one in *Madame Bovary*. Both Conrad and Flaubert present a brief but memorable *tableau*[23] not to make a direct contribution to the plot, but to prefigure later events without recourse to authorial commentary, and to set the action in a larger choric perspective.

22. *G*, 73. In addition to an illuminating comparison between *Madame Bovary* and *Almayer's Folly*, Albert Guerard gives a finely detailed critical account of Conrad's early narrative methods (*G*, 70–89).

23. There is a discussion of Conrad's use of Flaubert's "tableau" method in Horst Gödicke's *Der Einfluss Flauberts und Maupassants auf Joseph Conrad* (Hamburg, 1969), pp. 98–108.

These few passages must suffice to illustrate both the similarities between *Madame Bovary* and *Almayer's Folly*,[24] and, more important, the considerable extent to which Conrad had absorbed Flaubert's mystique of the novelist as artist and some of the main features of Flaubert's narrative technique.

But Conrad was also trying to please a much larger public than Flaubert; the resulting combination of the romantic and exotic parts of the novel with the more serious issues concerning Almayer, produced a narrative which is much less unified than anything in Flaubert, or, indeed, in Maupassant, and which demonstrates that the values and methods of Flaubert were so wholly (and designedly) antithetic to those of popular fiction that they could not coexist without mutual harm.

iii. Problems: Language, Narrative Method, and Characterisation

Almayer's Folly, like everything else that Conrad wrote, is very much worth reading for its own sake; it also illuminates not only the varied literary traditions which shaped Conrad's early fiction and the characteristic importance of the role of memory, but the many obstinate technical problems which he later found ways to surmount or evade. Among these technical problems the most refractory was certainly that of language.

The narrative begins with Almayer, having been called to dinner, still irresolutely lingering on the verandah of the Folly: he is

> . . . looking fixedly at the great river that flowed—indifferent and hurried—before his eyes. He liked to look at it about the time of sunset; perhaps because at that time the sinking sun would spread a glowing gold tinge on the waters of the Pantai, and Almayer's thoughts were often busy with gold. . . . There was no tinge of gold on it this evening, for it had been swollen by the rains, and rolled an angry and muddy flood under his inattentive eyes, carrying small drift-wood and big dead logs, and whole uprooted trees with branches and foliage, amongst which the water swirled and roared angrily.
>
> One of those drifting trees grounded on the shelving shore, just by the house, and Almayer, neglecting his dream, watched it with languid interest. The tree swung slowly

---

24. Edward Crankshaw argues, I believe justly, that Conrad "attempted to take not only the principles but the method of *Madame Bovary* to himself" in *Almayer's Folly*, and that "later the method was abandoned" although Conrad retained his "faith in the principles" (*Joseph Conrad: Some Aspects of the Art of the Novel* [London, 1936] p. 67; see also pp. 82–86). John Galsworthy, on the other hand, could trace no definite influence either on *Almayer's Folly* or Conrad in general (*Castles in Spain*, p. 119).

round, amid the hiss and foam of the water, and soon getting
free of the obstruction began to move down stream again,
rolling slowly over, raising upwards a long, denuded branch,
like a hand lifted in mute appeal to heaven against the river's
brutal and unnecessary violence. Almayer's interest in the fate
of that tree increased rapidly. He leaned over to see if it
would clear the low point below. It did; then he drew back,
thinking that now its course was free down to the sea, and he
envied the lot of that inanimate thing now growing small and
indistinct in the deepening darkness.

As narrative writing it is more than competent. The traditional
opening description of the place and time of day has been skillfully
combined with an initial prefiguring of character, situation, and
theme; and these are given considerable visual and psychological effectiveness, somewhat in Flaubert's manner, by being presented
through combining concrete images of the external world with the
internal reverie of the protagonist. The visual imagery is not particularly arresting in itself, and it is not left to make its meaning clear
without explanatory comment—Conrad still tells rather more than
shows: nevertheless the passage has impressive cumulative power,
and by making us identify with the developing sequence of Almayer's
observations we both participate in his consciousness and yet anticipate the fate to which he is still blind, but which is presaged in the
imagery.

Almayer's fate began in the past, with his dreams of gold; but now
the sun is setting on a stormy present, with the angry flood suggesting
the capsizing of Dain's boat, and hence the final wreck of Almayer's
hopes; while the future is prefigured when our attention, along with
Almayer's, is captured by the mute appeal of the denuded branch.
Almayer has always been a drifter; now the tide of events is hurrying
him towards a destiny which, could he foresee it, would force him into
a posture of equally forlorn supplication. It is a strong dramatic irony
that Almayer should have "envied the lot" of the uprooted tree because "its course was free down to the sea"; only two days later he will
go down the river to the sea with Nina and Dain, but from there he is
bound not for a voyage to Europe and his dream, but for a return to
Sambir and his death.

That we look for larger implications in the passage is partly because
its prose is so full of insistent verbal emphasis. The most obvious
manifestation of this emphasis is repetition, for instance in the four
uses of the word "gold" in the first paragraph (there are more in the
omitted portion), and in the duplication of "angry" and "angrily" at its
end. Tautology and anaphora are the easiest of rhetorical devices for

demanding attention; and Conrad uses them a good deal throughout
Almayer's Folly—for instance, in the passage quoted earlier about the
"look" of a woman's surrender.

In both passages the repetition is too heavily done. Some of it may
be the inadvertent residue of Conrad's difficulties with the English
language. For instance, Conrad could easily have avoided one of the
verbal repetitions by writing "Almayer's interest in *its* fate," which
would also have been less cumbrous than "interest in the fate of that
tree." What makes "of that tree" so obtrusive is the demonstrative
"that." "The" would have sufficed, but Conrad often had trouble with
the article, probably because there are none in Polish; and here the
difficulty may have been compounded by the fact that French often
uses the demonstrative ("cet arbre") where the indefinite article would
be normal in English. Another and more general result of not being a
native may also underlie Conrad's tendency to repetition: it is the
anxious overexplicitness of anyone using a foreign language; he says
it twice to make doubly sure.

Somewhat similar considerations probably explain Conrad's excessive repetition of sounds, both those which are probably accidental, as
in the "t" sounds of the phrase just quoted, and those consciously
intended for effect, as in the "s's" and "g's" of "the sinking sun would
spread a glowing gold tinge." Conrad would not have detected the
awkward jingle as easily as a native speaker would have done, especially as he had learned much of his English from reading rather than
hearing. Garnett reports that when Conrad "read aloud to me some
new written MS. pages of *An Outcast of the Islands* he mispronounced
so many words that I followed him with difficulty. I found then that
he had never once heard these English words spoken, but had learned
them all from books!" (*E G*, xix).

Conrad's difficulties with spoken English affected his style in other
matters besides an overemphatic patterning of words and sounds.
Ford diagnosed the "slightly stilted nature of Conrad's earliest prose"
as the result of his knowing only two of the three English languages.
Conrad had mastered the official literary tongue—"that of the *Edinburgh Review* which has no relation to life," as Ford put it;[1] and he was
also fairly familiar with the slang of the streets and the forecastle,
although Ford thought Conrad "consciously guarded himself"
against it in his early writing. Of the third language, which Ford called
the "dialect of the drawing room or the study," Conrad had had
relatively little experience; and it is, of course, precisely that middle
style which lays the basis for rapidity and ease in written prose.

1. "Introduction," *The Sisters*, pp. 22–24.

The stiltedness to which Ford refers is partly a matter of vocabulary. Here very few of Conrad's lapses are of the kind which would have been avoided by consulting a dictionary; they mainly seem the result of Conrad's late exposure to educated colloquial English, sometimes combined with the contamination of his previous exposure to Polish and French. Thus when Conrad wrote "they had dwelt together in cordial neighbourhood" (44), his dictionary would not have explained that, whereas *voisinage* in French is very currently used for "neighbourly intercourse," this particular sense of "neighbourhood" is so rare in English as to sound anomalous, unidiomatic, and awkward.

Many of Conrad's difficulties with grammar and syntax are of a similar nature. He once unidiomatically joked: "I know nothing of grammar myself as he who runs may see" (*B*, 72); and he later ungrammatically confessed to an "inability, distaste, and horror of grammar."[2] Most writers, one imagines, have been much less influenced by their formal knowledge than by their intuitive linguistic sense, absorbed through a lifetime's experience; and so it is not surprising that Conrad had particular difficulty in the more indeterminate areas of English grammatical practice. One obvious example, that of tense sequences, is found in the passage already quoted about the woman's look of surrender: "Men that had felt in their breasts the awful exultation such a look awakens become mere things of to-day. . . ." Sequence demands that it be either "have" at the beginning or "became" at the end, while the sentence as a whole requires the present—"Men who feel. . . ." Behind Conrad's difficulties here one could no doubt trace the equally complicated but much more definite rules for tense agreements in French, and the quite different but equally categorical rules in Polish.[3]

Another major difficulty in Conrad's English has to do with word order. The inflected nature both of French, and even more, of Polish, syntax makes the reference of modifiers, whether adjectives, adverbs, phrases, or clauses, much less dependent on word order than is the case in English. In the passage quoted above, for instance, where Conrad writes that Almayer "erased carefully with his hand all traces of Nina's footsteps," the awkwardness would vanish if one of the modifiers—the adverb "carefully"—or both—"with his hand carefully"—were placed before, not after, the verb "erased." Conrad was probably influenced here by the French and Polish practice of

2. Conrad also said that when he learned English: "I . . . absolutely refused to learn grammar . . . . After all, grammar is so arbitrary, why bother about it?" (Mégroz, *Joseph Conrad's Mind and Method*, p. 29).

3. On the general influence of the Polish language and literary style on Conrad, see I. P. Pulc, "The Imprint of Polish on Conrad's Prose," *Joseph Conrad: Theory and World Fiction* (Lubbock, Texas, 1974), pp. 117–39.

more regularly putting adverbs and adverbial phrases after the verb. In English there is often a choice, and Conrad often got it wrong, sometimes to the point of extreme gaucheness; he writes elsewhere in *Almayer's Folly:* "Mahmat had to produce the bangle, and saw with rage and mortification the lieutenant put it in his pocket" (145).

Another murky area of syntax where Conrad had lasting difficulties was that of prepositional usage. Thus when, in a rather exalted passage, he wrote "the heavens were suddenly hushed up in the mournful contemplation of human blindness," only considerable previous colloquial experience could have made him omit "up." He could not easily have learned from a grammar or a dictionary that when "hush" is fused with "up" it becomes a transitive verb, with a colloquial meaning similar to "shut up," which is inappropriate and possibly blasphemous when applied to the heavens.

Conrad's difficulties with prepositions, with the placing of modifiers, and with levels of diction, combine to provide the ludicrous climax to an already tangled sentence describing Nina's first glimpse of Dain: she espies him with half her face shyly hidden behind a curtain, thus "leaving only half a rounded cheek, a stray tress, and one eye exposed, wherewith to contemplate the gorgeous and bold being so unlike in appearance to the rare specimens of traders she had seen before" (55). It sounds awful, but awful in exactly the way that any literal translation from an inflected language sounds in English.

Conrad was helped in the revision of *Almayer's Folly* by Edward Sanderson, one of the friends he had made on the *Torrens,* and by Sanderson's mother; a friend reported that they both "took a hand, and considerable trouble, in editing the already amazingly excellent English" of the manuscript (*J B*, 134). Many of the stylistic faults which were left untouched involved either marginal matters of syntax and idiom that would have been very difficult to explain, or an over-literary style which probably came from an instinctive effort to imitate the more formal and ornate linguistic models of the French and Polish literature that Conrad had grown up with.

The more obvious residue of this in *Almayer's Folly* is the frequent use of long and involved sentence structure, exemplified in Conrad's description of Nina's half-face. The passage also illustrates the heavy use of qualifiers in Conrad's early style, where almost every noun had its adjective, and often two or three. In the opening passage about the Pantai, for instance, Conrad's phrase about the "river's brutal and unnecessary violence" has an artificial and strained quality which is quite absent in the French translation: "la violence brutale et inutile de la riviere."⁴ The device of paired or tripled qualifiers is most obtru-

---

4. *La Folie-Almayer*, trans. Geneviève Seligmann-Lui (Paris, 1947), p. 8.

sive when they are placed after the noun or verb, as in the earlier "the great river that flowed—indifferent and hurried—before his eyes." There Conrad's measured cadence perhaps suits the content and thus justifies the departure from common usage; but more often the use of paired and post-positioned qualifiers, usually adjectives, suggests a gauche striving for elegance which is a rather wearisome hallmark of Conrad's early writing.

Repetition and over-qualification in their various forms are the commonest defects in the prose style of *Almayer's Folly;* and they tend to become most prominent when Conrad is least sure of himself or is trying to force a climax. The two sometimes coincide, as in the sentence describing Dain's emotions on first seeing Nina: "Dain . . . forgot . . . the object of his visit and all things else, in his overpowering desire to prolong the contemplation of so much loveliness met so suddenly in such an unlikely place—as he thought" (55). The elaborate balance of three phrases of similar form and cadence—"so much loveliness," "met so suddenly," and "in such an unlikely place"— seems inappropriate to the subject; and the very attempt at stylistic elegance draws attention to such lapses from it as the rather vague archaism of "all things else," and the awkwardly otiose explanatory parenthesis "as he thought."

It goes without saying that Conrad would not be a great novelist if he had not written great prose. In *Almayer's Folly,* his prose is rarely that, although the weaknesses under discussion are certainly not its dominant feature. They have been given considerable attention here for two reasons: partly because critics have often raised the matter in overgeneral terms, or passed over it too easily; and partly because an examination of the style of his first novel enables one to see more clearly how, although Conrad never wholly lost some of the awkwardness of idiom and syntax illustrated here, his prose became much more fluent, colloquial, and effective with each succeeding novel. To use Ford's terms, Conrad steadily got closer to the language that lies between the opposite levels of the *Edinburgh Review* and the street. In any case, his highly individual style, of which there are already many signs in *Almayer's Folly,* surely owes something to the lateness of his exposure to English. Conrad's very difficulties with the language probably made him take less for granted, while in the end the pervading unconscious presence in his mind of other languages and rhetorical traditions probably provided countermodels which helped him achieve the very eloquent and original prose style of his mature work.

Conrad early worried that *Almayer's Folly* might be difficult for the reader to follow because it contained "a good deal of retrospective writing" (*P R*, 17).[5] There is, of course, nothing inherently new in the use of retrospective narration; all stories require some anterior explanation, as careful readers of *Paradise Lost* may have observed. What is new in *Almayer's Folly* is the extent of the retrospective narrative, and the way Conrad uses it.

Chapters two to four are a continuous flashback; but a great deal of anterior information is also conveyed not only in the first chapter, where it is given through Almayer's reverie about his past, but in the last seven chapters of the novel—Conrad's account of Taminah's love for Dain in chapter eight, for instance, or of Nina's relation to her father in chapter eleven. So if we take account of other, briefer retrospective passages, the novel probably contains almost as much narrative of past events as of present; this is a formal reflection of the fact that the three days into which the present-tense action of the novel is compressed are really only the final stage in the working out of an already predetermined fate.

In general Conrad handles the retrospective method with considerable skill. There is occasionally some doubt as to when some particular scene occurred chronologically, but for the most part the time setting of past events is clearly conveyed; and *Almayer's Folly* often anticipates Conrad's later experiments with a fluid chronological sequence, and with the multiplication of narrative points of view.

A comparison of *Almayer's Folly* with *Madame Bovary* helps to bring out the connection between Conrad's use of retrospective narration and his handling of the narrative point of view. Flaubert tells Emma's life mainly in the fictional present, in more or less direct chronological order, and from a fairly consistent point of view—that of an impersonal but omniscient narrator. But the story of Almayer, who made a choice in the past to live only for the future, would be very boring told chronologically in Flaubert's way, if it were possible. Instead, Conrad keeps the reader's interest in Almayer alive by making frequent shifts in chronological sequence and point of view, shifts which are usually designed to maintain the narrative suspense or to enforce the irony of the situation. For instance, we first see the mutilated corpse through Almayer's eyes, and like him assume it to be Dain's; Conrad keeps up the mystery either by not recounting the scenes where other characters—Nina, Mrs. Almayer, Babalatchi and the slave-girl, Taminah—learn the truth, or by postponing these scenes and recounting them later, out of their chronological order. For instance, just to maintain suspense about the identity of the corpse, Conrad makes two changes of narrative point of view, both of them involving

5. The early reviewers were "almost unanimous in condemning Conrad's handling of the action" (*J D G*, 273–74).

switches in time. Thus we get the full disclosure that the corpse is not really Dain's only in the eighth chapter, when we are given Taminah's doings on the previous night in the form of a retrospective flashback told from her point of view. Then in the next chapter we go forward in time to see the Dutch officers hold their enquiry, and Almayer produce the dead body. The reader already knows that it is not Dain's and can therefore appreciate the irony that Almayer still thinks it is; Almayer's ignorance, in turn, makes possible the climactic scene later that night when Taminah awakens him from his drunken stupor to announce that Dain is alive, and has taken Nina away with him, together with Almayer's last hopes of getting the gold.

The manipulation of chronology and point of view to achieve suspense helps the romantic and adventurous side of the plot; but it also has the effect of keeping us from any continuous closeness to the minds of the characters. With most of them this involves no particular difficulty. Lakamba, Babalatchi, and the rest are undoubted successes as characters, but only because they are flat and the plot does not require them to have a real or developing inner life. Romance, adventure, and melodrama are alike in requiring only that the individual performers be easily recognisable; the most successful characterisation in these genres usually comes with people like Babalatchi, or the eccentrics in Dickens or Stevenson, who are picturesquely different, not only from all the rest of the cast, but from any actual human being; and this, of course, means that their moral and psychological life does not carry over to that of the reader, and that they are essentially separate from the other characters in the novel.

Conrad's protagonist, Almayer, on the other hand, must have a wider truth to life if he is to represent the novel's central subject, which is of an individual and subjective nature; and this purpose also requires that the relationship between Almayer and Nina be much more inward and complex than those current in romance. Suspense, however, demands that the reader be kept guessing as to Nina's real feelings towards Almayer, and to some extent towards Dain: and so Conrad is forced to manipulate his narrative focus to avoid taking us inside Nina's mind. This is most obvious when, after Nina has avowed her love, Conrad shifts into the role of intrusive and yet secretive commentator to tell us that, "a faint smile seemed to be playing about her firm lips. Who can tell in the fitful light of a camp fire? It might have been a smile of triumph, or of conscious power, or of tender pity, or, perhaps, of love" (172). The teasing evasion does not particularly matter here; but Nina's actual feelings towards her father are more important, because the relationship is part of the psychological and moral center of the novel. In fact, however, we are given no sense of the earlier psychological process which separated Nina from her father, or of how she reacts internally to his harrowing appeals and confidences during the course of the novel. Conrad's manipulation of point of view has the ultimate effect of feeding our curiosity about the plot at the cost of starving our understanding of its protagonists. One later solution to this general problem was the use of Marlow, who established the connection between a narrative point of view which never fully satisfies our curiosity, and Conrad's larger assertion that it is impossible to fully understand or express individual experience; but in *Almayer's Folly*, where the narration is authorial, the reader can hardly help asking the question: does Conrad keep us guessing to maintain our interest, or because he does not know the answer? Are the shifts in chronology and point of view conscious strategies for concealing a secret, or unconscious devices for concealing that there is none?

The problem takes a special form with Almayer. His moral being is essentially as simple as that of the other characters, though for a different reason: he is so near the end, and his whole biographical trajectory has been so uniformly downwards, that there is little reason for us to be deeply involved in any particular stage of it. So, as the critics have objected ever since he appeared, Almayer is not a complete or developing character. This may not be a legitimate critical requirement for all fictional characters; but in the case of a full-length novel which is primarily based on the subjective aspirations and deceptions of a single protagonist, it is surely difficult to find any other sufficient basis for a serious and continuing interest on the part of the reader.

As we have seen, both the nature of the story and Conrad's way of telling it virtually preclude Almayer from having any real communication with anyone else. Direct access to Almayer's inner life thus becomes Conrad's main alternative; but this, in turn, is made difficult by the rather distant narrative point of view which Conrad has established in response to the other needs of his plot.

There are moments when Conrad takes us into Almayer's mind with convincing power, but even there a note of cold detachment inhibits our response. For instance, when Babalatchi has persuaded Almayer that the corpse from the river is really Dain, Conrad writes:

> It seemed to him that for many years he had been falling into a deep precipice. Day after day, month after month, year after year, he had been falling, falling, falling; it was a smooth, round, black thing, and the black walls had been rushing upwards with wearisome rapidity. A great rush, the noise of which he fancied he could hear yet; and now, with an

awful shock, he had reached the bottom, and behold! he was alive and whole, and Dain was dead with all his bones broken. It struck him as funny. A dead Malay; he had seen many dead Malays without any emotion; and now he felt inclined to weep, but it was over the fate of a white man he knew; a man that fell over a deep precipice and did not die. He seemed somehow to himself to be standing on one side, a little way off, looking at a certain Almayer who was in great trouble. Poor, poor fellow! Why doesn't he cut his throat? (99–100)

There is a remarkable power in the basic image, in the irresistible forward movement of the thought, and in the dramatisation of Almayer's state of mind. We see how Almayer unconsciously protects his delusions by imagining a total separation between himself as a detached observer of his fate, and himself as a suffering and broken man. But there is something too formal about the way Conrad puts himself into the irrational stresses of Almayer's mind: "and now he felt inclined to weep"—the implied distance between character and narrative voice undermines the emotion involved. This distance becomes even more evident when Conrad makes Almayer continue to soliloquise: "Why does he not die and end this suffering? He groaned aloud unconsciously and started with affright at the sound of his own voice." Here the jump from the "he" of Almayer's imagined other self to Conrad's narrative "he" for the physical Almayer who has been reported to groan, draws attention to the gap between the internal and external approach to characterisation: and the archaic cliché of "started with affright" finally destroys our sense of the psychological reality of Almayer's sufferings.

Conrad is least effective when he is dealing with Almayer in his more conscious and social roles. His speech becomes particularly stagey at moments of crisis, as in his last scene with Nina (188–94), or his confrontation with the Dutch ship's officers (138–44). The main exception is significant: Almayer is most convincing when he echoes Conrad's own sardonic accents: for instance, when Almayer finally uncovers the drowned corpse to the Dutch officers: " 'Cold, perfectly cold . . . Sorry can do no better. And you can't hang him, either. As you observe, gentlemen,' he added gravely, 'there is no head, and hardly any neck' " (143). Nothing we have heard Almayer say before has prepared us for this composed and laconic graveyard humour; but it is recognisably a variant of Conrad's own mordant voice as narrator.

Both here and later Conrad either deliberately preferred or unconsciously required a way of distancing himself from the inner lives of his main characters; and the most successful parts of *Almayer's Folly*

achieve this through retrospective narration, where Conrad's control
of the chronological perspective enables him to deploy the ironical
multiplicity of his vision. This is most evident in the flashback sections
of the narrative, which are also in harmony with the creative mood
out of which the novel arose. In general Conrad was always to be at his
best when he found modes of writing which gave free play to the
movements of the remembering mind; and in fiction this freedom
could most easily be achieved by the use of intermediate narrators.
Thus Almayer's sufferings seem most real when they are reported at
second hand, as in one passage from the brief coda of the novel which
is allotted to Almayer's final efforts to forget Nina and all his former
dreams. It occurs after Almayer has told his solicitous visitor, Captain
Ford, "I am a firm man"; Conrad then adds: "Ford looked at his
face—and fled. The skipper was a tolerably firm man himself—as
those who had sailed with him could testify—but Almayer's firmness
was altogether too much for his fortitude"(204).

This tightly ironic indirection is only one of Conrad's many ways of
avoiding the more inward narrative methods which would have been
needed to enable the personality of Almayer to bear the psychological
and moral weight which his central role in the novel requires. One
reason for this indirection probably had its origins in the contradictions of Conrad's own attitude toward Almayer, contradictions which
can be discerned both in Conrad's title and in his epigraph.

The primary reference of "folly" is, of course, to the lavish house
Almayer builds when he briefly imagines that his fortunes will rise
again. But this literal reference is largely peripheral to the action of
the novel itself, since the possible British takeover of Sambir is raised
at the end of one retrospective paragraph only to be dashed early in
the next. The decaying house remains, of course, as an appropriate
material symbol for Almayer's folly in the other main sense—it is a
monument to his foolishness. There may, however, be a significant
ambiguity in the shade of meaning Conrad intended for the word
"folly." In its obvious interpretation the title embodies a dismissive
irony at Almayer's silly dreams for the future, and in particular his
fatal mistake in agreeing to Lingard's plan; but folly in the sense of
mere foolishness seems to have too little moral weight to bear the
main burden of the novel's theme. Here a matter of linguistic connotation may be involved. In French, quite apart from its special meaning for an absurdly costly building or enterprise, the primary sense of
folie is not foolishness but mania or madness. This much stronger
usage was lost when the word was naturalised in English; but Conrad's
prior knowledge of French may have led him to assume that his title
would cover a wider range of meanings than it does, including that of

actual insanity. After Nina's departure, Almayer's mental state can justly be described as madness; but that final collapse is merely the culmination of Almayer's lifelong schizophrenic division between his inner picture of himself and what he actually is and does; his whole existence has been a continuously accelerating process of protecting his ego ideal by insulating it from reality. The stronger French connotation of *folie* would have included this theme of progressive psychotic breakdown, whereas the main English senses of "folly" tend to trivialize the import of the novel's title.

In any case Conrad does not go very deeply or consistently into Almayer's consciousness, perhaps because it would have meant a full exploration of the hidden identification between himself and his first hero. One aspect of this unresolved identification is suggested in the epigraph of *Almayer's Folly*, taken from Amiel: "Qui de nous n'a eu sa terre promise, son jour d'extase et sa fin en exil."[6] The opening verbal gesture of the novel invites us to an act of universal spiritual recognition; who has not dreamed of the Promised Land and failed to attain it? But in the novel this imputed universality of theme hardly stands up to examination. We can accept the inevitability of disillusionment and still feel disinclined to pay much heed to the particular case of Almayer; after all, he dies, not in heroic exhaustion and on the brink of victory like Moses, but in petulant disappointment at the failure of the future to behave as he thinks it ought, and make him very rich. That this is a common, perhaps universal, dream, does not make it less crass; as for the attempt to make his dream come true, most of the

6. The original is from Henri-Frédéric Amiel's little-known collection of poems and prose meditations *Grains de Mil* [*Grains of Millet*] (Paris, 1854), p. 196. The sentence occurs in a brief chapter entitled "Les Visions de Jeunesse," which begins by asking: "Why does one so rarely experience in later life one of those prodigious reveries, such as every adolescence has known, where one carries the whole world in one's breast, where one touches the stars, where one possesses the infinite?" Conrad's epigraph occurs in a passage where Amiel makes Moses a symbol of the disillusionment brought by a lifetime spent in the "muddy ruts of triviality": "Unhappy Moses! you also beheld the enchanting foothills of the promised land shimmering in the distance, and you were constrained to spread your weary bones in a ditch scooped out from the desert!—Who among us does not have his Promised Land, his day of ecstasy and his end in exile? And so how pallid a counterfeit of that once-glimpsed life is actual existence, and how those fiery lightning flashes of the prophetic visions of our youth serve to cast a yet duller shade on the twilight of our shabby and monotonous adulthood!" Conrad's somewhat less idiomatic version of Amiel's original French—"Lequel de nous n'a sa terre de promission, son jour d'extase et sa fin dans l'exil?"—suggests he was quoting from memory. The context in Amiel obviously establishes the epigraph as more appropriate to Conrad's youthful romantic reveries than to Almayer's more material aspirations. (Though see David Leon Higdon, "Conrad and Amiel," *Joseph Conrad Today* [1977]: 66–67). I am deeply indebted to Georges Poulet who so quickly discovered and communicated to me the source of Conrad's epigraph after other Amielians and I had searched in vain.

evidence supports the early and explicit verdict of the narrator that Almayer is a case of "feebleness of purpose" (25).

His hero's leaden sense of posthumous survival was no doubt deeply familiar to Conrad; but the unexamined residues of his own past were still too problematic to enable him to view Almayer either with consistent sympathy or resolute detachment: Conrad was unable either to affirm or to deny that "Almayer, c'est moi." When he had finished *Almayer's Folly*, Conrad felt that he had "buried a part of myself in the pages" (*P*, 66); but although the memory of Olmeijer was vivid, and apparently urgent, his personal meaning for Conrad seems to have remained obscure.

To avoid the problem Conrad fell back, as Flaubert did, on the psychological defence of maintaining a detached and ironic attitude to the feelings of his protagonists. In *Almayer's Folly* the models of detachment offered by Maupassant and Flaubert not only worked against the close identification required for popular fiction, but also against the deeper probing of the buried motives which might explain why the man who had impelled him into authorship should then have become the object of his implacable disdain. Conrad used much of his already formidable technical skill not to confront, but to avoid confronting, this basic irresolution; so in the end Almayer eludes us, and we are left with a novel which invites the verdict which Flaubert gave on *Salammbô:*[7] the pedestal is too big for the statue. That disproportion no doubt enacts the pathos of what happened to Almayer's grandiose intentions; but, like Conrad, we shrink from committing too much of our sympathy to a hero who comes out of the past only to tell us that the present is merely epilogue.

7. *Correspondance,* vol. 5, p. 69.

CHAPTER 3

The Nigger of the "Narcissus"

i. 1895–1897: Becoming an Author

Fisher Unwin had accepted *Almayer's Folly* on the enthusiastic recommendation of its two house readers, first W. H. Chesson,[1] and then Edward Garnett, who was to become a lifelong friend. Born of a distinguished intellectual family and son of the Keeper of Printed Books at the British Museum, Edward Garnett was a writer himself, but has gone down in history mainly as a publisher's reader who spent his life fighting on behalf of new literary talent—his numerous other protégés included W.H. Davies, W.H. Hudson, John Galsworthy, and later D. H. Lawrence, Henry Green and Stephen Spender.[2] Garnett soon became Conrad's intimate and indispensable literary adviser; always willing to give prompt and detailed criticisms of Conrad's work in progress, and to help him with publishers and editors, he earned Conrad's praise as "the true knight-errant of oppressed letters" (*E G*, 259).

Conrad even claimed that it was Garnett who made him an author. They met for the first time in November 1894, together with Unwin. Garnett relates that when, as publishers will, Unwin referred to "your next book," Conrad "threw himself back on the broad leather lounge and in a tone that put a clear cold space between himself and his hearers, said: 'I don't expect to write again. It is likely that I shall soon be going to sea'" (*E G*, viii). Garnett, feeling "disappointed and cheated," urged that "the life Conrad had witnessed on sea and land must . . . fade utterly from memory did he not set himself to record it in literature." What Conrad remembered was Garnett's adroit psychological strategy: "He said to me, 'You have written one book. It is very good. Why not *write another*?' . . . Another? Yes, I would do that. I *could* do that. Many others I could not. Another I could."[3]

Another, indeed, Conrad had actually begun many months before while the *Almayer* manuscript was still awaiting its fate in Unwin's

1. Ugo Mursia, "The True 'Discoverer' of Joseph Conrad's Literary Talent . . ." *C* 4 (1972): 5–22.
2. See especially Carolyn G. Heilbrun, *The Garnett Family* (London, 1961).
3. *E G*, vii. Conrad gives a somewhat different account in the Author's Note to *An Outcast of the Islands* (vii–viii).

office (*P*, 76–78). This new manuscript was to become *An Outcast of the Islands*, but, like all Conrad's later novels, it was originally intended only as a short story. That he had gone on writing cannot, however, be taken as meaning that Conrad was already committed to authorship as a career. He continued to seek a command for several years, and told his cousin, Charles Zagórski, that he had received one definite offer in March 1896, which he turned down because "the conditions were so unsatisfactory" (*J B*, 156–57; 168–69). If so, Conrad may also have been influenced by the fact that he was about to get married.

Conrad's works deal much less than those of most novelists with women, love, sex, and marriage; most of his critics have felt that where Conrad attempted these subjects he failed; and several have connected this with his own unresolved sexual conflicts.[4] Biographical evidence is scanty. What little information exists about Conrad's adolescent affairs in Poland is much too unreliable to allow any conclusions about his early sexual experiences. Conrad's subsequent twenty years in the merchant service presumably rule out his complete sexual innocence, although it is difficult to imagine him partaking with plenary indulgence in the traditional dissipations of mariners ashore.[5] Conrad's sea-going years probably influenced his sexual attitudes in two main ways. First, his works tend to reflect the nautical mythology which divides women into two wholly separate categories—the idealised asexual mother figures, and the venal sexual aggressors. Second, Conrad's life as a seaman must have deepened his earlier deprivations, and intensified his yearnings for a wife, a home, and a rooted existence. Such are the typical dreams of the sailor about his next landfall; their disillusionment is a common theme of Pierre Loti's novels, notably in *Ramuntcho* (1897).

Both these attitudes to women seem to have surfaced during the two-month stay of the *Otago* in Port Louis, Mauritius, in 1888. Having obtained his first command, Conrad's mind apparently turned to the customary next rung on the ladder of established life—marriage; and he briefly courted on Eugénie Renouf, the twenty-six-year-old daughter of an old family of French settlers, only to discover that she was already engaged to a pharmacist (*J B*, 97–99). At the same time Conrad may have had an equally unsuccessful association with the other kind of woman. He certainly knew a young girl called Alice Shaw, the daughter of a stevedore; and his largely autobiographical

4. The classic expression of this view is Thomas Moser's *Joseph Conrad: Achievement and Decline.*

5. The only—and not at all dependable—account of Conrad ashore in his early days only mentions drinking in Lowestoft public houses (Edmund A. Bojarski, "Joseph Conrad, alias 'Polish Joe,' " *English Studies in Africa* 5 [1962]: 59–60).

story, "A Smile of Fortune," set in Mauritius, shows a young sea captain obsessed with the silent lures of one Alice Jacobus, the daughter of a business acquaintance (*J B*, 99–100).

Back in Europe, Conrad became very friendly with the French widow of one of his Polish relatives, Aleksander Poradowski, a maternal uncle once removed who had been an exile since 1863. Marguerite Poradowska was beautiful, distinguished, very well-connected and a writer of some talent. There ensued what Bobrowski regarded as a dangerous flirtation (*N*, 148), and was certainly a close friendship. Conrad wrote ninety-two letters to Marguerite Poradowska between 1890 and 1895; then there is a five-year gap, a gap which may be connected with Conrad's marriage.

Jessie Emmeline George was nearly sixteen years younger than Conrad. The daughter of a London family on the lower fringes of the middle class, she was one of nine children who had been left in straitened circumstances by the death, three years before, of the father, variously described as a bookseller or warehouseman. Jessie worked in the city as a typist—a "typewriter" as the term then was; and although Conrad described her in a letter as "plain" (*N*, 215), a photograph of the period shows a plumply attractive, well-dressed and poised young woman.

Conrad apparently met Jessie George late in 1894, but it was not until a year later that they saw very much of each other. What evidence there is about the courtship suggests, not that Conrad was in love with Jessie but that he felt the need to make a drastic change in his life. In *Lord Jim*, Marlow offers what may be a clue to Conrad's frame of mind when he says that "the majority of us don't believe" in "stories of love" but "look upon them as stories of opportunities" (275). The most probable, and lacerating, reason for Conrad's particular choice is that he wanted to get married and that Jessie "was the only woman he knew in England."[6]

Both *Almayer's Folly* and *An Outcast of the Islands* express the sense of loneliness, demoralization, and failure which pervaded Conrad's life after he left the *Torrens* in the summer of 1893, a sense which deepened after the death of Bobrowski early in 1894. Conrad had come to a dead-end. As he wrote to Garnett on 7 June 1895: "Don't you think, dear Garnett, I had better die? True—there is love. That is always new ... Still one must have some object to hang his affections upon—and I haven't" (*E G*, 10). Conrad's wooing of Jessie combines

6. R. C. Curle to me, 16 September 1955. Zdzisław Najder has discovered that Conrad briefly courted, and was expected to propose marriage to, a twenty-year-old French girl, Emilie Briquel, whom he met at Geneva in May 1895 ("Conrad and Love," *Polish Perspectives* 11 [1972]: 26–42).

these two notes of despairing fatalism and ironic frivolity. According to Jessie, Conrad proposed to her in the National Portrait Gallery with the words: "Look here, my dear, we had better get married and out of this. Look at the weather" (*J C C*, 12). Soon afterwards Conrad staggered his mother-in-law to be by explaining that "one of his chief reasons for haste was that he hadn't very long to live and further that there would be no family" (*J C C*, 15). Later, Conrad took Jessie to meet the Garnetts; Edward Garnett, believing that Conrad's "ultra-nervous organization appeared to make matrimony extremely hazardous" (*E G*, xxii), expressed his deep misgivings. Conrad's answer, written the day before the wedding, is pitched at the loftiest level of impersonal abstraction: "If one looks at life in its true aspect then everything loses much of its unpleasant importance and the atmosphere becomes cleared of what are only unimportant mists that drift past in imposing shapes. When once the truth is grasped that one's own personality is only a ridiculous and aimless masquerade of something hopelessly unknown the attainment of serenity is not very far off. Then there remains nothing but the surrender to one's impulses, the fidelity to passing emotions which is perhaps a nearer approach to truth than any other philosophy of life" (*E G*, 23). All the truths of the further vision were negative; they even undermined the belief that what one did in life really mattered; and so the solicitations of the nearer vision took over, and urged Conrad to yield to the emotional impulses of the moment and the standard social pattern of "settling down."

Jessie was very much a woman of the nearer vision. She was not particularly intelligent, sensitive, or educated; there was no question of her providing Conrad with a base in English society, much less with any intellectual or literary rapport; on the other hand, she was loyal, responsible, and, as Conrad was not,[7] an excellent manager in domestic matters. In the new ménage Jessie was to have her job aboard, as cook, steward, typist, and later mother: ex-Captain Conrad kept her at it and up to it, while for his part he assumed the financial burden, not, certainly, without complaint, but with energy and resolution.

The marital record of the great modern writers falls sadly short of any ringing endorsement of the new models of sexual fulfilment and human freedom which they and their century proposed. Those few of them who married, and more or less stayed married to the same person—Yeats, Mann, Joyce, and Lawrence—established a pattern much like Conrad's; despite many important differences, all their

7. Gertrude Bone wrote that "Conrad, less than anyone I have ever met, had the home-making faculty. He, the voyager, sought his home here and there in the mind of a friend" (Heilbrun, *Garnett Family*, p. 65).

marriages followed a special version of a deeply bourgeois model; the author's wife, allotted a subordinate role, accepts it and survives through a sturdy, amused, and even sometimes faintly contemptuous, toleration of the husband's vagaries.

Such was to be Jessie's role. In her later years she was increasingly immobilised as the result of an early knee injury; this, in turn, made her get very fat; and then, in Virginia Woolf's phrase, "Conrad married to a lump of a wife"[8] became the couple's public image in metropolitan literary circles. Yet most people who knew them well believed that only a woman with Jessie's phlegmatic calm, not to say complacency, could have survived Conrad's excitable and unpredictable temperament for the twenty-eight years of what was always a difficult marriage. Lady Ottoline Morrell summed Jessie up as "a good and reposeful mattress for this hypersensitive, nerve-racked man."[9]

After the civil ceremony on 24 March 1896, the Conrads went to the coast of Brittany, where they stayed nearly six months. The period was on the whole a happy and productive one, though darkened by signs of coming economic crisis. Conrad heard that he had lost most of his capital through the failure of a South African goldmine, in which he had recklessly invested the fairly considerable legacy—some £1500—which Bobrowski had left him; and now that writing had become his main source of support, he was discovering that it paid very little.

Conrad had finished *An Outcast of the Islands* on 16 September 1895, and it was published by Fisher Unwin the following March. Conrad had "written another" in a very literal sense; the matter of Sambir was taken back nearly twenty years in time from *Almayer's Folly*, and with largely the same characters. The outcast himself, Peter Willems, is a somewhat more active, but very much more despicable, version of the youthful Almayer. Intensely proud of being white, Willems marries a half-caste in the hope of pleasing his employer and thus making his fortune; but he is caught stealing money, and is ruined. Out of pity Lingard offers him a new start in Sambir, where Almayer naturally resents the new rival. Isolated from everyone, and repelled by the threatening tropical environment, Willems is overpowered by a sense that he has been "left outside the scheme of creation," although other

8. Of 23 June 1920 (*A Writer's Diary* [London, 1953], p. 27).
9. *Memoirs of Lady Ottoline Morrell . . . 1873–1915*, ed. Robert Gathorne-Hardy (New York, 1964), p. 233. When Ottoline Morrell asked Henry James to arrange for her to meet Conrad, James, trying to dissuade her, explained, "Dear lady, he has never met 'civilised' women!"

people "lived, they lived!" (65). Both here and later Willems's sense of
cosmic despair often echoes that of Conrad: "It was not death that
frightened him: it was the horror of bewildered life where he could
understand nothing and nobody round him ... not even himself"
(149). In this void, Willems succumbs to a beautiful Malay girl, Aissa;
but his "ecstasy of the senses" (140) is soon brought to an end by the
hopelessness of his outcast status, and his sense that Aissa has "destroyed ... his dignity of a clever and civilized man" (334). Willems is
eventually forced to betray his benefactor by revealing Lingard's secret channel up the river to the Arab traders. When Lingard scornfully refuses his appeals for help, Willems's situation becomes impossible, and Aissa finally shoots him.

The psychological motives and the central action of *An Outcast* are
much stronger and more unified than those of *Almayer's Folly;* and it is
in general a more successful novel. But it is also more consciously
literary, and much slower in development, being nearly twice as long
for what is essentially a simpler plot; there are times, especially towards the end, when we feel that the words are going on, but little
else. On the other hand, there are a good many passages in the novel
where Conrad finds his fully mature narrative voice. The opening
retrospect, for instance, concerning Willems's theft, gives a sense of
relaxed but mordant high spirits, expressed with faultless linguistic
sophistication: "When he stepped off the straight and narrow path of
his peculiar honesty, it was with an inward assertion of unflinching
resolve to fall back again into the monotonous but safe stride of virtue
as soon as his little excursion into the wayside quagmires had
produced the desired effect. It was going to be a short episode—a
sentence in brackets, so to speak—in the flowing tale of his life"(3).
There are still a lot of qualifiers, but here their appropriately conventional quality gives them a cumulatively derisive force ("unflinching resolve," "little excursion," "wayside quagmires," "flowing tale");
there is a perfect conjunction between the easy intimacy of the
cadences—especially in the long main clause of the first sentence—
and the self-complacent assurance of the tone; while the two closing
metaphors—"sentence in brackets" and "flowing tale"—make their
point with easy sardonic wit. Conrad's irony is less sentimental than
Daudet's and less distant than that of Flaubert or Maupassant; and it
encourages the reader to participate in the mockingly collusive sympathy with which Conrad portrays the only-too-familiar moral
chicanery by which the self whitewashes its misdeeds.

After finishing *An Outcast of the Islands* Conrad started a very different kind of story, though one which continued the sad inward burden
of the first two novels. It concerned a young Russian introspective

who wanders about the world in search of truth and himself. He settles in Paris, and was there apparently destined to marry a Basque orphan girl and to fall in love with her sister. Garnett, however, found the early pages unsatisfactory, and the manuscript was laid aside early in 1896, after Conrad had only written some 10,000 words. This fragment, called *The Sisters,* remained unpublished until after his death.

When the Conrads went to Brittany, the main current work in progress was the third part of the Malayan trilogy, which focussed on Lingard in his early and heroic days; at that time it was called *The Rescuer.* Things went well in the early stages, but by May Conrad had bogged down completely, partly as a result of some exceptionally severe attacks of gout and malaria. He was, however, able to produce a short story, "The Idiots," based on children the honeymoon couple saw roaming the lonely Breton countryside. There is, no doubt, some psychological insight into Conrad's apprehensions about his marriage to be gained from the nature of his first new creative impulse after marrying Jessie. The story concerns a simple Breton husband who successively fathers four half-witted children, always in the hope that the next one will be normal; when he tries to start engendering the fifth, his wife kills him rather than submit; and in the end she throws herself over a cliff in the belief that his ghost is haunting her.

"The Idiots" has a certain grim power, but its main importance is that it shows Conrad turning towards the short story, a form of writing which made lesser demands on his time and creative energy, but produced a larger and more immediate financial return. After being rejected elsewhere, "The Idiots" was eventually sent to *The Savoy,* the successor to *The Yellow Book,* whose editor, Arthur Symons, had expressed an interest in getting a contribution from Conrad (*L G,* 16–18). The story was accepted and appeared in October 1896; for a mere 10,000 words Conrad received forty-two pounds, over twice what he had been paid for *Almayer's Folly,* and very nearly as much as the fifty-pound advance Unwin had given him for *An Outcast.*[10.]

"The Idiots" was to remain Conrad's only work of fiction written from the stimulus of immediate observation; his next two short stories, "An Outpost of Progress" and "The Lagoon," went back to much earlier scenes. "The Lagoon" is a short and melodramatic Malayan tale, which Conrad described to Garnett as "a tricky thing with the usual forests river—stars—wind sunrise, and so on—and lots of second hand Conradese in it. I would bet a penny they will take it" (*E G,* 47). "They"—the revered *Cornhill Magazine*—indeed did.

10. There is, among other things, a good account of the economics of Conrad's fiction-writing in Lawrence Graver's study *Conrad's Short Fiction.*

"An Outpost of Progress" also found ready publication; it was accepted by a rather prestigious new magazine called *Cosmopolis*, which paid him his highest fee yet, £50. Conrad was very pleased with the story, and rightly; it has a concentrated economy that he had not previously achieved, and by drawing upon his Congo voyage Conrad succeeded in freeing himself from the Malayan trammels. The plot concerns two average lower middle-class Belgians who go out to the Congo to get rich. In their isolated outpost they live "like blind men in a large room" (*T U*, 92); but after five months the "fellowship of their stupidity and laziness" breaks down; fear, greed, and pettiness finally erupt into a quarrel about sugar—rations have got short. Finally one of them, Kayerts, blind with terror, shoots the other; left completely alone, Kayerts breaks down and hangs himself on the cross marking the grave of the former head of the outpost. Next morning the company steamer arrives, and when the corpse of Kayerts is discovered, "irreverently, he was putting out a swollen tongue at his Managing Director" (117). The neat ironic surprise at the end is, like that of "The Idiots," reminiscent of Maupassant at his most mechanical; while Conrad's basic theme—the practical incapacity, and the intrinsic moral and intellectual nullity, of the typical products of modern urban society—is rather close to that of Flaubert's *Bouvard et Pécuchet*. Still, "An Outpost of Progress" was easily the most powerful and professional thing Conrad had yet done.

The Conrads returned to England in September 1896, and soon moved into an unattractive rented house in an Essex village called Stanford-le-Hope, which was near the Thames estuary and Conrad's old yachting friend G. F. W. Hope. There Conrad settled down to finishing a story which was in a wholly new vein. He had started it in Brittany in June, and by the end of the year he was talking of his "Beloved Nigger"; as its writing drew to a close he was, for once, genuinely pleased: "I think it will do! It will do!" (*E G*, 67).

The breakthrough was providential, for the financial situation had become even more desperate; as Conrad put it to Garnett in October 1896: "I am sitting on my bare ass in the lee scuppers" (*E G*, 52). He tried to negotiate better terms with Unwin for a coming volume of his collected short stories, and when that failed he changed publishers and went to Heinemann. There was another change to Conrad's economic advantage. The best return on novels came through supplementing the royalties from book sales by prior serial publication, which was paid at a rate equivalent to that for short stories. Conrad had not attempted to sell his first two novels to the magazines; but he tried with *The Nigger of the "Narcissus"*, and by the end of the year had the satisfaction of hearing that W. E. Henley, the influential editor of the *New Review*, was favourably impressed by the first two chapters. Henley's definite acceptance of his new work many months later marked a great step forward in Conrad's literary career.

ii. The Preface

In most respects, then, Conrad could look back on his first two years as an author with considerable satisfaction. He had published two novels and a short story; two more short stories had been completed and accepted; and he had finished another novel, *The Nigger of the "Narcissus"*, which was much finer than anything he had done. Conrad wrote of it in 1914 that "It is the book by which, not as a novelist perhaps, but as an artist striving for the utmost sincerity of expression, I am willing to stand or fall";[1] and Henry James was to call it "the very finest and strongest picture of the sea and sea life that our language possesses—the masterpiece in a whole great class."[2]

In his note "To My Readers in America," for the 1914 edition of *The Nigger of the "Narcissus"*, Conrad wrote that "after writing the last words of that book . . . almost without laying down the pen I wrote a preface, trying to express the spirit in which I was entering on the task of my new life" (*N N D*, ix-x).

The interval between completing the novel and writing the preface was probably greater than Conrad suggests, since he first mentions the preface only some six months later, and at a time when he had just finished revising the proofs. Conrad sent the preface to Garnett in August 1897, along with a letter in which he expresses more than his usual trepidation: "I want you not to be impatient with it and if you think it at all possible to give it a chance to get printed. That rests entirely with you . . . I've no more judgment of what is fitting in the way of literature than a cow. . . . I shall not draw one breath till your sublime Highness has spoken to the least of his slaves. We demand mercy" (*E G*, 87).

Four days later another letter shows that Garnett had suggested cutting out a substantial passage.[3] Conrad at once agreed, "patched the hole," and eventually had the pleasure of seeing the preface printed as an afterword to the last instalment of the serial publication of *The Nigger of the "Narcissus"* in Henley's *New Review* for December

---

1. *The Nigger of the "Narcissus"* (Garden City, N.Y., 1914), pp. ix-x; hereafter cited as *N N D*. This note is not reprinted in the Dent Collected Edition.

2. British Library, Ashley Ms. 4792 (26 June 1902).

3. The cancelled paragraphs are available in *J D G*, 237–38, and in *Conrad's Manifesto: Preface to a Career. The History of the Preface to The Nigger of the "Narcissus" with Facsimiles of the Manuscripts*, ed. David R. Smith (Philadelphia, 1966), which reproduces Conrad's heavily-revised manuscript, now in the Philip H. and A. S. W. Rosenbach collection.

1897. For the time being, however, that was all. Just as the brief prefatory note he had written for *Almayer's Folly* remained unpublished until the collected edition twenty-five years later, so the preface to *The Nigger of the "Narcissus"* was excluded from the subsequent volume publication, "on advice," Conrad wrote in his 1914 note, "which I now think was wrong" (*N N D*, x).

That Conrad had a special attachment to the preface is shown by the fact that he had a private limited edition printed in 1902; but his affection was accompanied by genuine misgivings. In 1914 Conrad told Richard Curle that he feared that the preface might sound "declamatory, even windy" (*R C*, 19); and he was also dubious about his capacity for writing literary criticism in general. Most of the critical pieces reprinted in Conrad's *Notes on Life and Letters* and in the posthumously collected *Last Essays*, were originally short articles, reviews, and introductions written to order; Conrad desperately needed the money, and found he could turn out casual literary essays with little effort and without affecting his other work. At their best, these short critical pieces are eloquent and perceptive; but Conrad's aim is merely to convey a personal train of thought provoked by a few random recollections. "Critical wandering . . . is all I am capable of," he wrote to Garnett in 1901 (*E G*, 179).

Samuel Hynes has argued that Conrad was "intellectually simple," and that "he didn't theorize . . . because his mind was not equipped to do so."[4] Possibly; Conrad's education had certainly stopped far short of any training in philosophical thought, and he was decidedly hostile to theories and systems; but the main quality of his mind was not simplicity but its opposite, scepticism. Conrad's casual literary comments, and his letters to friends about their current manuscripts— those to Galsworthy, Garnett, and Clifford, for example—reveal an impressive ease in going to the essence of critical problems. A more dauntless pursuer of subversive paradox might be tempted to say that Conrad was a good literary critic who was bad at writing literary criticism; the reverse phenomenon, of course, is much commoner.

At all events, Conrad wrote in 1919 that despite his reservations about the preface, "My convictions in the main remain the same."[5] Since then scores of anthologists and critics have accorded the preface classic status, though usually only by giving it their most bated breath, or intoning "To make you see" as though it were a charm against literary blindness. The general assumption seems to be that Conrad's meaning is self-evident. The belief that it is not so may perhaps justify

4. Samuel Hynes, "Conrad and Ford: Two Rye Revolutionists," in *Edwardian Occasions* (New York, 1972), p. 49.

5. Letter to Rollo Walter Brown, 9 September 1919 (Houghton Library).

a fairly detailed consideration of the preface, and of how it reveals that from the beginning of his career Conrad was quite aware of his own independent and eclectic position among the various literary traditions of the nineteenth century.

The basic terms of Conrad's attitude to writing were set by the substantially new ontological problems about literature with which history had confronted poets and critics at the end of the eighteenth century. The thought of Newton and Locke had made it necessary to face the question of what kind of truth was embodied in literature; the social tendencies represented by such movements as the French revolution and Utilitarianism had made it necessary to face the question of the social value of literature to mankind at large; and the prevailingly mechanistic models of the mind, notably that of associationist psychology, had raised the most difficult issue of all: what mental process could account for the creation and understanding of literature?

Such, in the very broadest terms, was the nature of the challenge to poetry as Wordsworth, Coleridge, and Shelley conceived it; and their responses took fairly similar forms. Literature embodied kinds of humanly necessary truths about life which were not attainable elsewhere; it therefore had a higher kind of utility than the material and the quantitative; and it was produced by, and communicated to, a part of man's mind, usually described as the imagination or the sensibility, which was not accessible to scientific psychological study, but which was nevertheless necessary to explain the grounds not only of man's aesthetic and literary interests, but of much of his religious, moral, and social life. Conrad's preface centers on these three large issues.

The first three paragraphs of the preface differentiate the kind of truth sought by the artist from that sought by the scientist or the philosopher. The general argument is close to Wordsworth's in the Preface to the *Lyrical Ballads,* where he asserts that the real contradistinction of poetry is not prose but "Matter of Fact, or Science."[6] Conrad assumes that all three modes of thought—philosophical and scientific as well as artistic—seek the truth, and seek it in "the visible universe." They are, however, concerned with different kinds of truth: "The thinker plunges into ideas, the scientist into facts"; the artist, on the other hand, "descends within himself" to find his kind of truth and "the terms of his appeal."

6. *Poetical Works of William Wordsworth,* ed. E. de Selincourt (Oxford, 1944), p. 392, n. 2. References to Wordsworth's Preface will hereafter be incorporated by a page number in the text.

The artist does not, however, descend into the self to make that his main study. Conrad defines art as "a single-minded attempt to render the highest kind of Justice to the visible universe, by bringing to light the truth, manifold and one, underlying its every aspect." Here, as David Goldknopf has argued, Conrad seems oblivious to the ancient epistemological problem of how "we go from the ephemeral and notoriously fallible evidence of the senses to the truth which is assumed, wishfully or not, to underlie that evidence."[7] As professional philosophers, we are justly affronted by Conrad's cavalier circumvention of so illustrious a metaphysical puzzle. Yet actually the preface does offer, in very general terms, a view of "how we go," if not from the Many to the One, at least from the irreducible pluralism of all the visible aspects of the universe to "the very truth of their existence." When Conrad asserts that the artist seeks truth in "that part of our being which is not dependent on wisdom," he presumably means that whereas science and ethics offer explanations and rules that are in different ways useful for man's actual conduct of life, the artist is concerned not with practical and contingent truths but with the inward contemplation of the general and enduring nature of human experience, a contemplation which occurs in another "part of our being."

Much of the preface is based on the assumption that the nature and the interests of this other "part of our being" are common to the artist and his audience. Conrad was convinced that everything began with the sense-impressions made by external reality on the individual consciousness; but he had to avoid reducing writing to a simple circuit which merely transferred the author's immediate sensory impression to the reader, as if the work were a photograph being developed in words and handed over to the recipient. What was needed was some intermediate psychological center in which the individual remembers and compares all the impressions made by the external world, and arrives at their larger meaning and importance. The essential logic of the third paragraph, therefore, is to equate the "lonely region of stress and strife" inside the artist, with a parallel intermediate faculty in the audience which responds to the appeal of art.

The special concerns of this more inward faculty are suggested in Conrad's famous words about how the artist

> speaks to our capacity for delight and wonder, to the sense of mystery surrounding our lives; to our sense of pity, and beauty, and pain; to the latent feeling of fellowship with all creation—and to the subtle but invincible conviction of

7. *The Life of the Novel* (Chicago and London, 1972), p. 82.

solidarity that knits together the loneliness of innumerable hearts, to the solidarity in dreams, in joy, in sorrow, in aspirations, in illusions, in hope, in fear, which binds men to each other, which binds together all humanity—the dead to the living and the living to the unborn.

The thought of this passage is fairly clear, although it may not be true.

The general argument is a familiar one since the Romantics. Wordsworth had found it necessary to distinguish between the way the mind responds to art and the way it responds to science: scientific knowledge, he wrote, does not connect us by any "habitual and direct sympathy . . . with our fellow-beings"; the knowledge of the poet, on the other hand, "cleaves to us as a necessary part of our existence, our natural and unalienable inheritance" (396). It is this natural inheritance of man's inward nature which provides the essential basis for Wordsworth's universalist claims for poetry. The poet was merely "a man speaking to men" (393); he spoke of their "general passions and thoughts and feelings" (397); and these in turn were connected, Wordsworth wrote, "with the operations of the elements, and the appearances of the visible universe; with storm and sunshine, with the revolutions of the seasons, with cold and heat, with loss of friends and kindred, with injuries and resentments, gratitude and hope, with fear and sorrow."

The general interests of man's inward nature listed by Wordsworth are very similar to those on which Conrad grounds the artist's appeal. Like Wordsworth, Conrad was opposed to the more extreme forms of romantic individualism; both attempt to bridge the basic division between the artist and the general public; and Conrad's idea of solidarity in effect echoes Wordsworth's democratic formulation of the role of the artist in civilisation: "In spite of difference of soil and climate, of language and manners, of laws and customs: in spite of things silently gone out of mind, and things violently destroyed; the Poet binds together by passion and knowledge the vast empire of human society, as it is spread over the whole earth, and over all time" (396).

History has remorselessly apprised us of the objections to these high claims: that literature does not really do these things; that it has done so less and less since Wordsworth wrote; and that "human society" is not in fact "bound together" by literature or by anything else. But it would be a very literal reading of Wordsworth or Conrad to see them as naively credulous either about society in general or about the extent to which they personally could alter the situation by their writings. We must interpret their prefaces—like most literary manifestoes—as orectic and conative in nature; orectic, because their view of the ultimate function of literature is a matter of what they desired rather than what they thought to be a fact; conative, because they are really talking about the creative direction which they themselves are trying to take as writers. In both cases it is ultimately their broadening of the current views of the content and function of art which matters most; and this in turn is surely connected with the reasons which led both Wordsworth and Conrad to win audiences of readers that were exceptional both in the diversity of their composition and the intensity of their allegiance.

Conrad's use of the term "solidarity" to denote the community of human interests which art expresses raises two kinds of difficulty. The first is a question of its existential status. The usual meaning of solidarity is given as "the fact or quality, on the part of communities, etc., of being perfectly united or at one in some respect, especially in interests, sympathies, or aspirations" (O E D). This meaning, like many of the uses of "solidarity" as political slogan, suggests a conscious and effective identity of orientation on the part of the assertedly solidary individuals; but as we all know, the identity may not exist, or may not exist very effectively. Conrad seems to acknowledge this when he writes that the "feeling of fellowship with all creation" is only "latent."

The other difficulty in Conrad's use of the word "solidarity" is that whereas its meaning is normally restricted to collective human activities, the preface uses it in a much wider sense to denote man's common experience in general, whether collective or individual, and whether concerned with the human or the natural world. Here we can certainly agree that throughout history mankind has known many of the same individual experiences—both natural and human: we all see the same sky as our neighbours; we all undergo or observe birth and death, joy and sorrow, youth and age; and this community of fundamental experience no doubt supplies the essential basis for the appeal of art over the ages. But the extent to which that appeal is felt, or to which it promotes a consciousness of being bound together, is a very different matter.

No one knew better than Conrad that actual human behaviour reveals solidarities that are at best irresolute and only occasionally conscious; indeed this knowledge supplies the basis of the central conflicts enacted in The Nigger of the "Narcissus". But Conrad made the most minimal concessions to these negative realities in the preface. When he writes of the "invincible conviction of solidarity that knits together the loneliness of innumerable hearts," the word "invincible" no doubt implies that solidarity exists under the threat of defeat; but such terms as "knits" and "binds" surely imply a more direct and transitive action than we have experienced. The popularity of what the preface says about solidarity is no doubt partly the result of its telling us what we want to believe, but it can hardly be accepted as a statement of a universal existential truth.

Conrad's preface is composed of three main units; and they all have a structure which may be described as partly expository and partly musical. The first three paragraphs sounded his main themes, and the fourth gave them a personal modulation. The next section, comprising paragraphs five to eight, is essentially a set of variations on the original themes from a different point of view, and like the first section it also concludes with an application to Conrad's particular case. The last three paragraphs constitute not so much an independent section as an extended coda which intermixes Conrad's personal apologia with a recapitulation of his main critical ideas.

In the second section, the opening fifth paragraph is typical of the way in which Conrad almost conceals the extent to which the essay's structure follows conventional expository order. The paragraph begins: "Fiction . . . must be . . . like all art, the appeal of one temperament to all the other innumerable temperaments whose subtle and resistless power endows passing events with their true meaning, and creates the moral, the emotional atmosphere of the place and time." This is essentially a transitional summary of what has gone before; but it is not immediately recognisable as such because Conrad had not previously named the particular psychological faculty in which the artist sought truth and the reader responded. In calling this center "temperament" Conrad made what was in some ways an unfortunate choice, because the word has developed a somewhat pejorative connotation in English. Conrad certainly did not intend an unfavourable connotation here;[8] he used "temperament" in a sense closer to its original English meaning—to denote the idiosyncratic mixture of elements in the total personality which controls its response to sensory, emotional, intellectual, and aesthetic experience.

The term was then very current in critical discourse, but Conrad's use of it may have been particularly influenced by Maupassant. In his "Le Roman," an introductory essay to *Pierre et Jean* (1888), which Conrad is known to have read and which has been argued to have influenced his preface,[9] Maupassant, using "temperament" as roughly equivalent to the "sensibility" or what used to be called the "soul,"

8. Although by 1902, at least, Conrad was aware of this more trivial sense of the word in English, writing of "the haphazard business of a mere temperament" (*B*, 155).
9. George J. Worth, "Conrad's Debt to Maupassant in the Preface to *The Nigger of the 'Narcissus'*," *Journal of English and Germanic Philology* 54 (1955): 700–704. Paul Kirschner does not accept Worth's argument (*The Psychologist as Artist*, pp. 272–73).

asserts that not only novels, but critical theories, and ultimately even our perception of reality, are essentially the product of the individual temperament.[10] Conrad's usage is very similar, but with the significant difference that he does not follow Maupassant's Naturalist emphasis on the physiological elements which differentiate one individual temperament from another.

Conrad next turns to how the literary work can reach the temperament, or "the secret spring of responsive emotions"; and here he carries through his idea of a direct appeal to the senses by calling for a prose which will "aspire to the plasticity of sculpture, to the colour of painting, and to the magic suggestiveness of music—which is the art of arts."

The sixth paragraph draws the deduction that the artist must be single-minded in the pursuit of these aims, to the exclusion of any other possible demands of his readers; as Conrad puts it in the much-quoted words, "My task . . . is, by the power of the written word to make you hear, to make you feel—it is, before all, to make you *see*."

The force of the word "make" is worth noting; one of the characteristics of Conrad's fiction is the sense we get of a steady narrative pressure to make us look at the situation from a particular point of view. The later renown of Conrad's formula, however, probably arose in part because it chimed with the post-Jamesian emphasis on narrative as showing rather than telling, and in part because of the formula's note of resonant finality which derives from the richly persuasive connotations of the word "see"; these obviously include the perception not only of visual impressions, but of ideas, as in "to see the point," and even of spiritual truths, as in "a seer."

"To make you see" has been interpreted as implying a specifically impressionistic position. This is very doubtful, as will later appear; but the preface is certainly impressionistic in one important, though limited, sense, because it places so much emphasis on the translation of the artist's sense-perceptions into vivid and evocative language. Conrad also emphasises that although art's appeal must be made through, it is not essentially addressed to, the senses; the ultimate aim of art, he affirms, is to make us see "that glimpse of truth for which you have forgotten to ask"; and this kind of seeing must presumably operate through the temperament or the imagination rather than through the eyes.

In the seventh paragraph, Conrad expands his earlier idea that the subject of art is "more enduring" than that of scientific or discursive thought. What the artist has to make us see is a "passing phase of life"

10. *Oeuvres complètes de Guy de Maupassant* (Paris, 1909), vol. 21, pp. ix–xvi.

before time consigns it to oblivion; but "to snatch . . . the rescued fragment . . . from the remorseless rush of time," Conrad writes, is "only the beginning": the fragment must then be held up "before all eyes in the light of a sincere mood." Here "mood" is presumably the condition of the temperament when it is most deeply responsive to "the moral, the emotional atmosphere of the place and time," and can therefore make the passing moment yield "the substance of its truth." To put it in other terms, in "a sincere mood" the artist's temperament can rescue the universal meaning from the evanescent concrete particular offered by sensory experience. How this is done, Conrad does not say; but after all, three-quarters of a century and many foundation grants later, we still await reliable information.

The second temporal aspect of the artistic process is dealt with in the eighth paragraph. It follows from what Conrad has said about how the course of time "demolishes theories," that the artist "cannot be faithful to any one of the temporary formulas of his craft"; these formulas—"Realism, Romanticism, Naturalism, even the unofficial sentimentalism"—all contain an "enduring part" which is true; but once the artist has learned from them, he still has a long way to go, and it must be on his own. In that "uneasy solitude," Conrad continues, even "the supreme cry of Art for Art . . . loses the exciting ring of its apparent immorality . . . and is heard only as a whisper, often incomprehensible, but at times and faintly encouraging."

In the first draft, the third and last part of the preface opened with a paragraph, later cancelled, which began: "It may seem strange if not downright suspicious that so much should be said in introduction to the unimportant tale of the sea which follows."[11] Conrad's deprecatory apology made a nice transition to the present paragraph nine, which begins: "Sometimes, stretched at ease in the shade of a roadside tree, we watch the motions of a labourer in a distant field, and after a time, begin to wonder languidly as to what the fellow may be at." As it now stands, the logical connection between the labourer in the distant field and the immediately preceding passage about the faintly encouraging whisper of art for art's sake, is very remote: the logic of the connection presumably lies in the hard and lonely struggle faced by both agricultural and literary workers; if the casual observer understands what either worker is trying to do, his activities will become more interesting and his failures more excusable. It is a charming exemplum; and Conrad's plea for indulgence in having fallen short of his aim in *The*

11. *Conrad's Manifesto*, pp. 38–39. The change was part of Conrad's general aim in the revision to be less embarrassingly personal—"apology" was changed to "preface," and "confession of weakness" became "avowal of endeavor" (pp. 62–64).

Nigger of the "Narcissus" is much more persuasive when made through the serene indirection of its present metaphorical form.

In the last two paragraphs Conrad restates the difference between the aim of art on the one hand, and of philosophy and science on the other. Art offers neither "the clear logic of a triumphant conclusion," nor "the unveiling of one of those heartless secrets which are called the Laws of Nature." What art does offer is stated in terms which recapitulate both the rescue of the ephemeral moment from the temporal flux which was discussed at the end of the second section, and the subsequent image of the labourer in the field. The aim of art, Conrad writes, is "To arrest, for the space of a breath, the hands busy about the work of the earth, and compel men entranced by the sight of distant goals to glance for a moment at the surrounding vision of form and colour, of sunshine and shadows; to make them pause for a look, for a sigh, for a smile—such is the aim, difficult and evanescent, and reserved only for a very few to achieve. But sometimes, by the deserving and the fortunate, even that task is accomplished. And when it is accomplished—behold!—all the truth of life is there: a moment of vision, a sigh, a smile—and the return to an eternal rest."

It is not clear who or what makes the return to an eternal rest. Conrad's referent seems to have slipped; the "it" which is accomplished could either be the "task," meaning the work of art itself, or its success in compelling men to pause; but neither referent applies very well as far as a "return to the eternal rest" is concerned.

The reason for the difficulty can be surmised. Conrad wanted to end the preface on the theme of time; to mention the difficulty of achieving even a momentary arrest of the reader's attention seemed an appropriately humble final gesture; and then the note of closure would be sounded by ending the whole preface with the word "rest." Adding the word "eternal," however, brought in the idea of death; and thus Conrad inadvertently suggested that his book would die forever as soon as it had been read, or even that its readers would return, not to their "labours at the work of the earth," but to their "eternal rest." In either case the meaning was muddied, and Conrad ended the preface on a note of elevated but eventually obscure finality.

The preface is a highly personal, and in many ways anomalous, contribution to the criticism of fiction. It says nothing about such hallowed matters as plot or character; neither word, indeed, is even mentioned; nor is "novel" or "novelist." Conrad's essential concern is with the creation and the appreciation of art in general, and with how

The Nigger of the "Narcissus" in particular can be understood in a larger human perspective. The main lines of Conrad's perspective are fairly similar to Romantic literary theory; but in some important respects his thought is closer to later ideas.

On some matters, for instance, the preface seems to echo Pater's views. Conrad apparently admired Pater; he had read *Marius the Epicurean* a month or so before writing the preface;[12] and in any case Pater's ideas were very much in the air during the nineties. On the other hand, the resemblance concerns a few points for which Pater was very widely known. Conrad's words about "the magic suggestiveness of music—which is the art of arts," would probably have been taken by his original readers as an echo of Pater's famous dictum *"All art constantly aspires towards the condition of music"*;[13] while Conrad's view of art as snatching "a passing phase of life . . . from the remorseless rush of time," is similar to Pater's aesthetic doctrine, in which art has supreme value as a lasting expression of individual experience, which in itself can only be momentary. Thus Marius believes that "what is secure in our existence is but the sharp apex of the present moment between two hypothetical eternities, and all that is real in our experience [is] but a series of fleeting impressions."[14]

In most respects, however, Conrad could well have picked up the main parallels between the preface and Pater either from memories of Schopenhauer, or from the latter's many admirers, who incidentally included Maupassant[15] as well as Pater.[16] Conrad himself was also an admirer, and there is some general resemblance of attitude on a good many points.[17] Schopenhauer had been very influential in giving music supreme status among the arts, and also in grounding artistic genius on the capacity to achieve "pure perception." More generally, he thought that—apart from death or suicide—the best available escape from the immersion of the will in the ceaseless flux of the illusions of temporal experience was the attitude of detached aesthetic contemplation.[18] In effect Schopenhauer had long before done to philosophy what Pater, following the Romantics and Matthew Arnold,

12. Conrad acknowledges receipt of *Marius* on 26 May 1897, and says he is "licking [his] chops in anticipation" (*E G*, 56; 83). I have seen no evidence that Conrad had read Wordsworth's Preface, but he was probably aware of its general position.

13. "The School of Giorgione," *The Renaissance*, 1877 (London, 1920), p. 135.

14. *Marius the Epicurean*, 1885, rev. ed. 1892 (London, 1939), p. 110.

15. A. Baillot, *Influence de la philosophie de Schopenhauer en France: 1860–1900* (Paris, 1927), pp. 228–30.

16. The connection between their aesthetics is analysed in William K. Wimsatt and Cleanth Brooks, *Literary Criticism: A Short History* (New York, 1962), pp. 488–89.

17. See Kirschner, *The Psychologist as Artist*, pp. 266–77.

18. In Sections 36 and 52 of *The World as Will and Representation*, trans. E. F. J. Payne (New York, 1958), vol. 1, pp. 185, 255–67.

did to religion—undermined its claims to be man's supreme source of truth, and put those of art in its place.

Most of the ideas in the preface, however, are formulated in a highly personal way. Even Conrad's emphasis on time may be less a reflection of its dominating role in late nineteenth-century thought than of his own characteristic concern with memory, already observed in *Almayer's Folly,* and further demonstrated in *The Nigger of the "Narcissus".* J. Hillis Miller, indeed, goes much further, and sees the concern with time as central to Conrad's general vision of reality. For him, the closing paragraph of the preface is "the most somber moment of all in Conrad's long dialogue with the darkness"; and he interprets the "return to an eternal rest" as "a double return, the return of the darkness to its uninterrupted repose in the flux at the heart of things, and the return of man, after his evanescent glimpse of truth, to the forgetful sleep of everyday life."[19] Hillis Miller, however, does not reconcile this with the more positive aspect of the concern with time in the preface, notably with its view of art as mankind's most enduring record. That Conrad took the idea seriously is shown in his essay on Henry James, where he returned to this theme, and described the novel as "rescue work" in which "vanishing phases of turbulence" in the human world may be "endowed with the only possible form of permanence in this world of relative values—the permanence of memory" (*N L L,* 13).

If Conrad sees the source of fiction as impressions recollected in maturity, he finds its permanent value as a memorial record in the long chain of human solidarity. This persistent concern is where Conrad most radically diverges, not only from Pater and Schopenhauer, but from Flaubert, Maupassant, and the Symbolists. It is true that Conrad does not return directly to the theme of solidarity in his concluding paragraphs; but the urgency of his rhetoric on the subject strongly suggests that his deepest interest in the preface was to articulate the hope that his presented vision would "awaken in the hearts of the beholders [the] feeling of unavoidable solidarity." Indeed, there is much to support the view that the most powerful motive, not only in the preface but in Conrad's writing in general, was for an art that would make real the yearning of the orphan, the exile, and the sceptic for the only kind of human brotherhood that was available to him now that his days at sea were over, and that he was forever separated from "those men of whom ... I can't even now," he wrote in 1912, "think otherwise than as brothers" (*N L L,* 224). The preface to *The Nigger of the "Narcissus"* expresses in personal—as the novel expresses

19. *Poets of Reality* (New York, 1969), p. 39.

in narrative—terms, the essential continuity of spirit with which Conrad aspired to bridge the gap between the old tasks of his life and the new.

There is nothing in the preface which is contradicted in Conrad's later criticism, and he frequently returned to its main ideas. His scepticism about intellectual formulas continued, and with it a disinclination either to endorse or reject most critical theories. In this the preface remains characteristic. Conrad refuses to accept the aesthetic and symbolist doctrines of the separation of art from life, and he maintains his own version of a correspondence theory of literature: after all, what we are to be "made to see" is the real world of man and nature. Nevertheless the conclusion of the preface is not inconsistent with the art-for-art's-sake attitude of the primacy of aesthetic response to momentary experience. Similarly, although Conrad stresses the importance and the difficulties of the expressive and formal problems of writing, he was not a formalist and would have rejected, had he ever considered, the idea of the autonomy of the literary work.

The language of the preface is much more elevated, and much less strict, than that to which we have become accustomed in literary discussion; we must go elsewhere for definitions and techniques that will help us to analyse fiction; and we must go elsewhere in Conrad for what little he is willing to disclose about his own methods as a novelist. Conrad's main effort in the preface is not in the ordinary sense critical at all; it is, rather, to set his own personal feelings about writing fiction within the psychological, moral, and historical perspective of other activities in the ordinary world. It is probably because Conrad so directly confronts this general problem of the wider human context of literature, and because he convinces most of us that we are genuinely sharing in his own anxious and unrigorous, but committed and eloquent response to it, that Conrad's preface has achieved, and deserves, its fame.

iii. From Memory to Fiction

The Nigger of the "Narcissus" is based on a particular voyage. On 28 April 1884 Conrad signed on as second mate of the Narcissus, a full-rigged iron sailing ship of 1336 tons; it left Bombay on 3 June and arrived at Dunkirk on 16 October 1884 after an exceptionally long passage of 136 days. We know a great deal about the voyage and the crew of the Narcissus, both from Conrad's later accounts and from independent documentary records;[1] and seeing what was altered or

1. For a full account of the Narcissus, see J A, 160–70; for photographs, J A, plate

omitted provides some understanding of how Conrad's imagination operated on his memories to shape the plot, the characters, and the themes of *The Nigger of the "Narcissus"*.

As regards the plot of the novel, the most obvious change from the actual voyage was where it ended. At first Conrad told his friend, and later biographer, Jean-Aubry, that "the voyage of the *Narcissus* was performed from Bombay to London in the manner I have described" (*L L*, I, 77–78); but by the time Conrad came to the end of his account he changed over to the correct version: "As to the conclusion of the book, it is taken from other voyages which I made under similar circumstances. It was, in fact, at Dunkirk, where I had to unload part of her cargo, that I left the *Narcissus*." There is something very grudging about Conrad's correction, since it was actually not only Conrad but the whole crew who were paid off at Dunkirk. The change itself was surely necessary. To have retained the original French port of disembarkation, though faithful to fact, would obviously have been an artistic irrelevance; there was a much richer general representativeness in making the whole ship's company disperse at the same time, in England, and at the port of London.

In many other respects Conrad kept to the facts of the voyage, from the mustering of the crew in Bombay to the landfall in the English channel. Conrad also made the basic movement of the plot correspond to the actual voyage, and, more generally, to the wind patterns normally prevailing from June to October on the course of the *Narcissus*. When the ship leaves Bombay it encounters delaying headwinds, which would be the normal succession of the south-west monsoon and then the south-east trades as the *Narcissus* sails south through the Indian Ocean. In chapter three the great westerly gale occurs when the ship's course takes it into the roaring forties south of the Cape of Good Hope. In chapter four the *Narcissus* runs first into the south-east trades, which give her "a famous shove to the northward" (99), and then into the ominous calm of the doldrums as she nears the equator. In chapter five this calm continues until the ship finally meets the headwinds of the north-east trades which make progress very slow until the Azores; and there the *Narcissus* is at last far enough north to pick up the west wind for the exhilarating rush home.

To a general action which follows the successive phases of the ship's life as they are determined by the changes of sea and sky at each stage of its voyage, and as Conrad had experienced them on the *Narcissus* and on many other voyages, three important events are added: the

---

24; Conrad's certificate of discharge is reproduced in Jean-Aubry (*L L*, vol. 1, facing p. 82); the Agreement and Account of the Crew of the *Narcissus* is reproduced in part by Baines (*J B*, between pp. 292 and 293).

near-capsizing of the *Narcissus,* the sickness and death of Wait, and the abortive mutiny. These events are obviously less typical, but they can be seen as dramatically heightened versions of commoner occurrences which may threaten the physical, the psychological, and the social survival of any ship's crew. Two of the events seem to have been invented to embody stresses which Conrad had only experienced in much less extreme forms; but there is some historical basis for the death of Wait.

It is known that an able-bodied seaman named Joseph Barron, who joined the *Narcissus* at Bombay, died at sea on September 24, which is about the time the *Narcissus* would have been approaching the Azores. There is, however, no evidence that Barron was black; he signed the Agreement only with a cross, and his place of birth was given as Charlton, which cannot be identified with any confidence.[2] Conrad's account of the matter was given in 1914: "From that evening when James Wait joined the ship—late for the muster of the crew—to the moment when he left us in the open sea, shrouded in sailcloth, through the open port, I had much to do with him" (*N N D,* ix). Ten years later Conrad explained the change of name to Jean-Aubry, saying that he had "forgotten the name of the real Nigger of the *Narcissus,*" but that "as a matter of fact, the name ... James Wait ... was the name of another nigger we had on board the *Duke of Sutherland,* and I was inspired with the first scene in the book by an episode in the embarkation of the crew at Gravesend on board the same *Duke of Sutherland*" (*L L,* I, 77). For the voyages Conrad took on her in 1878–79, the *Duke of Sutherland* does not seem to have had anyone called James Wait on board; but there was (in addition to a first mate called Baker) a seaman with the name of George White, who came from Barbados (*J A,* 166) and who may well, therefore, have been black; at the muster at Gravesend the name White could easily have been mistaken for Wait, if pronounced with a cockney diphthong and a silent "h."

The documentary evidence, then, offers some circumstantial support for what Conrad said about the origins of James Wait. On the other hand, it seems virtually certain that neither the near-capsizing of the ship nor the beginning of a mutiny actually occurred either on the *Narcissus,* or indeed on any ship that Conrad sailed on; if they had,

2. Jerry Allen suggests the county of Charlton in Georgia (*J A,* 165); but in the ship's agreement form foreigners usually entered only their country under "Town or Country where born," in which case one would expect U.S.A. to be the entry. In any case, James Wait's speech seems British rather than American; and "Charlton" might perhaps be a mistranscription of Charlestown, on Nevis, one of the Leeward Islands next to St. Kitts, where Wait is said to come from (37).

Conrad would surely have said so in one of his many reminiscences about his sea-career, or in his various accounts of the inception of the novel. One can, however, surmise that when, south of the Cape, the *Narcissus* did run into the "awful gale in the vicinity of the Needles" which Conrad mentions (*L L*, I, 78), his imagination may well have been busy with pictures of the ship going down on her beam ends. As to the near-mutiny, there is some indication that the kind of exacerbated tension between captain and crew which could easily lead to mutiny may have been specially associated in Conrad's memories with this particular period of his life. On the outward voyage of the *Narcissus* from Penarth to Bombay there had apparently been a good deal of trouble in the crew: two seamen deserted at Capetown; a third was put in prison there; and when the *Narcissus* arrived at Bombay the first mate and six seamen left it.

Conrad himself, of course, was not on the *Narcissus* for its outward voyage; but on his way out to India on the *Riversdale* he got on bad terms with his autocratic captain, and this ended in a humiliating episode. When they arrived at Madras, the captain was supposedly sick; Conrad was sent ashore to fetch a doctor; he incautiously gave it as his opinion that the master was drunk; but his diagnosis was not confirmed, and as a result Conrad was forced to write a retraction. Even so, he was dismissed, with the master "declining" to testify as to Conrad's "Character for Conduct" on his certificate of discharge.[3] Since the captain very soon ran his ship aground under circumstances which led to his being suspended from command for a year, it is likely that he was in fact dangerously incompetent; and so during the voyage immediately preceding that on the *Narcissus*, Conrad may well have personally experienced violent feelings of mutinous resentment against his captain, feelings which, however unjustly, led to Conrad's receiving the only black mark on his official record as a sailor (*J B*, 75).

In general, then, the action of *The Nigger of the "Narcissus"* mainly follows the facts of the historical voyage, or deviates from them only in transferring or heightening events associated with other ships that Conrad had sailed on. There is a similar reliance on remembered experience as regards the characters. Jean-Aubry related that Conrad told him that "most of the personages I have portrayed actually belonged to the crew of the real *Narcissus,* including the admirable Singleton (whose real name was Sullivan), Archie, Belfast and Donkin" (*L L*, I, 77). The crew did in fact include an Arch Maclean, and a James Craig who came from Belfast; the Agreement and Account of

3. G. Ursell, "Conrad and the *Riversdale*," *Times Literary Supplement,* 11 July 1968.

the crew of the *Narcissus* also confirms various other details—the captain was a Scot, though called not Allistoun but Duncan, and there were several Scandinavians aboard. On the other hand, there was no Sullivan on the *Narcissus,* although on Conrad's next ship, the *Tilkhurst,* there was fifty-four-year-old Daniel Sullivan, whose age was indeed almost patriarchal for a seaman by the normal standards of the time. Conrad actually used the name Sullivan in the manuscript, but then changed it, probably to avoid its Irish connotations, which would have been highly inappropriate for his hero's laconic stoicism. In choosing the name Singleton, Conrad combined paying a compliment to Garnett[4]—it was his mother's surname—with introducing the appropriate connotations of single-mindedness.

Conrad's other main changes from the actual crew of the *Narcissus* are equally clear examples of a reshaping to avoid irrelevant details and to intensify meaning. There was, for instance, no one identifiable as a Russian Finn on the *Narcissus,* and Wamibo is very different from the two Finns Conrad mentions as shipmates elsewhere, who were "very good" carpenters (*N L L*, 181); Conrad presumably wanted a picturesquely primitive but inarticulate seaman who could illustrate the idea that intense loyalty to the ship and the crew could transcend the barriers of language. Wamibo was an addition to the international composition of the crew which Conrad otherwise much reduced. There were, for instance, four men from Norway, three from Sweden, and one each from Canada, Australia, Guernsey, and, of course, Poland, among the twenty-four officers and crew of the original *Narcissus*; but Conrad had artistic reasons for wanting to give the impression of a more predominantly British crew than had been the case.

Conrad made another important change in the composition of the crew of the *Narcissus.* Its average age had actually been well under thirty, with only the cook and sailmaker over forty. In the novel, however, and quite apart from Singleton, we get the impression of a considerably older group; this is no doubt because Conrad's larger theme dictated that we get an impression of the men of the days of sail as an ancient and diminishing breed, which, of course, in larger historical terms they in fact were.

While most, though not all, of the names of the characters in *The Nigger of the "Narcissus"*, were drawn from those of Conrad's shipmates, we cannot know how true he was to their real characters. Nor need we. What is essential to Conrad's achievement is that the novel's plot and the characters were drawn from much deeper and more

---

4. See Neill R. Joy, "A Note on the Naming of Singleton in *The Nigger of the 'Narcissus',*" *C* (1976): 77–80. The novel is dedicated to Edward Garnett.

intimate sources in his own past than had been the case with any of his previous works. The creative method of *The Nigger of the "Narcissus"* is characteristically personal without being directly autobiographical. This method was to become the basis of five more of Conrad's most attractive and successful works, although the extent to which they approached autobiography varied considerably. All six works take their shape from a single voyage; three of them, "Youth," *Heart of Darkness* and *The Shadow-Line,* were much closer than *The Nigger of the "Narcissus"* to particular events in Conrad's own life. They were also closer to his main personal preoccupations, as was "The Secret Sharer." The fifth, *Typhoon,* stands closer to *The Nigger of the "Narcissus"* because its focus is primarily on the life of the ship as a whole. All six works, however, are alike in that they are more immediately and exclusively rooted in remembered experience than Conrad's other fiction. It may well be for this reason that they were also written with relative ease, and as a respite from a longer work with which Conrad was having difficulty.

In one minor respect *The Nigger of the "Narcissus"* resembles *Almayer's Folly:* like Olmeijer, the *Narcissus* was still alive and going about its business under that name when the novel came out. Memory, it seems, not only preceded creation but continued to dominate it by requiring that some verifiable tokens of what had once been should remain unchanged and recognisable. It is as though, like some primitive nomad, Conrad could only construct his imaginative edifice on the foundation of some preexistent real features in the landscape of memory; so deep was this original impulse that Conrad often forgot that he had actually carried some of the rocks from elsewhere, or rearranged them out of all recognition; and sometimes, as with the duel, what he remembered was something he had imagined. It was, then, something much deeper and more private than a concern for documentary realism which so often led Conrad to deny or denigrate the merely invented elements in his fiction, and on the other hand to exaggerate the extent to which even some of the arbitrary or unimportant details of his fiction were literally true. Conrad knew that for him there really was a paradox in the metaphysics of creation, that he worked best not by inventing situations and characters, but by so intensely and questioningly remembering the past that it finally disclosed much more than had actually happened.

Conrad's use of past experience as the basis of his fiction involved a kind of action which is characteristic of modern fiction, but which is hardly a plot at all in the traditional sense. The action is typically left to shape itself in conformity with one of the familiar processes of existence—a day in the life of Dublin in the case of *Ulysses,* and here a voyage. Any long sea voyage is intrinsically rich in structure and meaning; it has a beginning, a middle, and an end; its various routines, events and actors are already endowed with established wider meanings—weighing anchor and landfall, storm and calm, captain and steersman. Nor is this all, for, in literature as in life, a voyage typically involves discoveries of unknown realities both in the self and in the outside world. These discoveries more readily acquire a symbolic significance because they occur far away from the normal matrix of man's habits and relationships; and this is true both when the journey is primarily individual, as in the *Odyssey,* or *Robinson Crusoe,* and when it is primarily collective, as in the various versions of the Ship of Fools, or in *The Nigger of the "Narcissus".*

iv. Solidarity in *The Nigger of the "Narcissus"*

The World of Nature

Both the traditions of fiction which he inherited and his own early work had provided a literary basis for Conrad to realise his aim of "awakening" in the hearts of the beholders "the feeling of solidarity which binds . . . all mankind to the visible world." From Walter Scott and Balzac, to Flaubert, Tolstoy, and Hardy, the novel had developed the description of the environment and its human implications into an important and established feature of narrative. In *Almayer's Folly* and the works that followed Conrad had already shown what were to be the characteristic directions both of his descriptive method and of his intellectual attitude towards the natural world. *The Nigger of the "Narcissus"* takes both the method and the attitude much further; visual presentation is used more precisely and consistently, and Conrad's emphasis on the determining power of the natural environment is applied in a much more persistent and symbolic way.

"I aim at stimulating vision in the reader," Conrad wrote in 1897 (*B,* 10), and this meant basing the narrative on a succession of concrete physical impressions. Such a concentration on sensory particulars was the dominant consideration in Conrad's revision of *The Nigger of the "Narcissus".* For instance, the manuscript originally opened: "Mr. Baker the chief mate of the ship 'Narcissus' came out of his cabin on to the dark quarterdeck. It was then just nine o'clock" (*J D G,* 136). In the published version this became: "Mr. Baker, chief mate of the ship 'Narcissus,' stepped in one stride out of his lighted cabin into the darkness of the quarter-deck. Above his head, on the break of the poop, the night watchman rang a double stroke. It was nine o'clock." This version is almost twice as long, but dull factual summary has been transformed into an active sequence of sensations, mainly visual but also aural, as in "a double stroke," and kinetic, as in "in one stride" and "rang."

Conrad's most significant visual addition is "stepped out of his lighted cabin into the darkness." This also serves to establish the novel's central symbolic contrast between light and darkness. The contrast continues when we look at the forecastle: "in the illuminated doorways, silhouettes of moving men appeared for a moment, very black, without relief"; the first seaman we see clearly, "with his spectacles and a venerable white beard," is "Old Singleton, the oldest able-seaman on the ship, set apart on the deck right under the lamps" (6). Baker has already been connected with the imagery of light when he orders a "good lamp" for the muster (3); and it is through Baker's agency that the men in the forecastle come from the darkness into the lamp's emblematic circle of light, and are there formally transformed into the crew of the *Narcissus*. One man, however, is missing. Then an invisible late arrival sonorously pronounces the word "Wait!" He comes down towards Baker, but is too tall for the lamplight to illuminate his face. The ominous mystery is only dispelled when the ship's "boy, amazed like the rest, raised the light to the man's face. It was black" (17).

The contrast of black and white gathers more and more associations throughout the novel. One of them is particularly important. When the *Narcissus* goes to sea it leaves the tug, which is described as "an enormous and aquatic black beetle, surprised by the light, overwhelmed by the sunshine, trying to escape with ineffectual effort into the distant gloom of the land. . . . On the place where she had stopped a round black patch of soot remained, undulating on the swell" (27). This equation of shore life with darkness is part of Conrad's general thematic contrast between land and sea, which is insistently—often over-insistently—present throughout the narrative.

Ever since it was separated from darkness at the Creation, light, as a necessary condition for being able to see, has been a prime example both of how the natural world structures the human, and of how man uses his perception of nature to evoke a community of response. That community begins in the simplest of routines, such as "Good morning" and "Good evening"; but it extends into a larger structuring of antithetical social and moral ideas. Thus light is a symbol of clear understanding and collective order, while night, as the scene of evil deeds and invisible dangers, becomes the symbol of doubt and chaos. These associations are invoked in the way the characters are presented. Thus the two prime representatives of order in the *Narcissus* when she sets out—Baker and Singleton—are both associated with light, as opposed to the darkness of the land, of the ship while she is tied to it, of Donkin's machinations ("Go for them . . . it's dark!" he hisses during the mutiny [123]), and of the menacing blackness of James Wait. The series of correlations between physical and moral properties continues until the end; and it exemplifies Conrad's use of particular and concrete details to establish the basic moral polarities.

This larger purpose is no doubt one reason why, as in *Almayer's Folly*, Conrad's natural description is very little concerned with the purely aesthetic qualities of the world of appearances. In *The Nigger of the "Narcissus"*, Conrad's presentation of the sea, for instance, pays little attention to its varying smells, colours, or wave patterns. Instead, the main focus is on the imperative power which the sea, like other forces of nature, exercises on the lives of the men who sail upon it.

These meanings are magnificently evoked when the *Narcissus* sets out to sea: "The passage had begun, and the ship, a fragment detached from the earth, went on lonely and swift like a small planet. Round her the abysses of sky and sea met in an unattainable frontier. A great circular solitude moved with her, ever changing and ever the same" (29). The passage holds the reader with a deepening sense of man's lonely voyaging towards unattainable frontiers until it concludes in a kind of cosmic vertigo at the featureless immensity of time and space: "The smiling greatness of the sea dwarfed the extent of time. The days raced after one another, brilliant and quick like the flashes of a lighthouse, and the nights, eventful and short, resembled fleeting dreams."

None of the meanings of the natural world are intrinsic; they have all been created and named by man; and so natural description inevitably tends to involve attributing human properties, especially feelings, to natural objects—the pathetic fallacy, as Ruskin called it in *Modern Painters*. When Conrad talks of the sea "dwarfing" or the days "racing," however, the use of the pathetic fallacy is inconspicuous. After all, "dwarfing" and "racing" are both established metaphorical usages for scale and speed; they do not really impute any anthropomorphic intention to natural forces; and their use here—even in the veiled threat behind the deceptively benevolent appearance of the "smiling greatness of the sea"—has the positive effect of referring us continually to the human perceivers of the sea—the ship's crew. This focus on the human observer is even more obvious in the boldest, most successful, and most abstract of Conrad's images in the passage: "a great circular solitude moved with her." The words arrest the reader's attention, and fix it on the centre of the moving circle which is both the ship and the eye of someone on it observing the vast circumference of his isolation.

Conrad's attitude to nature is in one sense the opposite of

Wordsworth's. He does not feel love for the landscape, or try to persuade himself that his feelings are in any sense reciprocated; man's essential emotional and spiritual bonds to nature are very different, since the ties which most obviously "bind" mankind to the visible universe are really the shackles which the laws of the cosmos impose upon human aspiration, the iron conditions within which men must attempt to live.

This was Conrad's own general attitude. "The sea," he later wrote, "is uncertain, arbitrary, featureless, and violent. Except when helped by the varied majesty of the sky, there is something inane in its serenity and something stupid in its wrath" (*N L L*, 184). The solidarity of seamen, then, is essentially provoked by a common enemy; and the essence of Conrad's literary use of the sea is reverence for the heroism of man's "continuous defiance of what [the sea] can do."

Conrad's attitude to the visible world also reflects the nineteenth century's growing sense of nature's unconscious but absolute tyranny over human affairs; and he expresses this antagonism through the traditional techniques of metaphor, transferred epithet, simile, personification, pathetic fallacy, and, above all, overt authorial commentary.

Conrad's tendency to editorialise, to force the reader to accept his way of seeing things in an obtrusive and insistent way, has been widely attacked.[1] The most frequent target in *The Nigger of the "Narcissus"* is the extended passage of authorial commentary which occurs after the storm has subsided, and the ship is once again underway:

> On men reprieved by its disdainful mercy, the immortal sea confers in its justice the full privilege of desired unrest. Through the perfect wisdom of its grace they are not permitted to meditate at ease upon the complicated and acrid savour of existence [, lest they should remember and, perchance, regret the reward of a cup of inspiring bitterness, tasted so often, and so often withdrawn from before their stiffening but reluctant lips]. They must without pause justify their life to the eternal pity that commands toil to be hard and unceasing, from sunrise to sunset, from sunset to sunrise; till the weary succession of nights and days tainted by the obstinate clamor of sages, demanding bliss and an empty heaven, is redeemed at last by the vast silence of pain and labour, by the dumb fear and the dumb courage of men obscure, forgetful, and enduring (90).[2]

1. Marvin Mudrick, for instance, speaks of the passage's "unctuous thrilling rhetoric" ("The Artist's Conscience and *The Nigger of the 'Narcissus'*," *Nineteenth-Century Fiction* 11 [1957]: 297).
2. Conrad deleted the passage in brackets when revising for the collected edition,

Our modern distrust of the purple passage tends to make us very unsympathetic to Conrad's stylistic intention here. Since T.E. Hulme and the Imagists we have demanded in poetry—and, *a fortiori*, in prose—tautness of rhythm, hardness of outline, exactness of diction; and in this paragraph Conrad uses every device of sound and sense for the very opposite purpose of inducing feelings of rather vague exaltation. His aim is clearly to produce a chiaroscuro effect between one detailed picture—the righting of the ship—and another—the resumption of ordinary life aboard the *Narcissus*; in the respite between the two we are given a reflective pause in which the "magic suggestiveness of music" that Conrad praised in the preface induces a general mood of awe at the endless confrontation of man and nature. The passage seemed to Virginia Woolf—herself a supreme exponent of poetic prose—an example of her general assertion that in Conrad's prose "the beauty of surface has always a fibre of morality within."[3]

To make full sense of this particular passage we must, of course, read it with the sort of flexible and cooperative interpretation we normally give only to some kinds of poetry; in particular, we must allow Conrad his steady reliance on ironic, elliptical, and paradoxical personification of an inanimate object. We must, for example, see that the apparent paradox of "desired unrest" depends on the narrator's view that "life" in general, which all men literally "desire" because its only alternative is death, is nevertheless, like the sea, always a condition of "unrest." We must also accept the pathetic fallacy of Conrad's attributing, albeit ironically, "mercy" and "grace" to the sea; this serves to prepare for the final modulation whereby what has been revealed as the in-fact pitiless power of the sea is implicitly equated with God's supposedly merciful attributes; even so, the irony in Conrad's phrase "eternal pity" remains somewhat obscure until we get to the balancing phrase, "an empty heaven," and realise that Conrad wants to juxtapose his rejection of the consoling religious illusions of "the sages" against the only redemptive reality which he will acknowledge, that "vast silence of pain and labor" which the sea forces men to endure.

The gnomic compression, the largeness of reference, the tone of religious elevation, the continuous latent irony, all suggest a familiar literary analogue: the Greek chorus. The Greek chorus's statement of the general theme depends for its distinctive effect on the impact, at the point of rest in the action, of a plurality of voices and an inten-

---

which tended in general towards greater economy and sobriety of expression (*J D G*, 140–41).

3. In "Mr. Conrad: A Conversation," *The Captain's Death Bed* (London, 1950), p. 77.

sified musicality. There must be a plurality of voices, and not an individualized narrator, because the function of a chorus in general, as of the passage here, is to achieve what Yeats called "emotion of multitude"; there must also be an intensified musicality because the hieratic repetition and balance of cadence and rhythm is itself the formal expression of Conrad's controlled exaltation at the prospect of the laborious but triumphant monotony offered by the tradition of unceasing human effort. The moral tenour of the passage is equally choric in nature: it asserts that, contrary to the crew's longings and to the more sentimental hopes consciously promoted by those clamorous sages Donkin and Podmore, the destiny of the successive human generations is not to find any adequate reward either in this life or the next, but only to labour in their unending confrontation of the environment. The confrontation is unsought and yet obligatory; it is the basis of human solidarity; and its most dangerous enemies are those who seek to confuse, defer, or evade its exactions.

In this and other choric passages Conrad is not technically speaking in his own voice, since the whole novel is told by an unnamed and uncharacterised narrator; and when this narrator pauses to generalise about the experience as a whole, it is surely appropriate that his invocation of solidarity should be pronounced in a noticeably more distant and elevated voice. Conrad's intrusive authorial commentary, however, is much more difficult to justify in other passages where it does not stand alone but is more directly linked to concrete events and actions. Thus in the storm, when we are told that "the ship tossed about, shaken furiously, like a toy in the hand of a lunatic" (53), we cannot but feel that the personification is artificial; the pathetic fallacy in the simile of the "toy in the hand of a lunatic," which is intended to convey the utter vulnerability of the *Narcissus* and its crew to the senseless malignity of the storm, actually trivialises both the ship and the sea. A similar objection arises when we seek Donkin returning to the deck after precipitating the death of Wait and stealing his possessions. Conrad writes: "The immortal sea stretched away, immense and hazy, like the image of life, with a glittering surface and lightless depths. Donkin gave it a defiant glance and slunk off noiselessly as if judged and cast out by the august silence of its might" (155). We know why Conrad should feel like this; but Donkin seems rather small game for the sea.

There can, then, be different critical judgments on particular examples of Conrad's use of the pathetic fallacy, or of the voice of generalised authorial commentary for this purpose; but in general they are surely successful only to the extent that the imperative power of the natural upon the human world has already been confirmed by concrete impressions and events in the novel; it is only through narrative that Conrad can "awaken in the hearts of the beholders" a full awareness of the crew's pain and labour, fear and courage, forgetfulness and endurance.

Conrad's treatment of the relationship of man and nature in *The Nigger of the "Narcissus"* is certainly consistent with the general aims he expressed in the preface; for instance, we see many ways in which the crew is "bound to the visible world." Whether the crew feels tied by rewarding bonds or constricting shackles, however, is not raised directly, and most of what transpires merely suggests an automatic and unconscious acceptance of their common subjugation to the power of nature.

The most complete acceptance of that power is attributed to Singleton, the most experienced sailor aboard. He is instinctively alert to every stir of the sea and the wind, which are "as much part of his existence as his beating heart" (26); this alertness makes him perform the first nautical action of the novel: when the cable moves and the *Narcissus* comes to "unsuspected life," Singleton is there to tighten the brake of the windlass; and the first chapter ends with him growling the symbolic command: "You . . . hold!" It is also Singleton who voices the danger of trying to rebel against the natural forces which oppose man's wishes. The *Narcissus* is nearly lost because Captain Allistoun "would not notice that" he was asking the ship "to do too much" (52); and when Singleton observes this, we are told, he "broke his habitual silence and said with a glance aloft: —'The old man's in a temper with the weather, but it's no good bein' angry with the winds of heaven.' "

The crew, then, and their symbolic representative Singleton, seem to feel bound to nature only in the negative sense that for the most part they accept their common servitude to its power. The other question, that of whether the visible world binds the men on the *Narcissus* to each other, receives no more inspiriting an answer.

The World of Men

The first English edition of *The Nigger of the "Narcissus"* had as its subtitle "A Tale of the Sea," but that of the original serial version and the first American edition was "A Tale of the Forecastle," which is much closer to Conrad's basic subject: the essential psychological and moral continuity of the narrative is supplied by the processes of the crew's collective life.

Such collective subjects suffer from at least one serious literary difficulty: the ordinariness of ordinary life. However wide our sympathies and interests, it is difficult not to stifle a yawn at the thought of reading many pages documenting how a group of people work harmoniously together in their normal quotidian routine. At the level of plot, as we have seen, Conrad's solution of the problem was to add various exciting or psychologically absorbing invented episodes; but there remained the problem of finding an appropriate narrative method which would make the ordinary life of the crew seem simultaneously real, interesting, and representative. Conrad's solution was a special kind of participant narrator who functions as a collective voice.

The advantages of making the whole narrative seem to proceed from someone who can present the life of the forecastle with direct physical immediacy and close emotional involvement can be judged by comparing the opening of The Nigger of the "Narcissus" with that of Salammbô. To show the soldiers feasting in Hamilcar's gardens after their victory, Flaubert uses authorial narration in a fairly straightforward way, combining vivid description of different parts of the scene with whatever explanatory commentary is necessary for the reader to be able to understand the action and dialogue when they begin; the total effect is that of a large and clearly structured pictorial composition, which in reading seems motionless and artificial.[4] Conrad's method is less obviously pictorial, and at first reading somewhat confusing. The descriptive order is not rigorously linear as regards chronology: we have the vivid picture of Baker stepping out of his cabin, but then we move back to a retrospective account of various earlier preparations; next we plunge into the arrival of the crew, in which long paragraphs compress action, dialogue, and scene into a kaleidoscope of brief but vivid moments; and from this initial chaos of densely real, evocative fragments mixed with brief expository summaries, there gradually emerges a penumbral sense of a community in the unplanned and unconscious process of creating itself. The very difficulty of piecing the fragments together forces the reader into the position of feeling that he, like the narrator, is actually there on the ship; but the reader also gradually comes to realise that he is being made to see more of the ship's life than any single individual could. This realisation is related to the fact that the narrator, though a participant, is not a single identifiable character, sleeping in a certain bunk, member of a certain watch, and primarily interested in his own personal doings and those of his friends. Only a participant, a member of the crew, could provide the necessary sensory, emotional, and intellectual closeness to the life of the forecastle; but no one person could plausibly have access to so much else. The narrative of solidarity had to be able to enact individual responses to all the collec-

4. The parallel is briefly treated by Baines (J B, 182).

tive realities, both natural and human, in the life of the ship; and at the same time it had to be able to make us see these realities in their larger perspective.

Conrad's handling of this mixed narrative point of view involves many difficulties. There are the changes of voice needed when the narrator goes from presenting particular impressions and scenes to generalising summary and philosophical comment: here Conrad's rhetorical skill has been illuminated by Albert Guerard (G, 114–23). There are also various inconsistencies of a logical kind, especially when the narrator briefly goes into the minds of particular characters, as he does occasionally with Wait (113) and Donkin (155), or when he mysteriously witnesses scenes where only certain specified characters were present, as when Podmore (113–17) and Donkin (147–55) talk privately to Wait, or Allistoun to Baker in the officers' cabin (137). Marvin Mudrick has termed such passages "gross violation[s] of the point of view."[5] Conrad certainly flouts the modern shibboleth of a consistent narrative point of view; but this doctrine was developed by a generation of formalist critics long after his day, and in any case there seems no adequate reason to accept this or any other literary technique as an eternal and universal prescription. On the contrary, we must surely ask whether the modern pieties about point of view are immune from the logic of Dr. Johnson's objection to an earlier critical prescription—the unities of time and place: "Delusion, if delusion be admitted, has no certain limitation":[6] the reader knows that The Nigger of the "Narcissus" is just a story; and Conrad is surely at liberty to use his pretended narrator in whatever way will best serve his turn.

While the crew settles down, finding bunks, unpacking, accepting new arrivals, and exchanging casual gossip, the first speaker to hold the attention of the forecastle is "Belfast," the voluble and emotional young Irishman. He is bragging about how he once insulted a second mate and threw tar all over him (8); the boast is patently untrue but it expresses some of the crew's joint aspirations and illusions; and these are to prove the basis of that kind of solidarity whose essence is a shared hostility to another group—in this case to the officers, "blast their black 'arts."

We are thus immediately introduced to one of the central contradictions in the nature of human solidarity. On the one hand this

    5. Mudrick, "The Artist's Conscience," p. 291.
    6. Samuel Johnson, Preface, *Johnson on Shakespeare*, ed. Arthur Sherbo, Yale Edition of the Works of Samuel Johnson (New Haven, 1968), vol. 1, p. 77.

kind of hostility is universal, and undoubtedly effective in cementing in-group cohesion; on the other hand it may go so far as to endanger the existence of the larger group to which they belong and on which they depend. The newly-arrived Donkin proves himself a master in exploiting this divisive effect: "I can look after my rights! I will show 'em" (9), he at once announces; and he extorts the crew's pity for his total lack of clothes, bedding, or tobacco, by claiming he lost them through standing up for his rights against Yankee oppression on his previous ship. As soon as the crew have given Donkin some kit, he goes on to make another kind of appeal to in-group hostility. "Those damned furriners should be kept under" (13), he proclaims, and, under the well-tried banner of xenophobia, is about to start a fight with the most defenceless target at hand, the Finn, Wamibo, who knows no English. However, the boatswain's summons intervenes: "Lay aft to muster all hands!" As they prepare to assemble, an un-named voice complains, "Is there no rest for us?" Donkin is quick to use this complaint to mobilise the crew's resentment: "We'll 'ave to change all that."

Even before the crew of the *Narcissus* has officially established its collective identity at the muster, three threats to the solidarity of the ship's society as a whole have surfaced: hostility to the officers; lazi-ness; and pity. All these forms of collective resentment—against inequality, against work, and against unjust suffering—continue: at the muster some men answer their names in "an injured intonation" (16); and when the voyage starts, the crew's resentment is expressed in many forms, down to such trivial details as the theft on Wait's behalf of the officers' Sunday fruit-pie (38), and the mild comedy of the discussion round the mainmast of what constitutes the essential "characteristics of a gentleman" (32).

Some friction and bitterness is no doubt inevitable among the dif-ferent groups in any social hierarchy; on the *Narcissus* it is obviously strengthened by the enormous class disparities of income, accommo-dation, food, dress, and speech, which characterised Victorian Eng-land, which were particularly glaring on shipboard, and which the narrative is far from minimising. We gradually become aware, however, that there are both counterforces and limits to the crew's resentments, although they are never fully articulated. There is, for instance, their respect or affection for particular officers on a per-sonal basis. The "hearts" of the crew, we are told, go out to Captain Allistoun "when he pressed [the *Narcissus*] hard" to make her "hold to every inch gained to windward" (51); and most of the forecastle is positively fond of the first mate, Baker, quoting his sayings, and con-ceding that "on a fitting occasion" he could "jump down a fellow's throat in a reg'lar Western Ocean style" (21). The existence of these tacit limits is shown when Donkin's policy of being "systematically insolent to the officers" (40) leads him to transgress them; the crew rejoices "when the mate, one dark night, tamed him for good," although next morning they respond to the "etiquette of the forecastle" by preserving "a ceremonious silence" at the sight of Donkin's missing front tooth. In general the crew's ambivalence is manifested by the contradiction between their talk and their behaviour. This is demonstrated during the storm: when the *Narcissus* is blown over on her beam ends, they all—even Baker—want the masts cut, and they say so; yet they at once obey Allistoun's decision against it, even though they justifiably fear that the ship may go down as a result. The crew's feeling of resentment against their officers has much more bark than bite.

The storm also reveals that the crew's dislike of work is less deep-seated than they say or think. Every time the officers summon them to further efforts, it seems an unbearable personal affront, even when righting the ship is the issue; and yet when Baker and the boatswain collect a party of them from the safety of the poop for the dangerous task of setting a sail forward, they go, and they do it, although it is also true that "the others lay still with a vile hope in their hearts of not being required to move till they got saved or drowned in peace" (85). Where a fellow-shipmate is concerned, however, the crew can act on their own independent initiative, as in their immediate resolve that, despite the real danger to their own lives, Wait must be rescued. The operative attitude of the crew to work, in short, seems in one respect very like their attitude to authority—their rebellious talk is more an expression of in-group solidarity than a manifesto calling to action. It functions as a psychological safety-valve to prevent explosion, and does not in itself pose any real threat to the order of the society of the *Narcissus* as a whole.

The sentiment of pity, however, proves much more dangerous. This at first seems paradoxical because feeling for the sufferings of others is both a fundamental Christian virtue, and the basis of most efforts to bring about a more just social order. On the *Narcissus*, however, its psychological effects on the crew are shown to be much more destructive of individual and group stability than their resentment either against the privileges of the officers or the labours which they exact.

At first the crew's pity for Donkin's destitution, and later for Wait's plight, helps to establish the social unity of the forecastle, and to promote their common action in an unselfish cause. Pity is also shown to serve a variety of individual psychological needs, from Belfast's hunger for an object of devotion, to the commoner human relish for exercising feelings of superiority and contempt. The real danger of pity, however, slowly becomes apparent as Wait imperiously exploits the crew's sympathy. His demand for quiet and comfort puts an end to whatever alleviations their lot offers—to their laughter, to their evening talks, even to Archie's concertina; and in the vacancy thus created, Wait becomes the obsessive object of their private thoughts: "a stalking death, thrust at them many times a day like a boast" (36).

Many critics, it is true, have seen Wait as a much more active and even transcendental agent of moral disorder. His portentous first appearance, the way Conrad's title[7] singles him out as the apparent chief protagonist, and his alignment on the wrong side of the novel's symbolic polarity of light and dark, all these no doubt prompt the impulse to seek larger hidden malignities in Wait. His blackness, for instance, has often been given a moral extension, and made the basis of parallels to such characters as Babo in Melville's *Benito Cereno;* Wait is then interpreted as a symbol of the irruption of absolute evil on the *Narcissus,* or is given a more universal moral meaning, as when Guerard writes that Wait "comes in some sense to represent our human 'blackness' " (*G*, 107).

These interpretations of Wait, however, run counter to the origins of the story, to its general moral and intellectual tenour, and to Conrad's own explicit statement.

Conrad's interest in the actual person on whom Wait was based probably had somewhat similar psychological origins to his interest in Almayer: both were strikingly isolated and deluded figures of pathos. Conrad's initial identification with a solitary and marginal exile is suggested by what he wrote in 1914: "I had much to do with him. He was in my watch. A negro in a British forecastle is a lonely being. He has no chums" (*N N D*, ix). This sympathy for an outcast surely weakens the case for seeing Wait as evil; and so does the way Conrad treats his colour. The narrative begins by insisting on Wait's blackness. At his first appearance, Wait's colour dramatically establishes his difference and his threat: and the narrator speaks of "the tragic, the mysterious, the repulsive mask of a nigger's soul" (18). This may perhaps seem to establish an association of "black" and "nigger" with

---

7. It was the title with which Conrad began, and he later usually referred to the novel as the "Nigger." On the other hand, Conrad apparently suggested "thirteen different titles" to the publisher, perhaps because the present title gives Wait a misleading importance, though there was also the objection to the word "nigger" as racially offensive. In America the title of the first edition was *The Children of the Sea;* this was an equally misleading title because, as Conrad wrote, it is "absurdly sweet" (*J D G*, 232–34 and notes); but it at least establishes the crew rather than Wait as the novel's protagonist.

evil; but there are at least four reasons to believe otherwise. First of all, the racial prejudice in the word "nigger," which was in any case less blatant in the English usage of the day than in the American, and for which Conrad can be blamed only in the sense that he must here share in the indictment that white society as a whole deserved, need not carry any individual moral aspersion. Secondly, the effect of "repulsive" is largely counterbalanced by the two preceding qualifiers "tragic" and "mysterious." Thirdly, we must remember that the whole phrase is only the expression of the crew's first, and primarily visual, reaction to Wait's appearance. And, lastly, we must note that, after all, they see only "a mask," and that there is no reason to believe that the soul behind it is black, or even significantly darker than other people's. In any case, even if the first ominous appearance of Wait suggests demonic evil and the various other traditional associations of blackness—mourning, obscurity, and death are certainly present—the colour issue later recedes. The crew assimilate Wait to their group with the jocular nickname of "Snowball"; and thereafter it is only Donkin who makes an issue of Wait's colour, calling him "a black-faced swine" (45).

Wait's initial air of mysterious command also evaporates. His curious pride is discovered to be the very natural defense of a lonely alien; he is aboard only in obedience to one of the bleakest and most universal of the laws of existence: as he tells Baker, "I must live till I die—mustn't I?" (44). In the later chapters the sense that Wait is larger than life is steadily undermined, particularly in his climactic confrontations with Podmore, Allistoun, and Donkin. The ordinariness of his secret must undoubtedly seem deflating to those who see Wait as an emissary from some spiritual chamber of horrors; but it is really an essential part of the book's thematic development: the uncanny influence Wait exercised on the crew came from an irrational projection of their own collective fears. On the *Narcissus*, order and disorder alike are temporary, contingent, man-made; and disorder will triumph until the crew learns that, behind the mysterious and menacing authority of a St. Kitts Negro, there is only a common human predicament. Wait is a symbol, not of death but of the fear of death, and therefore, more widely, of the universal human reluctance to face those most universal agents of anticlimax, the facts; and the facts find him out, as they later will the crew, and everyone else.

Most of the crew believe that their behaviour towards Wait is dictated by their generosity of spirit and their fellow-feeling; but that is surely the illusion projected by self-pity at the thought of their own mortality. The crew in effect unconsciously enact Wait's reluctance to face the idea of death. At first they wishfully assume—against all the physical evidence, beginning with Jimmy's echoing cough—that his "monstrous friendship" (36) with the fate he parades so unceasingly must be based on some occult power. At other times they like to think he is merely a malingerer, an evader of their other harsh fate, work. Belfast, the emotional extremist, expresses the crew's oscillations of attitude when he alternates between compassionate tears for Wait and a rage to "knock his ugly black head off—the skulking dodger!" Wait himself also oscillates about how serious his condition is. On the one hand, he tries to believe that he will recover, but meanwhile finds it to his advantage to pretend otherwise. Like many sick people he feels morally entitled to any power or privilege he can extort from his suffering, and at the same time derives a malicious pleasure from his success in exploiting others. For instance, he laughs to think how on his last voyage, "I got my money all right. Laid up fifty-eight days! The fools!" (111). On the other hand, no malingerer is ever wholly well, and Wait really knows he has every reason to avoid facing the truth.

During the gale the crew have other things to think about besides Wait; but when calm supervenes the full ambivalence of their feelings comes to a head, and they are torn between pity for the sick man, urging them one way, and hostility to the shirker, pushing them the other. This demoralising absorption with Wait erodes their effectiveness as a crew; and it will not be restored until they are ready to accept Singleton's pitiless wisdom. It is given fairly early, as soon as he has become aware of the troubled atmosphere of the ship, and of its cause; he faces the issue squarely, asks Wait "Are you dying?" (42), and receives the answer "Can't you see I am?" Singleton passes this conviction on, and the narrator comments that the crew then feels relieved, because "at last we knew that our compassion would not be misplaced."

In *The Rebel*, Camus roots the instinct for rebellion in man's resentment against his fate—the fact that he must die.[8] The crew's mutiny ultimately arises from the process whereby they convert their latent revolt against their own mortality into a form of in-group solidarity—their pity for the dying Wait; but two further aggravations of the situation are needed to precipitate the crisis. First, Podmore, the pious cook, who is as much above pity as Donkin is below it, yields to the "pride of possessed eternity" (115), "prayerfully divest[s] himself of the last vestige of his humanity," and tells Wait that since he is "as good as dead already" (117) he must at once repent to avoid the certain fires of hell. This terrifies Wait, and forces him back on his

8. Albert Camus, *L'Homme revolté* (Paris, 1951), p. 374.

delusion that he can cheat death; he declares to Allistoun: "I've been better this last week ... I am well ... I was going back to duty ... to-morrow—now if you like—Captain" (119). Allistoun, who has been "looking at him, fixedly," bluntly refuses: "You have been shamming sick ... There's nothing the matter with you, but you choose to lie-up to please yourself—and now you shall lie-up to please me."

The crew, not understanding Allistoun's real motive, are completely outraged; all three elements of the forces that divide the crew from their officers—pity, and resentment of Allistoun's unjust denial both ōf their comrade's legitimate wishes and of their own right to have the work shared out equally—are at last united to urge revolt; the crew talk menacingly, the helmsman deserts his post, and finally Donkin throws a belaying-pin at Allistoun.

It is not only the crew who fail to understand Allistoun's real motives; when he explains them to Baker and Creighton, they are "more impressed than if they had seen a stone image shed a miraculous tear of compassion" (127). Allistoun had seen what Wait could not face: "When I saw him standing there, three parts dead and so scared ... the notion came to me all at once, before I could think ... I thought I would let him go out in his own way. Kind of impulse. It never came into my head, those fools...."

Allistoun's intuitive insight urged him to shield Wait from trying to work because he would fail, and then be forced to face the unwelcome truth before the whole ship. It is ironical that the only act of total sympathetic understanding of Wait's situation should precipitate the most violent attack on the solidarity of the social order of the *Narcissus* as a whole, and that this attack should be directed at Allistoun because he has manifested the most understanding form of that very pity in whose name the mutiny occurs.

The ironic miscarriage of sympathy continues after the mutiny has petered out. In preventing Wait from experiencing his moment of truth in public, Allistoun has merely exposed him to hearing the truth in private, and under even more terrible conditions, from Donkin.

After Allistoun has shamed him by forcing him to replace the belaying-pin he had thrown, Donkin has been "ignored by all" the crew (143). This virtual ostracism is a powerful motive in driving him to visit Wait: to be able to insult the dying man makes Donkin feel "even with everybody for everything" (150). "Blamme if yer don't look dead already" Donkin taunts Wait, "Yer no one at all!" Wait is too ill to protest when Donkin continues to abuse him, but he finally sobs out: "Overboard! ... I! ... My God!" (153). Even before it has come, Wait tastes the full bitterness of death from the cruelty of Podmore and Donkin, the two pretended saviours of their fellow men.

After Wait's death the commentator remarks: "A common bond

was gone; the strong, effective and respectable bond of a sentimental lie" (155). That Conrad's purpose in *The Nigger of the "Narcissus"* was primarily to enact the complexities and contradictions of solidarity is shown not only by this obituary perspective, but by what he later said about his intentions. As regards the role of Wait, he wrote that "in the book he is nothing; he is merely the centre of the ship's collective psychology and the pivot of the action" (*N N D*, ix). This primary emphasis on the crew is corroborated by Conrad's comparison of the aims of *The Nigger of the "Narcissus"* and *The Red Badge of Courage*. Crane, Conrad wrote, had dealt with "the psychology of the mass— the army; while I ... had been dealing with the same subject on a much smaller scale and in more specialized conditions—the crew of a merchant ship, brought to the test of what I may venture to call the moral problem of conduct" (*L E*, 95).

Conrad added that Crane would have been "eminently fit to pronounce a judgment on my first consciously planned attempt to render the truth of a phase of life," but he "doubted whether anything of my ambitiously comprehensive aim would be understood" by most readers. Conrad also conceded that "I myself would have been hard put to it if requested to give my complex intentions the form of a concise and definite statement." These "complex intentions" certainly include a sense of the strength of the various forces which are arrayed against solidarity, and especially of the almost universal and continuous power of individual egoism. This is shown in the crew's relief when Singleton assures them that Wait will die, and that therefore their compassion has not been thrown away; but egoism has another and more indirect connection with pity: it may seem to be based on a wholly altruistic concern for the welfare of others, but in reality it is intimately connected with the individual's unconscious fear of his own sickness and death. The fear affects everyone. When Wait is in his death-throes, even the callous Donkin feels sympathetic tears coming into his eyes; but their real cause, the narrator comments, is "the thought that he himself, some day, would have to go through it all" (154).

The impulse of pity is, then, universal; but it is a particularly dangerous and unpredictable threat to solidarity because it can spring from the same unconscious fears of death as are, in the view of Camus, the motivating force of the impulse to rebel.

The Ideological Perspective

Before considering the final resolution of the conflicts which threaten solidarity on board the *Narcissus,* their general intellectual background requires attention.

The word solidarity came into English in 1848, the Year of Revolutions and of the Communist Manifesto; and that date is as good as any to mark a new stage in Europe's accelerating slide towards the characteristic political and social organisation of the modern world. In the last two decades of the nineteenth century, it looked as if man's future could only be a perpetual state of conflict in the international, national, religious, economic, political, and social domains. As a result, thought turned increasingly to the problem of what force, if any, could be expected to avert a complete collapse of civilisation.

There were, very broadly, two kinds of proposed political solutions. The first, that of the philosophical radicals, utopians, and socialists, was rooted in a faith in human progress, and the belief that some particular change in the economic and social system would bring it about. Conrad was completely unsympathetic to these views. Thus in The Nigger of the "Narcissus", Donkin, who is the only avowed "votary of change" on board, is obviously Conrad's somewhat overwrought parody of the socialist attempt to achieve equality and justice by mobilising working-class solidarity; we note that though the crew "abominated" Donkin, they "could not deny the luminous truth of his contentions" (101); and the narrator mocks how they dream "enthusiastically of the time when every lonely ship would travel over a serene sea, manned by a wealthy and well-fed crew of satisfied skippers" (103).

Conrad was much closer to the opposite view, which held that any decent social order would have to be imposed from the top. This position is represented by Captain Allistoun, who tells the mates: "I am here to drive this ship and keep every man-jack aboard of her up to the mark" (133). Conrad's conservative tendencies, however, were in uneasy conflict both with his sceptical realism about human history, and with his basic social attitudes which, though certainly not democratic, were in many ways deeply egalitarian and individualist. In his essay on "The Crime of Partition" (1919), Conrad writes that the "qualities and defects" of "the Polish nation" tended "to a certain exaggeration of individualism and, perhaps, to an extreme belief in the Governing Power of Free Assent" (N L L, 132); and this national inheritance continually serves to qualify Conrad's otherwise pronounced emphasis on a disciplined social order.[9]

The conflict is very evident in The Nigger of the "Narcissus". In a letter to Galsworthy, Conrad doubted "whether ship-life, though pervaded by a sort of rough equality, is truly democratic in its real essence" (L L,

---

9. Avrom Fleishman has recently placed Conrad in the organicist political tradition of Edmund Burke in his Conrad's Politics: Community and Anarchy in the Fiction of Joseph Conrad (Baltimore, 1967); but Conrad shows little of the Burkean reverence for any form of government or for the political process in general.

II, 63–64); and what we see on board the *Narcissus* is neither democratic in itself nor likely to support any democratic political position. This has provoked Marvin Mudrick, for instance, into writing that Conrad gives us "a hand-me-down 'aristocratic' universe in which everybody in charge deserves to be and everybody else had better jump."[10] But although *The Nigger of the "Narcissus"* certainly shows the need for continuous pressure by the officers, neither they nor Conrad's attitude to them seems essentially authoritarian; the officers are not presented as larger than life; they are merely a normal and necessary part, not only of the *Narcissus*, but of a world where nobody works or accepts any social constraint willingly.

In a wider ideological sense Conrad seems to go no more than halfway with the great reactionary culture-critics of the late nineteenth century. For instance, much of the moral perspective of *The Nigger of the "Narcissus"* is consonant with the critical, if not with the programmatic, side of Nietzsche, whom Conrad apparently disliked, although not as obsessively as he did Dostoevsky.[11] Many aspects of Nietzsche's thought, and particularly his characteristic equation, in *The Twilight of the Idols* (1889) and *The Antichrist* (1895), of altruism, pity, and decadence as the lamentable historical results of Christianity, are present in *The Nigger of the "Narcissus"*. But where Nietzsche writes that "active pity for all the failures and all the weak" is "more harmful than any vice,"[12] Conrad shows both sides of the problem. On the one hand, the results of the crew's pity for Wait demonstrate that the increasing sensitivity to the sufferings of others which comes with Christianity has made it much more difficult to maintain the cohesion of the social order; and there is something very Nietzschean about the terms in which Wait's influence on the crew is described: "Through him we were becoming highly humanised, tender, complex, excessively decadent: we understood the subtlety of his fear, sympathised with all his repulsions, shrinkings, evasions, delusions—as though we had been overcivilised, and rotten, and without any knowledge of the meaning of life" (139). On the other hand, whereas Nietzsche proposes as an alternative the proud warrior morality of the superman, Conrad does not. He deprecates the divisions that pity produces in the crew, but he makes Allistoun share their feeling.

10. "The Artist's Conscience," p. 294. Mudrick's position is attacked in my "Conrad Criticism and *The Nigger of the 'Narcissus'*," *Nineteenth-Century Fiction* 12 (1958): 257–83.

11. In "The Crime of Partition" Conrad's reference to Nietzsche occurs within the controlling context of the Poles' hatred of their German oppressors: "The Germanic Tribes had told the whole world . . . in tones Hegelian, Nietzschean, war-like, pious, cynical, inspired, what they were going to do to the inferior races of the earth" (*N L L*, 124–25). Conrad's contempt for Dostoevsky is expressed in his letters to Garnett (*E G*, 260–61; 269).

12. *The Portable Nietzsche*, ed. Walter Kaufman (New York, 1954), p. 570.

Nietzsche scorned the sociologists of his time because they took as their norm the varieties of "social decay"[13] which were all that contemporary society offered them. *The Nigger of the "Narcissus"* can be read as a study of social decay, and Conrad's attitude is primarily that of the sociologist trying to give an objective analysis of the crew as a collective entity with its own autonomous set of social institutions, traditions, and ways of thought. What emerges from Conrad's picture is a view of the problems of solidarity which is very close to the thought of Tönnies (1855–1936) and Durkheim (1858–1917).

In 1887 Ferdinand Tönnies published his *Gemeinschaft und Gesellschaft*, usually translated as *Community and Society*. Very broadly, he distinguishes between two antithetical ideal types of social forms: *Gemeinschaft* includes such prototypes of community as the village or the family in a peasant economy, whose membership is obligatory rather than the result of individual choice, and which has a traditional and hierarchical kind of organisation; *Gesellschaft*, on the other hand, includes such associations as the companies of capitalists or the trade unions of workers, football clubs, or political parties; these "societies" arise primarily from the free, conscious, rational, and willed choice of their members; and they exist only to serve the specific interests of individual members, and not those of the community at large. For Tönnies, the uniquely distinctive feature of the modern social order was the extent to which the *Gesellschaft* society, with its rational and individualist mental attitudes, predominated over the *Gemeinschaft* community.

The tensions on board the *Narcissus* embody much of this now familiar division. On the one hand, the old *Gemeinschaft* elements are stronger than elsewhere: the ship is largely governed by customary procedures and traditional hierarchies. On the other hand, the new order of the *Gesellschaft* society is beginning to disturb the balance: neither the officers nor the men are wholly isolated from the models of urban and industrial life on land, and to some extent they follow those models by constituting themselves as separate societies which pursue their own group interests. What most provokes the crew is how their egalitarian feelings are "oppressed by the injustice of the world" (102). This sense is articulated and exploited by Donkin in his "altruistic indignation" at the way "we are put upon" (112). Donkin represents the ideology of working-class solidarity, which had led to the foundation in 1887 of the National Amalgamated Sailors' and Firemen's Union, a typical association of the *Gesellschaft* kind, concerned with advancing the group interests of seamen. The union, or

13. *Portable Nietzsche*, p. 541.

at least the bitter struggles which led to its foundation, are briefly referred to on the *Narcissus* when Knowles talks of how a crew in Cardiff got "six weeks' hard for refoosing dooty" at the instigation of the "Plimsoll man," who wrongly told them the ship was overloaded (107).[14] Samuel Plimsoll was the first president of the union, and had become famous as "the sailor's friend" through his fight for the Unseaworthy Ships Bill in 1875, which made the white painted load line, or Plimsoll mark, mandatory on British ships.

Conrad himself had personal knowledge of both sides in the conflict. He had worked his way up from the forecastle; and later, as an officer, he had become aware of the extent to which the economic demands of his shipowners were contrary to his responsibility as an officer to the ship's community as a whole. This division of loyalties emerged from Conrad's testimony before the Board of Trade's departmental committee on the manning of merchant ships, which was enquiring into the great increase in the numbers of merchant ships lost at sea. Very few masters were willing to testify at the enquiry. Conrad did, on 3 July 1894; but although he stood his ground when his view that the crew of the *Adowa* had been dangerously small was challenged by the interrogators, his evidence in general shows him trying to avoid offending the shipowners. He suggested, for instance, that the *Torrens* would have been a safer vessel with "a couple more hands" on its crew, but when pressed for a more absolute judgment, he answered, "I really cannot say that she was badly manned."[15]

The tensions between conflicting group allegiances on board the *Narcissus* are also treated in a way which is very close to the thought of the main founder of modern sociological thought, Émile Durkheim, and particularly that of his first book, *De la division du travail social,* which came out in 1893.

Durkheim, who had read Tönnies,[16] made a somewhat similar contrast between ancient and modern societies. Earlier societies had tended to require from the individual a substantial identity of at-

14. Plimsoll had waged his campaign largely through countless charges of overloading, not always true, against the shipowners; and there were many cases of seamen being imprisoned for refusing to work on allegedly unseaworthy ships. But the allusion may be partially based on a much publicised incident during a bitter seaman's strike at Cardiff in 1892, when the founder of the sailor's union, Joseph Havelock Wilson, was sentenced to six weeks' imprisonment, technically for unlawful assembly (David Masters, *The Plimsoll Mark* [London, 1955], p. 258). See also Norris W. Yates, "Social Comment in *The Nigger of the 'Narcissus'*," *P M L A* 79 (1964): 183–85, and J. Havelock Wilson, *My Stormy Voyage Through Life* (London, 1925).

15. Published in Edmund A. Bojarski's, "Conrad at the Crossroads: From Navigator to Novelist with Some New Biographical Mysteries," *The Texas Quarterly* 11 (1968): 22–23.

16. Steven Lukes, *Émile Durkheim: His Life and Work* (New York, 1972), pp. 143–47.

titudes and behaviour over a wide range of national, religious, intellectual, moral, economic, and social matters; and the most drastic penalties—death, disgrace, or banishment—were used to enforce individual conformity in whatever the society defined as essential to its collective life. Durkheim called this kind of solidarity "mechanical": human beings were treated as substantially interchangeable components of the social machine. Modern society, on the other hand, was characterised by what Durkheim called "organic solidarity." The metaphor is based on the different ways that mechanical and organic entities function. Plants and animals are not aggregates of identical units; they function through the interplay of different but complementary parts, as in the case of sexual reproduction. Modern society, Durkheim argued, was organic in the sense that individuals and groups may be very different and even largely autonomous, and yet, through the division of labour, can satisfactorily exercise intricately complementary economic functions which are necessary for the life of society as a whole. But the complexity of organic solidarity makes it peculiarly vulnerable to conflict or breakdown; and Conrad's picture of the stresses on the crew of the *Narcissus* is very close to what Durkheim classified as one of the "abnormal forms" of modern social organisation, in which the inequality between individuals is too extreme to allow organic solidarity to operate properly.[17] Durkheim called the result *anomie,* "lacking law," because collective beliefs no longer operate adequately; and this lack of any effective consensus of values and attitudes combines with the inequity of the contractual relations between employers and employed to make a stable social equilibrium impossible. Conflict is endemic, and, as Durkheim put it in terms very applicable to what we see happen on the *Narcissus,* "Truces, arrived at after violence, are never anything but provisional, and satisfy no one. Human passions stop only before a moral power they respect."[18]

Conrad is unlikely to have read Durkheim, who, like Tönnies, was relatively little known in 1896. On the other hand, the term solidarity was very much in the air, partly because it had been popularised as the name of a French political movement, with which Durkheim was loosely associated, that advocated measures to ameliorate the various conflicts which prevented solidarity; and the political leader of the movement, Léon Bourgeois, published a much discussed book, *La Solidarité,* in 1896.[19] In any case, the treatment of the problems of

17. Émile Durkheim, *The Division of Labor in Society,* trans. George Simpson (New York, 1964), pp. 374–88.
18. *Division of Labor,* p. 3.
19. Lukes, *Durkheim,* pp. 350–54.

solidarity in *The Nigger of the "Narcissus"* suggests not only that Conrad was very sensitive to one of the main social preoccupations of his day, but that his analysis was consistent with the new understanding of modern social problems pioneered by his two contemporaries, Tönnies and Durkheim.

Conrad's treatment of the psychology of the crew of the *Narcissus* is also similar to yet another celebrated work of the period, Gustave Le Bon's *La Psychologie des Foules* (1895). Le Bon saw the crowd as much more than the sum of its aggregate parts; by a process of "emotional contagion" it turns individuals into a new and autonomous social entity which is more dogmatic, singleminded, intolerant, irresponsible, and changeable than any of its constituent individuals; it is also much more emotional, more credulous, more illogical, and more convinced of its righteous power. The crew of the *Narcissus* is not a crowd; but in the mutiny it manifests most of these tendencies; and its behaviour in general exemplifies Le Bon's aphorism: "Whoever can supply them [the crowd] with illusions is easily their master; whoever attempts to destroy their illusions is always their victim."[20] We are, indeed, made to wonder whether the most powerful form of solidarity manifested in the novel is not the solidarity "in illusions" which Conrad mentions in the preface.

The Final Balance

The discrepancies between our ideal expectations and what actually happens aboard the *Narcissus* moved Jocelyn Baines to wonder that "Conrad should have declared his wish to 'enshrine my old chums in a decent edifice' and then put a curse on the edifice" (*J B*, 186). A more ringing endorsement of human solidarity might certainly have been anticipated, given Conrad's stated intentions in the preface, and the fact that, at least in comparison with what obtains elsewhere, conditions on the *Narcissus* were in many respects exceptionally auspicious. Its twenty-six men compose a group of very manageable size: a ship is a relatively homogeneous community, since everyone's daily life has a very large proportion of shared and public elements;[21] and even the great inequality of status and style between officers and crew is qualified by four exceptional circumstances. First, as the narrator comments, "discipline is not ceremonious in merchant ships, where the sense of hierarchy is weak, and where all feel themselves equal before the unconcerned immensity of the sea and the exacting appeal

20. Gustave Le Bon, *The Crowd*, ed. Robert K. Merton (New York, 1960), p. 110.
21. See Vilhelm Aubert and Oddvar Arner, "On the Social Structure of the Ship," *Acta Sociologica* 3 (1958): 200–219.

of the work" (16); secondly, the separation between officers and crew is not in general based on inherited educational or economic advantages; thirdly, all those on board share an immediate mutual dependence in which everyone's survival is continuously at stake; and lastly, they are all united by a strong and unique symbolic tie—their ship.

Conrad himself had been attracted to the *Narcissus* as soon as he saw her in Bombay harbour (*L L*, I, 76); the crew shares his feeling—"We knew she was the most magnificent sea-boat ever launched" (51). Conrad's epigraph emphasises the power of this emotional bond: "My Lord in his discourse discovered a great deal of love to this ship."[22] In a later essay, "Well Done," which is concerned with how the "sense of immediate duty" is generated, Conrad wrote that "in everyday life ordinary men require something . . . material, effective, definite, and symbolic on which to concentrate their love and their devotion"; and he concluded that in fact "what awakens the seaman's sense of duty, what lays that impalpable constraint upon the strength of his manliness, what commands his not always dumb if always dogged devotion, is not the spirit of the sea but something that in his eyes has a body, a character, a fascination, and almost a soul—it is his ship" (*N L L*, 191).

Both Conrad's aims, then, and the circumstances of the life presented in *The Nigger of the "Narcissus"*, would appear to be ideally suited to give the most favourable possible picture of human solidarity in modern society; and yet even on the *Narcissus* solidarity between officers and men is never conscious and whole-hearted; it seems to operate fully only in moments of acute crisis; and most of its manifestations are wayward, fragile, and impermanent.

In the storm, it is true, the crew's psychology exhibits a moral unanimity which has a much more humanly affirmative character than that described by Le Bon. The structure of command, of course, is still needed; but some members of the crew are also shown as capable of spontaneous collective and individual effort, not only in the rescue of Wait but also in Podmore's miraculous production of coffee. Conrad places the storm in the central position of the narrative, and this, combined with power of the writing, makes the solidarity exhibited there the most powerful and enduring experience in the book.

This effect is achieved largely through Conrad's brilliant visualisation of symbolic meanings. For instance, when the *Narcissus* overturns, the reader watches alongside the crew as "the topsail sheet parted, the end of the heavy chain racketed aloft, and sparks of red fire streamed down through the flying sprays. The sail flapped once with a jerk that

22. From Samuel Pepys, *Diary*, 30 March 1660. The epigraph is often omitted.

seemed to tear our hearts out through our teeth, and instantly changed into a bunch of fluttering narrow ribbons that tied themselves into knots and became quiet along the yard" (59). The threat of death is vividly present in the red fire, and in the sudden and mysterious transformation of the sail into some quiet knots along the yard. Later, when Baker has led a party forward to hoist the fore-topmast staysail as a first step to righting the ship, the sense of collective resurrection is all the stronger for being presented as a distant visual occurrence whose human cause seems quite inexplicable to the rest of the crew, miserably huddled by the poop; they only see a group of men who "were restless with strange exertions, waved their arms, knelt, lay flat down, staggered up, seemed to strive their hardest to go overboard. Suddenly a small white piece of canvas fluttered amongst them, grew larger, beating. Its narrow head rose in jerks—and at last it stood distended and triangular in the sunshine.—'They have done it!' cried the voices aft" (85).

The reader's heart beats with the sail; but the real test of solidarity must be what happens under more normal conditions. As soon as calm and safety supervene on the *Narcissus*, the crew's larger solidarity vanishes, and is replaced by other group manifestations which are mainly of a divisive and potentially destructive kind. Mainly, but not entirely; the limits to the crew's rebellious feelings remain; and at the critical moment of the mutiny Allistoun is in effect saved by the crew. When Donkin throws the belaying pin, it is the suddenly mobilised collective action of the forecastle which stops him from throwing another; this is largely a spontaneous reaction, although it is crystallised by one of their number, Archie, who threatens the worst of all betrayals of the code of the forecastle: "If ye do oot ageen I wull tell!" (123).

In general the crew composes a reasonably viable society. From a practical point of view, the in-group solidarity of the forecastle seems to arise very easily and spontaneously both in the early physical arrangements of settling in, and in the later development of a variety of symbolic reinforcements: Tom the cat is the crew's mascot; the sayings of Baker, Podmore, and Singleton are their oral tradition. The community life they set up is conspicuously kind, and in the main tolerant and good-humoured. Aggression, laziness, and egotism are all there, of course, but they are not dominant in practice, although they may seem to be in the crew's verbal codes and even in their gropings toward a political consciousness.

From the ideological point of view, the crew, both as individuals and as a group, seem to exist in a state of unresolved tension: "We oscillated between the desire of virtue and the fear of ridicule; we wished to save ourselves from the pain of remorse, but did not want to be made the contemptible dupes of our sentiment" (41). There is no possibility of collective action rationally directed towards a common purpose. Between "timid truth and audacious lies" (30), the crew enact a perpetual ideological stalemate; any resolution of their moral and social conflicts is blocked by an uneasy awareness of their own "intellectual shortcomings" (102); as a group they endure in a state of feeling "oppressed by the injustice of the world, surprised to perceive how long we had lived under its burden without realising our unfortunate state, annoyed by the uneasy suspicion of our undiscerning stupidity."

After the mutiny, the crew's sense of inadequacy makes them equally receptive to the illusions of Wait, the propaganda of Donkin, and the superstitions of Singleton. There is certainly little evidence that they have learned from experience. For instance, after Wait's death Singleton waxes scholastic in explaining how "the sight of an island (even a very small one) is generally more fatal than the view of a continent. But he couldn't explain why" (156). This comical concern with ontology now infects the forecastle with theological dissensions almost as bitter as those which led to the mutiny. Pacific Knowles, good-tempered Davies, and finally even the watch below, come to blows over the question of whether the barometer had begun to fall, and thus herald the long-awaited breeze, before or after the precise moment of Wait's death.

After this we learn little more of the crew's state of mind until they arrive in London Dock. The two Norwegians stay together; poor young Charley is carried off by his blowzy mother so that his pay can keep her in drink; Belfast goes off alone cherishing a new delusion about Wait: "I never touched him—never—never," he sobs (171), seeing himself as the saint in a miracle of his own belated invention; while the rest of the crew go off to the *Black Horse*, whose varnished barrels will dispense "the illusions of strength, mirth, happiness."

Then they drift "out of sight," to go on being, one imagines, what they are, and acting as we have seen them act.

This impenetrability to the lessons of experience is by no means the only accepted interpretation of the novel's ending. No doubt in obedience to the modern critical superstition that in literature, at least, all suffering and error are automatically digested into maturity of understanding, many critics have read *The Nigger of the "Narcissus"*, and especially its resolution, in much more positive terms. James E. Miller, for instance, writes that after the men have been paid off, and they refuse Donkin's offer of a drink, "The rejection of Donkin's ignorance is finally complete, and Singleton's primitive wisdom is at last triumphant. The crew has passed from diversity based on ignorance through a false unity based on the lie perpetrated by Donkin, to, finally, the true 'knot' of solidarity based on genuine insight into the meaning of life and death."[23]

The balance of the evidence surely resists so consoling a conclusion. Though Donkin is certainly spurned after his attack on Allistoun, the crew's general reaction after the mutiny amounts to no more than tacit shame, and their delusions about Jimmy do not abate. They are, it is true, inclined to reject Singleton's oracular confidence that Wait, the cause of the head winds, would die at the first sight of land, but this is not because they reject superstition, but because thinking about death "caused pain" (142). Nor does Wait's death promote any genuine insight; it merely shakes "the foundations of our society" (155) without any suggestion that something better is in prospect. If we look back over the novel as a whole, and consider the course taken by the various ideological forms of solidarity among the crew, we must surely conclude that, despite much that is admirable, the predominant tendency has been a random, foolish, and wasteful expenditure of intellectual, emotional, and social energy; fruitless conflict is apparently the predestined and unalterable condition of individual and social life.

Conrad, in fact, seems to deny that there is any inherent meaning or direction in the processes of time; man's lot, to judge by *The Nigger of the "Narcissus"*, is one of endemic ideological and class conflict. These conflicts apparently lead neither to a further unfolding of the Hegelian idea, nor to the eventual triumph of a better social order; conflict is not a temporary stage towards something better, but a law of existence.

This perspective is fairly close to the thought of another sociologist, who was Conrad's contemporary and somewhat akin to him in spirit. For Georg Simmel (1858–1918), it was in the very nature of society to be kept in motion by perpetually opposing forces. As he wrote in an essay on "The Conflict in Modern Culture" (1918): "The future does not replace conflicts with their resolutions, but only replaces their forms and contents with others."[24]

It is, of course, only from the point of view of optimistic political ideologies that Simmel or Conrad must be regarded as pessimists. Few dispassionate and informed observers would be inclined to question

23. James E. Miller, Jr., *"The Nigger of the 'Narcissus'*: A Re-examination," *P M L A* 66 (1951): 917.

24. *Georg Simmel: On Individuality and Social Forms*, ed. Donald Levine (Chicago, 1971), p. 393.

the justness and balance of Conrad's picture of the crew's behaviour, or to give it a particularly low rating in comparison with other examples of social life. The curse which Baines detects and Miller tries to exorcise is only the curse which practice invariably lays upon theory; and if the modes of solidarity which operate in *The Nigger of the "Narcissus"* offer little hope of political or social progress, they certainly offer no darker a prospect for the future of civilisation than history was subsequently to enact.

v. The Affirmations of Retrospect

Conrad later wrote that "the problem that faces" the crew of the *Narcissus* "is not a problem of the sea, it is merely a problem that has arisen on board a ship where the conditions of complete isolation from all land entanglements make it stand out with a particular force and colouring" (*L L*, II, 342). This assertion is conspicuously inapplicable to the last few pages of *The Nigger of the "Narcissus"*, which voice a much more affirmative view of solidarity than what has gone before, but in specifically nautical terms. Much of this more positive perspective comes from Conrad's authorial rhetoric, and there are times when it reveals an obvious discrepancy between his nostalgic affection for his sailor comrades and what he has actually shown them doing in the narrative.

Both the overloaded rhetoric and the internal contradictions become very apparent when the *Narcissus* sails up the English channel. England is no longer, like other lands, all darkness and dirt, but a bright creature of the sea: it is the "ship mother of fleets and nations! The great flagship of the race; stronger than the storms! and anchored in the open sea" (163). To be loyal to the British merchant service, Conrad had to be both against the land, and for his adopted country; so England became a boat. As he looked back on his years at sea, Conrad no doubt felt that he should record the personal feelings with which he had often responded to the first sight of England on returning from a long voyage; and so he put the passage in, regardless of the extent to which it complicated, if it did not destroy, the opposition between land and sea which is persistently present in the narrative. Of course, the dualism which assigns all the virtues to the sea, and all the vices to the land, is itself contradicted by what transpires; Conrad writes that the "true peace of God begins at any spot a thousand miles from the nearest land" (31); but on board the *Narcissus* the peace of God is far to seek even on the high seas.

These inconsistencies of attitude, however, do not affect Conrad's vivid and concrete presentation of the arrival of the *Narcissus* in port;

and this is succeeded by a touching description of the dispersal of the
crew. It closes in a passage where the narrator's valedictory salute is
beautifully conveyed through visual implication only. The lowering
darkness of London lifts for a fleeting moment, and we see:

> . . . overhead the clouds broke; a flood of sunshine streamed
> down the walls of grimy houses. The dark knot of seamen
> drifted in sunshine. To the left of them the trees in Tower
> Gardens sighed, the stones of the Tower gleaming, seemed to
> stir in the play of light. . . . The sunshine of heaven fell like a
> gift of grace on the mud of the earth. . . . And to the right of
> the dark group the stained front of the Mint, cleansed by the
> flood of light, stood out for a moment dazzling and white like
> a marble palace in a fairy tale. The crew of the *Narcissus*
> drifted out of sight (172).

The next paragraph begins "I never saw them again," and this brief
personal statement provokes a thoughtful pause in which we can reflect on the symbolic purport of the sunburst on the Mint. The
aureole of blessedness and the dazzling brightness of the dying hero's
apotheosis are familiar ways in which a sudden effect of light in the
natural world is correlated with a symbolic recognition of
transcendent human qualities; and it traditionally occurs at the moment of death, as it does here when we are seeing the crew of the
Narcissus for the last time.

In the last paragraph of the novel the requiem continues in the
form of a direct apostrophe by the narrator to his former shipmates:

> A gone shipmate, like any other man, is gone for ever; and
> I never met one of them again. But at times the spring-flood
> of memory sets with force up the dark River of the Nine
> Bends. Then on the waters of the forlorn stream drifts a
> ship—a shadowy ship manned by a crew of Shades. They pass
> and make a sign, in a shadowy hail. Haven't we, together and
> upon the immortal sea, wrung out a meaning from our sinful
> lives? Good-bye brothers! You were a good crowd. As good a
> crowd as ever fisted with wild cries the beating canvas of a
> heavy foresail; or tossing aloft, invisible in the night, gave
> back yell for yell to a westerly gale (172–73).

The rhetorical inflation is obvious, and some of its details jar. We
have not, for instance, been shown the crew of the *Narcissus* giving
"back yell for yell to a westerly gale"; and if this means a shout of
proud defiance hurled at the winds, it is surely a mode of affirming
heroic solidarity more appropriate to a sea-scout regatta than to the
grim endurance which hardly managed to handle the sails of the
Narcissus during the storm. Both the language and the substance are

forced, as they also are in the earlier sentence: "Haven't we, together and upon the immortal sea, wrung out a meaning from our sinful lives?" Conrad would no doubt like some final "meaning" to have emerged from the voyage, but it is far from clear that anything very permanent has; and in any case the phrase "wrung out" suggests a conscious intention of so doing by the "we," a suggestion which is no more supported by what the narrative shows us of the crew's intellectual preoccupations than it is made more convincing by the quasi-colloquial elevation of Conrad's style.

One can recognise, and honour, the reverence in Conrad's retrospective celebration of the crew of Shades, so reminiscent in attitude of what he had said earlier about Almayer. One can also understand that, as he finished the novel, Conrad should have felt that his picture of the voyage of the *Narcissus* fell far short of what his heart wanted to say. It is an ancient literary problem: as Auden asks, "O who can ever praise enough / The world of his belief?"[1] Like everyone else, Conrad felt that for the world of his belief, his words could never be enough.

Conrad had also, as usual, been in a hurry to finish; and afterwards he was very much aware of the weakness of his last pages, writing to Stephen Crane that "artistically the end of the book is somewhat lame. I mean after the death [of Jimmy]. All that rigmarole about the burial and the ship's coming home seems to run away into a rat's tail—thin at the end. Well! It's too late now to bite my thumbs and tear my hair."[2]

On one matter, at least, Conrad need not have worried, for, long before the conclusion, he has made us see the intensity of his admiration and affection for the comrades of his years at sea, and conveyed it through a perspective which also took account of the darker view of the processes of time which pervades the preface.

In general our picture of life depends very largely on the durational scale we are using when we make our judgment. From a distance of months or years, a few special moments may stand out whose absolute quality almost obliterates all those other unremembered moments which brought the commoner message that as usual no one had quite come up to snuff. *The Nigger of the "Narcissus"* shows us some of these redeeming spots of time, and it also suggests another kind of affirmation, which belongs to a much vaster temporal scale: the centuries cannot but recount a tale which does indeed bind "the dead to the living and the living to the unborn" through the "solidarity . . . in toil" of the "disregarded multitude of the bewildered, the simple and the voiceless."

1. *Collected Poetry* (New York, 1945), p. 226.
2. 16 November 1897 *(The Bookman* [New York]) 69 (1929): 230.

In *The Nigger of the "Narcissus"*, not only the privileged moments, but the millennial continuity of human solidarity are primarily associated with the heroic figure of Singleton, "old as Father Time himself" (24). Singleton has been at sea for forty-five years, and since the age of twelve. He is the lonely relic of an earlier, heroic age of seamen, men who "had been strong, as those are strong who know neither doubts nor hopes"; and he is specifically contrasted with the younger generation who compose the rest of the crew: "They are less naughty, but less innocent; less profane, but perhaps also less believing; and if they had learned how to speak they have also learned how to whine. But the others were strong and mute; they were effaced, bowed and enduring, like stone caryatides that hold up in the night the lighted halls of a resplendent and glorious edifice."

The idea that Singleton represents an evolutionary stage in human history which is destined to vanish for ever is consistent with what Herbert Spencer saw as a general law of the "evolution of the simple into the complex, through successive differentiations."[3] Conrad's deepest sympathies, unlike Spencer's, go out to the past; and so, in the inexorable "change from the homogeneous to the heterogeneous," he sᵔts Singleton against the succeeding generation. Unlike the other members of the crew of the *Narcissus*, Singleton is absolute in his unthinking commitment to the spirit of a simpler phase of society, to the *Gemeinschaft* allegiances of Tönnies and to the mechanical solidarity of Durkheim.

We first see Singleton, quite oblivious to the turmoil in the forecastle, holding Bulwer-Lytton's *Pelham* "at arm's length before his big, sunburnt face . . . intensely absorbed, and as he turned the pages an expression of grave surprise would pass over his rugged features" (6). Like many old people, Singleton shows little interest in whatever activities going on around him do not seem necessary; and he is conspicuously unadapted to life on land, or in the modern world. Singleton is wont to boast "with the mild composure of long years well spent, that generally from the day he was paid off from one ship till the day he shipped in another he seldom was in a condition to distinguish daylight"; and when he is paid off from the *Narcissus*, he can "hardly find the small pile of gold in the profound darkness of the shore" (168). Unable to sign his name, he "painfully sketched in a heavy cross"; and the pay-clerk, a sober, hygienic, and educated representative of the new social order, recoils from Singleton as an affronting anachronism, "a disgusting old brute."

3. "Progress: Its Law and Cause" (1857), *Essays: Scientific, Political, and Speculative* (New York, 1892), vol. 1, p. 10.

Conrad does not pretend that Singleton is a viable model in the contemporary world. We are certainly not intended, for instance, to accept the superstitious certitudes which help Singleton to maintain his stoical composure; his credulity is part of his emblematic role as representative of the ancient traditions of the sea. When Shakespeare's Pericles is told that the storm will not abate until the ship is cleared of his wife's dead body, he objects, "That's your superstition"; to this, the seaman replies: "With us at sea it hath been still observed; and we are strong in custom" (II, i). Singleton is sure that the *Narcissus* will never make headway until it is relieved of Wait's body; when it is, the breeze comes, and Singleton mumbles: "I knowed it—he's gone, and here it comes" (161).

Superstition is the way in which the archaic forms of solidarity are strengthened, particularly when, as in such dangerous and unpredictable occupations as the mariner's, there is a special need to believe in the existence of an unalterable relationship between man and the power of the natural world. Conrad did not believe that the state of Wait's body affected that of the weather, but he used the episode to enact an important aspect of the older ideological tradition.

Singleton makes a more convincing contribution to the theme of solidarity as an emblem of the continuity of the generations. Like the aging warriors of epic, such as Nestor, or, even more, like later heroes of ordinary toil, such as Wordsworth's leech-gatherer, Singleton has been reduced by time to a human shape that has become indistinguishable from what it has done; a lifetime of steady service has created a seaman who, as Conrad wrote, is "in perfect accord with his life" (*C G*, 53). All his loyalty and his love go to his ship. After the *Narcissus* has been righted, and Allistoun asks if the steering gear works, Singleton answers "Steers . . . like a little boat," speaking "with hoarse tenderness, without giving the master as much as half a glance" (91). The ship, an instrument of human need, has supplanted humanity itself as the only center of Singleton's being; the collective inheritance of man's past struggles for survival has become a deeply-rooted but wholly impersonal instinct.

Conrad's nostalgic reverence for the life of sailing ships as an archaic survival based on a simple and unthinking commitment to solidarity, is expressed by making Singleton, not Captain Allistoun, the guardian spirit of the *Narcissus*. More than that, he is the guardian spirit of the whole tradition of human toil. We see this most vividly after the storm, when, soon after the ship has at last been righted, we finally become aware of Singleton again. He has been at the wheel for thirty hours: "Apart, far aft, and alone by the helm, old Singleton had deliberately tucked his white beard under the top button of his glistening coat. Swaying upon the din and tumult of the seas, with the whole battered length of the ship launched forward in a rolling rush before his steady old eyes, he stood rigidly still, forgotten by all, and with an attentive face. In front of his erect figure only the two arms moved crosswise with a swift and sudden readiness, to check or urge again the rapid stir of circling spokes. He steered with care" (89).

Conrad's sudden and drastic narrowing of the narrative horizon brings home our utter, but usually forgotten, dependence on the labors of others. To make us see the ultimate and universal basis of human solidarity Conrad has reserved his greatest art to make us pause at the spectacle of a man who steers with care; and this vivid moment constrains us, in Auden's words, to "Give / Our gratitude to the Invisible College of the Humble, / Who through the ages have accomplished everything essential."[4]

There is surely a special moral for readers and critics here: for, in making us look up to Singleton at the wheel, Conrad compels us, in a humbling moment of awed vision, to acknowledge our solidarity with those who cannot write and who read only Bulwer-Lytton.

4. *Collected Poetry,* p. 344.

CHAPTER 4

Heart of Darkness

i. 1897–1898: In the Doldrums

The course of Conrad's life between January 1897, when *The Nigger of the "Narcissus"* was finished, and December 1898, when *Heart of Darkness* was begun, established the essential pattern of the rest of his writing career, and especially of the period up to 1913, when the success of *Chance* finally brought him some measure of financial security. Until then the tale of Conrad's days largely reduces itself to a few depressing themes: harassing economic anxiety, accompanied by much borrowing of money, guilt at unpaid debts, and exasperation at importunate creditors; painfully slow progress in writing, punctuated by occasional periods of intense productivity but more often by bouts of disabling physical illness or psychological prostration; and at the end, anxiety and dissatisfaction about each completed work, which there is no time to amend.

Conrad's earlier works had begun to win him a circle of devoted friends. For instance, *Almayer's Folly* had brought him Garnett; then an anonymous reviewer of *An Outcast of the Islands* called it "perhaps the finest piece of fiction" of the year, but added that its "greatness" was masked by "a glaring fault . . . Mr. Conrad is wordy" (*J B*, 165–66). Conrad wrote to the reviewer, was surprised to receive an answer from H. G. Wells, already a very successful author, and a fairly close friendship ensued. Then, in the summer of 1897, the appearance of "An Outpost of Progress" produced an enthusiastic letter from R. B. Cunninghame Graham—Scottish aristocrat, radical member of Parliament, horseman, world traveller, adventurer, and just then beginning his career as a prolific and widely-admired writer.[1] Their friendship grew rapidly, and for Conrad it became a supremely important psychological assurance: Arthur Symons reports that Conrad once said to him, "in a tone of tragic and almost passionate pathos I shall never forget: 'Could you conceive for a moment that I could go on existing if Cunninghame Graham were to die?'" (*C G*, 4).

Another important friendship began in the autumn of 1897. Stephen Crane had admired *The Nigger of the "Narcissus"* in its serial

1. There is a fine analysis of his friendship with Conrad in Cedric Watts's introduction to his edition of *Joseph Conrad's Letters to R. B. Cunninghame Graham.*

form, and asked to meet Conrad; the two quickly became intimate and remained so until Crane's early death in 1900. Crane soon tried to further Conrad's career by using his American connections; he wrote in the New York *Bookman* that with *The Nigger of the "Narcissus"* Conrad "comes nearer to an ownership of the mysterious life on the ocean than anybody who has written in this century." Crane also took issue with the "inexorably respectable" English journal, the *Academy*, because it had not given its prize for the best book published in 1897 to *The Nigger of the "Narcissus"*. Crane ranked it above two very notable contenders for that year—Henry James's *What Maisie Knew* and Rudyard Kipling's *Captains Courageous*.[2]

Unfortunately there was very little Crane or anyone else could do to make Conrad a popular writer. Even favourable reviewers tended to object that *The Nigger of the "Narcissus"* had no story and no love interest—"no plot and no petticoats," as Israel Zangwill put it (*S C H*, 95). Surprising as it must seem today, the novel was also criticised as belonging to "the school of fiction-brutality"; its seamen were characterised by one reviewer as "generally worthless personages" (*J D G*, 288;286); and although Conrad had already removed most of the "bloody's" at his publisher's urging (*E G*, 100), the few shameless relics moved the *Literary World* to find the story "in many places absolutely repellent by reason of the robustness of the adjectives employed" (*J D G*, 288). Even the most favourable reviews were often such as to discourage sales. The *Spectator,* for instance, wrote: "Mr. Conrad is a writer of genius; but his choice of themes, and the uncompromising nature of his methods, debar him from attaining a wide popularity" (*J B*, 205–6).

Conrad had anticipated that it would be difficult to earn a living by his pen. In March 1896, for instance, he had written to his cousin, Charles Zagórski: "If I have ventured into this field it is with the determination to achieve a reputation—in that sense I do not doubt my success. I know what I can do. It is therefore only a question of earning money . . . That I do not feel too certain about" (*N*, 216).

When Garnett had advised Conrad against going on with "The Sisters" in 1896, he was in effect warning him against trying to be a more ambitious and highbrow kind of novelist; and Conrad, to make his "abasement . . . very complete," promised that in the future he would obey all Garnett's "expoundings of the ways of the readers" (*E G*, 23–24; 27). In "Karain," his first short story of 1897, Conrad had more or less accepted Garnett's typecasting: it was an engrossing and neatly-structured Malayan tale, but it also, as Conrad wrote to

2. "Concerning the English 'Academy,' " March 1898, 22–24.

Cunninghame Graham, had "something magazine'ish about it" (*C G*, 82). Then in the summer of 1897 Conrad tried to break out of his rut into another kind of fiction, but one very different from "The Sisters." "The Return," set in fashionable London society, is a short story about the moral vacuum between a husband and wife; she leaves him, but returns; in their ensuing conversations, it appears that neither side can satisfy, or even understand, the other's needs; and the husband eventually leaves, never to return. The story is not as lifeless as most critics (including Garnett and Conrad himself later) have thought; but it is a laboured piece of writing and, at 20,000 words, much too long. Conrad lacked the touch required for presenting intimate crosscurrents of feeling between men and women in an interesting and convincing way; and he was particularly weak in dialogue, on which the development of his subject largely depended. Very predictably "The Return" proved unacceptable in the magazine market; and so, for the second time, Conrad was forced to the bitter conclusion: "It is evident that my fate is to be descriptive and descriptive only. There are things I *must* leave alone" (*E G*, 94).

In immediate terms that meant going back to *The Rescuer*, whose title, in the summer of 1897, was finally changed to *The Rescue*. *The Rescue* was both exotic in background, and a tale of the sea—the second of the Conrad stereotypes which had been established by the renown of *The Nigger of the "Narcissus"*. Conrad had set himself what he thought was the modest task of merely making *The Rescue* "good enough for a magazine—readable in a word" (*E G*, 108). Very soon, however, he was alarmed to discover "how mysteriously independent of myself is my power of expression" (*B*, 27); and the increasing paralysis of his capacity to write, which dogged him from the summer of 1897 to the spring of the following year, made his material anxieties seem even more frightening.

Conrad's need for money also exacerbated the conflict between his own literary outlook and that of the reading public. The deepening chasm between the highbrow and the mass audience subjected most of the great twentieth-century novelists to similar pressures; but none experienced them quite as nakedly and directly as Conrad. Some had private means, like André Gide, E. M. Forster and Virginia Woolf; others found patrons, like James Joyce; a few, like D. H. Lawrence, were willing to accept a much lower standard of living; and none started their writing careers so late. When Garnett had spoken of the "necessity for a writer to follow his own path and disregard the public's taste," Conrad had retorted: "But I *won't* live in an attic! . . . I'm past that, you understand? I *won't* live in an attic!" (*E G*, xiii). Conrad economised by residing in the country, but he lived in reasonable comfort, and was sometimes extravagant. At the same time his fierce independence and ferocious contempt for commercial activities made every concession to the tastes of the public stick in his throat: one major difficulty with *The Rescue* was probably the inner resistance to expending so much of his being on what he regarded as "an infamous pot-boiler" (*E G*, 133).

Another reason for Conrad's inability to make any progress with *The Rescue* has been given by Thomas Moser, who points out that the problem became most acute at the point where the plot called for his hero, Tom Lingard, to fall in love with the married society lady, Edith Travers. Conrad put the problem off for a time by changing his plan and substituting a long retrospect about the Malay side of his story. Later, when Conrad put *The Rescue* aside again, early in 1899, it was also at a point where the crisis in the relationship between the lovers could no longer be postponed (*M*, 64–65). Nor could the novel be given a wholly different direction, for, in his quest for a larger audience, Conrad was very much aware that what was then called love was not less saleable in the literary marketplace than what is now called sex.

There were other reasons for Conrad's difficulties with *The Rescue*, including the problem of making Lingard's life and character consistent with what had already been written in *Almayer's Folly* and *An Outcast of the Islands;* and all this was on top of other pressures which would in themselves have sufficed to make the years 1897 and 1898 psychologically and financially desperate. One of his more personal anxieties, as he wrote Garnett, was that on 3 December 1897, Conrad had gone "over the rise of forty to travel downwards—and a little more lonely than before" (*E G*, 109). The mid-life crisis was particularly acute for Conrad for many other reasons. The death of the surviving relative to whom he felt closest, Charles Zagórski, had made a further break in his ties with Poland. Conrad now had no capital left, and no Bobrowski to appeal to; and at the same time he had assumed a serious new responsibility, for, on 17 January 1898, a son had been born—Alfred Borys Konrad Korzeniowski. Meanwhile, Conrad's attacks of gout and nervous exhaustion were taking a more serious turn; in February 1898 he told Graham that he had been "beastly seedy—nerve trouble—a taste of hell" (*C G*, 77); in March he wrote to Cora Crane cancelling a meeting—"it is nervous trouble and the doctor advises me to keep very quiet";[3] and in April he excused a two-month silence to Charles Zagórski's widow, Aniela, by pleading

3. *Stephen Crane: Letters*, ed. R. W. Stallman and Lillian Gilkes (New York, 1960), p. 176.

"the bad state of my health," and added: "We live with difficulty, from day to day . . . The work is not easy and every day seems more difficult to me" (*N*, 225).

Conrad's most despairing letters were to Garnett. He wrote on 29 March 1898:

> I sit down religiously every morning, I sit down for eight hours every day—and the sitting down is all. In the course of that working day of 8 hours I write 3 sentences which I erase before leaving the table in despair . . . it takes all my resolution and power of self-control to refrain from butting my head against the wall. I want to howl and foam at the mouth but I daren't do it for fear of waking that baby and alarming my wife (*E G*, 126–27).

In August, Conrad was still forcing himself to write: "Pages accumulate and the story stands still," he told Garnett, and added "I feel suicidal" (*E G*, 133). Even when his condition improved, the fear of collapse remained: as he wrote to Garnett later that August: "Looking back, I see how ill, mentally, I have been these last four months. The fear of this horror coming back to me makes me shiver. As it is it has destroyed already the little belief in myself I used to have" (*E G*, 134–35).

As the year 1898 drew on, the situation was made more desperate by the fact that Conrad had mortgaged his future output to pay current debts. He had sold the serial rights of *The Rescue* to the publisher Samuel McClure of New York for £250, of which £100 was an advance. Then, in August, the editor of the *Illustrated London News*, which had bought the English rights, announced that he intended to start running a serial, at a month's notice, that October. On this Conrad wrote defeatedly to Cunninghame Graham, "Half the book is not written and I have only to 1st November to finish it!" (*C G*, 102). But though Conrad could force himself to cover pages with words, that was all; in October, he wrote to Garnett, "I've destroyed all I did write last month" (*E G*, 141). It was the writer's version of the punishment of Sisyphus; and in the whole of 1898, the only new fiction Conrad completed was one short story, "Youth."

Like *The Nigger of the "Narcissus"*, "Youth" and Conrad's next two works, *Heart of Darkness* and *Lord Jim*, were all intended as short stories. They offered Conrad an escape from his unavailing labours on *The Rescue;* and, apart from brevity and the likelihood of a rapid financial return, they had three other great advantages: first, that women characters were of minor importance; second, that they used Marlow as narrator; and third, that they were written for *Blackwood's*, or *Maga,* as *Blackwood's Edinburgh Magazine* was variously called.

This connection had begun in May 1897, when *Blackwood's* accepted "Karain"; and it is ironically typical of his circumstances that Conrad's first act in his association with the prestigious Edinburgh publisher was to insist, feeling "very vile" (*L L*, I, 206), that he be given a higher price for "Karain." Conrad stipulated the sum of £40, which was eventually accepted; from then on Conrad and William Blackwood, the sixty-one-year-old head of the firm, got on very well. Blackwood's first letter to Conrad assured him that he was "very pleased to hear that you liked to live for a bit with your work before passing it finally for Press"; and Blackwood later added that "Maga ... does not grudge expense in revision of proofs when that is conscientiously done" (*B*, 4–5;7). Throughout their correspondence, friendliness, admiration, gratitude, flattery and old-world courtesy rub shoulders with fuss about proofreading and publication-schedules. On Conrad's side there are also fulsome praises of current articles in *Blackwood's,* artful evasions about his over-extended writing plans, and more or less direct appeals for money.

William Blackwood—the fifth of the line since the magazine's beginning in 1817—continued the firm's established policy of cultivating and encouraging its chosen set of authors. For instance, having heard from Meldrum that another story was "on the stocks," he sent an unsolicited advance of £5, and Conrad proceeded to wax effusive about Blackwood's "manner" of handling this, which "superficially viewed appears a business transaction" (*B*, 23). For a man as sensitive as Conrad it was "an unspeakable relief" to be dealing with a publisher whose approach was not entirely commercial, and to be writing, as he put it, "for *Maga* instead of for 'the market' " (*B*, 140). The rate of payment was as high as all but the most popular magazines, where Conrad had fastidious—though they could not be insuperable— reservations about appearing; and his new audience was very congenial.

Blackwood's Magazine had published many of the greatest Victorian novelists. Always rather traditional in its literary tastes, it had now become very conservative and masculine in tone; as Conrad later commented: "One was in decent company there and had a good sort of public. There isn't a single club and messroom and man-of-war in the British Seas and Dominions which hasn't its copy of Maga."[4] The joint influence of this imagined audience and of William Blackwood's personal style no doubt accounts for the bluff heartiness which occasionally injects a jarring note into Marlow's storytelling; there is no

4. Letter to James Pinker, November 1911, quoted in *L G*, 22.

real parallel to it in Conrad's previous fiction. But the immediate
literary benefits for Conrad in becoming a *Blackwood's* author were
immense; whereas writing *The Rescue* had become a hated constraint,
imposed by necessity for an audience he despised, Conrad could now
feel, as he sat down to write for *Blackwood's*, that there were people out
there beyond the four walls of his room whom he could imagine
himself speaking to. The advent of this fixed, dependable, and familiar element into Conrad's creative life probably encouraged him to
write more freely than ever before, using the conversational manner
that he had been accustomed to in his former days at sea, and dealing
with matters that were directly connected with his personal sense of
life.

Blackwood had accepted Conrad's higher terms for "Karain" on the
understanding that he would have first refusal on any future short
story. Conrad did not submit "The Return" to *Blackwood's*, however,
probably because he thought it would be rejected as unsuitable; but he
had no doubts about "Youth." It was accepted; and on 3 June 1898
Conrad sent the last part of the story, together with the news that he
would be sending *"Jim"* in a few days (*B*, 21). Conrad had at last found
a way out of his endless struggles with *The Rescue*; and there was much
more at stake than the alleviation of his immediate economic anxieties: not only the restoration of his self-confidence as a writer, but
with it the beginning of his greatest creative phase, and the one by
which Conrad would always be primarily remembered.

In a letter to Garnett of 4 June 1898, Conrad mentions plans for
three more tales, which would make up the volume of short stories he
had promised *Blackwood's* (*E G*, 130–31). None of them seems to have
been *Heart of Darkness*, but one projected five thousand word story
entitled "Dynamite," was probably the basis of the last of Conrad's
Marlow tales, the long novel *Chance,* which was only to be published
fifteen years later.

There was another personal stimulus for this sudden renewal of
Conrad's creative power. *Blackwood's* London representative, David
Meldrum, was an exceptionally perceptive, able and generous man,
and somewhat like Garnett in his enthusiasm for promising writers;
and he must have given Conrad the reassurance that he particularly
needed in 1898, by conveying to him the faith in Conrad's genius
which animates his letters to William Blackwood. Meldrum held the
volume of short stories called *Youth—A Narrative; and Two Other Stories*
(1902), which also contained *Heart of Darkness,* to be "the most notable
book we [Blackwood's] have published since George Eliot"; and
he was immediately convinced that *Heart of Darkness* was "a very wonderful piece of writing. . . . And such a 'Show up' for the French!"
(B, 172; 43).

"Youth" is a relatively slight story about Conrad's early voyage as second mate on the *Palestine* in 1881–2. An old and leaky barque (renamed the *Judea*) is rammed by a steamship in Newcastle harbour, and further damaged by gales in the English channel. She puts in for repairs, which prove endless, at Falmouth. Then, soon after finally setting out for Bangkok, the cargo of coal catches fire. After a long struggle to control the fire, there is an explosion off Sumatra and the crew has to abandon ship and take to the boats.

The thematic perspective of the story offers a neat ironic counterpoint to its main events. The middle-aged Marlow relates his memories of his first voyage as a second mate at the age of only twenty. For the young Marlow, the *Judea* is not "an old rattle-trap," but "the test, the trial of life" (12); his youthful enthusiasm makes him much too self-preoccupied to feel the tribulations of the ship very deeply; everything is an adventure, and when they at last have to take to the boats, he is delighted because he has a command at last, even though it is only that of a small lifeboat. He navigates to a little tropical port, and next morning wakes up to his first view of the fabled East.

Recalling this, the older Marlow, no doubt echoing Conrad's own memory of a more hopeful initiation than his own fortieth year had brought him, exclaims: "Only a moment; a moment of strength, of romance, of glamour—of youth!" (42). The primary narrator, who reports Marlow's reminiscences, echoes his theme with almost equal banality in the conclusion, commenting that men are always "looking anxiously for something out of life, that while it is expected is already gone—has passed unseen, in a sigh, in a flash—together with the youth, with the strength, with the romance of illusions."

Apart from a few such moments of trite rhetoric, "Youth" is a distinct success. It has clarity, humour, and ease; the supporting cast is convincing; and although the character of Marlow is not presented with any particular moral or psychological depth, he is an effective voice for two very typical Conradian subjects—gallant defeat and disillusioned romanticism. Both of these are present in Conrad's most famous anthology piece, which describes the sinking of the *Judea*; the death of a ship has an immediate symbolic appeal, which is here made more explicit by the fact that the ship's motto is "Do or Die." The passage concludes:

> Then the oars were got out, and the boats forming in a line moved round her remains as if in procession—the long-boat leading. As we pulled across her stern a slim dart of fire shot out viciously at us, and suddenly she went down, head first, in a great hiss of steam. The unconsumed stern was the last to sink; but the paint had gone, had cracked, had peeled off, and there were no letters, there was no word, no stubborn

device that was like her soul, to flash at the rising sun her
creed and her name (35).

As in many of the descriptive passages of *The Nigger of the "Narcissus"*, Conrad relies a good deal on personification, and a strong repetitive parallelism. The striking repetition of "had" in the three verbs
that follow "paint"—"had gone, had cracked, had peeled off"—is
taken further in the emphatic triple series of negative complements—"no letters," "no word," and "no stubborn device"—until we
are forced to see the sinking in its larger meaning, and mourn the
passing of the heroic challenge to the power of nature which the *Judea*
had once flashed at every sunrise.

"Youth" derives much of its charm and its great popularity from
the relative simplicity of its story, characters, and theme; and there
are too few examples in literature of a simple thing beautifully done
to make us value it only for the way it leads into the later Marlow
stories. Yet lead it does, though not directly. After finishing "Youth,"
Conrad spent the summer and autumn of 1898 mainly on further
struggles with *The Rescue*; but he was also working more or less surreptitiously at some new stories: an early version of *Lord Jim*, and at
least one other. He had probably envisaged this new story many
months earlier (*E G*, xviii), but the first definite mention comes on 18
December, when he wrote to Garnett: "Now I am at a short story for
Blackwood which I must get out for the sake of the shekels" (*E G*,
142). Three days later Conrad told Meldrum "I am writing something
for *Maga* a tale (short) in the manner of *Youth*, to be ready in a few
days" (*B*, 35). By a lucky chance, on 30 December William Blackwood
sent Conrad his "best wishes for a happy new year," and said that "I
should be specially pleased if you had anything on the stocks, or
nearly ready, to send me for Maga's Thousandth number."

It was coming out in February, and this gave Conrad very little
time, but he agreed, and the writing went quickly. On 2 January 1899
Conrad told Meldrum that the story would have been finished the day
before "had it not been our boy fell ill," that this delay by no means
lessened his need for another advance, and—as if to assure Meldrum
that *Blackwood's* would not lose money on *Heart of Darkness*—that it
had "a mere shadow of love interest just in the last pages" (*B*, 37; 38).
Four days later Conrad was acknowledging £40 "on account of short
stories," and promising to send off 12,000 words the next day. But the
story, Conrad explained, had "grown upon me a bit," and would now
be too long for one number (*B*, 40). On 9 January he sent another
sixty-eight pages to Meldrum, who at once assured Conrad that he
had received enough of *Heart of Darkness* for the first instalment in
February. On 6 February Conrad sent a telegram: the story had
"grown on him" again, and he would like it to run in three instalments

if possible. The complete story was sent off on 7 February, Blackwood having agreed it should appear in three parts. On the 19th, Blackwood sent his congratulations and sixty pounds; within a week Conrad had revised the proofs, "compressing the end not a little," and had received from William Blackwood an unsolicited advance of another hundred pounds to "relieve you of any further anxiety" (*B*, 51; 52).

So after nearly two unproductive years, in little more than two months, and in the midst of several further anxieties, Conrad had managed to write, revise, proofread, be more than paid for, and even see beginning in print what was to prove one of the earliest and greatest works in the tradition of modern literature.

ii. Sources: The Congo and Kurtz

Nearly ten years before, Conrad had resigned his command of the *Otago*, and returned from Australia to London. There, while making arrangements for his first visit to Poland since he had left in 1874. he started to look for another job. When nothing offered at home he applied for a foreign command with the newly-formed *Société Anonyme* [i.e., limited liability company] *Belge pour le Commerce du Haut-Congo*. He was interviewed by its director, Albert Thys, in November 1889, and was apparently promised an appointment, but then nothing happened for some time. Conrad therefore asked Marguerite Poradowska—as Marlow asks his "aunt" in *Heart of Darkness*—to intervene on his behalf with some of her influential friends. While he was paying a two-month visit to Bobrowski in the Ukraine, Conrad heard that matters were at last progressing; and on his return to Brussels at the end of April he was appointed to a command which had become vacant owing to the sudden death of one of the Company's captains, Freiesleben.

After hectic last minute preparations Conrad sailed from Bordeaux on 10 May 1890, and arrived at Boma, the capital of the Congo Free State, on 12 June. From Boma, he took another smaller steamer some forty miles up the lower Congo to Matadi. After a two-week stay, Conrad left on foot for Kinshasa, near Stanley Pool. He was accompanied by a Belgian official called Harou, and thirty-one black native porters. Conrad had started keeping a diary, and it shows that the exhausting journey of some 230 miles was made very difficult and depressing because Harou was ill, and the caravan had to stay seventeen days at a depot, Manyanga.[1] On 2 August Conrad arrived at

---

1. Conrad's Congo diary is reprinted in *Last Essays;* the second notebook, entitled "Up-river book," consisting of sailing directions from Kinshasa to Bangala, is available, together with the first, in *Congo Diary and Other Uncollected Pieces* by Joseph Conrad, ed.

Kinshasa, which was the main base for navigation on the upper
Congo, and corresponds to Marlow's Central Station. He found that
the steamer which he was supposed to command, the *Florida*, had
been damaged; unlike Marlow, however, Conrad did not spend three
months repairing his command, but instead left Kinshasa the next day
as supercargo on another steamer, the *Roi des Belges*. This was the
normal arrangement for new arrivals, and was intended to initiate
them in the navigation of the very difficult upper reaches of the
Congo. The *Roi des Belges* was going nearly a thousand miles upriver
on a routine voyage to various trading posts, delivering supplies and
picking up ivory; and at its final destination near Stanley Falls it also
had to collect an agent of the company called Klein, who was ill.

At the Stanley Falls station, which roughly corresponds to Marlow's
Inner Station and is now called Kisangani, the captain of the *Roi des
Belges* took sick, and during the voyage down Conrad was in command
for a few days, possibly as many as ten. During the whole journey
Camille Delcommune, the local manager and a deputy director of the
company, had been on board. He apparently took a strong dislike to
Conrad, which was more than reciprocated. Soon after they arrived
back at Kinshasa on 24 September, Conrad decided that Delcommune
would never give him the promised command; he therefore took
advantage of a violent attack of dysentery to break his three-year
employment contract on medical grounds. After retracing the gruel-
ing overland journey, during which he was desperately ill, Conrad
arrived at Matadi on 4 December; he continued to Boma, and took
ship for Europe shortly after. He had been in the Congo for only six
months.

Heart of Darkness is much less directly autobiographical than
"Youth," especially in its mode of presentation. The difference is
manifest in the treatment of proper names. In both stories Marlow
follows Conrad's actual itinerary quite closely; but whereas in "Youth"
nearly all the real place-names are used, in *Heart of Darkness* only a few
unimportant places are specified; as Marlow comments, their
names—Gran' Bassam, Little Popo—"belong to some sordid farce"
(61), and they serve only to prepare us for the grotesque world he is
entering. For most places Conrad uses general descriptive phrases:
Brussels becomes the sepulchral city, Matadi the Company Station,

---

Zdzisław Najder (Garden City, N.Y., 1978). We also know a good deal about Conrad's
Congo journey from various surviving letters and from Conrad's reminiscences in two
other works: *A Personal Record* (13–14), and "Geography and Some Explorers" (*L E*,
1–21). The biographical facts are most fully set out in Norman Sherry's *Conrad's Western
World (S W W)*.

and so on; even the Congo is never named, and remains "that river."
These are obvious examples of the principle which Conrad had
applied only in one key place in "Youth," where the port of Marlow's
final landing, Muntok, is not named because, as Conrad later explained to Curle: "explicitness . . . is fatal to the glamour of all artistic
work, robbing it of all suggestiveness, destroying all illusion" (R C,
142).

Conrad's procedure is much the same with the characters. In
"Youth," the names of the captain and first mate, Beard and Mahon,
are retained; but in *Heart of Darkness* most of the characters are given
type names—the director, the brickmaker, and so on. There are,
however, two curious exceptions: Freiesleben, the captain whom Conrad replaced, appears under the spelling Fresleven; more important,
by a paradoxical variation on Conrad's change of the *Palestine* into the
Judea, Klein, who is still so called in the manuscript, was eventually
given the German word for "short" instead of "little," and renamed
Kurtz—a much more sonorous and menacing sound.

Many of Conrad's changes in other matters were fairly obviously
dictated by the need for narrative economy and thematic focus. There
was no point, for instance, in making Marlow repeat Conrad's three
separate visits to Brussels to arrange the job; one was enough. Similarly, having portrayed Marlow's journey up-river, it would have been
anticlimactic, as well as repetitive, to give the return journey in any
detail. Even for the journey up, Conrad omitted a great deal, a process which was continued at the proof stage, most notably in the
cancelling of four pages of the manuscript which described Boma.[2]
The reader's imagination could hardly operate if it were stunned by a
lot of unfamiliar place-names and incidental information about them;
instead Conrad distils his experiences into the generalised picture of
three main stations and journeys. These pictures are themselves
highly selective; they emphasise the prevailingly sombre mood of the
story, and omit the various pleasant incidents which Conrad mentions
in his notebook, not to mention the hope he expressed on one occasion of having "a shot or two at buffalo or elephant" (P, 18).

Conrad clearly subordinated personal experience to thematic focus
in his treatment of two of his own most vivid memories of the Congo.
Some time before Conrad wrote *Heart of Darkness,* he recounted "a
very full synopsis" to Garnett; but when the printed version came out,
Garnett was surprised to discover that "about a third of the most

2. Variants in the manuscript (which is almost complete) are available in the edition
of *Heart of Darkness* by Robert Kimbrough (Norton Critical Edition, New York, 1971;
hereafter cited as *H D N*). See also Jonah Raskin, "*Heart of Darkness:* The Manuscript
Revisions," *Review of English Studies,* n.s. 18 (1967): 30–39.

striking incidents had been replaced by others" (*E G,* xviii). Garnett
particularly regretted the omission of a scene which "described the
hero lying sick to death in a native hut, tended by an old negress who
brought him water from day to day. . . . 'She saved my life,' Conrad
said; 'The white men never came near me.' "[3] To describe this episode
would have given a prominence to Marlow's illness which, like an
extended account of his return journey, would inevitably have
weakened the emphasis on Kurtz's illness and death, and diverted to
Marlow some of the suffering and pathos which had to be reserved
for the African victims of the colonisers.

Conrad's treatment of another Congo memory was more complicated. In 1914, when he was asked what had most deeply impressed
him among all the things he had seen in his life, he replied, "A certain
woman, a Negress. That was in Africa. Hung with bracelets and
necklaces, she was walking in front of a railroad station."[4] There is no
direct representation of this in *Heart of Darkness;* and there was no
railway station in the Congo Free State at this time; but part of this
memory probably went into the portrayal of Kurtz's abandoned native mistress with "brass wire gauntlets to the elbow" and "innumerable necklaces" (135). In this brief scene she becomes the most affirmative image in the narrative, the embodiment of the confident natural
energy of the African wilderness.

Heart of Darkness is no more a direct representation of conditions in
the Congo in 1890 than it is of Conrad's actual experiences there; but
it is an expression of the essence of the social and historical reality of
the Congo Free State as his imagination recreated it.

One large area of omission concerns the difference between the
conditions in the particular areas of the Congo which Marlow describes and those which Conrad actually saw. Here the historical record, which is surprisingly detailed,[5] and the remarkable researches of

3. The similarity of this incident to others recounted by earlier travelers, notably
Mungo Park, has led Eloise Hay to question whether it actually happened to Conrad
(*E K H,* 121).

4. Edmund A. Bojarski, "Joseph Conrad's Sentimental Journey: A Fiftieth An-
niversary Review," *Texas Quarterly* 7 (1964): 164. Arthur Symons reports another version, in which Conrad told him: "The superb native woman I saw in Singapore" (*Conrad
Memorial Library,* pp. 170-71).

5. One has the impression that at this period very few people connected with the
Congo, from Stanley and Thys down to the ordinary missionaries, soldiers, explorers,
ship's captains, journalists, and commercial agents, did not publish their reminiscences,
keep diaries, or even write novels. There were also many official sources, in which
Conrad's arrivals and departures, for instance, were recorded. These various sources
have been thoroughly studied by Hunt Hawkins in his "Joseph Conrad and Mark
Twain on the Congo Free State," an unpublished dissertation (Stanford, 1976), to
which I am much indebted.

Norman Sherry, have made it clear that Marlow much underrates the actual extent of colonial development in the Congo in 1890, though not its appalling human results.

In 1876 Leopold II of Belgium who, in response to the smallness of his kingdom and the spirit of the age, had been looking round for an empire for some time, promoted the formation of the "International Association for the Suppression of Slavery and the Opening Up of Central Africa." At its founding international conference in Brussels, he announced: "To open to civilization the only area of our globe to which it has not yet penetrated, to pierce the gloom which hangs over entire races, constitutes, if I may dare to put it in this way, a Crusade worthy of this century of progress."[6] Leopold had in mind a crusade in the only large area of Africa which remained unclaimed by the chief colonial powers; and, mainly through the energy of the famous journalist-explorer Henry Morton Stanley, a chain of stations was set up along the Congo river, whose upper reaches were only just being explored. The association's concern with free trade, human better-ment, and the abolition of slavery was merely propaganda; once Leopold had secured a toehold he used shameless economic and polit-ical manipulation to exploit the rivalries of the great powers then engaged in carving up Africa, and to win international recognition of his position as sovereign of the Independent State of the Congo. This was ratified by the Berlin Conference of 1885, and Leopold soon became the sole effective owner and ruler of an empire of nearly a million square miles.

Conrad had gone out to the Congo at the very time when Leopold and his backers, largely spurred by financial difficulties resulting from the high initial costs of colonial development, were forcing the pace of exploitation with increasing ruthlessness.[7] To raise revenue and achieve a complete monopoly of trade, customs duties and various other taxes were imposed on all the independent trading concerns on the Congo. This direct threat to international business interests led to increasing protests, and in 1897 the London *Times* and the House of Commons were much occupied by Leopold's misdeeds.

Heart of Darkness was, among other things, an early expression of what was to become a worldwide revulsion from the horrors of Leopold's exploitation of the Congo; as Conrad told Blackwood in his first letter about the story, "the subject is of our time distinctly." He went on, however, to say that it was "not topically treated" (*B*, 37); and

6. Neal Ascherson, *The King Incorporated: Leopold II in the Age of Trusts* (London, 1963), p. 94.

7. Ascherson, *King Incorporated*, pp. 147–49, 174–75, 184, 187, 195–98.

the closest *Heart of Darkness* gets to immediately topical matters is its
treatment of the conflict of attitudes among Belgian colonial interests.
Unlike Conrad, Marlow remains several months at the Central Station; he imputes this to the general manager's deliberate design of
delaying the rescue of Kurtz by wrecking Marlow's steamer just before his arrival—"the affair was too stupid . . . to be altogether natural" (72). The manager wants to destroy Kurtz because he belongs to
"the new gang—the gang of virtue" (79) in the great Trading Company. Most directly Kurtz represents the same faction as Albert Thys,
Marlow's "pale plumpness," a very influential leader of the Belgian
private enterprises in the Congo. These private trading concerns were
also threatened by Leopold's monopoly, and they therefore found
allying themselves with genuine Belgian reformers, and posing as a
"party of virtue," a useful defensive tactic.[8]

Some of the main differences between *Heart of Darkness* and Conrad's actual experience on the Congo serve both political and literary
purposes. For instance, to emphasise the inefficiency of Belgian colonisation and increase the isolation of Marlow and Kurtz, the story
gives no idea of how far colonisation had proceeded. Thus, at what
Marlow calls the Company Station, Matadi, there were actually some
170 Europeans present, and much commercial activity in which German, Dutch, French, and English concerns were involved; and contrary to the impression given by Marlow, the railway to Kinshasa was
in fact being built. Later, Marlow's journey up-river is made even
more lonely than it would have been; much of the area traversed was
populated, and on its way up the *Roi des Belges* must have passed not
only many trading and military settlements, but at least three out of
the twenty-three ships then plying on the upper river.[9] The contrasts
between reality and fiction become most extreme in the treatment of
the Inner Station. During Conrad's stay at Stanley Falls, Georges Antoine Klein was only one of the many European traders present. Instead of consisting only of a single building, the Inner Station was in
fact quite a large settlement, which was beginning to acquire many of
the trappings of civilisation; by 1893, at least, they included a hospital,
a police barracks, and a jail (*S W W*, 65).

Making Marlow go to a much more isolated kind of place than
Stanley Falls actually was at the time served at least three important
narrative purposes.

First, Marlow could be given a more active and exciting role as

8. Ascherson, *King Incorporated*, pp. 197–98, 244–60; and especially Ruth Slade,
King Leopold's Congo (London, 1962), pp. 193–203.
9. *S W W*, 30, 51; Hawkins, "Conrad and Twain on the Congo," p. 157.

Kurtz's resourceful rescuer. For instance, the *Roi des Belges* was almost
certainly not attacked; if it had been, the event would undoubtedly
have been reported in the weekly bulletin of Congo news called
Mouvement Géographique. But in *Heart of Darkness,* the attack serves to
turn Marlow into something of a boy's adventure-story hero when he
strikes terror into Kurtz's followers by blowing the steam-whistle. This
device had actually been used with success by Stanley and others, but
that had been on unexplored tributaries, and by 1890 the novelty
would certainly have lost its power for anyone on the Congo near
Stanley Falls (*S W W,* 54–55).

Second, for thematic emphasis Marlow must be made to stand out
from the corrupt inhumanity of all the white colonisers. This process
begins down river, where Marlow makes no mention of meeting anyone he likes, as Conrad did Casement, or of various fellow Europeans
who treated him well. The moral polarity between Marlow and the
colonisers must be unmediated, and so must the very different opposition between Kurtz and Marlow. There is, for instance, no mention
of the complicating fact that the dominant conflict in the area was
actually between the Belgian authorities and the long-established
Congolese Arabs, who raided the local villages for slaves as well as
ivory, and therefore, like Kurtz, posed a threat which the official
commercial interests were determined to remove.

The third, and most important reason, for the difference between
Stanley Falls as Conrad saw it and the Inner Station as Marlow presents it is that the threatening vastness and silence of the jungle
deepens the isolation of Kurtz, and is therefore an essential condition
of Kurtz's own literal and symbolic roles.

In his "Author's Note" Conrad wrote that, compared to "Youth"
Heart of Darkness is "experience, too; but it is experience pushed a little
(and only very little) beyond the actual facts of the case for the perfectly legitimate, I believe, purpose of bringing it home to the minds
and bosoms of the readers" (vii).

With Kurtz, Conrad certainly went much more than a little beyond
"the actual facts of the case" as far as biographical evidence goes.
Conrad said very little about his origins beyond affirming, when a
journalist asked him in 1923 if Kurtz was a real person, "I saw him
die."[10] The man Conrad "saw die" must have been Klein, who was
taken aboard the *Roi des Belges* at Stanley Falls, and who died on board
of dysentery and was buried, not "in a muddy hole" as Marlow says

10. Dale B. J. Randall, "Conrad Interviews, No. 2: James Walter Smith," *C* 2 (1969):
88.

(150), but in a proper grave in the cemetery at the Baptist mission at Tchumbiri.[11] Klein, however, had only been a few months at Stanley Falls, and was a subordinate agent of the company of no particular interest or importance.

One can surmise that merely "seeing him die" gave Conrad an unbearably painful memory. From the departure on September 6th until Klein's death 15 days later, there would, in the very cramped quarters of the *Roi des Belges,* have been no escape from the sounds, the smells and the sight of a man in the last stages of dysentery—a disease peculiarly repulsive in its physical manifestations, and usually marked by an unimaginable degree of emaciation; this may have supplied Marlow's description of Kurtz: "the cage of his ribs all astir, the bones of his arm waving. . . . an animated image of death carved out of old ivory" (134).

Still, Klein was no Kurtz. There is the illness and death; there is the suggestion of Kurtz's international origins in the fact that, for all his German name, Klein was French, and worked for a Belgian company; but there is little else. As a result there have been many attempts to find some more convincing model for Kurtz.

The most detailed argument is that of Norman Sherry, who has shown that some features of Kurtz's character and career were similar to those of one Arthur Eugene Constant Hodister (*S W W,* 95–118). At the time of Conrad's stay in the Congo, Hodister was an important official; in addition, he was an intrepid explorer of the tributaries of the Upper Congo, a very successful collector of ivory, and a man of great prestige, both among the Arab traders and the African indigenes. Hodister was also a genuine reformer and an eloquent speaker against the horrors of slave-raiding. In 1891 he became director of another Thys enterprise, the *Syndicat Commercial du Katanga,* a new company which was to trade with the Congolese Arabs in largely unexplored areas; the hope was that the spread of trade and law would weaken the dependence of the Arabs on the slave trade, and thus hasten its end. Hodister led out a large expedition for the purpose, but it was savagely destroyed in a large-scale Arab revolt. The *Times* reported of Hodister and his comrades that "their heads were stuck on poles and their bodies eaten."

There are at least two kinds of difficulty in seeing Hodister as the person on whom Kurtz was based: the many important differences between them; and the many partial similarities between Kurtz and numerous other people who were in the Congo during the period. Three of these, Emin Pasha, Major Barttelot, and Charles Henry

11. *S W W,* 77–78. Sherry even provides the death certificate and two photographs of the grave.

Stokes, have one important element in common with Hodister: they met their deaths as a result of the eventually unsuccessful Arab revolt against the extension of Belgian, and more broadly, of European, power in the vast upper reaches of the Congo and its tributaries.[12]

Emin Pasha (1840–1892; born Eduard Schnitzer) had been appointed governor of a province of the Sudan by General Gordon; after Gordon's defeat, Emin was isolated, and in 1887, Stanley, backed by Belgian and British colonial interests, led his lavish and much-publicised expedition to relieve him. Like Kurtz, however, Emin did not want to be rescued, as Albert Guerard has pointed out (*G*, 34), and Stanley was accused of bringing him back by force, as Marlow does Kurtz. Later, while leading a German expedition in central Africa, Emin was obliged to retreat towards the Congo, and, like Hodister, was killed by Arab leaders and their local allies not very far from Stanley Falls in October 1892.

Major Edmund Musgrave Barttelot, the commander of Stanley's rearguard for the Emin Pasha relief expedition, was a victim of the same conflict. Things went wrong at his camp at Yambuya on the Aruwimi, north of Stanley Falls; a relief convoy was unduly delayed; and Barttelot was shot by a Manyema tribesman. There was much public controversy about his death, and some, including Stanley, alleged that under the pressure Barttelot had gone mad, and brought his fate on himself by savage beatings, rapes and murders (*J A*, 275–81).

Charles Henry Stokes (1852–1895), a British missionary who became a very successful ivory trader, avoided paying Leopold's taxes by using the German ports in East Africa as his export outlet. This made him very unpopular with the Belgian authorities, and early in 1895 Stokes was arrested and summarily executed by a Belgian officer, Lothaire, on the no doubt well-founded charge of supplying arms to Kibonge, a leader of the Arab revolt.[13]

Much more could be said about the similarities and differences between these four men and Kurtz. Emin Pasha "went native" in the sense that he passed as a Muslim; and both Hodister and Stokes "went native" in the sense that they had native mistresses. Of the four, only Barttelot, a Sandhurst man, was apparently innocent of any sympathy for the indigenes; he was certainly brutal, and the closest to Kurtz in having been accused, though probably wrongly, of an ever-deepening relapse into murderous and sadistic savagery.

---

12. See Slade, *Leopold's Congo*, pp. 89–114.
13. S. J. S. Cookey, *Britain and the Congo Question, 1885–1913* (London, 1968), pp. 31–34; George B. Alexander, "The Real Mr. Kurtz," an unpublished manuscript, to which I am much indebted.

Given the extensive publicity about the deaths of all these men in the years after his own voyage to the Congo, it is likely that Conrad read something about all four;[14] it is possible that some or even all of them had some residual effect upon his portrayal of Kurtz. Still, none of them enacted the essential trajectory of Kurtz's life, and we must surely see Klein as Conrad's only definite, though very inadequate, biographical source. But the essence of Kurtz's fate was of a very different kind; and insofar as its origins were African at all, it was more likely to be a distillation, not of these four careers, but of two other kinds of human destiny which the Congo offered in much greater abundance and variety.

First, and most obviously, the final phase of Kurtz's life could be placed in a much commoner perspective—that of white men "going native." This myth had arisen as soon as the white man had started going out to make his fortune in the far places of the earth. In Africa the myth had taken a particular form—that of "going fantee." The phrase, based on the name of a Gold Coast tribe, came into English in 1886, meaning "to join the natives of a district and conform to their habits" (O E D); and there was a French equivalent, that of being stricken by la Soudaneté. The process was already a commonplace in popular stories; and it provided the perspective in which at least two initiated readers saw the character of Kurtz. Hugh Clifford, a man of very wide colonial experience in Asia and Africa, saw Kurtz as the most convincing picture of the "why" of the process he called "denationalisation," which in itself had already "been treated often enough in fiction."[15] This was also the diagnosis of the only person who both knew the Congo well and put on record his reaction to Heart of Darkness.

Captain Otto Lütken, a Danish sea captain who had commanded ships on the upper Congo for eight years, wrote an article and a subsequent letter on "Joseph Conrad in the Congo" in 1930. He testified to the truth of Conrad's descriptions (with the exception of Stanley Falls), but thought Conrad did not do justice "to the memory of certain brave men of my acquaintance, who, many of them, had at least a dream of working for the cause of Civilisation."[16] Lütken,

14. Roger Jones mentions a member of Barttelot's rearguard, James S. Jameson, who in one respect at least, is closer to Kurtz than the other candidates. During the outcry that followed the decimation of Stanley's rearguard, all kinds of rumours, many of them originating with Stanley, were spread; one of them even (falsely) alleged that Jameson indulged in cannibal orgies, and purchased a ten-year-old African girl so that he could pursue his artistic interests by sketching cannibals eating her (Roger Jones, The Rescue of Emin Pasha [London, 1972], pp. 351–56).
15. The Spectator, 29 November 1902, p. 828.
16. London Mercury 22 (1930): 350.

nevertheless, greatly admired Conrad, and particularly the characterisation of Kurtz: "It is in the picture Conrad draws of Kurtz, the 'tropenkollered' ['maddened by the tropics'] white man, that his authorship rises supreme. The man is lifelike and convincing—heavens, how I know him! I have met one or two 'Kurtzs' in my time in Africa, and I can see him now."

But there was a second and even more common kind of human destiny which illustrated the obvious discrepancy between the ideal of Western civilisation, and the degradation which it suffered in Africa; and in this context *Heart of Darkness* is unique in being the first to connect the process of "going fantee" with an even more general consequence of the colonial situation: the fact that the individual colonist's power, combined with the lack of any effective control, was an open invitation to every kind of cruelty and abuse.

None of the possible sources for Kurtz seems to have equalled his murderous exploits, but there were other whites in Africa who did. Hannah Arendt has suggested the parallel of Carl Peters, the German explorer of East Africa, who was eventually dismissed for mistreatment of natives in 1897.[17] In 1899 there occurred an even more spectacular parallel, the career of the French professional soldier, Captain Paul Voulet. He led an expedition from Senegal towards the Nile, leaving a broad trail of murdered and enslaved inhabitants, and of plundered and destroyed African towns; finally he briefly set up his own virtually independent kingdom near Lake Chad.[18]

But to create a character who revealed the brutal discrepancy between the colonising ideal and the reality, Conrad needed no other historical model than the two founders of the Congo Free State, Leopold and Stanley. Their civilising pretensions were flagrantly contradicted by what they did; and the brutal callousness with which Stanley plundered and destroyed everything that stood in his way led to some of the first public protests in England against what was happening in the Congo.[19]

It is essential to the very nature of what Conrad was doing in *Heart of Darkness* that there should be not one but innumerable sources for Kurtz. Some of these have nothing to do with Africa or with Conrad's experiences there; but among those sources that do, Stanley is probably of central importance, though not so much as a basis for the character of Kurtz as for the moral atmosphere in which he was created.

17. *The Origins of Totalitarianism* (New York, 1958), p. 189.
18. See Jacques-Francis Rolland, *Le Grand Capitaine* (Paris, 1976).
19. Cookey, *Britain and the Congo Question*, p. 35.

In his essay "Geography and Some Explorers" (1924), Conrad writes of his early admiration for such "militant geographers" as James Cook, Sir John Franklin, Mungo Park, and David Livingstone. As a boy he had paid his "first homage" to the explorers of the Great Lakes, Burton and Speke, by entering the "outline of Tanganyika on my beloved old atlas"; it dated from 1852, and "the heart of its Africa was big and white" (*L E,* 14). Conrad had also put his "finger on a spot in the very middle of the then white heart of Africa," and "declared that some day I would go there" (16). Some eighteen years later he moored close to Stanley Falls. It was because Stanley had discovered them, and then gone down the Congo to the sea, that the heart of Africa was no longer white on the map. So it is not surprising that when Conrad realized "with awe, 'This is the very spot of my boyish boast,' " his elation was short-lived. For, Conrad recounts, "a great melancholy descended on me," as he reflected that the "idealized realities of a boy's daydreams" had been befouled by the actualities of the Congo Free State. There now stood at his side, "no great haunting memory," such as the explorers of the past would have left, but the corruption of that ideal by Stanley; the only memory Conrad could think of was "the unholy recollection of a prosaic newspaper 'stunt' and the distasteful knowledge of the vilest scramble for loot that ever disfigured the history of human conscience and geographical exploration."

Conrad's confrontation of this stark contradiction between the ideal and the real in the political, historical, and moral domains was no doubt the main spiritual burden of his voyage up the Congo; and the depth of his disillusionment must have been increased by the physical and mental crises which he endured there. In the last stages of the breakdown of his own health in the Congo, Conrad had faced alone the fact of his own mortality. He later considered the physical and moral assault of his African experience the turning point of his life: before then, he told Garnett, he had " 'not a thought in his head . . . I was a perfect animal' " (*E G,* xii).

When, nine years later, Conrad came to write *Heart of Darkness,* he was calling upon memories that were much more recent than those which had given rise to Almayer or James Wait, and of incomparably greater and more direct importance for his own personal life. Those memories, in turn, were evoked and expressed at the end of a year so depressing and unsettled that he had written to Garnett: "I am afraid there's something wrong with my thinking apparatus. I am utterly out of touch with my work—and I can't get in touch. All is darkness" (*E G,* 134).

iii. Ideological Perspectives:
Kurtz and the Fate of Victorian Progress

There are many reasons why the literary critic tends to be suspicious of the history-of-ideas approach: one easy way of not attending to *King Lear* is to underline a few passages which seem to confirm that the Great Chain of Being is really there; and in general the search for such portable intellectual contents as can conveniently be pried loose from a literary work deflects attention from what it can most genuinely yield, and at best gives in return a few abstract ideas whose nature and interrelationships are much more exactly stated in formal philosophy. In any case the greatest authors are rarely representative of the ideology of their period; they tend rather to expose its internal contradictions or the very partial nature of its capacity for dealing with the facts of experience. This seems to be true of Shakespeare; it seems to be even truer as we approach the modern world, where no single intellectual system has commanded anything like general acceptance.

One can, however, accept such arguments and yet remain suspicious of the way that modern literary criticism has turned the tables on philosophy's old objection to the cognitive validity of art. Now it is art which claims exclusive access to the higher forms of knowledge, and philosophy which obscures them: the ancient notion was that ideas were the proper inhabitants of man's mind; T. S. Eliot's resounding paradox that Henry James "had a mind so fine that no idea could violate it"[1] transformed them into dangerous ruffians threatening the artist with a fate worse than death. In this perspective, however, Eliot found Conrad a very special case: "Mr. Conrad," Eliot wrote in 1919, "has no ideas, but he has a point of view, a 'world'; it can hardly be defined, but it pervades his work and is unmistakable."[2]

The remark is characteristically oblique but it nudges us toward a fundamental discrimination. On the one hand Conrad disclaimed, and rightly, that he possessed anything approaching a conscious intellectual system. "I don't know what my philosophy [of life] is," Conrad wrote in 1905 to Garnett, and continued jocularly: "I wasn't even aware I had it.... Shall I die of it do you think?" (*E G*, 199). But if Conrad disclaims being a thinker, he strikes us as very thoughtful; and if we cannot call him a philosopher, the intimations of his fictional world steadily invite ethical and even metaphysical response.

1. "In Memory of Henry James," *The Egoist* 5 (1918): 2.
2. "Kipling Redivivus," *Athenaeum*, 9 May 1919; quoted from Leonard Unger, *The Man in the Name* (Minneapolis, 1956), p. 230.

During the composition of *Heart of Darkness* Conrad had a particular reason to be conscious of the problem of the role of ideas in literature. In January 1898 Arthur Symons, speaking of *The Nigger of the "Narcissus"* and Kipling's *Captains Courageous,* had complained: "Where is the idea of which such things as these should be but servants? . . . everything else is there, but that, these brilliant writers have forgotten to put in" (*J B*, 183). Symons's charge stung Conrad to the quick; he wrote three letters to friends asking if they thought the criticism just; and, in an interestingly indirect form of self-justification, he apparently even composed a defence of Kipling from Symon's attack—a defence, however, which has not survived.

Conrad's first description of *Heart of Darkness* makes it clear that he conceived it in an ideological context: "The *idea* in it," he wrote to William Blackwood, "is not as obvious as in *youth*—or at least not so obviously presented. . . .The criminality of inefficiency and pure selfishness when tackling the civilizing work in Africa is a justifiable idea" (*B*, 36–37). This letter was written very early, and refers only to the story's obvious anti-colonial theme; but there are many other ideas in *Heart of Darkness,* which is Conrad's nearest approach to an ideological summa.

That summa emerges from the conflict between Marlow, in whom Conrad the seaman presents his lingering wish to endorse the standard values of the Victorian ethic, and Kurtz, in whom Conrad the seer expresses his forebodings that the accelerating changes in the scientific, political, and spiritual view of the world during the last decades of the old century were preparing unsuspected terrors for the new.

Marlow's Victorian Ethic

Conrad had arrived in England during the last years of the ascendancy of the Victorian world order. That order, as we can now see more clearly, had essentially been a rearguard action against the destructive implications of the most characteristic new features of nineteenth-century civilisation: the growth of science, industrialism, utilitarianism, democracy, socialism, and individualism. But for a long time a host of optimistic rationalisations were used to conceal the fundamental challenges which the new intellectual and social forces posed to traditional values. Neither Conrad nor Marlow had any faith in the rationalisations, but they adhered to many of the values.

During the late fifties, John Stuart Mill, in his essay on "The Utility of Religion," found it to be characteristic of "an age of weak beliefs" that "such belief as men have" should be "much more determined by their wish to believe than by any mental appreciation of evidence."[3] Conrad's past had bequeathed him this same wish to believe in defiance of all the evidence; and this had led him to adopt a fairly conscious dualism of attitudes, a dualism in which, very roughly, ontology is opposed to ethics. Conrad expressed this opposition with paradoxical mockery in an 1895 letter to Garnett: "I suffer now from an acute attack of faithlessness in the sense that I do not seem to believe in anything, but I trust that by the time we meet I shall be more like a human being and consequently ready to believe any absurdity—and not only ready but eager" (*E G*, 11–12). In 1897 he gave the contradiction a more direct and positive form in his first letter to Cunninghame Graham: "It is impossible to know anything tho' it is possible to believe a thing or two" (*C G*, 45).

In *Heart of Darkness*, Marlow is driven to make a similarly obscure but crucial distinction between truth and belief. On the journey upriver, his glimpses of primitive tribal dances strike a responsive chord, and he accepts that "wild and passionate uproar" as a form of "truth stripped of its cloak of time" (96–97). It is, Marlow says, an "ugly" truth and one that modern civilised man must resist: but to resist, however, he must, paradoxically enough, "be as much of a man as these on the shore. He must meet that truth with his own true stuff—with his own inborn strength. Principles won't do. Acquisitions, clothes, pretty rags—rags that would fly off at the first good shake. No; you want a deliberate belief."

What is that deliberate belief? Marlow only tells us that he does not go "ashore for a howl and a dance" because he is committed to his job as captain: "There was," he says, "surface-truth enough in these things to save a wiser man." Marlow's ethic here is in accord with one of the most pervasive of the Victorian moral imperatives. "Except for 'God,' " Walter Houghton writes, "the most popular word in the Victorian vocabulary must have been 'work'."[4]

The most influential Victorian prophet of the faith in work was Thomas Carlyle, particularly in *Sartor Resartus* (1834), whose "clothes philosophy" may have supplied Marlow's metaphor of "pretty rags." The second book of *Sartor Resartus* presents a symbolic and discursive quest for truth, in which Carlyle's protagonist, Professor Teufelsdröckh, is saved from his spiritual torment and despair through a moral progression that has several stages. First, Teufelsdröckh pronounces the "Everlasting No" to the current views

---

3. *Nature, The Utility of Religion, and Theism,* 3rd ed. (London, 1885), p. 70.
4. *The Victorian Frame of Mind, 1830–1870* (New Haven, 1957), p. 242.

of life which present the universe as merely "one huge, dead, im-measurable Steam-engine, rolling on, in its dead indifference, to grind [him] limb from limb." Having rejected a purely mechanist position, he must learn that the "most truly fearful Unbelief" is the "unbelief in yourself"; and the individual can begin to believe in himself only when he has understood "the folly of that impossible Precept, *Know thyself*; till it be translated into this partially possible one, '*Know what thou canst work at.*' "[5]

Work can give the individual a stable psychological base; it can also give him a social ethic, a reaching out to the "Not-me" which may render him a useful member of the "Family of Man." This in turn will entail the "Renunciation" of the quest for purely selfish gratifications; and then Teufelsdröckh can at last pronounce "the EVERLASTING YEA." We are told that this means "Love God," which Conrad would not have regarded as a useful injunction; but in practice, Carlyle's everlasting yea amounts to little more than a personal commitment to two precepts from Goethe's *Wilhelm Meister's Apprenticeship:* "Doubt of any sort cannot be removed except by Action"; and *"Do the Duty which lies nearest thee."*[6]

Carlyle's preachments about work, duty, and renunciation are es-sentially an early, comprehensive, and, of course, very influential statement of a constellation of values which characterised Victorian life as a whole.[7] Here too these values were often placed in the context of a defence against temptation, hedonism, and loss of faith. Thus, work was a defence against the powers of evil; renunciation saved man from the self-absorbed despair which resulted from the vain pursuit of happiness; while duty was humanity's last stay against the demoralizing loss of Christian faith, as in George Eliot's famous decla-ration to F. W. H. Myers when, taking as her text the three words *"God, Immortality, Duty,"* she "pronounced, with terrible earnestness, how inconceivable was the *first*, how unbelievable was the *second*, and yet how peremptory and absolute the *third*."[8]

Carlyle and Conrad were very different; and Conrad apparently found *Sartor Resartus* too hyperbolic for his taste (*Y*, 7); but his views on the spiritual role of work for the individual were very similar. The

5. *Sartor Resartus: The Life and Opinions of Herr Teufelsdröckh,* ed. P. C. Parr (Oxford, 1913), pp. 119; 118.

6. *Sartor,* pp. 134; 122; 131; 140. The Novalis and Goethe quotations are identified on pp. 254, 256–57. The relationship of Carlyle and Conrad is briefly discussed in Alan Sandison, *The Wheel of Empire* (London, 1967), pp. 136–40, and in *C G*, 26. See also Alison L. Hopwood, "Carlyle and Conrad: *Past and Present* and 'Heart of Darkness'," *Review of English Studies* 23 (1972): 162–72.

7. See Houghton, *Victorian Frame of Mind,* pp. 173–74, 234, 238–39.

8. Cited from Houghton, *Victorian Frame of Mind,* p. 238.

process whereby Teufelsdröckh is saved from seeing the world as merely "a mad primeval Discord" through an acceptance of work, duty, and renunciation, is very close to the way Marlow is saved from the heart of darkness, except that Marlow's word for renunciation is "restraint," and for duty, "fidelity." Neither Conrad nor Marlow pitch their claims for these defences at anything like so transcendental a level as Carlyle; nevertheless, the same practical virtues, in a much attenuated and largely instinctive form, constitute virtually the whole of the meagre moral armament with which Marlow confronts Africa and Kurtz.

Most of the ideological content of *Heart of Darkness* is of a very different nature, and amounts either to a rejection of many of the other standard Victorian assumptions, or to a warning against their ultimate implications, implications to which Marlow is very alive, and to which Kurtz succumbs. In this, Conrad is largely reflecting the much bleaker and more threatening ideological perspective on human life which followed from new developments in physical science, in evolutionary theory, and in political life, during the last half of the nineteenth century.

The Material Universe

The extraordinary increase in industrial production and technological discovery made many Victorians come close to believing that the logic of material progress would itself resolve all the intractable problems that formerly bedevilled human history. The Prince Consort expressed a widely shared belief when he declared that the Great Exhibition of 1851 was the manifest symbol of "a period of most wonderful transition, which tends rapidly to accomplish that great end to which indeed all history points—*the realisation of the unity of mankind.*"[9]

Conrad had no such illusions. Rejecting the quantitative values of commercial and industrial society, he saw only danger in "the modern blind trust in mere material and appliances" (*N L L*, 218); he viewed the Victorian hope that progress would automatically result from "the peaceful nature of industrial and commercial competition" as an "incredible infatuation"; and of the 1851 Great Exhibition, the historic apogee of that infatuation, he remarked that it was "crammed full with that variegated rubbish which it seems to be the bizarre fate of humanity to produce for the benefit of a few employers of labour" (*N L L*, 106).

There was no such dismissive scorn in Conrad's attitude to scientific

9. Cited by Houghton, *Victorian Frame of Mind,* p. 43.

knowledge itself. For a literary man he was rather well informed about natural science: he had learned some elementary astronomy and physics as part of his nautical education; he had a lifelong interest in engineering; and he was quite curious about new scientific ideas. Man's new knowledge about the natural world, however, was far from affording Conrad any consolation; indeed, recent developments in astronomy and physics tended in quite the opposite direction.

Their main effect was to force man to confront his infinitely minute and equally transitory role in the total scheme of things. Our earth had probably originated as an incidental by-product of cooling gases from the sun; and the formulation of the second law of thermodynamics by Lord Kelvin in 1851 seemed to mean that, like all else, the earth would end in cold and drought through the diffusion of heat-energy.[10] This astrophysical pessimism became a standard feature of late Victorian thought. As Edward Carpenter wrote about the universe of his youth: "one of its properties was that it could run down like a clock, and would eventuate in time in a cold sun and a dead earth—and there was an end of it!"[11] The previous century had inferred a divine watchmaker from the perfection of the celestial machine; it was now discovered not only that there was no watchmaker, but that the spring was running down.

For Conrad there were two kinds of inference to be derived from the new cosmology, and both were negative.

First, in the words of the preface to The Nigger of the "Narcissus", Conrad deduced that "those heartless secrets which are called the Laws of Nature" (xi–xii) really dealt with matters that are essentially irrelevant to the deepest human concerns. Like Matthew Arnold in his essay "Literature and Science" (1883), Conrad viewed contemporary attempts to force a marriage between natural science and human culture as misguided; he asserted that "life and the arts follow dark courses, and will not turn aside to the brilliant arc-lights of science" (N L L, 74).

Secondly, Conrad derived from the facts of natural science a view of man's situation very close to that of modern Existentialism: the individual consciousness is inevitably separate from its environment and the fate which it dictates. "What makes mankind tragic," he wrote

10. Popularised by Balfour Stewart's The Conservation of Energy in 1873. In his The Triumph of Time: A Study of the Victorian Concepts of Time, History, Progress, and Decadence (Cambridge, Mass., 1966), Jerome Buckley discusses the impact of this idea on decadence (pp. 66–69). In the nineties the idea is found in such disparate works as Wells's The Time Machine (1895) and Villiers de L'Isle-Adam's Axël (1890), whose hero calls the earth "that drop of frozen mud" (Pt. IV, section 2).

11. The Drama of Love and Death (1912), quoted in Samuel Hynes, The Edwardian Turn of Mind (Princeton, N. J., 1968), p. 136.

to Cunninghame Graham on 31 January 1898, "is not that they are the victims of nature, it is that they are conscious of it. . . . There is no morality, no knowledge and no hope; there is only the consciousness of ourselves which drives us about a world that whether seen in a convex or a concave mirror is always but a vain and fleeting appearance" (*C G*, 70–71).

The laws of nature undermined man's political as well as his individual aspirations. At the end of 1897 Conrad expressed this view in a significant blend of scientific and industrial metaphors:

> There is a—let us say—a machine. It evolved itself (I am severely scientific) out of a chaos of scraps of iron and behold!—it knits. I am horrified at the horrible work and stand appalled. I feel it ought to embroider—but it goes on knitting. You come and say: "this is all right; it's only a question of the right kind of oil. Let us use this—for instance—celestial oil and the machine shall embroider a most beautiful design in purple and gold." Will it? Alas no. You cannot by any special lubrication make embroidery with a knitting machine. And the most withering thought is that the infamous thing has made itself; made itself without thought, without conscience, without foresight, without eyes, without heart. It is a tragic accident—and it has happened. . . . It knits us in and it knits us out. It has knitted time, space, pain, death, corruption, despair and all the illusions—and nothing matters. (*C G*, 56–57)

The kind of natural world which was revealed to Conrad's further vision by science was very close to the steam-engine view of the universe which symbolised the "Everlasting No" for Carlyle; human hopes were powerless against what Conrad called "the curse of decay—the eternal decree that will extinguish the sun, the stars one by one, and in another instant shall spread a frozen darkness over the whole universe" (*C G*, 53). The bleak determinism of the new cosmology deprived the individual of any rational grounds of action; as Conrad wrote in a later letter:

> [Reason] demonstrates . . . that . . . the fate of a humanity condemned ultimately to perish from cold is not worth troubling about. If you take it to heart it becomes an unendurable tragedy. If you believe in improvement you must weep, for the attained perfection must end in cold, darkness and silence. In a dispassionate view the ardour for reform, improvement for virtue, for knowledge, and even for beauty is only a vain sticking up for appearances as though one were anxious about the cut of one's clothes in a community of blind men. (*C G*, 65)

To this sweeping and summary mode of argument we can logically object that the life of a planet is after all much longer than that of a man, and that Conrad is really confusing two wholly different orders of temporal magnitude. But the habit of combining cosmological and human history had long been deeply entrenched in the way man looked at the world; it was, for instance, a basic assumption of Christianity. Conrad and his contemporaries belonged to the first generation that had not felt supported by the traditional view of man's flattering eminence in the history, as well as the design, of the cosmos; it was a heavy blow to be deprived of the old assumption that there is a humanly significant order and purpose throughout time and space, and that one is therefore entitled to think in terms which assume some continuity or analogy between the laws governing stellar galaxies and those governing human existence. Once science had denied this analogy, it is understandable that Conrad and many of his contemporaries should have drawn negative moral and political lessons from the newly-revealed vulnerability of man's situation in the temporal and spatial order.

The main visible residues of the new astrophysical pessimism in *Heart of Darkness* are a few passages about the menacing transience of man and his planet measured against the universe's scale of time and space. Marlow's first remark, as the sun sets over London, is: "And this also . . . has been one of the dark places of the earth" (48). Dismissing from our minds both the present lights on the shore and the glories of the national past enacted along the estuary of the Thames, Marlow harks back to the darkness which had here confronted the first Roman settlers in Britain; we are made to see civilisation, not as a stable and normal condition, but as a brief interruption of the customary rule of darkness, an interruption as brief as "a flash of lightning in the clouds"; and, Marlow reflects, "We live in the flicker" (49).[12]

Conrad is thinking here of historical rather than astronomical time, but later the threatening instability and darkness of the new cosmology becomes an immediate presence in the narrative. At the company station the roar of the rapids upstream gives Marlow a dizzy sense, "as though the tearing pace of the launched earth had suddenly become audible" (66). Earlier, the primary narrator has recounted how: "the sun sank low, and from glowing white changed to a dull red without rays and without heat, as if about to go out suddenly, stricken to death

12. In a cancelled passage in the manuscript of *Heart of Darkness* the rapid passing of a big steamer on the Thames leads the primary narrator to comment: "And the earth suddenly seemed shrunk to the size of a pea spinning in the heart of an immense darkness full of sparks born, scattered, glowing, going out beyond the ken of men" (*H D N*, 7).

by the touch of that gloom brooding over a crowd of men" (46). Conrad's insistent precision gives the mysteriousness of natural impressions a chilling symbolic resonance: it is really the London smoke which makes the sun seem to change colour, but watching the process evokes a moment of primitive fear that the sun may desert the human world, and abandon it to "cold, darkness and silence."

Evolution and Imperialism

In the last half of the nineteenth century it was not the physical but the biological sciences which had the deepest and the most pervasive effect upon the way man viewed his personal and historical destiny. The outcry against Darwin's *On the Origin of Species, by Means of Natural Selection, or The Preservation of Favoured Races in the Struggle for Life* (1859) was partly caused by the idea that the species of plants and animals were the accidental products of natural selection and not of a special creation by God as the book of Genesis had it. This was seen as the last stage of the process by which man had been deprived of the assurance that he was the most important constituent of a universe which God had designed for him. After Darwin, if man looked back at his own lineage, he discovered, not created Adam, but a long succession of unplanned mutations leading to the higher apes.

Conrad grew up in the heyday of evolutionary theory; Alfred Wallace was one of his favorite authors; and several aspects of evolutionary thought are present in *Heart of Darkness*. The most specific evidence occurs during Marlow's voyage up the river. Already at the Central Station, he imagines he is hearing an "ichthyosaurus . . . taking a bath" (86); later he recalls that "going up that river was like travelling back to the earliest beginnings of the world, when vegetation rioted on the earth and the big trees were kings" (92–93). The primeval world which Marlow encounters is a very far cry from that of noble savages: "We were wanderers on prehistoric earth, on an earth that wore the aspect of an unknown planet. We could have fancied ourselves the first of men taking possession of an accursed inheritance, to be subdued at the cost of profound anguish and of excessive toil" (95).

This evocation of primordial human history is part of Conrad's reflection of a wider, though indirect, aspect of evolutionary theory in *Heart of Darkness*. Many political and social theorists were fervid believers in what may be called the Victorian religion of progress. Long before Darwin, the traditional view of man's supremacy in the divine plan had been replaced with the idea that an equivalently splendid status could be attained through the working-out of humanity's secular destiny. In Arthur Lovejoy's phrase, the "temporalisation of the

Chain of Being"[13] substituted the law of historical progress for the lost belief in the perfection of God's original design. The idea of evolution suggested a way in which traditional ideas about the privileged splendour of human destiny could be salvaged: if man had not been put on top to begin with, it was patent that he had already come a long way up the chain of evolutionary being; and there was no limit to what he might later achieve if he worked hard and kept moving.[14]

The program for the future, therefore, seemed very clear. As regards individual morality, the puritan outlook was in effect reinforced; there were now even more imperative reasons for widening the gap between civilised man and his animal antecedents; in the famous exhortation of Tennyson's *In Memoriam*, man must "Arise and fly / The reeling Faun, the sensual feast; / Move upward, working out the beast, / And let the ape and tiger die" (Section 118). As regards economic and political matters there developed a loose body of beliefs that became known as Social Darwinism.[15] Darwin himself, though not wholly consistent, had doubted whether any political or social deductions could be drawn from his theories; but Herbert Spencer, who had already introduced the word "evolution" into general currency in 1854, warmly welcomed *The Origin of Species* because it helped fill out his own grand system of the progressive development of every part of the universe—from the stars to the plants. Spencer applied the biological analogy for the sociological part of his scheme; he asserted in *First Principles* (1862), that the "Survival of the Fittest," a term which Darwin later accepted as "more accurate" than natural selection,[16] was a law which validated the current competitive economic order and its attendant inequities, because they were a necessary stage in the process of social evolution.

The same mode of evolutionary argument also supported the ideology of colonial expansion. Merely by occupying or controlling most of the globe, the European nations had demonstrated that they were the fittest to survive; and the exportation of their various economic, political and religious institutions was therefore a necessary step towards a higher form of human organisation in the rest of the world. It was also widely thought—by Spencer, for example—that the dominance of the white races was itself the result of inherited superiority, and in *The Descent of Man* (1871), Darwin himself spoke of

13. In *The Great Chain of Being* (New York, 1960), ch. 9.
14. See William Irvine, *Apes, Angels, and Victorians: Darwin, Huxley, and Evolution* (New York, 1959), especially pp. 178–202, 264–359.
15. See Gertrude Himmelfarb, *Victorian Minds* (New York, 1970), pp. 314–32.
16. *The Origin of Species, by Charles Darwin: A Variorum Text*, ed. Morse Peckham (Philadelphia, 1959), p. 145.

"high" and "low" races, and of "stronger" and "weaker" nations. Later in the century the assumption that all evolution occurred in a single upward line of development was extended by such Social Darwinists as Benjamin Kidd, in his *The Control of the Tropics* (1898), to include the necessary domination or destruction of inferior peoples by white civilisation. The wide acceptance of such racial doctrines did much to enlist popular support for the imperialist adventures of the end of the nineteenth century; as Victor Kiernan has written, the "mystique of race was Democracy's vulgarization of an older mystique of class."[17]

Imperialism as a topic of wide public interest was a fairly recent development. It was only in 1877 that Queen Victoria, against some opposition, had been given the title of Empress of India.[18] In the same year the prime mover in the rise of British imperialist doctrines, Cecil Rhodes, wrote his first will: it left his fortune, as yet prospective, to a clandestine society devoted to expediting God's evident intention of making his chosen people, the Anglo-Saxon race, crown the evolutionary process by adding the Americas, Africa, and other promising places, to the British Empire.[19] In the eighties, public interest in the Empire was spurred on by the discovery of gold in the Transvaal, and by increasing resentment at German imperial expansion. The final adoption of an imperialist programme as British government policy occurred when the leadership of the Liberal party passed from Gladstone to Rosebery in 1894, and especially when the Conservative ministry of Lord Salisbury took office the next year, with Joseph Chamberlain as colonial secretary. There followed a number of collisions among the great powers over the division of Africa, culminating in the Jameson Raid of 1895, and the Fashoda Incident in 1898, when the French attempt to link their African territories from east to west by establishing a claim to part of the Sudan was turned back by Kitchener.

It was in this atmosphere of intensifying international conflict over Africa, and the consequent spread of jingoist fervour in England, that Conrad wrote *Heart of Darkness*. The new enthusiasm for empire had been fostered by a small group of writers, of whom the most popular was Rider Haggard and the most famous, Rudyard Kipling. Kipling, a personal friend of Rhodes and Jameson, was already the established poet laureate of empire, and the chief propagandist for the values

17. V. G. Kiernan, *The Lords of Human Kind: Black Man, Yellow Man, and White Man in an Age of Empire* (Boston, 1969), p. 230.

18. See Richard Koebner and Helmut Dan Schmidt, *Imperialism: The Story and Significance of a Political Word, 1840–1960* (Cambridge, 1964), pp. 118–23.

19. On the imperialist program, see Richard Faber, *The Vision and the Need* (London, 1966); on the opposition, Bernard Porter, *Critics of Empire* (London, 1968).

which the imperial mission required—group duty, military discipline, and technological efficiency. Kipling's preoccupation with "The Law" is not unlike Conrad's with solidarity; but although Conrad's seaman values might seem to place him on the side of Kipling, he did not really belong there. Conrad's closest friends were fervid anti-imperialists: "Kipling," Edward Garnett wrote to Cunninghame Graham in 1898, "is *the* enemy . . . *the genius of all we detest*" (*C G*, 20); Cunninghame Graham defined "the Imperial Mission" as "the Stock Exchange Militant"; and both men subsequently opposed the Boer War. Conrad's attitude was divided, and, like many historians,[20] his novels present as many "imperialisms" and "colonialisms" as there are particular cases. In so far as these cases had the common element of conquering, killing, and enslaving the native population, Conrad was opposed, if only because of what had happened to his own native country. He had been dubious about the British forward movement in Africa at the time of the British occupation of Egypt in 1882 (*L L*, I, 200); and he hoped for a Spanish victory in the 1898 Spanish-American War (*C G*, 84–85). But Conrad's commitment to his adopted country brought him into conflict with these sentiments, especially when the Boer War broke out in October 1899. On the one hand, Conrad mocked Kipling's view that it was "a war undertaken for the cause of democracy," and correctly believed that it was "an appalling fatuity" which "must be the beginning of an endless contest"; on the other hand, he hoped, vainly, that "British successes will be crushing from the first (*C G*, 126), partly because he was convinced that "liberty . . . can only be found under the English flag all over the world," and partly because he saw the war as essentially a "struggle against the doings of German influence" (*L L*, I, 288).[21]

Much the same ideological contradiction is present in *Heart of Darkness*. In broad terms it must be considered a powerful attack not only on Belgian colonisation but on Western expansion in general. For instance, Conrad cancelled the only allusion in the text to King Leopold ("some third rate king" [*H D N*, 7]) and thus gave a more universal implication to Marlow's judgment immediately following: "The conquest of the earth, which mostly means the taking it away from those who have a different complexion or slightly flatter noses than ourselves, is not a pretty thing when you look into it too much" (50–51). But when Marlow observes a map in the company's waiting room, he comments: "There was a vast amount of red—good to see at

20. See especially Ronald Robinson and John Gallagher, *Africa and the Victorians* (New York, 1961), pp. 13–26, 462–72.

21. C. T. Watts discusses Conrad's attitudes to imperialism in his introduction (*C G*, 19–24); see also Stephen Koss, *The Pro-Boers* (Chicago, 1973), pp. xiii–xxxviii.

any time, because one knows that some real work is done in there, a deuce of a lot of blue, a little green, smears of orange, and, on the East Coast, a purple patch, to show where the jolly pioneers of progress drink the jolly lager-beer" (55). The red of the British Empire gets a patriotic pat, but there is no comment on the other colonisers until the purple patch of the German colonies in Central Africa receives its contemptuously ironic kick.

This passage may have been intended to placate the more jingoistic of his potential readers. Conrad had early expressed the same anxiety in a letter to Blackwood in which he wondered "whether the *subject*" of *Heart of Darkness* would "commend itself to you" (*B*, 36). But although Conrad probably thought that *Blackwood's* would have been unhappy if he made any overt criticism of British imperialism, it is unlikely that he wished to do so. We must not forget that in the nineteenth century no real political alternative had been suggested to Western penetration of the other continents; the only practical issue was what form it should take. The ultimate choice was that which, anticipating Kurtz, a witness before the parliamentary committee on aborigines had expressed as early as 1837: "The main point which I would have in view would be trade, commerce, peace, and civilization. The other alternative is extermination; for you can stop nowhere."[22]

Conrad was equally complicated in his attitude to the ideas of racial superiority which were widely promulgated during the later phases of Anglo-Saxon and German imperialism.[23] He certainly did not adopt Kipling's belligerent superiority towards "the lesser breeds without the law," and he exposed the combination of Social Darwinism and Imperialism in his hostile portrayal of Travers in *The Rescue*. On the other hand, Conrad habitually uses the derogatory racial terms which were general in the political and evolutionary thought of his time. This might pose a serious problem if *Heart of Darkness* were essentially concerned with the colonial and racial issue in general. But it is not. As in his earlier Malayan fiction, and in "An Outpost of Progress," Conrad was primarily concerned with the colonisers, and there the general purport of his fiction is consistent and unequivocal: imperial or colonial experience is disastrous for the whites; it makes them lazy; it reveals their weaknesses; it puffs them up with empty vanity at being white; and it fortifies the intolerable hypocrisy with which Europeans in general conceal their selfish aims. Conrad made

22. Quoted in *Imperialism*, ed. Philip D. Curtin (New York, 1971), p. 289.
23. John E. Saveson argues that Conrad's views changed from an early similarity to Spencer's ideas to the less ethnocentric positions of Schopenhauer and Hartmann ("Conrad's View of Primitive Peoples in *Lord Jim* and *Heart of Darkness*," *Modern Fiction Studies* 16 (1970): 163–83).

Babalatchi sum up the message of "you white men" very concisely in *An Outcast of the Islands:* "Obey me and be happy, or die!" (226).

The Belgian Congo, however, provided Conrad with a case where he could speak with absolute freedom, because it was neither British nor a threat to Britain's power in the world, and because the issues involved went far beyond those of race. The colony was ideal for another reason: unlike most others, it had been a conscious creation from the beginning, and a creation accompanied by a deafening international chorus mouthing the moral slogans of evolutionary political progress; but by 1898 this chorus was attacking the savagery of that same Leopold whom, in 1890, Stanley had called the "Royal Founder of this unique humanitarian and political enterprise."[24]

The inconsistencies in Conrad's attitudes to colonial and racial problems must in general be understood in their historical context: and those in *Heart of Darkness* are particularly influenced by the fact that it was written at a time when Britain had committed herself to stopping further French and German expansion in Africa, even at the risk of war. But *Heart of Darkness* is not essentially a political work; Conrad mainly followed his own direct imaginative perceptions; and insofar as he treated the Africans at all, it was essentially as human beings seen from the inward and subjective point of view which characterises *Heart of Darkness* as a whole.

This emerges from what is perhaps Conrad's most explicit statement on what Belgian colonisation meant for the Africans. He expressed it in a letter of 21 December 1903 to his friend Roger Casement, who was then writing his report on atrocities in the Congo. Conrad wished Casement every success in his campaign; he wondered how a civilisation which at home punishes its citizens for overworking a horse can allow "the moral clock" to be "put back many hours" in the Congo State; and he then gave the moral essence of the problem as he saw it:

> [The black man] shares with us the consciousness of the universe in which we live—no small burden. Barbarism per se is no crime ... and the Belgians are worse than the seven plagues of Egypt insomuch that in that case it was a punishment sent for a definite transgression; but in this the ... man is not aware of any transgression, and therefore can see no end to the infliction. It must appear to him very awful and mysterious; and I confess that it appears so to me too.[25]

24. H. M. Stanley, *The Congo and the Founding of its Free State,* 2 vols. (New York, 1885), vol. 2, p. 407.
25. Zdzisław Najder, "Conrad's Casement Letters," *Polish Perspectives* 17 (1974): 29.

The passage reminds us that Conrad's distance from immediate political involvement or any other fixed ideological position often has as its dialectical complement the revealing directness of his power of imaginative projection; and it is surely this power which makes *Heart of Darkness* even now endure as the most powerful literary indictment of imperialism.

The Nineties and the Savage God

Imperialist and social-evolutionary thought were the last stands of nineteenth-century optimism; but elsewhere, and especially in intellectual circles, there was little talk of progress. Except to Fabian inheritors of the utilitarian and positivist traditions such as H. G. Wells, science and technology no longer seemed to promise man a golden future; between Conrad's arrival in England in 1878, and the writing of *Heart of Darkness* twenty years later, it had become increasingly evident that the Victorian world order was collapsing.[26]

In literature, the general mood was one of anxiety and disillusionment. In 1884 Ruskin had pronounced that the Darwinian reduction of man to the status of "nothing more than brute beasts" was the chief "Storm Cloud of the Nineteenth Century,"[27] and that it threatened the doom of civilisation; later, G. K. Chesterton was to look back on the years 1885 to 1898 as "an epoch of real pessimism," and diagnosed the studied *ennui* of the decadents as a yawn to stifle their cry of despair.[28] A great many writings about the future prospects of the world were marked by a note of apocalyptic gloom. *Heart of Darkness* is but one of many late nineteenth-century works which, in different ways, implied the coming destruction of existing civilisation—Richard Jeffries's *After London* (1885), William Morris's *News From Nowhere* (1891), Grant Allen's *The British Barbarians* (1895), and H. G. Wells's *The War of the Worlds* (1898), are four other examples. There is the same sense of impending collapse in Max Nordau's *Degeneration*, which was immensely successful in its 1895 English translation; for Nordau, almost every manifestation of contemporary civilisation was evidence of the "fin de siècle,"[29] a phrase which had been given very

26. This is the subject of John A. Lester, Jr.'s *Journey Through Despair: 1880–1914: Transformations in British Literary Culture* (Princeton, 1968).

27. *Works* (London, 1903–1912), vol. 34, pp. 78–79. Stewart's *The Conservation of Energy* was another target (p. 76).

28. *George Bernard Shaw* (New York, 1909), pp. 246–47.

29. Nordau wrote a letter praising *The Nigger of the "Narcissus"*, and Conrad's wry remark that "praise is sweet, no matter whence it comes," along with other evidence, suggests that he knew of Nordau's work (*L L*, I, 255). The possible influence of Nordau's analysis of "atavistic degeneracy" upon *Heart of Darkness* is suggested in C. T. Watts's, "Nordau and Kurtz: A Footnote to *Heart of Darkness*," *Notes and Queries* 21 (1974): 226–27.

wide currency by Oscar Wilde's *Picture of Dorian Gray* (1891), where Lord Henry murmurs "Fin de siècle," and his hostess knowingly answers "Fin du globe."

The "fin de siècle" depression even extended to many of the evolutionists, and most notably to Darwin's greatest advocate, Thomas Huxley. His Romanes lecture in 1893 on "Evolution and Ethics," which had Spencer as its main antagonist, advanced a view of the radical disjunction between man's natural constitution and the aims of civilisation which is in many ways similar to the ideological purport of *Heart of Darkness*.

"The ethical process," Huxley asserted, "is in opposition to the principle of the cosmic process, and tends to the suppression of the qualities best fitted for success in that struggle." The ethical process builds up in man "an artificial personality," a conscience, largely through the operation of the "fear . . . of the opinion of their fellows," which is "the greatest restrainer of the anti-social tendencies of men." This socially imposed restraint is directly opposed to the instincts of "natural man," and to the qualities through which he has "worked his way to the headship of the sentient world."[30] Darwin also had believed that there was a struggle both in animals and men between the "derived" social virtues and the "lower, though momentarily stronger impulses"; but in *The Descent of Man* he had seen "no cause to fear that the social instincts will grow weaker," and had indeed asserted that "we may expect that virtuous habits will grow stronger, becoming perhaps fixed by inheritance."[31]

Huxley now took a darker view of the probable outcome of the conflict between the social and the lower impulses. "That baleful product of evolution," internal moral conflict, causes "pain or suffering" which inevitably becomes more acute as civilisation progresses. With lofty and compassionate irony, Huxley conceded that "after the manner of successful persons, civilised man would gladly kick down the ladder by which he has climbed. He would be only too pleased to see 'the ape and tiger die.' But they decline to suit his convenience; and the unwelcome intrusion of these boon companions of his hot youth into the ranged existence of civil life adds pains and griefs, innumerable and immeasurably great, to those which the cosmic process brings on the mere animal." Quite contrary to Spencer's earlier confidence that the law of progress meant that in the future "evil and immorality"

30. Thomas H. Huxley, *Evolution and Ethics, and Other Essays* (New York, 1894), pp. 31; 30; 29; 51; 52; 44–45. The general historical background of nineteenth-century evolutionary thought about society is examined in J. W. Burrow's *Evolution and Society: A Study in Victorian Social Theory* (Cambridge, 1966).

31. *The Descent of Man*, 2nd ed. (New York, 1898), p. 127.

would surely disappear and "man become perfect,"[32] Huxley affirms
that the "prospect of happiness or perfection is as misleading an illusion as ever was dangled before the eyes of poor humanity"; the
"constant struggle" between civilisation and "the State of Nature" will
continue until "the evolution of our globe shall have entered so far
upon its downward course that the cosmic process resumes its sway;
and, once more, the State of Nature prevails over the surface of our
planet."

Five years later, in 1898, even Spencer's sanguine faith that progress was "a beneficent necessity"[33] had evaporated; he was now inclined to believe that "we are in course of rebarbarisation."[34]

Kurtz's return to barbarism exemplifies the dangers in the attempt
to make technological and evolutionary optimism a functional substi-
tute for more traditional views of the social and moral order. In a
large historical perspective the evolutionary optimism of the mid-
century can be seen as having weakened the two main lines of demar-
cation which had traditionally defined man's estate; there was the
upper one which separated man from God and the angels; and there
was the lower one which separated him from the animals. But evolutionary thought had introduced a new mobility into the chain of
being, and this was widely supposed to make it possible for man to
transcend the upper barrier, as he had already transcended that
which separated him from the apes.

From the traditional religious point of view this faith in man's self-
propelled spiritual ascent was essentially heretical; nevertheless the
idea that the world's salvation could be expected from a boundless
increase in individual development had been supported by all the
strongest new forces in nineteenth-century life: by the developing
imperatives of Romantic individualism, with its Faustian ideal of absolute liberation from religious, social, and ethical norms in the pursuit
of experience; by the utilitarian view that leaving individuals free to
pursue their own good would increase the sum of human happiness;
by the democratic egalitarianism of liberal political theory; and by
evolutionary positivism which followed Herbert Spencer's belief that
the progressive differentiation of individuals was the sufficient aim of
the evolutionary process. The ultimate logic of these expectations was
the assumption that progress would eventually lead to man's self-

32. Herbert Spencer, *Social Statics: The Conditions Essential to Human Happiness
Specified, and the First of Them Developed,* 1850 (New York, 1865), p. 80.
33. "Progress: Its Law and Cause," in *Essays Scientific, Political, and Speculative* (New
York, 1892), vol. 1, p. 60.
34. Edward Clodd, *Grant Allen: A Memoir* (London, 1900), p. 199.

deification. This idea had been implicit in Comte's "religion of humanity" and in Ludwig Feuerbach's *The Essence of Christianity* (1841); later, Winwood Reade's very influential *The Martyrdom of Man* (1872) works towards a future in which, "Finally, men will master the forces of nature; they will become themselves architects of systems, manufacturers of worlds. Man then will be perfect; he will then be a creator; he will then be what the vulgar worship as a god."[35]

The assumptions of that latent megalomania are beautifully expressed in Auden's poem "In Father's Footsteps," which begins with a poignant valediction to the basic psychological strategy of the Victorian religion of progress:

> Our hunting fathers told the story
> Of the sadness of the creatures,
> Pitied the limits and the lack
> Set in their finished features;
> Saw in the lion's intolerant look,
> Behind the quarry's dying glare,
> Love raging for the personal glory
> That reason's gift would add,
> The liberal appetite and power,
> The rightness of a god.

The "rightness of a god" was a role almost automatically conferred on the white European when he left home and went out to govern colonies. In this both Kurtz's motives and his fate are deeply representative. He goes out, first of all, to make money; he is thus a representative of economic individualism in a free marketplace. Paradoxically, however, the Benthamite, utilitarian, and imperialist modes of thought turn out to be, not the contraries, but the complements of Romantic individualism in its later Bohemian and Decadent embodiments. Kurtz is a poet, a painter, a political radical, a man with the power of words; and in his final liberation from all the constraints of civilisation he becomes a symbolic parallel to the career of Arthur Rimbaud, who, in Verlaine's words, had aspired "to be that man who will create God,"[36] but who had turned his back on European civilisation in 1875, and ended up as a trader and explorer in Abyssinia, living in the manner of a native chief in Harrar.

Unlike Rimbaud, however, or Gauguin, who had left for Tahiti in

35. London, 1910, p. 515.
36. "*Je serai celui-là qui créera Dieu*," in "Crimen Amoris." Conrad had some knowledge of Rimbaud in 1898 (*C G*, 104; *B*, 46); the parallel of Kurtz and Rimbaud is extensively treated by Aniela Kowalska in her *Conrad: 1896–1900: Strategia wrażeń i refleksji w narracjach Marlowa* [Patterns of impressions and reflections in Marlow's narrative] (Lodz, Society of Arts and Sciences, 1973), pp. 35, 43–81.

1891, Kurtz is not a voluntary exile from civilisation; he is proudly bringing its benefactions to the dark places of the earth. But once Kurtz is freed from the pressures of his own kind, and the wilderness whispers "things about himself which he did not know" (131), he meets the ape and the tiger within himself and lets loose all his "forgotten and brutal instincts" (144). When the individual is liberated from the restraining power of what Huxley called the "artificial conscience" provided by the opinion of his fellows, it appears that "reason's gift" is powerless against the appetites Kurtz shares with those below him on the evolutionary chain of being.

The prophetic quality of this surrender to the archaic and irrational drives of the unconditioned ego has been analysed by Lionel Trilling. In his essay "The Modern Element in Literature," he writes that Conrad's "strange and terrible message of ambivalence toward the life of civilization" continues the tradition of Blake and Nietzsche; and Kurtz is therefore a portent of the future, for "nothing is more characteristic of modern literature than its discovery and canonization of the primal, non-ethical energies."[37] Trilling amplified this perspective in *Sincerity and Authenticity*. Kurtz is the "paradigmatic literary expression of the modern concern with authenticity," meaning the intransigent assertion of the inward impulses of the individual in defiance of social and traditional values, while Marlow is the exemplar of "the trait on which the English most prided themselves, their sincerity, by which they meant their single-minded relation to things, to each other, and to themselves." The contrast between the two men is implicit in Trilling's concluding protest at the recent tendency to turn madness itself into "the paradigm of liberation from the imprisoning falsehoods of an alienated social reality," despite the "great refusal of human connection" that such an attitude implies. Trilling's contemptuous summary of the ultimate direction of this mode of thought could also have been written about Kurtz: "An upward psychopathic mobility to the point of divinity."[38]

The romantic, anarchic, and psychopathic energies of Kurtz find their ultimate sanction in Western industrial supremacy; for Kurtz really asserts his claims to "the rightness of a god" through his monopoly of firearms. The idea is prefigured, ironically enough, in his report to the International Society for the Suppression of Savage Customs, where Kurtz begins from the premise that "we whites ... 'must necessarily appear to them [savages] in the nature of super-

37. 1961; collected as "On the Teaching of Modern Literature," in *Beyond Culture* (New York, 1965), p. 19.

38. *Sincerity and Authenticity* (Cambridge, Mass., 1974), pp. 106, 111, 171–72.

natural beings—we approach them with the might as of a deity' "
(118). The harlequin confirms this basis for Kurtz's power: "He came
to them with thunder and lightning, you know—and they had never
seen anything like it" (128). But it turns out that modern technology
heralds a deity of a very atavistic kind. Kurtz is really a monitory
variant of the biogenetic law which the German zoologist Ernst Haec-
kel had developed in his *History of Creation* (1867; translated 1892);
ontogeny recapitulates phylogeny but the direction of historical evolution is reversed. Following the traditional African practice of king-
ship, Kurtz takes on semi-divine attributes. Like the contemporary
African ruler Msiri at Bunkeya in the Southern Congo, he decorates
the fencepoles round his house with human heads;[39] and, as Marlow
almost brings himself to recount, human sacrifices "at certain midnight dances ending with unspeakable rites, which—as far as I reluc-
tantly gathered from what I heard at various times—were offered up
to him—do you understand?—to Mr. Kurtz himself" (118).

Marlow is horrified, and so, just before his end, is Kurtz, to understand what happens to a man who discovers his existential freedom
under circumstances which enable him to pervert the ultimate direction of nineteenth-century thought: not the disappearance but the
replacement of God. Many had thought that man's last evolutionary
leap would be forwards and up into the bright throne that he had
emptied: Kurtz's destiny suggests that the leap would in fact be down
and back into the darkness.

Man, in Sartre's definition, is "the being whose plan it is to become
God."[40] Conrad enacted the unreal exorbitance of the plan in the fate
of Kurtz: against it he set the humbler and irresolute moral alternative of Marlow's example. That example also is representative; Marlow's overriding moral commitment to civilisation, however deluded it
may be, and however unsatisfactory its supporting arguments, is
rather similar to that of Conrad's contemporary, Freud. Freud's observations had forced him to a position which dramatically undermined the established psychological foundations of the social and
moral order, since man was shown to be unconsciously dominated by
the omnivorous and ultimately unappeasable appetites of the id; and
so, in *Civilization and Its Discontents* and *The Future of an Illusion*, Freud
was moved to wonder whether any secular mechanism could ever
replace religion in controlling the aggressive drives which led men to
war and the hatred of civilisation. Freud had a much deeper belief in
systematic thought than Conrad, but they shared much the same vi-

---

39. Ascherson, *King Incorporated*, p. 159.
40. *L'Être et le néant* (Paris, 1943), p. 653.

sion of how they should direct their moral energies: they saw that culture was insecurely based on repression and restraint, and yet what seemed most worth their effort was to promote a greater understanding of man's destructive tendencies, and at the same time support the modest countertruths on which civilisation depends. As against the more absolute negations of Rimbaud and Nietzsche, or the equally absolute transcendental affirmations of Dostoevsky or Yeats, both Freud and Conrad defend a practical social ethic based on their fairly similar reformulations of the Victorian trinity of work, duty, and restraint.[41]

The general modern tendency has been to overlook this aspect of Conrad and Freud in favour of the more unsettling and nihilistic side of their vision; in effect, both of them have been attacked or praised more for what they saw than for how they judged it; their warnings against the truths they revealed have been overlooked. A very similar bias has been reflected in the modern critical tendency to take a view of Kurtz very different from Marlow's overt condemnation. The late nineteenth century had seen many celebrations of animal energy, pagan hedonism, and savage violence; it was in their name that the Symbolist Alfred Jarry wrote his gleefully destructive satire on civilisation, *Ubu-Roi*, in 1896. Its ridicule of all established attitudes and institutions seemed to Yeats the climax of a process in which he and the leading French symbolist poets and painters had participated; and it led him to ask apprehensively, "What more is possible? After us the Savage God."[42] Conrad was even more directly alarmed by the new modes of liberation. In 1907 the early protagonist of Symbolism in England, Arthur Symons, praised Conrad for the cruel, perverse, and diabolic quality of his imagination as he had exemplified it in Kurtz. This led Conrad to protest: "I did not know that I had 'a heart of darkness' and 'an unlawful soul.' Mr. Kurtz had—and I have not treated him with easy nonchalance."[43]

The tendency to see Kurtz as a modern variant of the Faustian hero is partly the result of identifying vision and wish; but it is characteristic of Conrad and Freud, as of most truth-tellers, that what they see is often just the opposite of what they want to see. For us, and no doubt for Conrad, Kurtz makes a vivid appeal to the imagination, while Marlow does not; but the contrast between Marlow's undramatic moral posture and the emblematic extremities of Kurtz's career itself

41. For Freud on work, see especially *Civilization and Its Discontents*, trans. J. Rivière (London, 1946), p. 34, n. 1.

42. *Autobiographies* (London, 1955), p. 349.

43. Arthur Symons, *Notes on Joseph Conrad with Some Unpublished Letters* (London, 1925), p. 15.

enacts one of the ideological lessons of *Heart of Darkness*: that nothing is more dangerous than man's delusions of autonomy and omnipotence. In "Youth," Marlow says that he prefers Burnaby's *Ride to Khiva* to Carlyle's *Sartor Resartus,* the soldier to the philosopher, on the grounds that: "One was a man, and the other was either more—or less" (*Y*, 7). In *Heart of Darkness,* against all the unreal psychological and social hyperboles of his waning century, Conrad affirmed the need, as Camus put it, "in order to be a man, to refuse to be a God."[44]

iv. Critical Perspectives

In the tradition of what we are still calling modern literature, the classic status of *Heart of Darkness* probably depends less on the prophetic nature of Conrad's ideas than on its new formal elements. These new narrative elements reflect both the general ideological crisis of the late nineteenth century and the literary innovations which accompanied it; but there are other and more direct reasons for considering them. Many readers of *Heart of Darkness* have found it rather obscure, and in particular, obscure in its answer to questions that would have been normal to ask, and easy to answer, in the case of most nineteenth-century fiction; questions such as: What is the heart of darkness? What does Kurtz actually do and why don't we see him doing it? What does it matter to Marlow, and why doesn't he tell the Intended? These questions about *Heart of Darkness* all receive answers, but only in terms of its own formal presuppositions. This qualification would actually apply to almost any literary work, but the terms of *Heart of Darkness* are especially difficult to decipher.

Conrad provides us with very little critical guidance. This is no doubt partly because of the intuitive way he wrote. As Edward Crankshaw put it, Conrad "seems to have worked in a state of semi-blindness, calculating as the need arose, crossing his bridges as they came, living, so to speak, from hand to mouth."[1] This mingling of the intuitive and the calculating in Conrad's mode of fictional creation was probably too complicated for him to describe, even perhaps to recall; and so he leaves us with miscellaneous critical explanations which are always incomplete, often unhelpful, sometimes wayward, and yet in their own way psychologically convincing. In this Conrad offers a total contrast to Henry James, whose prefaces are so con-

---

44. *L'Homme révolté,* p. 377.

1. Edward Crankshaw, *Joseph Conrad: Some Aspects of the Art of the Novel,* 1936 (New York, 1963), p. 10.

scious, logical, and comprehensive that as descriptions of what actually happened they seem too good to be true.

Conrad's most helpful comment on the method of *Heart of Darkness* occurs very early in the story, where the primary narrator explains that the meanings of Marlow's tales are characteristically difficult to encompass:

> The yarns of seamen have a direct simplicity, the whole meaning of which lies within the shell of a cracked nut. But Marlow was not typical (if his propensity to spin yarns be excepted), and to him the meaning of an episode was not inside like a kernel but outside, enveloping the tale which brought it out only as a glow brings out a haze, in the likeness of one of these misty halos that sometimes are made visible by the spectral illumination of moonshine (48).

The passage suggests at least three of the distinctive elements in *Heart of Darkness*. First of all there is the duplication of narrators; and the first one, who begins and ends the story in his own voice, feels called on to explain that the second one, Marlow, goes in for a very special kind of storytelling, which has two distinctive qualities. These two qualities are suggested metaphorically, and may be roughly categorised as symbolist and impressionist: the abstract geometry of the metaphor is symbolist because the meaning of the story, represented by the shell of the nut or the haze around the glow, is larger than its narrative vehicle, the kernel or the glow; but the sensory quality of the metaphor, the mist and haze, is essentially impressionist.

(a) *Impressionism*

Mist or haze is a very persistent image in Conrad. It appeared as soon as he began to write: there was an "opaline haze" over the Thames on the morning when he had recalled Almayer; and the original Olmeijer had first come into Conrad's view through the morning mists of Borneo. In *Heart of Darkness* the fugitive nature and indefinite contours of haze are given a special significance by the primary narrator; he warns us that Marlow's tale will be not centered on, but surrounded by, its meaning; and this meaning will be only as fitfully and tenuously visible as a hitherto unnoticed presence of dust particles and water vapour in a space that normally looks dark and void. This in turn reminds us that one of the most characteristic objections to Impressionist painting was that the artist's ostensive "subject" was obscured by his representation of the atmospheric conditions through which it was observed. Claude Monet, for instance, said of the critics who mocked him: "Poor blind idiots. They want to see everything clearly, even through the fog!"[2] For Monet, the fog in a painting, like the narrator's haze, is not an accidental interference which stands between the public and a clear view of the artist's "real" subject: the conditions under which the viewing is done are an essential part of what the pictorial—or the literary—artist sees and therefore tries to convey.

A similar idea, expressed in a similar metaphor, occurs twenty years later in Virginia Woolf's classic characterization of "Modern Fiction" (1919). There she exempts Conrad, together with Hardy, from her objections to traditional novels and those of her Edwardian contemporaries, H. G. Wells, Arnold Bennett, and John Galsworthy.[3] Her basic objection is that if we "look within" ourselves we see "a myriad impressions" quite unrelated to anything that goes on in such fiction; and if we could express "this unknown and uncircumscribed spirit" of life freely, "there would be no plot, no comedy, no tragedy, no love interest or catastrophe in the accepted style, and perhaps not a single button sewn on as the Bond Street tailors would have it." For, Virginia Woolf finally affirms, "Life is not a series of gig lamps symmetrically arranged; life is a luminous halo, a semi-transparent envelope surrounding us from the beginning of consciousness to the end."

The implications of these images of haze and halo for the essential nature of modern fiction are made somewhat clearer by the analogy of French Impressionist painting, and by the history of the word impressionism.

As a specifically aesthetic term, "Impressionism" was apparently put into circulation in 1874 by a journalist, Louis Leroy, to ridicule the affronting formlessness of the pictures exhibited at the Salon des Indépendants, and particularly of Claude Monet's painting entitled "Impression: Sunrise." In one way or another all the main Impressionists made it their aim to give a pictorial equivalent of the visual sensations of a particular individual at a particular time and place. One early critic suggested that "l'école des yeux" would be a more appropriate designation for them than "Impressionists";[4] what was new was not that earlier painters had been blind to the external world, but that painters were now attempting to give their own personal visual perceptions a more complete expressive autonomy; in the words of Jean Leymarie, what distinguished the French Impressionists was an intuitive "response to visual sensations, devoid of any

2. Quoted by Jean Renoir in *Renoir, My Father*, trans. Randolph and Dorothy Weaver (Boston and Toronto, 1958), p. 174.
3. *The Common Reader* (London, 1938), pp. 148–49.
4. Jacques Lethève, *Impressionnistes et Symbolistes devant la presse* (Paris, 1959), p. 63.

theoretical principle."[5] It was this aim which, as E.H. Gombrich has said, allots the Impressionist movement a decisive role in the process of art's long transition from trying to portray what all men know to trying to portray what the individual actually sees.[6]

The history of the words "impression" and "impressionism" in English embodies a more general aspect of the long process whereby in every domain of human concerns the priority passed from public systems of belief—what all men know—to private views of reality— what the individual sees. Beginning with the root meaning of "impression"—from *premere*, to "press" in a primarily physical sense, as in the "impression" of a printed book—the *Oxford Dictionary* documents a semantic flow towards meanings whose status is primarily psychological. The meaning of impression as "the effect produced by external force or influence on the senses or mind" was apparently established as early as 1632; and afterwards it proceeded to reflect the process whereby, from Descartes onwards, the concentration of philosophical thought upon epistemological problems gradually focussed attention on individual sensation as the only reliable source of ascertainable truth. The most notable single name connected with the process is probably that of David Hume, who opened *A Treatise of Human Nature* (1739–1740) with the ringing assertion, "All the perceptions of the human mind resolve themselves into two distinct kinds, which I shall call *IMPRESSIONS* and *IDEAS*." He had then attributed greater "force and violence" to impressions, as opposed to ideas, which he defined as merely the "less lively perceptions" which occur when we reflect on our original sense-impressions.[7] It was in protest against this empirical tradition in philosophy that the first English usage of "impressionism" occurred. In 1839 John Rogers, an eccentric word-coiner who entitled his attack on popery *Antipopopriestian*, wrote an ironical panegyric of the two main English prophets of "universal doubt": "All hail to Berkeley who would have no matter, and to Hume who would have no mind; to the Idealism of the former, and to the *Impressionism* of the latter!"[8]

It is appropriate that the word "impressionism" should be connected with Hume, since he played an important part in making the psychology of individual sensation supplant traditional philosophy as the main avenue to truth and value. One incidental result of this in the romantic and post-romantic period was that the religious, imag-

5. Jean Leymarie, *Impressionism*, trans. J. Emmons, 2 vols. (Lausanne, 1955), vol. 2, p. 28.
6. E. H. Gombrich, *The Story of Art*, 12th ed. (London, 1972), p. 406.
7. Bk I, "Of the Understanding," Pt. 1, sect. i.
8. 2nd ed. (New York, 1841), p. 188.

inative, emotional and aesthetic orders of being became increasingly private, a trend which in the course of the nineteenth century led both to the Aesthetic movement and to Impressionism. The most influential figure here is Walter Pater. In the famous "Conclusion" to *The Renaissance* (1868–1873), for instance, he speaks of how every person enclosed in "the narrow chamber of the individual mind" can directly experience only "the passage and dissolution of impressions, images, sensations"; these are "unstable, flickering, inconsistent," and the individual mind is therefore condemned to keep "as a solitary prisoner its own dream of a world."

This epistemological solipsism became an important part of the cultural atmosphere of the nineties; but by then the main English usage of the term "impressionism" was in reference to the French school of painters, and to their English counterparts who came to the fore with the foundation of the New English Art Club in 1886.[9] As in France, the term was very quickly extended to ways of writing which were thought to possess the qualities popularly attributed to the painters—to works that were spontaneous and rapidly executed, that were vivid sketches rather than detailed, finished, and premeditated compositions.[10] The literary use of the term remained even more casual and descriptive; although Stephen Crane was widely categorised as an "impressionist,"[11] and in 1898 a reviewer of Conrad's first collection of short stories, *Tales of Unrest*, described him as an "impressionistic realist,"[12] there was little talk of impressionism as a literary movement until considerably later.

It was Ford Madox Ford who gave wide currency to the view that he and Conrad, like Flaubert and Maupassant, had been writers of impressionist fiction. This view was expounded in Ford's 1913 essay "On Impressionism," which sees the distinctive trait of "the Impressionist" as giving "the fruits of his own observations alone";[13] but it is Ford's memoir of Conrad which gives his fullest account of literary impressionism. The memoir was published after Conrad's death, and so we do not know whether Ford's statement there that Conrad "avowed

9. See Holbrook Jackson, "British Impressionists," in *The Eighteen-Nineties* (London, 1939), pp. 240–50.

10. See *O E D*, and Todd K. Bender, "Literary Impressionism: General Introduction," in *Preliminary Papers for Seminar #8*, distributed for the Modern Language Association Annual Meeting, 1975 (University of Wisconsin, Madison, 1975), 1–21.

11. By Edward Garnett, for instance, in a 1898 essay reprinted in *Friday Nights* (London, 1922).

12. Cited by Bruce E. Teets and Helmut Gerber, eds., *Joseph Conrad: An Annotated Bibliography of Writings About Him* (De Kalb, Ill., 1971), p. 16.

13. Reprinted in *Critical Writings of Ford Madox Ford*, ed. Frank MacShane (Lincoln, 1964), p. 37.

himself impressionist" (*F M F*, 6) would have been contradicted by Conrad if communication had been possible. Garnett immediately registered an emphatic protest,[14] but later critics such as Joseph Warren Beach[15] and Edward Crankshaw[16] applied the term to Conrad, and he is now ensconced in literary history as an impressionist.

Conrad certainly knew something about pictorial and literary impressionism, but the indications are that his reactions were predominantly unfavourable.[17] Conrad's tastes in painting, as in music, were distinctly old-fashioned; he apparently disliked Van Gogh and Cézanne, and the only painter he ever mentioned as a model for his own writing was the peasant realist Jean-François Millet: in a letter to Quiller-Couch, Conrad wrote "it has been my desire to do for seamen what Millet (if I dare pronounce the name of that great man and good artist in this connection) has done for peasants."[18] As to literary impressionism, at the very least Conrad probably read a mildly derogatory article on "The Philosophy of Impressionism," which appeared in *Blackwood's Magazine* in May 1898,[19] and presumably knew Garnett's view of Stephen Crane as an artist of "the surfaces of life."

Conrad's own references to Crane's impressionism suggest that he shared Garnett's unsympathetic view of it. Thus, speaking of Crane's story, "The Open Boat," Conrad writes: "He is *the only* impressionist and *only* an impressionist" (*E G*, 107). This was in 1897, and Conrad's sense of the limitations of impressionism apparently hardened later; thus in 1900 he praised the "focus" of some Cunninghame Graham sketches, and added: "They are much more of course than mere Crane-like impressionism" (*C G*, 130). Conrad was to pay much more favourable public tributes to Crane later; but his early private comments make it clear that, much like Garnett, he thought of impressionism as primarily concerned with visual appearances. This is confirmed by Conrad's usage of the term in *The Mirror of the Sea* (1906). He writes there of a sailor asking "in impressionistic phrase: 'How does the cable grow?'" (21); here "impressionistic" can only mean describing how things look as opposed to stating what is "really happening."

14. *Nation and Athenaeum* 36 (1924), 366–68.

15. In *The Twentieth-Century Novel* (New York, 1932), Conrad and Lawrence are categorised under Impressionism; Joyce comes under Post-Impressionism, Virginia Woolf under Expressionism.

16. Crankshaw writes: "The label will do as well as any other" (*Joseph Conrad*, p. 9).

17. Conrad visited Marguerite Poradowska in the Paris apartment of her cousin, Dr. Paul Gachet, close friend of Van Gogh and Cézanne, and found his collection "nightmarish" (*R R*, 87).

18. Zdzisław Najder, "Joseph Conrad: A Selection of Unknown Letters," *Polish Perspectives* 13 (1970): 32.

19. By C. F. Keary, no. 991, pp. 630–36.

Perhaps the most distinctive quality of Conrad's own writing, like Crane's and unlike Ford's, is its strong visual sense; and Conrad's insistence in the preface to *The Nigger of the "Narcissus"* that art depends for its success on an "impression conveyed through the senses," is to that extent wholly consistent with impressionist doctrine. So, indeed, is much of the narrative itself, whose technique constitutes an original kind of multiple visual impressionism. This was immediately recognized by Arnold Bennett when he read *The Nigger of the "Narcissus";* he wrote admiringly to H. G. Wells in 1897 asking: "Where did the man pick up . . . that *synthetic* way of gathering up a general impression and flinging it at you?" (*S C H,* 82).

Heart of Darkness is essentially impressionist in one very special and yet general way: it accepts, and indeed in its very form asserts, the bounded and ambiguous nature of individual understanding; and because the understanding sought is of an inward and experiential kind, we can describe the basis of its narrative method as subjective moral impressionism. Marlow's story explores how one individual's knowledge of another can mysteriously change the way in which he sees the world as a whole, and the form of *Heart of Darkness* proposes that so ambitious an enterprise can only be begun through one man trying to express his most inward impressions of how deeply problematic is the quest for—to use Pater's terms—"an outer world, and of other minds." There is a certain kinship between the protagonist of Pater's *Marius the Epicurean* (1885) and Marlow, who comes to believe something fairly close to the "sceptical argument" of Marius; since "we are never to get beyond the walls of this closely shut cell of one's own personality," it follows that "the ideas we are somehow impelled to form of an outer world, and of other minds akin to our own, are, it may be, but a day dream."[20] *Heart of Darkness* embodies more thoroughly than any previous fiction the posture of uncertainty and doubt; one of Marlow's functions is to represent how much a man cannot know; and he assumes that reality is essentially private and individual—work, he comments, gives you "the chance to find yourself. Your own reality—for yourself, not for others—what no other man can ever know. They can only see the mere show, and never can tell what it really means" (85).

The other most distinctively impressionist aspect of Conrad's narrative method concerns his approach to visual description; and this preoccupation with the problematic relation of individual sense impressions to meaning is shown most clearly in one of the minor innovations of his narrative technique.

20. Pater, *Marius the Epicurean,* pp. 106, 110.

Long before *Heart of Darkness* Conrad seems to have been trying to find ways of giving direct narrative expression to the way in which the consciousness elicits meaning from its perceptions. One of the devices that he hit on was to present a sense impression and to withhold naming it or explaining its meaning until later; as readers we witness every step by which the gap between the individual perception and its cause is belatedly closed within the consciousness of the protagonist.

In both "The Idiots" and "An Outpost of Progress" the climax of the story is presented in this way. Thus in "The Idiots," when Susan Bacadou jumps over the edge of the cliffs to her death, a seaweed-gatherer merely sees that she "at once vanished before his eyes, as if the islet itself had swerved aside from under her feet" (*T U*, 84). This takes us directly into the observer's consciousness at the very moment of the perception, before it has been translated into its cause, into the term death or suicide, which make the sense-events of the outside world intelligible and communicable to the observer.

There is a much more elaborate version of this device in "An Outpost of Progress." Kayerts, terrified by the delusion that Carlier is coming to shoot him, suddenly hears

> the other push his chair back; and he leaped to his feet with extreme facility. He listened and got confused. Must run again! Right or left? He heard footsteps. He darted to the left, grasping his revolver, and at the very same instant, as it seemed to him, they came into violent collision. Both shouted with surprise. A loud explosion took place between them; a roar of red fire, thick smoke; and Kayerts, deafened and blinded, rushed back thinking: I am hit—it's all over. He expected the other to come round—to gloat over his agony. He caught hold of an upright of the roof—"All over!" Then he heard a crashing fall on the other side of the house, as if somebody had tumbled headlong over a chair—then silence. Nothing more happened. He did not die (112–13).

Persuaded that Carlier is still stalking him, Kayerts finally decides to end his suspense and face his doom: "He turned the corner, steadying himself with one hand on the wall; made a few paces, and nearly swooned. He had seen on the floor, protruding past the other corner, a pair of turned-up feet." Even now Kayerts does not decode the visual signs; and it is only when he sees Carlier's untouched revolver that Kayerts at least realizes that "He had shot an unarmed man."

This narrative device may be termed delayed decoding, since it combines the forward temporal progression of the mind, as it receives messages from the outside world, with the much slower reflexive process of making out their meaning. Through this device—here used somewhat crudely—the reader participates in the instantaneous sensations of Kayerts, and is "made to see" that he is too blinded by terror to know what he has done.

This passage seems to be the fullest example of delayed decoding in Conrad until Marlow's appearance in "Youth." Here is Marlow's description of the final explosion on the *Judea:*

> The carpenter's bench stood abaft the mainmast: I leaned against it sucking at my pipe, and the carpenter, a young chap, came to talk to me. He remarked, "I think we have done very well, haven't we?" and then I perceived with annoyance the fool was trying to tilt the bench. I said curtly, "Don't, Chips," and immediately became aware of a queer sensation, of an absurd delusion,—I seemed somehow to be in the air. I heard all round me like a pent-up breath released—as if a thousand giants simultaneously had said Phoo!—and felt a dull concussion which made my ribs ache suddenly. No doubt about it—I was in the air, and my body was describing a short parabola. But short as it was, I had the time to think several thoughts in, as far as I can remember, the following order: "This can't be the carpenter—What is it?—Some accident— Submarine volcano?—Coals, gas!—By Jove! we are being blown up—Everybody's dead—I am falling into the after-hatch—I see fire in it" (22–23).

The text gives a chronological sequence of momentary sensations in the protagonist's mind; and the reader finds it quite natural that there should be a delay before Marlow's brain finally decodes his impressions into their cause: "We are being blown up." Technically the passage is an improvement on that in "An Outpost of Progress," partly because it is done through concrete impressions of the outside world, and partly because there is nothing arbitrary in our being put into the protagonist's consciousness, since, as was not the case with Kayerts, we are in Marlow's mind throughout. Conrad's mastery of the device is also shown by the way he uses it for a comic effect; the very slowness of the decoding makes us smile at Marlow's impercipience—his initial blaming the carpenter, for instance, and the odd contrast between the pedantic precision of "my body was describing a short parabola" with the wild chaos of what is actually happening.

By the time Conrad came to write *Heart of Darkness,* then, he had developed one narrative technique which was the verbal equivalent of the impressionist painter's attempt to render visual sensation directly. Conrad presented the protagonist's immediate sensations, and thus made the reader aware of the gap between impression and understanding; the delay in bridging the gap enacts the disjunction between the event and the observer's trailing understanding of it. In *Heart of Darkness* Conrad uses the method for the most dramatic action of the story, when Marlow's boat is attacked, just below Kurtz's station. Marlow, terrified of going aground, is anxiously watching the cannibal sounding in the bows just below him: "I was looking down at the sounding-pole, and feeling much annoyed to see at each try a little more of it stick out of that river, when I saw my poleman give up the business suddenly, and stretch himself flat on the deck, without even taking the trouble to haul his pole in" (109).

As in the "Youth" passage, Marlow's initially inexplicable visual impression is accompanied by his irritation at an apparently gratuitous change in the normal order of things. Here, however, the effect is duplicated: "At the same time the fireman, whom I could also see below me, sat down abruptly before his furnace and ducked his head. I was amazed." Only now does the cause of these odd changes in posture begin to emerge: "Then I had to look at the river mighty quick, because there was a snag in the fairway. Sticks, little sticks, were flying about—thick: they were whizzing before my nose, dropping below me, striking behind me against my pilot-house." But it is only when Marlow has finished attending to his duty as captain, and negotiated the next snag, that his understanding can finally decode the little sticks: "We cleared the snag clumsily. Arrows, by Jove! We were being shot at!"

Meanwhile the pilgrims, and, to Marlow's fury, even his helmsman, have started "squirting lead" into the bush. Marlow is navigating and catching occasional glimpses of "vague forms of men" through the shutterhole of the pilot-house, when his attention is suddenly deflected:

> Something big appeared in the air before the shutter, the rifle went overboard, and the man stepped back swiftly, looked at me over his shoulder in an extraordinary, profound, familiar manner, and fell upon my feet. The side of his head hit the wheel twice, and the end of what appeared a long cane clattered round and knocked over a little camp-stool. It looked as though after wrenching that thing from somebody ashore he had lost his balance in the effort. The thin smoke had blown away, we were clear of the snag, and looking ahead I could see that in another hundred yards or so I would be free to sheer off, away from the bank; but my feet felt so warm and wet that I had to look down. The man had rolled on his back and stared straight up at me; both his hands clutched that cane. It was the shaft of a spear . . . He looked at me anxiously, grip-

ping the spear like something precious, with an air of being afraid I would try to take it away from him (111–12).[21]

A third sudden and unfamiliar action is enacted through the protagonist's consciousness, and the delay in his decoding of it makes the reader simultaneously experience horror and sardonic amusement. Amusement, because we feel a certain patronising contempt for those who do not understand things as quickly as we do, and because there is a gruesome comedy in the mere visual impression of the helmsman's "air of being afraid I would try to take [the spear] away from him." This macabre note has already been prepared for: if the poleman lies down, and then the fireman sits down, it is only natural that Marlow should assume that the dead helmsman's recumbent posture must be just a third example of the crew's deserting their duty just for their personal safety.

Still, the passage is obviously not primarily comic. Conrad's main objective is to put us into intense sensory contact with the events; and this objective means that the physical impression must precede the understanding of cause. Literary impressionism implies a field of vision which is not merely limited to the individual observer, but is also controlled by whatever conditions—internal and external—prevail at the moment of observation. In narration the main equivalents to atmospheric interference in painting are the various factors which normally distort human perception, or which delay its recognition of what is most relevant and important. First of all, our minds are usually busy with other things—Marlow has a lot to do just then, and it is only natural that he should be annoyed by being faced with these three new interferences with his task of keeping the boat from disaster. Secondly, our interpretations of impressions are normally distorted by habitual expectations—Marlow perceives the unfamiliar arrows as familiar sticks. Lastly, we always have many more things in our range of vision than we can pay attention to, so that in a crisis we may miss the most important ones—in this case that the helmsman has been killed. Conrad's method reflects all these difficulties in translating perceptions into causal or conceptual terms. This takes us deeply into the connection between delayed decoding and impressionism: it re-

21. Beerbohm hit off Conrad's use of delayed decoding for the climax of his story. The protagonist is "silenced by sight of what seemed to be a young sapling sprung up from the ground within a yard of him—a young sapling tremulous, with a root of steel" (*A Christmas Garland*, London 1950, p. 133). The closest analogy seems to be this passage, although Jocelyn Baines says that "Max Beerbohm based his witty parody of Conrad in *A Christmas Garland*" on "Karain" and "The Lagoon" (*J B*, 190) and Addison C. Bross argues, in "Beerbohm's 'The Feast' and Conrad's Early Fiction," (*Nineteenth-Century Fiction* 26 [1971]: 329–36), for "An Outpost of Progress" as a closer source.

minds us, as Michael Levenson has said, of the precarious nature of the process of interpretation in general; and since this precariousness is particularly evident when the individual's situation or his state of mind is abnormal, the device of delayed decoding simultaneously enacts the objective and the subjective aspects of moments of crisis. The method also has the more obvious advantage of convincing us of the reality of the experience which is being described; there is nothing suspiciously selective about the way it is narrated; while we read we are, as in life, fully engaged in trying to decipher a meaning out of a random and pell-mell bombardment of sense impressions.

The attempt to transcribe the process of individual perception was one of the most widely diffused tendencies in all the arts during the period between 1874, the date of the first Impressionist exhibition in Paris, and 1910, the date of the exhibition of new painting in London for which Roger Fry coined the term Post-Impressionism. Conrad's device of delayed decoding represents an original narrative solution to the general problem of expressing the process whereby the individual's sensations of the external world are registered and translated into the causal and conceptual terms which can make them understandable to the observer and communicable to other people. More generally, Marlow's emphasis on the difficulty of understanding and communicating his own individual experience aligns *Heart of Darkness* with the subjective relativism of the impressionist attitude. Nevertheless, it is very unlikely that Conrad either thought of himself as an impressionist or was significantly influenced by the impressionist movement. Conrad wanted to pay as much attention to the inside as to the outside, to the meaning as to the appearance; and this is one of the reasons why, in the last analysis, he is so different both from the French Impressionists and from Pater, Crane, or Ford.

Behind this difference is another which gives a unique quality to the impressionist elements in Conrad. For Conrad, the world of the senses is not a picture but a presence, a presence so intense, unconditional, and unanswerable that it loses the fugitive, hypothetical, subjective, and primarily aesthetic qualities which it usually has in the impressionist tradition. Ramon Fernandez, in one of the very few indispensable essays on Conrad, remarks that his way of describing the external world is the exact opposite of traditional narrative description such as Balzac's: Conrad's art, he writes, "does not trace the reality before the man, but the man before the reality; it evokes experiences in their subjective entirety because the impression is the equivalent of the entire perception, and because the whole man experiences it with all the powers of his being." Conrad's "great originality," Fernandez concludes, "is to have applied this impressionism to the knowledge of human beings."[22]

(b) *Symbolism*

In the narrator's description of Marlow's unseamanlike conduct as a storyteller, the symbolist aspect derives from the main geometrical feature of the illustration. It is based on the contrasted arrangements of two concentric spheres. In the first arrangement, that of the typical seaman's yarn, the direction given our minds is, to use a term from Newtonian physics, "centripetal": the story, the narrative vehicle, is the shell, the larger outside sphere; it encloses a smaller sphere, the inner kernel of truth; and as readers of the yarn we are invited to seek inside it for this central core of meaning. Marlow's tales, on the other hand, are typically "centrifugal": the relation of the spheres is reversed; now the narrative vehicle is the smaller inside sphere; and its function is merely to make the reader go outside it in search of a circumambient universe of meanings which are not normally visible, but which the story, the glow, dimly illuminates. This subordinate yet necessary role of the story was made even clearer in the manuscript, which included the two phrases here italicised: "the meaning of an episode was not inside like a kernel but outside *in the unseen,* enveloping the tale which *could only bring* it out as a glow brings out a haze."[23]

The outer sphere of larger meaning, then, is presumably infinite, since, unlike the husk of a nut, the haze lacks any ascertainable circumference; but to be visible the haze needs the finite glow; and so the two together constitute a symbol in Carlyle's view of it: "the Infinite is made to blend itself with the Finite, to stand visible, and as it were, attainable there."[24]

When Virginia Woolf speaks of the aim of modern fiction as the expression of life seen as "a luminous halo, a semi-transparent envelope," and proceeds to applaud Conrad for conveying this "unknown and uncircumscribed spirit," her words, like those of Conrad's narrator, suggest an analogy both to Carlyle and to later symbolist theories of literature. But Virginia Woolf's views of modern fiction, as we have seen, are also consistent with the general impressionist position; both her terms and those of Conrad's narrator, in fact, imply

22. "L'Art de Conrad," *Nouvelle Revue française* 12 (1924): 732; conveniently available in English in *The Art of Joseph Conrad,* ed. Robert W. Stallman (East Lansing, Mich., 1960), pp. 8–13.

23. I am indebted to Dave Thorburn, and Marjorie Wynne of the Beinecke Library, for sending me a copy of the holograph.

24. *Sartor Resartus,* Bk. 3, ch. 3, p. 158.

something like a symbiotic relationship between the symbolist and impressionist perspectives.

There is some doubt, however, whether either impressionism or symbolism stand for meanings which are sufficiently clear to be worth using. The case of symbolism is particularly obstinate, because the term is used much more widely, and with less reference to any specific historical movement. The issue can perhaps best be approached by considering two general questions: first, why did no one talk about literature as symbolic until the last century or so? And second, why have so many modern critics assumed that their main task is to find symbolic meanings in whatever literature they find worth discussing?

Historically, the impressionist and symbolist tendencies are alike in being antitraditional assertions of the private individual vision. In this they are essentially reflections of much vaster changes, which first became apparent in the romantic period, and took more urgent forms during the intellectual crisis of the late nineteenth century, a crisis by now most familiar to literary history in its twin manifestations of the death of God and the disappearance of the omniscient author.

In its simplest terms, symbolism involves a process whereby particular objects or events are attributed some larger, nonliteral meaning. This larger meaning is connected to its verbal sign either by arbitrary convention or by a natural extension of its normal properties. The use of the fixed conventional kind of symbolism—the apple of discord, for instance—was hardly a problem before the romantic period, because everything in the outside world was widely agreed to constitute a fixed order, in which each item had its appropriate religious, moral, or social role: the connection between the object and its meaning was public and established—most obviously in mythology and allegory; and the fixed and public quality of these established linkages is indicated by the fact that the earliest sense of the word "symbol" was "a creed or confession of faith" (O E D).

In the romantic period, and by a historical process broadly parallel to that which led to the impressionist effort to render an individual visual representation of the external world, many poets felt impelled to discard symbols of a fixed and conventional kind, and instead to assign their own personal symbolic meanings to natural objects, to mountains, birds and flowers. These meanings began from the properties of the object, but they were often taken further by the writer's imagination.[25] In its extreme form, the correspondence between the

25. In this very summary and simplified account I am particularly indebted to Frank Kermode, *Romantic Image* (London, 1957), M. H. Abrams, *Natural Supernaturalism: Tradition and Revolution in Romantic Literature* (New York, 1971), Marcel Raymond, *De Baudelaire au Surréalisme* (rev. ed., Paris, 1969), and Jean-Jacques Mayoux, *Vivants*

particular, literal object and its imagined symbolic meaning was of a mystical or esoteric kind, as often in Blake; more commonly the meaning, while not hermetic, extended far beyond the inherent representativeness of the object; and that meaning was based on the assumption that the poet had privileged access to previously unknown immanent connections between the external world and spiritual reality.

What the romantic poets and their nineteenth-century successors had in common was a similar reaction to the tendency to identify truth with individual impressions. They found their literary subjects in particular individual experiences, but they sought to go beyond what a mechanistic psychology could deduce, and make us imagine their particular subject as representative of more universal human meanings or spiritual states, as Wordsworth, for instance, makes his leech-gatherer embody Resolution and Independence. Romantic symbolism in general moves from the particular and the transitory towards that larger world of meanings and values which in earlier periods had been ordered and enriched by a common religious, mythological, social, moral, and aesthetic order. This centrifugal direction of romantic poetry—Blake's "To see a world in a grain of sand," for instance—was continued by Baudelaire, who gave historic expression to the idea that the phenomenal world was a mysterious source of larger and quasi-religious symbolic meanings in his poem "Correspondances" (1857):

> La Nature est un temple où de vivants piliers
> Laissent parfois sortir de confuses paroles;
> L'homme y passe à travers des forêts de symboles
> Qui l'observent avec des regards familiers.[26]

Neither Baudelaire, nor the most famous of what have come to be called the French Symbolist poets—Verlaine, Rimbaud and Mallarmé—called themselves Symbolists; nor did the painters, Gustave Moreau (1826–1898), Puvis de Chavannes (1824–1898), and Odilon Redon (1840–1916). The ideas and much of the vocabulary of Symbolism, however, had been worked out long before the movement was named, as it belatedly was in poetry when Jean Moréas wrote his manifesto in 1886, and in painting at the Cafe Volpini exhibition in 1889.[27]

---

piliers: le roman anglo-saxon et les symboles (Paris, 1960). Tzvetan Todorov's comprehensive analysis in *Théories du symbole* (Paris, 1977) appeared too late to be used. Its first six chapters place the changing nature of the symbol during the romantic period in the more general perspective of the breakdown of the Western tradition of rhetoric.

26. Nature is a temple where living pillars occasionally let out confused words; man passes there through forests of symbols that watch him with familiar looks.

27. See Jean Leymarie, *Impressionism*, vol. 2, pp. 86–88, and Guy Michaud, *Message*

It is a rather misleading coincidence that the first Symbolist manifesto should have occurred in the same year as the last Impressionist exhibition, for one movement did not in fact succeed the other. They were contemporary. The leading figures of both came to the fore at the same time in the seventies, had won their battles by the end of the eighties, and were for the most part admiring allies rather than enemies or rivals. Many of their ideas and methods were common property; they agreed in rejecting intellectual conceptualisation and traditional assumptions in the name of a directly apprehended personal and subjective vision; and it was only in their views of what that subjective vision should look for that there was an important theoretical divergence.

The Impressionist painters were not much concerned with thought, apart from some quasi-scientific notions about colour and perception; they were content with the objective world as it appeared, or seemed to appear, to their senses; and their essential aim, to produce a truer pictorial representation of the world's appearances, makes them in this respect the continuers of the realist tradition in painting and literature. Thus the foremost theoretician of Realism, Edmond Duranty, gave an early welcome to Impressionism in his book *La Nouvelle peinture* (1876); while the chief of the Naturalists, Zola, was an admiring friend of the Impressionists, although he thought they should be called *Naturalistes*.[28]

This concern of the Impressionists with the representation of the world as it is actually perceived was not accepted as a primary aim by the Symbolists. They approached their task from the opposite end of the same newly intensified polarity between the individual consciousness and the external world; their overriding objective was to discover the coherent meanings and values for which they inwardly yearned, but which they could not find in external reality. The fundamental intellectual mode of the Symbolists, therefore, was not science and observation but religion and imagination. The world of visible objects was valued only insofar as it offered concrete manifestations which corresponded to spiritual and imaginative meanings. As Jean Moréas wrote, Symbolist poetry "seeks to clothe the Idea in a perceptible form [*forme sensible*], a form, however, which would not be an aim in itself, but which, while being used to express the Idea, would remain secondary to it."[29] This implied movement from the verbal sign to its spiritual idea is necessarily centrifugal; and there is, therefore, a general

poétique du symbolisme (Paris, 1947), pp. 165, 123–24, 143–44.

   28. John Rewald, *History of Impressionism* (New York, 1946), pp. 271–300.

   29. Cited by Franco Russoli, "Images et langages du Symbolisme," in *Le Symbolisme en Europe* (Paris, 1976), p. 17.

analogy between the Symbolist view of literature, and that which Conrad's narrator ascribes to Marlow in *Heart of Darkness.*

In the nineties, England was very much more receptive to foreign literature and philosophy than it had been earlier in the Victorian period;[30] in many circles Mr. Podsnap's "Not British" had become a term, no longer of anathema, but of acclamation. As a result, Symbolism, like Impressionism, was much in the air; and so, quite apart from his own wide reading in French, there can be no doubt that, by the time he wrote *Heart of Darkness,* Conrad could hardly have avoided knowing something about the French Symbolists. Under Verlaine's preferred term of Decadents, for instance, they had recently been the subject of a series of essays by Arthur Symons, which were soon to be collected in his influential *The Symbolist Movement in Literature* in 1899. On the other hand, Conrad was not in general very receptive to poetry; and although he knew Arthur Symons, who had published "The Idiots" in his magazine, the *Savoy,* Conrad apparently disliked being tarred with the decadent brush (*L G,* 18).

It is virtually certain, therefore, that whatever similarities may exist between Conrad and the French Symbolists are not the result of any direct literary influence on Conrad or of his doctrinal adhesion. One can imagine Conrad giving guarded approval only to a part of what W.B. Yeats recalled as the general literary outlook of the contributors to the *Savoy,* among whom he mentioned Conrad by name. Their shared attitude, Yeats wrote in "The Trembling of the Veil," was to argue "something after this fashion: 'Science . . . has won its right to explore whatever passes before its corporeal eye, and merely because it passes. . . . Literature now demands the same right of exploration of all that passes before the mind's eye, and merely because it passes,'" "Merely because it passes" might have drawn a protest from Conrad, and Yeats's ensuing justification of his own attitudes certainly would. Yeats argues that, having been "deprived by Huxley and Tyndall" of a religion, and being consequently possessed by a "conviction that the world was now but a bundle of fragments," it was imperative to restore "Unity of Being" through some spiritual or occult order.[31] Conrad would have laughed scornfully, not at the problem but at the esoteric solutions proposed: his mocking attitude is suggested in a comment on the ideas of Sar Peladan, one of the most committed devotees of the occult among the French Symbolists, whom Conrad found "marvellously and deliciously absurd" (*N L L,* 70).

30. See Christophe Campos, *The View of France: From Arnold to Bloomsbury* (London, 1965), especially pp. 164–73.
31. *Autobiographies* (London, 1955), pp. 325–26; 115; 189; 90.

There is, however, much in Conrad's letters which suggests that he shared many of the basic attitudes of the French Symbolists. These attitudes may be summarily divided into two categories: the ontological—the kinds of basic reality, knowledge, or vision, which literature seeks beyond the "bundle of fragments" offered by the external world; and the expressive—the characteristic formal methods by which the reader is induced to seek this vision beyond the work's overt statements.

Believing, with Rimbaud in "Soleil et Chair," that "notre pâle raison nous cache l'infini," the Symbolists commonly expressed their ontological concern by adopting as practices, subjects, or metaphors, those modes of perception which are the most opposed to rational observation or analysis—notably dreams, drug-induced hallucinations, and occult rituals. These, together with less extreme forms of intuition or imagination, were used as ways in which the spiritual order thought to subsist beneath or beyond surface appearances could be apprehended or made manifest. The basic analogy is that of the Platonic search beyond the transient inadequacies of the phenomenal world for the ultimate changeless ideas; and this analogy is present in some of Conrad's statements about his larger artistic aims. Thus in a letter of 27 January 1897, he wrote that in The Nigger of the "Narcissus" he had "tried to get through the veil of details at the essence of life" (L L, I, 200). The metaphor of the "veil" here is reminiscent, not only of much esoteric symbolist doctrine during the period, but also of the thought of one of its main philosophic sources, Schopenhauer. He habitually called the objective world Maya, the term for the world's "illusion of multiplicity" in Hinduism, and taught that through detached contemplation the individual could penetrate the veil of Maya and discover that "there is really *only one being*."[32]

Conrad thought along somewhat similar lines, except that for him the "essence of life" remained much more irreducibly plural, public, and contingent than it was for Plato or Schopenhauer. When an influential critic, W. L. Courtney, reviewed The Nigger of the "Narcissus" somewhat impercipiently, Conrad objected in terms that combine impressionist and symbolist attitudes. Denying the influence of "formulas and theories," and specifically disclaiming "all allegiance to realism, to naturalism," Conrad asserted that he wrote "straight from the heart," in an attempt "to give a true impression"; but he then went on to confess "that I also wanted to connect the small world of the ship

---

32. *World as Will and Representation*, vol. 2, p. 321.

with that larger world carrying perplexities, fears, affections, rebellions, in a loneliness greater than that of the ship at sea."[33]

In this attempt to connect the literal objects of his narrative with a "larger world" conceived at a rather high level of abstraction, Conrad is in general accord with the symbolist ontology; as regards expressive technique the parallels are somewhat closer. Several have already been noted—the yearning for the "magic suggestiveness of music" for instance, a priority which echoes Verlaine's "De la musique avant toute chose" in his "Art poétique." Conrad also often speaks of the mysteriously evocative power of words with an emphasis somewhat reminiscent of Mallarmé. Thus in November 1898, just before starting *Heart of Darkness*, he wrote "How fine it could be . . . if the idea had a substance and words a magic power, if the invisible could be snared into a shape" (*J B*, 223). It sounds like a Symbolist prayer; and in a letter of 9 October 1899 to Hugh Clifford, Conrad clarified his views on the evocative role of words. "Words," he wrote, "groups of words, words standing alone, are symbols of life, have the power in their sound or their aspect to present the very thing you wish to hold up before the mental vision of your readers" (*L L*, I, 280). Conrad was to retain this view of the quasi-magical power of words; in 1911 he wrote to an Italian admirer about his "ineradicable conviction that it is in the living word *que l'on saisit le mieux la forme du rêve*" [that one best captures the shape of the dream].[34]

Conrad, then, sometimes spoke about his larger creative aspirations in terms which recall those which Mallarmé used to summarise the poetic aims of the Symbolists: "*Nommer* un objet, c'est supprimer les trois quarts de la jouissance du poëme qui est faite de deviner peu à peu: le *suggérer*, voilà le rêve. C'est le parfait usage de ce mystere qui constitue le symbole."[35] Throughout his career Conrad retained the general aim of making the work suggest much more than it overtly

33. Cited from David R. Smith, " 'One Word More' about *The Nigger of the 'Narcissus,'*" *Nineteenth-Century Fiction* 23 (1968): 208–9. Smith shows how the general argument of the letter closely follows the preface to *The Nigger of the "Narcissus"*, but adds to it "about as clear a statement of his symbolic intent as [Conrad] ever made" (210). Conrad's letter went on to give his aim a Schopenhauerian note with the comment: "There is joy and sorrow; there is sunshine and darkness—and all are within the same eternal smile of the inscrutable Maya."

34. Carlo Angeleri, "Joseph Conrad: Una Lettera Inedita a Carlo Placci," *Paragone* 8 (1957): 55–58.

35. Stéphane Mallarmé, *Oeuvres complètes* (Paris, 1945), p. 869. "To *name* the object is to destroy three quarters of the enjoyment of the poem, which comes from guessing at it bit by bit: to *suggest* the object, that is the dream. It is the perfect practice of this mystery which constitutes the symbol." Conrad's relation to the symbolists, and much else, receives full and illuminating treatment in Donald C. Yelton's *Mimesis and Metaphor: An Inquiry into the Genesis and Scope of Conrad's Symbolic Imagery* (The Hague, 1967), especially pp. 28–67.

embodies; thus in 1914 he wrote: "It is a strange fate that everything that I have, of set artistic purpose, laboured to leave indefinite, suggestive, in the penumbra of initial inspiration, should have that light turned on to it and its insignificance (as compared with, I might say without megalomania, the ampleness of my conceptions) exposed for any fool to comment upon or even for average minds to be disappointed with" (R C, 142).

The parallels between Conrad's basic assumptions and those of the French Symbolists could be expanded and qualified; but the great diversity in the works and doctrines of the French Symbolists,[36] and Conrad's own reluctance to theorise, make it unlikely that a fuller analysis could go very much beyond the analogies which have already been advanced. The problems of how far, and in what senses, Conrad's fiction is symbolic, can perhaps be seen in somewhat more concrete terms by considering the role of Symbolism in the particular case of prose fiction.

There is a loose but demonstrable kinship among the works produced by the main Symbolist poets in France during the seventies and eighties; but it seems distinctly less helpful to talk about a symbolist movement in the novel. For one thing, only a single example, J. K. Huysmans's A Rebours (1884), comes readily to mind; and this being so, the Symbolist elements in Heart of Darkness can hardly be determined before first establishing its relationship to two earlier traditions in the fictional use of symbolism; there is the increasingly conscious, ambitious, and systematic use of symbolism in narrative during the nineteenth century; and there is also a minor tradition of what can be called the symbolic novel which began in the romantic period. Heart of Darkness reflects both these developments.

The commonest critical use of the term symbolic merely means that a particular act, character, or object is typical or representative. Balzac, for instance, had made particular clothes, furniture, and houses stand for the individual and social values with which his novels were concerned. Later, and as a result of the nineteenth-century novel's increasing self-consciousness as regards form, there was a tendency to make every narrative element, and especially the description of the external world, contribute to the significance of the novel as a whole. The fog in Bleak House obviously refers to much more than the London climate; it also stands for the blind and shapeless muddle of the law, and that of the society to which it belongs. This extension

36. See Kenneth Cornell, The Symbolist Movement (New Haven, 1951), especially the summary on pp. 195–200.

of symbolic meaning is still "natural," still inherent in the literal object; common experience has established "fog" as a mental as well as a physical metaphor; and Dickens's symbol is essentially centripetal because it leads us back into the central issues of the novel, and does not impel our imagination to look behind it for some immanent spiritual truth in the universe at large.

There is one tradition of fiction where the central symbol is more autonomous, and stands for a larger idea—the narrative of the symbolic quest. It is common enough in the romance, from the classical period, with the *Argonautica* of Apollonius Rhodius, to the medieval, with the Arthurian stories of the Holy Grail, and the renaissance, with *The Faerie Queene*. In all of these, however, the meaning of the symbolic object sought is quite clearly defined, and its great value is agreed on by the society at large. It was only in the romantic period that the quest plot turned on a central symbol which was both problematic and multiple in its meaning. The prime example is *Heinrich von Ofterdingen* (1799; trans. 1842), an unfinished poetic novel by Novalis, which deals with the search by the hero, named after a German *minnesinger* of the Middle Ages, for a certain blue flower.[37] It is, then, a quest for an object which, unlike the Golden Fleece, would hardly be sought for its literal value in the real world; the quest for the blue flower can only be a quest for what it symbolises. Just what that may be is not very clear, but it is commonly agreed to stand for many things, including ideal love, reality, the magical power of the poetic imagination, and that all-encompassing unifying principle of the universe which was sought both by the romantics and the symbolists.[38]

Novalis was immensely influential in the nineteenth century, particularly towards its close and among the symbolists; but *Heinrich von Ofterdingen* had no direct successors. The closest analogue is probably a play, Maurice Maeterlinck's *The Blue Bird (1909);* and in prose fiction many examples of the symbolic quest, such as *Sartor Resartus* or *Marius the Epicurean*, have tended to make the exceptions; the most famous of them, *Moby Dick* and *Heart of Darkness*, have two important features in common: they do not subordinate everything to the hero's quest; and the symbolic objects which the protagonists seek—the whale or Kurtz—are both dangerous and ambiguous.

Heart of Darkness, then, belongs to a specifically symbolic tradition of fiction, and it is the only one of Conrad's novels which does. As to his

37. For a brief account, see Abrams, *Natural Supernaturalism*, pp. 249–52.
38. Novalis's blue flower became the generally accepted romantic symbol of the ideal (Jutta Hecker, *Das Symbol der Blauen Blume im Zusammenhang mit der Blumensymbolik der Romantik* [Jena, 1931]); and Conrad uses the phrase—"the little blue flower of sentiment"—in his preface to *The Nature of a Crime* (London, 1924), p. 6.

theoretical position on the symbolic nature of the novel, and on the French Symbolists, Conrad expressed himself most directly, though not unambiguously, in a letter of 1918. In answer to a critic who had written to him about the "final effect" of a work of art, Conrad maintained the general position that "All the great creations of literature have been symbolic." "A work of art," he explained, "is very seldom limited to one exclusive meaning and not necessarily tending to a definite conclusion. And this for the reason that the nearer it approaches art, the more it acquires a symbolic character. This statement may surprise you, who may imagine that I am alluding to the Symbolist School of poets or prose writers. Theirs, however, is only a literary proceeding against which I have nothing to say. I am concerned here with something much larger" (*L L,* II, 205).

Conrad casually dissociates himself from the French Symbolists, not in order to say anything against their "literary proceedings," but to affirm a "much larger" view: that great works of art do not necessarily "tend to definite conclusions"; and that the extent of their "symbolic character" is directly proportional to the quality of their art.

It is possible that Conrad's use of the word symbolic here may mean no more than that in the greatest works of literature the characters and their destinies stand for much more than their particular selves and actions, and are representative of more universal feelings and situations. This would be a variant of the commonest usage of "symbolic" as meaning "widely representative"; and it would then carry the idea that all the components of the novel should have wider and more general implications. But Conrad seems to be implying something more: only a larger meaning for symbolic, surely, would justify his assumption that his statement may be found "surprising"; and the essence of his statement is presumably that the quality of art is proportional to its range of symbolic meanings. Such a view, of course, would be consistent both with the image of the glow and the haze, and with the general intention of the French Symbolists. But Conrad's letter is sufficiently obscure to allow of some doubt; and so as regards *Heart of Darkness,* the only real test must be that of its actual narrative practice. One passage, whose symbolism has been given conflicting interpretations, seems especially appropriate.

On his way to receive his appointment from the trading company, Marlow goes through

> A narrow and deserted street in deep shadow, high houses, innumerable windows with venetian blinds, a dead silence, grass sprouting between the stones, imposing carriage archways right and left, immense double doors standing ponder-

ously ajar. I slipped through one of these cracks, went up a swept and ungarnished staircase, as arid as a desert, and opened the first door I came to. Two women, one fat and the other slim, sat on straw-bottomed chairs, knitting black wool. The slim one got up and walked straight at me—still knitting with down-cast eyes—and only just as I began to think of getting out of her way, as you would for a somnambulist, stood still, and looked up. Her dress was as plain as an umbrella-cover, and she turned round without a word and preceded me into a waiting-room. I gave my name, and looked about (55).

Marlow is ushered into the presence of the director, and then

In about forty-five seconds I found myself again in the waiting room with the compassionate secretary, who, full of desolation and sympathy, made me sign some document. I believe I undertook amongst other things not to disclose any trade secrets. Well, I am not going to.

I began to feel slightly uneasy. You know I am not used to such ceremonies, and there was something ominous in the atmosphere. It was just as though I had been let into some conspiracy—I don't know—something not quite right; and I was glad to get out. In the outer room the two women knitted black wool feverishly. People were arriving, and the younger one was walking back and forth introducing them. The old one sat on her chair. Her flat cloth slippers were propped up on a foot-warmer, and a cat reposed on her lap. She wore a starched white affair on her head, had a wart on one cheek, and silver-rimmed spectacles hung on the tip of her nose. She glanced at me above the glasses. The swift and indifferent placidity of that look troubled me. Two youths with foolish and cheery countenances were being piloted over, and she threw at them the same quick glance of unconcerned wisdom. She seemed to know all about them and about me, too. An eerie feeling came over me. She seemed uncanny and fateful. Often far away there I thought of these two, guarding the door of Darkness, knitting black wool as for a warm pall, one introducing, introducing continuously to the unknown, the other scrutinizing the cheery and foolish faces with unconcerned old eyes. *Ave!* Old knitter of black wool. *Morituri te salutant.* Not many of those she looked at ever saw her again—not half, by a long way (56–57).

Several critics have made the two knitters a primary basis for a large-scale symbolic interpretation of *Heart of Darkness* in which Marlow's whole journey becomes a version of the traditional descent into hell, such as that in the sixth book of Virgil's *Aeneid*,[39] and in Dante's *Inferno*. This kind of critical interpretation assumes that the symbolic reference of the verbal sign must be closed rather than open, and that it arises, not from the natural and inherent associations of the object, but from a preestablished body of ideas, stories, or myths. The present passage certainly makes symbolic reference to associations of this kind; Marlow presents his own experience in the general perspective of the pagan and Christian traditions of a journey to the underworld: this is made sufficiently explicit when he talks of the knitters "guarding the door of Darkness," and of the two youths "being piloted over." But this is not the only symbolic reference of the passage, nor the most important; and there is no reason to assume that the movement from the literal to the symbolic must be centripetal. Only some such assumption could have impelled one critic to assert that there is a "close structural parallel between *Heart of Darkness* and the *Inferno*," and proceed to equate the company station with Limbo and the central station with the abode of the fraudulent, while making Kurtz both a "traitor to kindred" and a Lucifer.[40]

One obvious practical objection to this kind of symbolic interpretation is that it alerts our attention too exclusively to a few aspects of the narrative—to those which seem to provide clues that fit the assumed unitary and quasi-allegorical frame of symbolic reference. This leads us to interrogate the text only in those terms, and to ask such questions as: Why does Conrad give us only *two* fates? Which one is Clotho the spinner? and which Lachesis the weaver? Did the Greeks know about knitting anyway? Where are the shears? What symbolic meaning can there be in the fact that the thin one lets people *in* to the room and then *out* again—a birth and death ritual, perhaps? Lost in such unfruitful preoccupations, our imaginations will hardly be able to respond to the many other symbolic clues in the passage, or even to the many other meanings in those details which have secured our attention.

In fact a multiplicity of historical and literary associations pervades the scene in the anteroom; and this multiplicity surely combines to place the two knitters in a much more universal perspective. There is, most obviously, the heartless unconcern manifested throughout the ages by the spectators at a variety of ordeals that are dangerous or fatal to the protagonists. This unconcern is what the fates have in common with the two other main historical parallels evoked in the

---

39. Lillian Feder, "Marlow's Descent into Hell," *Nineteenth-Century Fiction* 9 (1955): 280–92.

40. Robert O. Evans, "Conrad's Underworld," *Modern Fiction Studies* 2 (1956): 59; 60.

passage—the French *tricoteuses* callously knitting at the guillotine, and the Roman crowds to whom the gladiators address their scornful farewell in Marlow's rather pretentious interjection: "*Ave!* Old knitter of black wool, *Morituri te salutant.*"

Within the context of *Heart of Darkness* as a whole the function of these three examples of symbolic reference is local and circumscribed; like Marlow's earlier historical allusions to Drake and Franklin they are dropped as soon as made; they are not intended to link up with other allusions into a single cryptographic system which gives the main symbolic meaning of the work as a whole. One reason for this is surely that any continuing symbolic parallel would undermine the literal interest and significance of the narrative at every compositional level, from the essential conflict of the plot, to the details of its narrative presentation.

The present passage, then, gives clear evidence of how Conrad aimed at a continuous immediacy of detail which had symbolic reference that was primarily of a natural, open, and multivocal kind. Marlow presents a highly selective but vivid series of details; they are for the most part given as raw and unexplained observations, and the autonomy and isolation of each particular image seems to impel the reader to larger surmise. There is, for instance, the approach of the thin knitter who "got up and walked straight at me—still knitting with downcast eyes—and only just as I began to think of getting out of her way, as you would for a somnambulist, stood still, and looked up. Her dress was as plain as an umbrella-cover."

If we submit ourselves to the evocative particularity of these intensely visualised details, their symbolic connotations take us far beyond our primary sense of the fateful, uncanny, and impassive atmosphere of the scene; we are driven to a larger awareness of a rigid, mechanical, blind, and automatised world. If we attempt to explain the sources of this awareness we can point to the way that the thin knitter does not speak to Marlow, nor even, apparently, see him; her movements are unrelated to other human beings. The knitter's appearance increases this sense of the nonhuman; her shape recalls an umbrella and its tight black cover; there has been no effort to soften the functional contours of its hard and narrow ugliness with rhythmic movements, rounded forms, or pleasing colours. It is not that the knitter reminds us of the classical Fates which really matters, but that she is herself a fate—a dehumanised death in life to herself and to others, and thus a prefiguring symbol of what the trading company does to its creatures.

Some of the images in the passage are representative in a limited and mainly pictorial way; the older knitter, for example, with her wart and her flat cloth slippers, becomes a stark visual image of physical and spiritual deformity combined with imperturbable self-complacence. But there is another, larger, and to some extent contrary, tendency, where the extreme selectivity of Marlow's memory draws our attention to his state of mind at the time. For instance, when Marlow comments about the tycoon: "He shook hands I fancy," his uncertainty suggests that his consciousness was occupied with other matters. Marlow omits much that would certainly be mentioned in an autobiography, or a naturalist novel; we are not, for instance, given the details of Marlow's contract, or the name of the people. This omission of proper names is a particularly typical symbolist procedure—in Maeterlinck, for instance, or in Kafka. The general reason for the strategy is clear: most of the details about the narrative object are omitted, so that what details remain, liberated from the bonds and irrelevancies of the purely circumstantial and contingent, can be recognised as representatives of larger ideas and attitudes.

Marlow despecifies the tycoon to reveal his essence; he calls him merely a "pale plumpness" because big bureaucrats typically eat too much, don't exercise outdoors, are featureless and somewhat abstract. But there is another essence involved in the situation; if Marlow so often despecifies the external and the factual aspects of the scene, it is because his own hierarchy of attention at the time was primarily internal and moral; what Marlow was actually registering with benumbed incredulity was his spiritual reaction to being initiated into the most universal and fateful of modern society's rites of passage—the process whereby the individual confronts a vast bureaucracy to get a job from it.

Marlow begins his rite of passage with a representative ecological sequence: approach through unfamiliar streets and arid staircases; passive marshalling from waiting room to grand managerial sanctum; and, forty-five seconds later, a more rapid return thence through the same stages, with a delayed and demoralising detour for medical examination. The sequence of routinised human contacts is equally typical: the impassive receptionists; the expert compassion of the confidential secretary; the hollow benevolence of the plump tycoon; the shifty joviality of the clerk; and the hypocritical pretences of the medical examiner.

Marlow registers but rarely comments; and we are thus left free to draw our deductions about the symbolic meanings of the passage. They are multiple, and they are not expounded but suggested; consequently our interpretative priorities will depend on our literary imagination as readers, and on our own way of conceiving reality.

One possible direction of larger symbolic reference concerns the implicit view of civilisation suggested in the passage. Some of the details of the scene suggest the way Marx saw one result of modern capitalism as the turning of people into mere objects in a system of economic relations; human beings become things and so their personal relationships take on a "spectral objectivity."[41] This interpretation is also consistent with Max Weber's related view that modern bureaucratic administration brings with it "the dominance of a spirit of formalistic impersonality."[42] Since both these interpretations find some support in the literal meanings of the passage, as well as in other parts of *Heart of Darkness*, they can reasonably be regarded as tributes to Conrad's power not only to penetrate the essential moral meaning of the institutions of the modern world, but to communicate that meaning symbolically.

The passage also implies a good deal about the unspoken subjective meaning of the ordeal for Marlow. When the scene ends we can look back and see that Marlow is left with a sense of a doubly fraudulent initiation: the company has not told him what he wants to know; but since Marlow has been unable to formulate the causes of his moral discomfort, much less ask any authentic question or voice any protest, his own tranced submission has been a betrayal of himself. These implications prefigure what we are to see as one of the larger and more abstract themes of the story—the lack of any genuinely reciprocal dialogue; even Marlow cannot or does not speak out. In this passage, for instance, Marlow's most extended dialogue at the company's offices is with the doctor. In part it merely typifies this particular aspect of bureaucratic initiation: the formulaic insult ("Ever any madness in your family?" [58]); the posture of disinterested devotion to scientific knowledge (measuring Marlow's cranium); and the pretendedly benevolent but actually both impractical and deeply disquieting counsel ("Avoid irritation more than exposure to the sun"). Such details might be said to operate partly in a centripetal way, since they point to specific later issues in the narrative—to Kurtz's skull and those on his fenceposts, and to the physical and mental collapse of Kurtz and Marlow at the end; but the details also have larger and more expansive centrifugal overtones. The horrors of the modern secular hell are not merely the affronting mumbo-jumbo of the medical priesthood; Marlow has illumined the haze which hangs like a pall over the society of which the doctor, the clerk, the knitters and the

41. The phrase, "gespenstische Gegenständlichkeit," is that of Georg Lukács (*Existentialismus oder Marxismus?* [Berlin, 1951]), p. 41, summarising one aspect of Marx's view of reification.

42. Max Weber, *The Theory of Social and Economic Organisation*, trans. A. M. Henderson and Talcott Parsons (New York, 1947), p. 340.

pale plumpness are the symbolic representatives; and we are led outwards to discern the ramifying absences of human communion.

We are left with an overpowering sense of Marlow's fateful induc-
tion into the vast overarching network of the silent lies of civilisation.
No one will explain them—not the servants of the company certainly,
if only because the jobs of the personnel depend on their discretion;
the great corporate enterprise has no voice, yet Marlow cannot help
attributing moral meanings and intentions to all the tangible manifestations of the power which controls his life.

The absence of shared understanding exists at an even higher level
of abstraction. Marlow hardly knows the meaning of what is happening to him; there is no Virgil in sight, much less a Beatrice; and no one
even seems aware that the problem exists. Later the narrative reveals
that this gap extends throughout Marlow's world; we go from the
silent, lethal madness of the trading company to that of the civilisation
for which it stands; Marlow is confronting a general intellectual and
moral impasse whose narrative climax is enacted when he is forced to
lie to the Intended; and this gap, in turn, can be seen in a wider
historical and philosophical perspective as a reflection of the same
breakdown of the shared categories of understanding and judgment,
as had originally imposed on Conrad and many of his contemporaries
the indirect, subjective, and guarded strategies that characterised the
expressive modes of Symbolism.

One could argue that the distinctive aim, not only of Conrad but of
much modern literature, is not so much "to make us see," but, somewhat more explicitly, "to make us see what we see"; and this would
ultimately involve a view of narrative in which every detail is inherently symbolic. The reader and the critic of such literature, therefore,
must assume that since each individual text generates its own symbolic
meaning, only a primary commitment to the literal imagination will
enable him to see the larger implications of all the particularities
which confront him. Thus in the present scene the knitters suggest
many ideas which are essentially generalised forms of the literal or
inherent qualities which Marlow has recorded; and each of these
symbolic meanings can in turn be extended in a centrifugal way to a
larger understanding of the world Conrad presents. The opposite
kind of critical reading starts from an esoteric interpretation of particular objects—the knitters are "really" the fates—and combines
them into a centripetal and cryptographic interpretation which is
based, as in allegory, on a single and defined system of beliefs, and is
largely independent of the literal meanings of the details presented
and of their narrative context. But the primary narrator's image has
warned us against proceeding as though there is a single edible kernel

of truth hidden below the surface; and it is surely curious, even sad-
dening, to reflect that, out of the dozen or more studies of the scene
with the knitters, none has interpreted it as part of a larger symbolic
vision of the great corporation and its civilisation.

The modern critical tendency to decompose literary works into a
series of more or less cryptic references to a system of non-literal
unifying meanings is in large part a misguided response to a very real
problem in the interpretation of much modern literature.

Many of the characteristics of that literature can be seen as the
result of the convergence of the symbolist and impressionist
traditions. The two movements were largely parallel manifestations in
the *avant garde* ferment which affected all the arts during the last
three decades of the nineteenth century; and this fusion of the
impressionist and symbolist tendencies continued into the twentieth
century. The Imagist movement, for instance, is primarily a development of the impressionist tendency, as Ford's connection with it suggests, but Imagism also had strong ties with the English symbolist
poets. In his 1913 Imagist Manifesto, Ezra Pound, who was in part
reacting against what he considered the vagueness of both impressionist and symbolist art, nevertheless telescoped the primary emphases of both tendencies when he defined his literary objective, the
image, as "that which presents an intellectual and emotional complex
in an instant of time," and went on to make the ringing polemic
affirmation "the natural object is always the *adequate* symbol."[43]

Pound's dual principles suggest how the impressionist and symbolist emphases combined to form the basis of the characteristic expressive idiom not only of modern poetry but of modern narrative
prose. The same two emphases, for example, underlie Marvin Mudrick's almost pardonable hyperbole that "After *Heart of Darkness,* the
recorded moment—the word—was irrecoverably symbol."[44] "The
recorded moment," with its emphasis on immediate sensation, is
primarily impressionist, and so is Mudrick's subsequent analysis of
how Conrad developed "the moral resources inherent in every recorded sensation."

The need to derive moral meaning from physical sensation partly
arises from the fact that both the impressionists and the symbolists, as
has already been noted, proscribed any analysis, prejudgment, or
conceptual commentary—the images, events, and feelings were to be

43. "A Stray Document," in *Make It New: Essays* (London, 1934), pp. 336–37. On
Pound's view of the relationship of imagism to impressionism, see Herbert N.
Schneidau, *Ezra Pound: The Image and the Real* (Baton Rouge, La., 1969), pp. 34–35.
44. "The Originality of Conrad," *Hudson Review* 11 (1958): 553.

left to speak for themselves. This laid a particular burden on the writer's power of expression, since his objects alone had to carry a rich burden of suggested autonomous meanings. The symbolist method therefore begins by making the same descriptive demand as that of impressionism: the writer must render the object with an idiosyncratic immediacy of vision, which is freed from any intellectual prejudgment or explanatory gloss; and the reader must be put in the posture of actively seeking to fill the gaps in a text which has provoked him to experience an absence of connecting meanings.

One way of doing this is to make the poem or the novel put the reader in the presence of an unfamiliar and inexplicable hierarchy of intense literary attention; for instance, it is the emphasis on some details and the absence of others which make it clear that the swans in Mallarmé's "Le vierge, le vivace et le bel aujourd'hui" or Yeats's "The Wild Swans at Coole" are presented not for their ornithological or autobiographical interest, but for some other purpose, some larger complex of connecting values and meanings. These values and meanings are not stated, but only the hypothesis of their hidden presence could explain the special emphases and unexplained transitions with which the writers' perceptions are conveyed; the obtrusive disparity between a particular image and the significance apparently attributed to it by the writer creates an insistent semantic gap, which the reader feels called upon to fill with his own symbolic interpretation.

There has presumably always been some gap between the verbal sign and its meaning; but the gap is much more obtrusive in the literature of the twentieth century. The expressive idiom of modern writing in general is characterised by an insistent separateness between the particular items of experience presented and the reader's need to generate larger connecting meanings out of them. This semantic gap does much to explain the importance and the difficulty of the modern role of the literary critic. He is faced with the task of explaining to the public in discursive expository prose a literature whose expressive idiom was intended to be inaccessible to exposition in any conceptual terms. He confronts an incompleteness of utterance, an indeterminacy of meaning, a seemingly unconscious or random association of images, which simultaneously demand and defy exegesis. In the fiction whose primary allegiance is to the impressionist tradition, such as that of Hemingway, for instance, the idiosyncratic sequence of apparently unconnected particularities in the narrative asks to be construed and translated into the realm of public discourse; but once translated into that expository language not much is left, and its residue of general meaning is likely, in the critic's rendition of it, to seem both meagre and ambiguous. The difficulty is similar but even greater for writing with stronger symbolist allegiances; it requires the critic, not only to supply physical causes or psychological motives, but to deduce some larger pattern of significance from the unstated implications of each literal detail. Having been solicited by history into donning the robes of the romantic seer, it is to be expected that the modern critic finds it easy to succumb to the temptation of discovering hidden allegorical configurations, thereby laying himself open to the charge of excessive abstraction or extravagant symbol-hunting.

If Conrad belongs to the symbolist tradition it is only in a limited, eclectic, and highly idiosyncratic way; even if one accepts in some very general sense the view that modern literature is mainly a continuation of the symbolist tradition,[45] and waives the until now insuperable difficulties of definition,[46] there seems little to be gained by categorising Conrad, along with Proust, Kafka, Joyce, Mann, and Faulkner, as a symbolist novelist,[47] especially if this is taken to involve dissociating him from the impressionist tradition to which he is more commonly assigned. The particular case of *Heart of Darkness*, however, is somewhat different; its narrative technique in most respects typifies, and indeed anticipates, the general expressive idiom of modern literature; but its plot, its themes, and some of the evidence about its intentions are closer to some of the central features of the French symbolist movement than any of Conrad's other works.

Its plot contains some very untypical elements of adventure and melodrama, but it is nevertheless based on a simple symbolic quest, in which the various forms of "darkness" which Marlow encounters have as many possible meanings as the blue flower in Novalis. The essence of the action is a process of expanded moral awareness; as Marlow says, his journey was significant only because it "seemed somehow to throw a kind of light on everything about me—and into my thoughts" (51).

The structure of *Heart of Darkness* is very largely based on naturally symbolic actions and objects: the plot—a journey, a death, and a

45. Influentially propounded by Edmund Wilson in *Axel's Castle: A Study of the Imaginative Literature of 1870–1930* (New York, 1931).

46. In his *The Symbolist Aesthetic in France: 1885–1895*, 2nd ed. (Oxford, 1968), A. G. Lehmann concludes that "the terms 'literary symbol' and 'symbolist' are terms which, introduced and fortified by a series of mischances, should never have been allowed to remain in usage" (p. 316).

47. These are all, for instance, classified as "romantic symbolists" in William York Tindall's *The Literary Symbol* (New York, 1955), p. 3. Mark Schorer described *Heart of Darkness* as "that early but wonderful piece of symbolist fiction" in his classic essay "Technique as Discovery" (*The World We Imagine* [New York, 1968], p. 19).

return; the characters—Kurtz, or the helmsman; the incidents—
Marlow's interview for the job, or the grove of death; the material
objects—the rivets, the staves of the pilgrims, the heads on the posts;
the scene—the Thames and the Congo; the atmosphere—light and
darkness. In all these elements the symbolic meaning of objects and
events is established through the expansion of their inherent properties, and they have a structural, rather than a merely illustrative,
function.

The analogy is equally close as regards subject matter. *Heart of
Darkness* shares many of the characteristic preoccupations and themes
of the French Symbolists: the spiritual voyage of discovery, especially
through an exotic jungle landscape, which was a common symbolist
theme, in Baudelaire's "Le Voyage" and Rimbaud's "Bâteau ivre," for
instance; the pervasive atmosphere of dream, nightmare, and hal-
lucination, again typical of Rimbaud; and the very subject of Kurtz
also recalls, not only Rimbaud's own spectacular career, but the typical
symbolist fondness for the lawless, the depraved, and the extreme
modes of experience.

More generally, we surely sense in *Heart of Darkness* Conrad's supreme effort to reveal, in Baudelaire's phrase about Delacroix, "the
infinite in the finite."[48] This intention is suggested in Conrad's title.
The Symbolist poets often used titles which suggested a much larger
and more mysterious range of implication than their work's overt
subject apparently justified—one thinks of the expanding effect of
T. S. Eliot's *The Waste Land,* for example, or of *The Sacred Wood.* This
centrifugal suggestion was sometimes produced by an obtrusive
semantic gap—a coupling of incongruous words or images that
forced us to look beyond our habitual expectations; there is, for instance, the initial puzzling shock of the titles of two of the great pre-
cursive works of symbolism which appeared in 1873, Rimbaud's *Une
Saison en enfer,* and Tristan Corbière's "Les Amours jaunes."

Compared with the particularity of Conrad's earlier and more
traditional titles, such as *Almayer's Folly* or *The Nigger of the "Narcissus",
Heart of Darkness* strikes a very special note; we are somehow impelled
to see the title as much more than a combination of two stock
metaphors for referring to "the centre of the Dark Continent" and "a
diabolically evil person." Both of Conrad's nouns are densely charged
with physical and moral suggestions; freed from the restrictions of the
article, they combine to generate a sense of puzzlement which prepares us for something beyond our usual expectation: if the words do
not name what we know, they must be asking us to know what has, as

48. *Oeuvres complètes,* ed. Ruff (Paris, 1968), p. 404.

yet, no name. The more concrete of the two terms, "heart," is attributed a strategic centrality within a formless and infinite abstraction, "darkness"; the combination defies both visualisation and logic: How can something inorganic like darkness have an organic centre of life and feeling? How can a shapeless absence of light compact itself into a shaped and pulsing presence? And what are we to make of a "good" entity like a heart becoming, of all things, a controlling part of a "bad" one like darkness? *Heart of Darkness* was a fateful event in the history of fiction; and to announce it Conrad hit upon as haunting, though not as obtrusive, an oxymoron as Baudelaire had for poetry with *Les Fleurs du Mal*.

(c) *Marlow and Henry James*

It was in connection with *Heart of Darkness* that Conrad made what appears to have been his most explicit attack on symbolism in fiction. In 1902, when the publication in book form had provoked critical discussion in the public press and in his private circle, Conrad responded to a friend's objections to what he called "my pet Heart of Darkness" by allowing only one criticism: "What I distinctly admit is the fault of having made Kurtz too symbolic or rather symbolic at all."[49] Conrad may have found it easier—not for the first time—to avoid discussing adverse criticism by presenting himself as a much simpler kind of writer than he was. He certainly continued in this vein: "The story being mainly a vehicle for conveying a batch of personal impressions I gave the rein to my mental laziness and took the line of least resistance. This is then the whole Apologia pro Vita Kurtzii—or rather for the tardiness of his vitality."

That Kurtz comes late upon the scene, and that he then proves rather one-dimensional and theatrical has been widely felt; but Conrad's pejorative use of "symbolic" here seems to imply the fixed and limiting conception of the word symbol, according to which Kurtz would merely "stand" for some set idea or ideas. This sense is quite contrary to the larger ambitions of Symbolist theory, and so Conrad's comments do not really bear on the question of whether his intentions in *Heart of Darkness* were or were not close to those of the Symbolists. The general view that Kurtz is not very fully characterised, however, could be taken as in some sense confirming the Symbolist presence in *Heart of Darkness*, since the novels of the French Symbolists tend to centre so much on the inner life of the protagonist that the other characters do not emerge very clearly. Kurtz is the victim of a similar

49. Letter of Conrad to Elsie Hueffer, 3 December 1902 (transcript courtesy of Frederick Karl).

subordination; both the form and the content of *Heart of Darkness* are centered on the consciousness of Marlow, and so Kurtz, in effect absorbed into Marlow's subjectivity, can have no independent existence. For *Heart of Darkness* is a "roman de la vie cérébrale,"[50] to use the phrase which Rémy de Gourmont applied to his Symbolist novel *Sixtine* (1890); it largely conforms to what de Gourmont thought "the only excuse for a man to write": "to unveil to others the kind of world which he beholds in his own personal mirror";[51] and Conrad's agent for this unveiling is Marlow.

In the Author's Note (1917) to the volume in which *Heart of Darkness* appeared in book form, *Youth—A Narrative: and Two Other Stories* (1902), Conrad devoted three of his eight paragraphs to Marlow, "with whom my relations have grown very intimate in the course of years." The terms in which this intimacy is expressed are both ironic and touching: "He haunts my hours of solitude, when, in silence, we lay our heads together in great comfort and harmony." About the origins of their relationship, however, Conrad says virtually nothing; he merely disclaims having had any "meditated plan for his capture," and adds: "The man Marlow and I came together in the casual manner of those health-resort acquaintances which sometimes ripen into friendships. This one has ripened." Conrad is equally noncommittal about Marlow's literary function. He limits himself to reporting without comment that others had "supposed" him to be "all sorts of things: a clever screen, a mere device, a 'personator,' a familiar spirit, a whispering 'daemon.' "

We must then, enquire into Marlow's origins and functions without any help from Conrad; and one way to begin is to consider how Conrad had handled the narrative point of view in his earlier writings, and especially in those closest in subject or time to *Heart of Darkness*.

Conrad's early works mainly employ impersonal third-person narration, and he continued to use it when, after finishing *An Outcast of the Islands* late in 1895, he attempted a change to a more subjective theme in his unfinished novel "The Sisters." Its subject, the intellectual and spiritual history of an isolated individual, was somewhat similar not only to that of *Heart of Darkness* but to that of J. K. Huysmans's *A Rebours;* and like Huysmans and other Symbolist novelists, Conrad had used the impersonal, distant, and omniscient point of view which tended to discourage the reader's active participation in the inner life of the protagonist. "The Sisters" was also a tale of individual quest, and even had something of the esoteric religious over-

---

50. Cited by Cornell, *Symbolist Movement,* p. 97.
51. Preface, *Le Livre des Masques: portraits symbolistes* (Paris, 1923), p. 13.

tones of the Symbolists. It opened, for example, with: "For many years Stephen had wandered amongst the cities of Western Europe. If he came from the East—if he possessed the inborn wisdom of the East—yet it must be said he was only a lonely and inarticulate Mage, without a star and without companions. He set off on his search for a creed—and found only an infinity of formulas."

"The Sisters" remained a fragment, and its failure must have influenced Conrad's development in many ways. Ford suggests in his introduction that Edward Garnett's very adverse criticism decisively turned Conrad away from "the misty problems of the Slav soul" and its "introspections passing in Paris," and set him firmly on the path of being an Anglo-Saxon novelist (*T S*, 29; 16). But it may be that the experiment also planted the idea that a different narrative point of view would be needed to "make us see" the individual's subjective life.

Between 1896 and the writing, some two years later, of the first two Marlow stories, "Youth" and *Heart of Darkness*, it is likely that the main innovations in narrative technique which influenced Conrad were those of Henry James.

Many critics have seen James as one of Conrad's masters; F. W. Dupee, indeed, calls Conrad James's "greatest disciple."[52] We know that Conrad had been an admiring reader while he was still at sea, and when *An Outcast of the Islands* came out, he thought of sending James a copy; but it was very difficult to pluck up courage. In one letter (16 October 1896) Conrad wrote to Garnett: "I do hesitate about H. James. Still I think I will send the book. After all it would not be a crime or even an impudence." Then, after two further letters from Garnett, Conrad finally announced (27 October 1896): "I have sent *Outcast* to H. James with a pretty dedication; it fills the flyleaf" (*E G*, 50; 54).

Conrad's self-mockery about the "pretty dedication" only partly prepares us for the lacerating embarrassment of its terms. The letter begins:

> I address you across a vast space invoking the name of that one of your children you love the most. I have been intimate with many of them, but it would be an impertinence for me to disclose here the secret of my affection. I am not sure that there is one I love more than the others. Exquisite Shades with live hearts, and clothed in the wonderful garment of your prose, they have stood, consoling, by my side under many skies. They have lived with me, faithful and serene—

---

52. *Henry James* (London, 1951), p. 281. See also Leon Edel, *Henry James: The Master, 1901–1916* (Philadelphia and New York, 1972), p. 46.

with the bright serenity of Immortals. And to you thanks are
due for such glorious companionship.[53]

The effusions continue until the letter closes with Conrad asking
James to accept his book, and thus "augment the previous burden of
my gratitude."

One senses the paralysing apprehension of an insecure worshipper
approaching a redoubtable deity, or of a lover whose very fear of
rebuff invites humiliation. However, after some four months, James
reciprocated by sending Conrad his just-published *The Spoils of Poynton,* with the characteristic inscription: "To Joseph Conrad in dread-
fully delayed but very grateful acknowledgment of an offering singu-
larly generous and beautiful" (*L L,* I, 201, n. 2). Then, a week later, on
19 February 1897, Conrad announced jubilantly to Garnett: "I had a
note from James. Wants me to lunch with him on Thursday next—so
there is something to live for—at last!" (*E G,* 76).

The meeting probably took place in James's London apartment—it
is there that Conrad later remembered that he had chanced upon the
Pepys epigraph for *The Nigger of the "Narcissus".* But it was only in
October 1898, and in the period immediately preceding the composition of *Heart of Darkness,* that James and Conrad became neighbours;
a period of quite close literary frequentation ensued. There is no
question of Conrad's profound reverence for James's achievement.
Conrad habitually addressed James, and James alone, as "cher
maître";[54] one imagines that for Conrad the veteran writer who had
been the friend of Flaubert and Turgenev was a captain under whom
he would willingly learn the last secrets of the novelist's craft.

The period was a momentous one in the careers of both men.
James, genial as never before, was producing the works which precede *The Ambassadors,* and in which his method of narration through
the registering consciousness of one of the characters is already
perfected—*The Spoils of Poynton* (1896), *What Maisie Knew* (1897), and
The Awkward Age (1898). Conrad, for his part, was finally turning away
from the French influence, as James had long before. The first story
which Conrad began after his meeting with James early in 1897 was
"The Return." It had a somewhat Jamesian subject—"the fabulous
untruth" of a society husband's "idea of life." In a letter to Garnett,

---

53. Dated 16 October 1896. I am indebted to Frederick R. Karl for giving me a copy
of this letter, and to the Academic Center Library at the University of Texas for
permission to publish part of it.

54. *Lettres françaises,* pp. 34, 77; also in dedication copies to James. For the later
development of the friendship, see Edel, *James: The Master,* pp. 47–56, and my "Conrad, James and *Chance,*" in *Imagined Worlds: Essays on Some English Novels and Novelists in
Honour of John Butt,* ed. Maynard Mack and Ian Gregor (London, 1968), pp. 301–22.

Conrad analyses the failure of the story in somewhat Jamesian terms: "if I did see it [the reason for his failure] I would also see the other way, the mature way—the way of art" (*E G*, 94; 98); but if "The Return" taught Conrad any permanent lesson, it was probably that he should avoid the Jamesian subject matter.

There remained, however, James's narrative technique, and especially that of his most recent novels. There is no doubt that Conrad deeply admired *The Spoils of Poynton*. Ford reports "the rapturous and shouting enthusiasm of Conrad over that story," and suggests that it "must have been the high-water mark of Conrad's enthusiasm for the work of any other writer."[55] The possible significance of this for the development of Marlow is that *The Spoils of Poynton* is, as J. W. Beach called it, "the first absolutely pure example of the James method."[56] It was there that James developed the indirect narrative approach through the sensitive central intelligence of one of the characters. Technically this was halfway towards avoiding both the intrusive authorial omniscience of earlier fiction and the obtrusive detachment of Flaubert. James went only halfway because he usually retained a discreet form of authorial narrative, and both his selection of a particular registering consciousness, and the terms in which he presented it, implied the author's full understanding of that consciousness. But the psychological and moral effects of James's way of registering the experience of the novel as a whole through the subjectivity of a protagonist were enormous: our sympathetic and authorially-endorsed closeness to the inward fineness of Fleda Vetch in *The Spoils of Poynton*, or of Maisie Farange's groping awareness of the horrors of the adult world in *What Maisie Knew*, did much to counter the refrigerating tendency of third-person narration as Flaubert had developed it.

Several critics have suggested that Conrad may have developed Marlow from James's use of a central observer. William York Tindall, for instance, though unwilling to go so far as to see Marlow as "a kind of bearded Maisie,"[57] concedes that Conrad may have got a "possible hint" from James. There is some circumstantial support for this view. For one thing, Conrad, though very evidently a conscious artist, had paid little attention to technical consistency as regards narrative point of view in his earlier fiction; and for another, we know that Conrad noticed and admired the formal perfection of James's narrative technique in *The Spoils of Poynton* as soon as he read it. In a letter of 13

55. Ford Madox Ford, *Portraits from Life* (Chicago, 1960), p. 11.

56. Joseph Warren Beach, *The Method of Henry James* (New Haven, 1918), p. 233.

57. "Apology for Marlow," in *From Jane Austen to Joseph Conrad: Essays Collected in Memory of James T. Hillhouse*, ed. Robert C. Rathburn and Martin Steinmann, Jr. (Minneapolis, 1958), p. 276.

February 1897 to Garnett, he commented on the novel's transparency: "The delicacy and tenuity of the thing are amazing. It is like a great sheet of plate glass—you don't know it's there till you run against it. Of course I do not mean to say it is anything as gross as plate glass. It's only as *pellucid* as clean plate-glass" (*E G*, 74). As we have seen, notably in the case of Maupassant, Conrad carefully studied the technique of new novels that he admired. There is no such direct evidence of his technical study of James, perhaps because Conrad was now past his apprenticeship; but the possibility remains that it was Conrad's reading of James's current novels which influenced him in adopting the very different narrative method of his next works— "Youth," completed in the summer of 1898, and *Heart of Darkness*, completed early in 1899.

Conrad's use of Marlow, of course, has no equivalent in James: it represents, above all, a much more extreme and overt break with the distance, impersonality, and omniscience of third-person narration; and it does so in the interests of a dual concreteness of visualization—dual because Marlow not only tells us what he saw and heard in the past, but as readers we see him telling his auditors about it in the narrative present. With Marlow, in fact, James's registering consciousness is wholly dramatized as regards both the tale and its telling; it is also internalised in the sense that it is as fully adapted to the direct relation of the individual's inner thoughts and feelings as to the description of the external world. One way of summarising these aspects of the function of Marlow in *Heart of Darkness* would be to say that Conrad takes the impressionist direction much further than anything in James, and in a number of ways.

James and Conrad are both impressionists in one broad sense: as E. K. Brown puts it, their novels focus the reader's attention not on "what will happen, but rather with what the happening will mean to the principal character or characters."[58] But whereas James as author selects and orders the "meaning" of what happens, in the Marlow stories and especially in *Heart of Darkness*, Conrad lets his protagonist muddle out the meaning of his own experiences as best he can. This total subordination to the subjective limitations of the vision of one particular character is very different from James, and Conrad emphasises the limitation by giving both Marlow's personal presence and the occasion of his narration a fully described impressionistic particularity in space and time.

The external aspect of the polarity between the inner and outer

---

58. "James and Conrad," *Yale Review* 35 (1945): 265.

world is much more marked in *Heart of Darkness* than in the other three Marlow tales; it is the only story which is told on board ship, and in a setting whose time and place—the coming of night on the Thames estuary—are themselves to become important elements in the narrative. The occasion is unique in another respect: the teller and his audience have been physically immobilised by the tide, and are isolated from all else; both circumstances favour intimacy of disclosure. This intimacy is also given a psychological basis: Marlow's hearers apparently know him well, whereas in "Youth" the narrator was not even sure how Marlow "spelt his name" (*Y*, 3). All these elements—the particularity of time and place, the physical isolation, the closeness of the group—combine to dramatise the telling; and the reader's attention is focussed on the physical immediacy of Marlow's presence as he sits far aft, cross-legged and leaning against the mizzenmast, with "an aspect of concentrated attention" on a face that is "lean . . . worn, hollow, with downward folds and dropped eyelids" (46; 114).

Henry James was no admirer of Marlow as a character, or of *Heart of Darkness*. James would refer to him in conversation as "that preposterous master mariner" (*F M F*, 161); and Marlow is indeed difficult to believe in as a fictional character. He belongs to a class of one, a class composed of British ship's officers whose minds and interests have been produced by the unique circumstances of Conrad's own national and personal history; he emerges before us weighed down by the knowledge and experience of a lifetime, and yet devoid of a biography—no birthplace, no home, no school, no fixed social or domestic ties. But James's deepest objection to Marlow, however, was probably on technical grounds. In a diary entry of 5 January 1903, Olive Garnett reports Elsie Hueffer as telling her that James "objected to the narrator mixing himself up with the narrative in 'The Heart of Darkness' & its want of proportion; said that we didn't really get hold of Kurtz after all the talk about him, but said the Russian was excellent."[59]

James's phrase about Marlow's "mixing himself up with the narrative" surely discloses a myopic resistance to the technique of *Heart of Darkness* that only James's invariable veneration for his own methods can explain. But there are probably much larger considerations behind James's objections, considerations affecting his own theory and practice as regards two of the crucial structural changes that were

59. Thomas C. Moser, "From Olive Garnett's Diary: Impressions of Ford Madox Ford and His Friends, 1890–1906," *Texas Studies in Literature and Language* 16 (1974): 525. James thought "The End of the Tether" the finest of the three stories in the *Youth* volume; it was the only one using third-person narration.

occurring in the tradition of the novel: Conrad goes much further than James both in the abandonment of authorial omniscience, and in the related transition from a closed to an open fictional form.

Both James and Conrad were very much aware that the way a novel ended reflected a general view of life, and they broke with the traditional closed form cf ending which attempted a complete resolution of the main problems of the novel's plot and characters. This is one structural aspect of Henry James's fiction which Conrad specifically endorsed. In a 1905 essay, Conrad wrote of how James had rejected "the usual methods of solution by rewards and punishments, by crowned love, by fortune, by a broken leg or a sudden death." This rejection, Conrad argued, involved a breach with the tradition of the novelist's god-like control of the life he portrayed:

> Why the reading public which, as a body, has never laid upon a story-teller the command to be an artist, should demand from him this sham of Divine Omnipotence, is utterly incomprehensible. But so it is; and these solutions are legitimate inasmuch as they satisfy the desire for finality, for which our hearts yearn, with a longing greater than the longing for the loaves and fishes of this earth. Perhaps the only true desire of mankind, coming thus to·light in its hours of leisure, is to be set at rest. One is never set at rest by Mr. Henry James's novels. His books end as an episode in life ends. You remain with the sense of the life still going on.[60]

Conrad was surely right in assuming that Henry James had denied his readers the satisfying illusion that the conflicts of life could ever be completely or finally resolved; on the other hand James had nevertheless regarded it as part of the task of art to produce out of life's continuing conflicts and endless bewilderments the appearance of resolution and finality. This appearance was generated by the perfection of the novel's own intrinsic formal organization. James summed up the matter in the famous words of the preface to *Roderick Hudson:* "Really, universally, relations stop nowhere, and the exquisite problem of the artist is eternally but to draw, by a geometry of his own, the circle within which they shall happily *appear* to do so."[61]

Conrad's praise of James had not suggested that his narrative technique as such incorporated the incompleteness of life; Conrad was, rather, recognising how James had represented the complexity and incompleteness of life in the content of his plot. The representation of life's incompleteness had also been an important part of Conrad's own

---

60. "Henry James: An Appreciation," 1905 (*N L L,* 18–19).
61. Preface to *Roderick Hudson* (Henry James, *The Art of the Novel,* ed. R. P. Blackmur [New York, 1934], p. 5).

aim in *The Nigger of the "Narcissus"*. As he wrote to Garnett, it expressed "the incomplete joy, the incomplete sorrow, the incomplete rascality or heroism" (*E G*, 61); and it was this aim, Conrad thought, which had made it so difficult to bring his novel to "the end, such as it is." But in *Heart of Darkness*, Conrad took the incompleteness of the fictional action and the indeterminacy of its moral implications much further.

Most obviously, the whole structure of the tale rejects linear chronological development. In this respect *Heart of Darkness* is very different from "Youth": Conrad was aiming, he wrote in his Author's Note, at "another art altogether" which would produce "a continued vibration that, I hoped, would hang in the air and dwell on the ear after the last note had been struck." In more general terms Conrad uses Marlow to give his tale neither the full close of the plot of earlier fiction, nor James's more limited completeness in the formal structure, but a radical and continuing exposure to the incompleteness of experience and the impossibility of fully understanding it.[62] This has been recognised by Alan Friedman, who argues, in *The Turn of the Novel*, that Conrad goes far beyond his contemporary novelists in making his structure and his narrative point of view reflect "the progressive emergence of a finally open experience as normative for fiction."[63]

What Conrad called the omnipotence of the author can obviously affect both the substance of *what* happens in the novel and *how* the fictional happenings are told. Henry James may have been sceptical about the possibility of seeing a character completely, but the form of his fiction did not fully embody this doubt. James disclaimed authorial omniscience, in the sense that the narrative usually presented the characters mainly from the point of view of the effect they made on others; as Ezra Pound noted of *The Awkward Age*: "Only real thing the impression of people, not observation or real knowledge."[64] But the liberty which James allowed to the impressionist approach to reality was limited; although the events and characters in *The Spoils of Poynton* were presented through the sensibility of the heroine, Fleda Vetch, these contents had first been selected and ordered by the author; and we feel as we do with the clarifying and unifying focus of Strether in *The Ambassadors*, that the central intelligence has fused its multiple impressions of others into a single, coherent, and reliable report. In any case James does not give us the impressions of his central intelli-

---

62. See Elsa Nettels's fine recent study, *James and Conrad* (Athens, Ga., 1977), especially pp. 65–66.
63. *The Turn of the Novel* (New York, 1966), p. 99.
64. "Henry James and Rémy de Gourmont," *Make it New*, p. 287.

gence directly, but as they have been translated into the lucidity of his own analytic style, and given the relatively impersonal and authoritative status which is implied by the use of the *style indirecte libre*. As a result the narrative, to a considerable degree, gives an impression of "happily appearing" to achieve completeness and reliability.

James, then, found a way by which the central intelligence could take over much of the direct responsibility of the author, and yet achieve a work which was as susceptible to complete understanding by the reader as if an omniscient author had been there to explain everything. James's objection to Marlow's "mixing himself up with the narrative" was probably based on how Conrad, by taking the sceptical aspect of impressionism much further, and making the observer an inseparable part of what he observed, interfered with the final effect of order and lucidity in narrative which James continued to require. Marlow is certainly very different from the Jamesian central intelligence; in effect he embodies what James thought the two essential faults of the first-person method—"the terrible *fluidity* of self-revelation," and the fact that the narrating "I" has "the double privilege of subject and object."[65]

It is because Marlow has this "double privilege of subject and object" that the reader cannot see him as a fictional object very clearly. Marlow is in effect his own author, and so there is no reliable and comprehensive perspective on him or his experience. Conrad's scepticism about understanding character had not really been embodied in his fiction until *Heart of Darkness;* but there Marlow prefigures how the modern novel was to reject much more fully than did James the assumption of full authorial understanding, and, in its formal posture at least, restrict itself to showing an individual consciousness in the process of trying to elicit some purely relative and personal meaning from its experience. What Marlow says is not lucidly pondered but random and often puzzled, leaving contradictions unresolved and allowing the less conscious elements of the mind, including those of reverie and dream, to find expression. Conrad's version of the Jamesian registering consciousness, in short, does not, as it does in James, induce the reader to zero in from every point within the story to view its centre more clearly; and this lack of any authorised objective clarity is one reason why we see Conrad as decisively closer to us than James.

One must concede part of James's general argument against first-person narration; there is indeed a "terrible fluidity" about the multiple roles which Marlow plays, even if the frame of *Heart of Darkness* prevents it from being a first-person narrative in a strict sense. Any

---

65. *Art of the Novel,* ed. Blackmur, p. 321.

final comparative evaluation of the two methods must largely depend
on the price we are willing to pay for formal perfection in art, and the
exclusions it dictates. By making us marvel at each move in his narrative strategy, James makes us forget or forgive the exclusions which
that strategy involves. Conrad, on the other hand, so hypnotises us
with the wide-ranging urgencies of Marlow's voice that we hardly
notice our increasing bewilderment at the almost unmanageable inclusiveness of what we are being left to piece together.

Behind this contrast there is another: Conrad did not share James's
belief that the secrets of the art of the novel had at last been uncov-
ered.[66] Like James and many of his French contemporaries, Conrad
thought Naturalism was a dead end; but, unlike James, he felt that
there was no other model in sight which offered much hope. Thus he
wrote to an admirer in 1902: "I doubt if greatness can be attained now
in imaginative prose work. When it comes, it will be in a new form; in
a form for which we are not ripe as yet. Till the hour strikes and the
man appears, we must plod in the beaten track." (*L L*, I, 308). Allowance must no doubt be made for the strategy of polite self-
deprecation which leads Conrad to place himself in the ranks of the
dull plodders; still, it is a fact that he never claimed to be an innovator,
and tended throughout his career to play down his characteristic fictional methods as mere devices of the craft. His consciousness of that
craft certainly fell far short of any fully conceptualised fictional system; and while this may have encouraged a freedom in yielding to
unformulated intuitions that played a part in making us, three generations later, see *Heart of Darkness* in the perspective of a profoundly
original anticipation of many of the formal, as well as the ideological,
aspects of the modern novel, it also explains why it stands rather alone
in the Conrad canon, and for reasons about which Conrad is almost
entirely silent.

Conrad's use of Marlow in *Heart of Darkness,* then, differs not only
from James's narrative point of view in many important respects, but
also from the other Marlow tales. Some of these differences point
forwards: Conrad's retreat from the omniscient author is applied
much more radically to his characterisation and his mode of narration, and through them to the meaning of the story as a whole. As
several critics have noted, Marlow's role turns *Heart of Darkness* into a
story about—among other things—the difficulty of telling the "full
story."[67] This difficulty is latent in both the Impressionist and Sym-

66. Michel Raimond, *La Crise du roman: des lendemains du Naturalisme aux années vingt*
(Paris, 1966), pp. 25–43.
67. Most recently, Tzvetan Todorov, "Connaissance du vide," *Nouvelle revue de
psychoanalyse* 11 (1975): 145–54.

bolist doctrines. Marlow is obsessively aware of it. "No, not very clear" (51), he ruminates aloud as he begins to recall his experience, and later he is driven to conclude that it is "impossible to convey the life-sensation of any given epoch of one's existence—that which makes its truth, its meaning—its subtle and penetrating essence" (82). Marlow's ironic consciousness of how far he is from being able to tell "the full story," and the overt enactment of this within the novel, are two of the ways in which *Heart of Darkness* anticipates the unauthoritative, self-reflexive, and problematic nature of such later fiction as Kafka's novels and Gide's *Les Faux-Monnayeurs*.

These comparisons, however, are themselves reminders of how far scepticism is from being the only or even the main burden of meaning in *Heart of Darkness*; Marlow is also the means whereby Conrad incorporates three of the oldest, and predominantly affirmative, elements in storytelling: the narrator as a remembering eyewitness; the narrator as the voice of his author's opinions; and the narrator as a friendly personal presence.

The most obvious of these traditional elements derives from the way that Marlow functions as a more direct expression of the preoccupation with writing as the. voice of memory that informs most of Conrad's earlier fiction. In this respect *Heart of Darkness* formally harks back to that most ancient of the forms of storytelling which begins "I remember"; and Conrad may have been influenced by a traditional Polish form of such tales, the *gawęda*, which is told by a clearly defined narrator, and is usually of a retrospective nature (*N*, 16–17). Conrad at first thought of entitling his projected collection of short stories, which would include "Youth" and *Heart of Darkness*, "Tales from Memory," because he wished "to convey the notion of something lived through and remembered" (*B*, 55). The kinds of memory in the two stories, however, were essentially different: in "Youth" memory is there mainly to give a nostalgic appeal to a story which is mainly told in a very traditional kind of way; but in *Heart of Darkness* memory is the means for depicting an intense confrontation of Marlow's past with his present; and the mood of that confrontation, as Conrad commented in his Author's Note, is "anything" but that "of wistful regret, of reminiscent tenderness."

The fact that Marlow is not the primary narrator, however, has the effect of giving him an objective status that is in accord with more recent modes of storytelling. It can, indeed, be argued that retrospection does not in fact involve a breach with the relativism of the more typically impressionist modes of modern fiction. Neither the immediate verbal rendering of sense impressions, nor the later development of the stream-of-consciousness novel, has any certain basis in experience; after all, no one has ever seen an impression, let alone a stream of them, and life offers no model for putting them into words. Memory is somewhat closer to our consciousness; and the act of putting memories into words is a common and observed phenomenon. Retrospective narration, then, though one of the oldest forms of narrative, has as good a claim to represent actual experience as more modern methods; and the way Conrad uses Marlow is peculiarly adapted to showing the individual engaged in trying to understand what has happened to him.

Conrad's use of Marlow as the voice of retrospection, then, combines old and new narrative methods. Marlow's memories of his lonely experiences on the Congo, and his sense of the impossibility of fully communicating their meaning, would in themselves assign *Heart of Darkness* to the literature of modern solipsism; but the fact that Marlow, like Conrad, is speaking to a particular audience makes all the difference; it enacts the process whereby the solitary individual discovers a way out into the world of others. One can surmise that Conrad found the narrative posture of moral and social neutrality intolerable; and so under cover of Marlow's probing of the meaning of the past, Conrad smuggled in the ancient privilege of the narrator by the backdoor, and surreptitiously reclaimed some of the omniscient author's ancient rights to the direct expression of the wisdom of hindsight.

Edward Crankshaw has argued that "Marlow was invented so that Conrad could moralize . . . freely without ruining his illusion . . . which was dependent on his, the author's, aloofness and impersonality."[68] Through Marlow, Conrad can unobjectionably express the sort of moral commentary on the action which had been proscribed by Flaubert and the purists of the art of the novel, and which had seemed somewhat obtrusive when Conrad did it directly, as he had occasionally in *The Nigger of the "Narcissus"*, for instance. But Marlow is much more than a device for circumventing the modern taboo on authorial moralising; he is also a means of allowing his author to express himself more completely than ever before; through Marlow Conrad discovered a new kind of relation to his audience, and one which enabled him to be more fully himself.

The first Marlow story, "Youth," was also the first story which Conrad ever wrote with a particular group of readers—that of *Blackwood's*—in mind. This defined audience may have given Conrad the initial psychological impetus towards dramatising a fictional situation in which a narrator rather like Conrad addresses an audience

68. *Joseph Conrad*, p. 73.

rather like that of *Blackwood's*. Marlow's listeners comprise a company
director, an accountant, a Tory lawyer, and a primary narrator, all of
them ex-seamen; in effect they are a composite of the two audiences
Conrad had himself encountered—those at sea and those he now
visualised as his readers. The connection between the two audiences
probably had its roots in Conrad's early years in London, and the
friends there who had provided him with a transition between his
lives on sea and on land. In the years 1890 to 1892 Conrad had done a
good deal of sailing, and no doubt yarning, in the Thames estuary
aboard a cruising yawl; he retained its actual name in *Heart of Darkness,* the *Nellie*; and though he did not give the name of its captain and
host, the *Nellie* in fact belonged to Conrad's old friend Hope, who was
indeed a director of companies (*S W W*, 122–24). Marlow himself, of
course, is also a composite, combining the two main roles in life that
Conrad had experienced—the seaman and the writer; and the moral
perspective which Marlow's commentary endorses is very largely
the professional and social ethic that he shares with his immediate
audience.

At all events, through the presence of Marlow's companions on the
Nellie, the old friendly commerce of oral storyteller and the listening
group is restored. This commerce had already been implicit in "Karain," a story published in, though not written for, *Blackwood's*. There
Conrad made his first full use of a participant narrator, an unnamed
character who occasionally raised questions about the meanings and
motives which the story involved; on one occasion he even steps out of
the frame to wonder about the reaction of his audience: "I wondered
what they thought; what he thought; . . . what the reader thinks?"
(*T U*, 52). This active interplay between narrator and immediate audience is itself an image of the further interplay which Conrad imagined between his story and its public; and it creates an intimacy between author and reader of a kind that is surely unique in modern
fiction.

This intimacy of communication is notably absent in Henry James's
The Turn of the Screw, which has been cited as a possible influence on
Heart of Darkness.[69] There both the "I," the primary narrator, and
Douglas, who tells the main story to its "compact and select auditory,"
completely disappear once the governess's tale begins; she has no
audience, and since her written diary belongs to the past, it has the

69. Edel, *James: The Master,* pp. 54–55; and Roger E. Ramsey, "The Available and the
Unavailable 'I': Conrad and James," *English Literature in Transition* 14 (1971): 137–45. In
view of James's resistance to *Heart of Darkness* there is a nice complementary irony in
Conrad's unenthusiastic comment on *The Turn of the Screw:* it "evades one, but leaves a
kind of phosphorescent trail in one's mind" (*L L*, vol. 1, p. 256).

kind of cold unanswerable authority which is automatically conferred when the source of a story is beyond recall.

Marlow's living voice, and the congenial setting which awakens it, profoundly affect the atmosphere of all his narratives. Henry James, writing in 1914 about *Chance*, described Marlow as a "reciter, a definite responsible intervening first person singular." But, as he went on to emphasize, Marlow was not just a reciter; there was a personal and spiritual "residuum"; and the effect of that "residuum," as James wonderfully put it, was not merely that "of such and such a number of images discharged and ordered, but that rather of a wandering, circling, yearning imaginative *faculty*, encountered in its habit as it lives and diffusing itself as a presence or a tide, a noble sociability of vision."

The eclectic insouciance of Conrad's use of Marlow goes far to justify Garnett's view that Marlow came into being because he "saved trouble" and "came natural" to Conrad (*E G*, xxx); one can understand James's distaste for the infinite pluralism of Marlow's narrative functions. Still, for all his fastidious objections to Marlow as a character and as a method, Henry James, like countless readers, is eventually won over by Marlow's "noble sociability of vision."[70] James's phrase in effect recognises that Marlow is a persuasive fictional voice for that movement towards human solidarity which Conrad had affirmed as his essential authorial purpose in the preface to *The Nigger of the "Narcissus"*.

v. The Tale

Interpretations of *Heart of Darkness* diverge very widely. For this reason, what follows concentrates on a fairly literal account of how Conrad's narrative, thematic, and symbolic structures develop, while taking some note, as occasion arises, of the main critical divergencies.

(a) *To the Central Station*

Heart of Darkness opens with a prologue of relaxed and yet compelling eloquence.

The primary narrator first gives a low-keyed description of the *Nellie's* coming to anchor, and of the five men aboard settling down to await the ebb of the tide; then he slowly modulates into an increasingly fixed absorption on the gathering gloom and what it suggests. Almost imperceptibly, this evocation of the time and the place sets up the novel's basic symbolic dualism; the light in the sky and the lumi-

70. *Notes on Novelists, with Some Other Notes* (New York, 1914), pp. 347; 350–51.

nous estuary are contrasted with the darkness along the banks of the Thames and over London. But the profound serenity of the sky just before the sun vanishes under the horizon illuminates the seaward reaches of the Thames; and, as though united by a common spiritual bond, the men on the *Nellie* look at "the venerable stream . . . in the august light of abiding memories." They are memories of the countless voyagers who set out from the Thames, and especially of the explorers, such as Drake and Franklin, with their famous "ships whose names are like jewels flashing in the night of time," and of the colonisers who bore "the sword, and often the torch, messengers of the might within the land, bearers of a spark from the sacred fire."

By now our attention has been alerted against assuming that the narrative depends exclusively on the symbolic meanings traditionally attributed to the contrast of black as bad and white as good: for instance, the two opposites are intermingled in the case of the "torch" of civilisation, since it came from "within the land," which we have just seen as dark. This symbolic interplay continues when the sun finally sets, lights appear on the shore, and Marlow steps out of the narrative frame: " 'And this also,' said Marlow suddenly, 'has been one of the dark places of the earth' " (48).

Characteristically, Marlow's opening remark both reverses and expands the general meditative direction: it reverses it because Marlow is thinking, not about the light of British civilisation, but about the darkness out of which it arose; and it amplifies it because the historical perspective becomes much longer when Marlow invokes the first Roman settlers on the Thames in "very old times." This idea is developed in a long paragraph which begins by making us see civilisation, not as the established norm, but as a brief interruption of the normal order of darkness, an interruption which is as brief and unsubstantial as "a flash of lightning in the clouds."

Marlow's backward plunge into England's remoter past soon proves to be an indirect approach to a much more immediate and personal preoccupation—the moral and psychological conflict between light and darkness which goes on inside the individual. The commander of the Roman trireme and his soldiers were no doubt "men enough to face the darkness"—the wilderness with its menace of isolation, disease, and death; but Marlow's need to probe into just what power could have kept darkness at bay inside each individual Roman, prefigures what is to prove an obsessional concern with how he and Kurtz reacted to what confronted them in Africa. The parallel becomes more overt when Marlow imagines the situation of some "decent young citizen in a toga" exiled to some post in the interior and surrounded by "utter savagery" (50): "There's no initiation either into such mysteries," Marlow explains, and goes on to ask his listeners to "imagine the growing regrets, the longing to escape, the powerless disgust, the surrender, the hate."

Until now the prologue has proceeded through counterpointing scenic description and prefigurative rumination; but after Marlow, as solo instrument, has restated the primary narrator's themes of the conflict between light and darkness, he develops them in variations which become increasingly sombre, urgent, and questioning.

Two of these variations—colonisation and atavistic regression—are clearly related to the dominant symbolic polarity of light and darkness. Colonisation has been briefly presented by the primary narrator as in the guise of light overcoming darkness; but this moral positive is soon undermined when Marlow presents it as a brief and cyclical interruption of the normal predominance of darkness over the course of historical time. After a little, Marlow pauses, apparently reflecting that he ought not to upset his listening friends with his gloomy ruminations. When he resumes it is to exclude the present company from his unflattering generalisations about human weakness: "None of us," he volunteers, "would feel exactly like this. What saves us is efficiency—the devotion to efficiency." The argument of efficiency was much used by the Social Darwinists to justify their economic and political views, and at the time Conrad was writing it had become a catchword of the Liberal Imperialists.[1] Marlow invokes the argument here to suggest that the work-ethic of the British colonist fortifies him against the darkness, while the Roman, lacking this devotion, was more vulnerable. The Roman practice of empire, Marlow affirms, was much cruder; they merely "grabbed what they could get for the sake of what was to be got." Marlow here condemns Roman colonisation, but in the original manuscript he implicitly prefers it to the hypocritical pretences used by the modern colonisers of the Congo: at least the Romans "didn't get up pretty fictions about it."[2] Marlow again gets on delicate ground by saying that "The conquest of the earth . . . is not a pretty thing when you look into it too much"; and once more he has to qualify what he has said by conceding that imperial conquest can be redeemed by "An idea at the back of it; not a sentimental pretence but an idea; and an unselfish belief in the idea—something you can set up, and bow down before, and offer a sacrifice to."

Unselfish belief in the idea, and a devotion to efficiency, constitute a rather weak and asymmetrical alliance of powers to set up against

1. See H. C. G. Matthew, *The Liberal Imperialists* (London, 1973), pp. 19–72.
2. The manuscript continued: "Was there, I wonder, an association on a philanthropic basis to develop Britain, with some third-rate king for a president. . . ." (*H D N,.* 7).

greed, violence, and the call of the wilderness. It is especially difficult to know what to make of efficiency, since the Romans were not notably inefficient in most senses of the term. Marlow's reasoning is probably empirical and psychological: the automatic British "devotion" to the "unselfish idea" of efficiency immunises the believer against all morbid solicitations. But this defence of "what saves us" leaves untouched Marlow's moral and social grounds for condemning "the conquest of the earth"; and there is no reason to believe that Conrad intended to dissociate himself from this contradiction of attitudes, since Marlow is usually, as Wayne Booth writes, a "reliable reflector of the clarities and ambiguities of the implied author."[3] Without assuming any ironic intention on Conrad's part, then, we must register both the conciliatory intention, and the intrinsic inadequacy, of Marlow's attempt to exclude his listeners and his country from the ugliness of imperialism; and we must also note that while Marlow nowhere retracts his views on "efficiency" and "a definite idea," they play a rather minor and extremely ambiguous role in the rest of the story.

Marlow breaks off his placatory qualifications before he has informed his listeners just what idea should be sacrificed to. There ensues "a long silence." Finally. Marlow makes explicit that his general ruminations have been prompted by a past personal experience, and he then introduces his tale with a general explanation of its nature: "to understand the effect of it on me you ought to know how I got out there, what I saw, how I went up that river where I first met the poor chap. It was the farthest point of navigation and the culminating point of my experience. . . . It was . . . not extraordinary in any way—not very clear either" (51).

The tale will be unclear; it will be subjective; and it will subordinate the facts of Marlow's biography to their effect on him, even though this is a break with the wishes of the audience. For when Marlow says, "I don't want to bother you much with what happened to me personally," the primary narrator protests on behalf of fiction's traditional interest in individual character: "many tellers of tales . . . seem so often unaware of what their audience would best like to hear."

This introduction serves both as the end of the prologue and as the prologue to Marlow's main narrative. It continues the symbolic and thematic structure already described, but Marlow now concentrates more on directly reported sights and actions; as a result the narrative texture becomes much richer in impressionistic particularity, although the reflective and discursive element remains.

The rest of the first section is mainly concerned with recounting a

3. *The Rhetoric of Fiction* (Chicago, 1961), p. 154, n. 6.

series of Marlow's progressive initiations. Freed from the priorities of conventional autobiography, each incident is selected and treated for its larger implications, as we have already seen in the case of the first extended episode, where Marlow gets his appointment from the trading company.

The four other main stages of the first section deal with Marlow's voyage out, the company station, the overland journey, and the central station. They are arranged in chronological order, with occasional flashbacks and anticipatory parentheses; and within each stage, the particular episodes which are given the greatest emphasis seem selected to amplify or complicate Marlow's internal process of moral discovery, rather than to recount his journey.

During the voyage out most of the episodes serve to reverse the conventional application of light and darkness to the colonialism-savagery dichotomy. This reversal had already been suggested when Marlow says of the unnamed city from which he sets out that it "always makes me think of a whited sepulchre" (55). The terms of this contrast between virtuous pretences and evil realities come from Christ's anathema on the professed moral leaders of his time: "Woe unto you, scribes and Pharisees, hypocrites! for ye are like unto whited sepulchres, which indeed appear beautiful outward, but are within full of dead men's bones, and of all uncleanness." (Matthew 23:27). So Marlow leaves a white civilisation which masks death and darkness to confront the Dark Continent; and this will bring about a complementary transvaluation of the habitual assumptions which he initially shared with his society.[4]

As the French steamer makes its way along the African coast, Marlow's journey slowly takes on the aura of an enigmatic quest. "A coast as it slips by the ship," he comments, always seems to be "whispering, Come and find out" (60). At first his main impression is of how the overwhelming vastness of the land dwarfs the ship and the settlements it visits; these are "no bigger than pinheads" on the "untouched expanse" of the jungle, which is "so dark-green as to be almost black." Between ship and land there runs the boundary limit of the "white surf"; and to Marlow, feeling imprisoned "within the toil of a mournful and senseless delusion," the occasional emissaries of the land who came out across the surf in their boats "gave one a momentary contact with reality." Unlike the customhouse clerks and their protecting soldiers, some of whom are said to have "got drowned

4. Out of the enormous bulk of writing about light and darkness in *Heart of Darkness* one study may be cited, Wilfred S. Dowden, "The Light and the Dark: Imagery and Thematic Development in Conrad's 'Heart of Darkness,'" *Rice Institute Pamphlet*, no. 44 (1957): 33–51.

in the surf," these black paddlers wanted no excuse for being there;
they "had bone, muscle, a wild vitality, an intense energy of movement, that was as natural and true as the surf along their coast."

The tonic dynamism of the blacks who belong here is immediately
juxtaposed to another sight, that of a French man-of-war:

> She was shelling the bush. It appears the French had one of
> their wars going on thereabouts. Her ensign dropped limp
> like a rag; the muzzles of the long six-inch guns stuck out all
> over the low hull; the greasy, slimy swell swung her up lazily
> and let her down, swaying her thin masts. In the empty im-
> mensity of earth, sky, and water, there she was, incomprehen-
> sible, firing into a continent. Pop, would go one of the six-inch
> guns; a small flame would dart and vanish, a little white
> smoke would disappear, a tiny projectile would give a feeble
> screech—and nothing happened. Nothing could happen.
> There was a touch of insanity in the proceeding, a sense of
> lugubrious drollery in the sight; and it was not dissipated by
> somebody on board assuring me earnestly there was a camp
> of natives—he called them enemies!—hidden out of sight
> somewhere (61–62).

The symbolic force of this episode, as of many others in Marlow's
narrative, partly depends upon the way that it emerges out of the less
particularised summary which is the staple of Marlow's narrative; in
that setting the images take on the bold autonomy of pictures in a
dream. Here, for instance, there is no immediate context of other
narrative interests to diminish our attention to the absoluteness of the
opposition between the greasy swell and the white surf, the limp flag
of the intruders and the bracing energy of the indigenes. The passage
conveys through direct impressions alone that the warship is a parallel
manifestation of the same lethargic malevolence that Marlow has earlier experienced at the trading company's offices. But there is development as well as repetition in the visual symbolism of the scene: the
vaunted claims of efficiency and power put forward by a colonising
civilisation at home, are exposed, out here, as a farcical display of
puffs, pops, and screeches; the only practical effect of the rhetoric of
civilisation is to delude people, who can actually see nothing, that
there must be "enemies" in the bush because there may be natives.

Until now Marlow has seen the waste, ineffectiveness and cruelty of
the colonial presence only at a distance, and from the outside; when
he arrives at the company station he is forced to confront their human
consequences at close quarters. A file of six emaciated blacks balancing baskets of earth on their heads slowly passes Marlow, "with that
complete, deathlike indifference of unhappy savages" (64). When he

hears "another report from the cliff," the sound of blasting reminds Marlow of "that ship of war I had seen firing into a continent"; and he is moved to comment: "It was the same kind of ominous voice; but these men could by no stretch of the imagination be called enemies. They were called criminals, and the outraged law, like the bursting shells, had come to them, an insoluble mystery from the sea."

To shield himself from seeing any more of the lacerating results of "these high and just proceedings," of which he is "after all . . . a part," Marlow turns off the path into the shade of a grove, only to discover that "I had stepped into the gloomy circle of some Inferno" (66). As soon as his eyes have become used to the deep shade, Marlow discovers that he has taken refuge in a place "where some of the helpers had withdrawn to die." These labourers on the railway are essentially the victims, not of calculated brutality, but of the blindness to their needs of an alien and more powerful order; they have been "brought from all the recesses of the coast in all the legality of time contracts" by the rationality of a capitalist order based on legal agreements and chronometric time, an order which is wholly incomprehensible to the blacks; they are being mercilessly destroyed by a system which is administered by whites who make a point of not noticing what they are really doing.

Marlow glances down, and sees a face close to his hand; it belongs to a young black whose sunken eyes look up at him slowly; and Marlow finds "nothing else to do but to offer him" a ship's biscuit he happens to have in his pocket. By that instinctive movement of pity and reparation, Marlow reveals his unconscious commitment; among all his fellow-whites he alone, apparently, sees and feels the situation for what it is and reacts humanly to its imperatives.

The dying man has "tied a bit of white worsted round his neck," and Marlow's characteristic preoccupation with the moral essence of everyone he meets, and with their ultimate grounds of belief, leads him to wonder: "Why? Where did he get it? Was it a badge—an ornament—a charm—a propitiatory act? Was there any idea at all connected with it? It looked startling round his black neck, this bit of white thread from beyond the seas." The bit of white thread is an eloquent example of how effectively Conrad animates objects with the life of their symbolic meanings, and thus provokes larger questions in the reader. Does the dying black's mysterious faith in a scrap of cloth, for instance, mean that he wonders whether he can propitiate the white intruders by using their machinemade tradegoods as a fetish?

By now the reversal of the symbolic associations of black and white has gone very far; it is soon given a further range of thematic complication. When Marlow gets to the company station, the first sight that

meets his eye is a man who proves to be a very problematic representative of Marlow's other moral positive—work and efficiency. The
"white cuffs" and "snowy trousers" of the company's chief accountant
look dazzling; and Marlow at first reflects, only half ironically, that "in
the great demoralization of the land he kept up his appearance.
That's backbone" (68). So far, so good, perhaps; especially when it
appears that the accountant is also "devoted to his books, which were
in apple-pie order." This devotion, however, excludes all other
human values. There is a sick company agent dying in his office, and
the accountant comments: "The groans of this sick person . . . distract
my attention." The cold bureaucratic attitude, Marlow later discovers,
does more than atrophy natural sympathy; it incites the accountant to
positive inhumanity, as when the noise made by the native carriers
leads the accountant to explain, in a premonitory echo of Kurtz:
"When one has got to make correct entries, one comes to hate those
savages—hate them to the death" (70). The heartless priorities of the
Western administrative order have helped the accountant to maintain
his professional efficiency, but they insulate him from the darkness
only at the cost of insulating him from everything else.

The episodes of the accountant and the dying African enact a symbolic confrontation of the most absolute kind between two world
views. This confrontation exists at many levels; at the most abstract of
them it opposes magic to mathematics. The thematic direction of
these two episodes prepares us for another metaphysical question:
Can any more valid faith be found in Africa than those of the accountant and the dying black?

The overland journey to the central station supplies some negative
answers. All that Marlow sees of the original native life are the deserted villages with their ruined grass walls; but he hears "the tremor
of far-off drums, sinking, swelling, a tremor vast, faint; a sound
weird, appealing, suggestive, and wild—and perhaps with as profound a meaning as the sound of bells in a Christian country." The
meanings of the Christian conquerors, however, are only represented
by a drunken white man supposed to be in charge of the upkeep of
the road; when Marlow asks him why he came out, he replies scornfully: "To make money, of course. What do you think?"

When Marlow arrives at the central station he soon learns that this
is indeed the only faith to be found among the colonisers. There is no
vestige even of a devotion to efficiency; the central station is run by
the same "flabby, pretending, weak-eyed devil of a rapacious and
pitiless folly" (65) as Marlow found earlier at the company station: the
brickmaker makes no bricks; the man in black moustaches fights the
fire by filling his leaking bucket with "about a quart of water" (76);

and in general, Marlow comments, "they were all waiting—all the sixteen or twenty pilgrims of them—for something; and upon my word it did not seem an uncongenial occupation."

Marlow's persistent description of the company agents as "pilgrims" is of some interest as an anticipation of a literary device which later became common in the symbolist tradition. The disappearance of an intelligible spiritual, social, and literary order had left a residual hunger for earlier periods where such an order was thought to have obtained; and so this order was used as an ironical touchstone to reveal the emptiness of the modern world. Joyce used Homer's *Odyssey*[5] in his *Ulysses,* and T. S. Eliot the legend of the Grail in *The Waste Land,* to act as implicit contrasts by which the world of the past exposes the inadequacies of the present; and Marlow calls the colonisers "pilgrims" for the same critical purpose, although the device is used less obtrusively, since it has a literal basis: like real pilgrims the colonisers whom Marlow sees "strolling aimlessly about" actually have staves, symbols of authority which white men generally were wont to carry in the colonies. Still, the appellation plants a large question in our minds: if a pilgrimage is a small human community united for the purpose of a single journey by a religious aim, what aim unites these modern pilgrims? Marlow makes the answer to this question very clear when he says of the officials of the central station, that they "wandered here and there . . . like a lot of faithless pilgrims bewitched inside a rotten fence. The word 'ivory' rang in the air, was whispered, was sighed. You would think they were praying to it" (76).

At the central station Marlow is surrounded by beings who are emotionally, morally, and spiritually void; and for this lack of human essence he finds another analogy, that of hollow men. The image complements the idea behind Marlow's use of the term pilgrims: their professions are hollow; like sepulchres they present only a facade which conceals the dead bones of belief. At the company station Marlow had seen the accountant as a hairdresser's dummy; here the brickmaker is a "papier-maché Mephistopheles" who makes Marlow think "that if I tried I could poke my forefinger through him, and would find nothing inside but a little loose dirt, maybe" (81); and the manager, who has risen to his position only because he is immune to disease, gloats that "men who come out here should have no entrails" (74). The hollowness of the manager is also spiritual. His smile sug-

5. One celebrated statement of the position is T. S. Eliot's essay "*Ulysses,* Order and Myth" (*The Dial* 75 [1923]: 480–83): "Manipulating a continuous parallel between contemporaneity and antiquity . . . is simply a way of controlling, of ordering, of giving a shape and a significance to the immense panorama of futility and anarchy which is contemporary history."

gests "a door opening into a darkness he had in his keeping"; but Marlow suspects that the reason the manager never gave away "the secret" of "what could control such a man," was that "perhaps there was nothing within him."

Marlow has learned as many negative truths as he can bear; they add up to the discovery that the "white patch" on the map which he dreamed about as a boy has indeed become "a place of darkness" (52), and that it is his fellow whites who have made it so. Even before he arrived at the central station Marlow had recalled the doctor's warnings against "the mental changes of individuals, on the spot" (72), and feared that he "was becoming scientifically interesting"; in that continuing fear Marlow goes to work repairing the wrecked steamer. It is only by "turning, so to speak, my back on that station," Marlow says, that he can keep some "hold on the redeeming facts of life" (75). He can draw some strength from devoting all his energies to his "battered, twisted, ruined, tin-pot steamboat" (85), and from the society of the mechanics with whom he works, and "whom the other pilgrims naturally despised."

Work necessarily involves a reality which none of the pilgrims are willing to encounter. Marlow does not absorb himself in work because he likes it for its own sake—"No man does," he says. His reasons are, rather, psychological and even metaphysical: "I like what is in the work,—the chance to find yourself. Your own reality—for yourself" (85). It is as a part of this search for his own reality that Marlow's battle to repair the steamboat takes on a special meaning: an absorbing need to meet Kurtz, with whom he hopes that dialogue will at last be possible. We have seen enough of Marlow's spiritual desolation to understand why he should be so intensely "curious to see whether this man, who had come out equipped with moral ideas of some sort, would climb to the top after all and how he would set about his work when there" (88).

(b) Marlow and Kurtz

With this question, the first section ends. Chapter is hardly the word. The needs of magazine publication dictated that *Heart of Darkness* should be divided into three parts; but although the first break was planned by Conrad, there was less time for planning the second, and it may well have been decided on by Blackwood (*B*, 47, 51).[6] In any case the narrative is continuous, and in this reflects the tendency

6. Although Philip Stevick uses *Heart of Darkness* as an example of how "Conrad's chapters are models of the art of division" (*The Chapter in Fiction: Theories of Narrative Division* [Syracuse, 1970], p. 156).

in the late nineteenth-century and modern novel to reduce the autonomy of the chapter as a compositional unit. *Heart of Darkness* is essentially composed of a single and unbroken narrative movement. This seamless continuity is particularly characteristic of the *novella,* whose length falls between that of the novel and the short story; the intermediate scale of the genre makes possible an ample, complex, but still manageable unity of movement, which no doubt helps to explain why the form of the novella was one in which many modern novelists, including James, Lawrence, and Mann, achieved their greatest triumphs; as did Conrad, whose *Heart of Darkness* is perhaps better called a long *novella* than a short novel.

When the first instalment of *Heart of Darkness* came out, Cunninghame Graham wrote to express his enthusiasm; but Conrad urged him to delay final judgment: "There are two more instalments in which the idea is so wrapped up in secondary notions that You—even You!—may miss it. And also you must remember that I don't start with an abstract notion. I start with definite images and as their rendering is true some little effect is produced. So far the note struck chimes in with your convictions—mais après? There is an après. But I think that if you look a little into the episodes you will find in them the the right intention though I fear nothing that is practically effective" (*C G*, 116).

Conrad does not say what these "secondary notions" were, and our only direct clues are that he specifically distinguishes them from the "note struck" in the first instalment, and fears that subsequent notes may not "chime" with Cunninghame Graham's convictions. The "note struck" is almost certainly the anti-colonial theme of the first part; what Conrad meant by his "secondary notions" can only be guessed at. One difficulty about most of the possible notions which present themselves is that they usually operate not as single ideas, but as parts of dualisms; another difficulty is that these dualisms are neither static nor symmetrical, but overlap or lead into others. Conrad's treatment of the colonial theme is typical. During the first part it is developed very largely as an implicit opposition between the public pretences in Europe and the contrary realities which Marlow discovers in Africa; but then this opposition becomes part of a more general dualism of progress versus atavism, until finally both dualisms collapse when Marlow discovers that Kurtz, the highest representative of European colonial progress, has been transformed into its opposite.

Two other persistent thematic dualisms offer themselves as possible "secondary notions," although, of course, there is no reason to believe that Conrad conceived them in these abstract terms. The first of them is that of work versus words; work receives considerable emphasis in the first part, while the theme of words is developed only in the last two. As to the second dualism, that of restraint versus liberation, both ideas surface only towards the end of the second part. All three of these thematic dualisms will be considered in conjunction with a brief account of the general progress of the narrative up to Kurtz's death.

The idea of atavistic reversion emerges in Marlow's imagination at the central station; and then, as the little steamboat plunges deeper into the jungle, its manifestations find a deeper resonance as his previous assumptions about the place of man in the continuum of space and time are irresistibly undermined. Along "the high walls of our winding way" Marlow sees: "Trees, trees, millions of trees, massive, immense, running up high; and at their foot, hugging the bank against the stream, crept the little begrimed steamboat, like a sluggish beetle crawling on the floor of a lofty portico" (95). As they go deeper inland Marlow gradually comes to feel "cut off for ever from everything you had known once—somewhere—far away—in another existence perhaps" (93). His old familiar world is disappearing, and Marlow contemplates the new in a spirit akin to that of Baudelaire's "Correspondances": the forest seems to have meanings and intentions; Marlow continually senses its "mysterious stillness watching me" in silent interrogation. The mute immensity of the primeval jungle makes him feel that he and his civilisation are insignificant and temporary intruders. At the central station, he says, "The silent wilderness surrounding this cleared speck on the earth struck me as something great and invincible, like evil or truth, waiting patiently for the passing away of this fantastic invasion" (76). Marlow is overwhelmed to realise "how big, how confoundedly big, was that thing that couldn't talk, and perhaps was deaf as well" (81). He had wondered "What was in there?" Now that he is "in there," Marlow still wonders.

Just as the paddlers off the African coast had seemed a touchstone that exposed the unnatural and hypocritical sickness of Western civilisation, so Marlow now finds a similar appeal in his occasional glimpses of the tribal life along the river banks. Nothing he hears or sees—an occasional "roll of drums behind the curtain of trees," or "a burst of yells, a whirl of black limbs, a mass of hands clapping, of feet stamping, of bodies swaying"—has a clear meaning; he does not know if "the prehistoric man was cursing us, praying to us, welcoming us—who could tell?" (96). Still, something is communicated which is vitally human: "What thrilled you was just the thought of their humanity—like yours—the thought of your remote kinship with this wild and passionate uproar. Ugly. Yes, it was ugly enough; but if you were man enough you would admit to yourself that there was in you just the faintest trace of a response to the terrible frankness of that noise." Marlow comes to believe that his subliminal responsiveness is an echo of the primitive residues in his own being; he has a "dim suspicion" that there was "a meaning" in that noise which his listeners—"you—you so remote from the night of first ages—could comprehend. And why not? The mind of man is capable of anything—because everything is in it, all the past as well as all the future."

Kurtz's mind is to prove as capable of a fearless acting out of the whole past of human barbarism, as of propounding its verbal opposite in eloquent platitudes about boundless progress in the future.

As for Marlow, he immunises himself against both barbarism and the ugliness of progress through work, as he twice explains to his listeners. On the first occasion he explains that it was really his work as captain which rendered him deaf to the solicitations of the wilderness "watching me at my monkey tricks, just as it watches you fellows performing on your respective tight-ropes for—what is it? half-a-crown a tumble—" (94). A voice growls, "Try to be civil, Marlow." Marlow quickly invokes the notion of efficiency in a breezy concession: "what does the price matter, if the trick be well done?" and he then goes on to praise his cannibal crew on the grounds that "They were men one could work with, and I am grateful to them."

Marlow's second interchange with his listeners occurs soon afterwards. He has confessed to feeling the mysterious appeal of primitive life, and asserted that, against this "truth stripped of its cloak of time," man must "meet that truth . . . with his own inborn strength" (97). This need is only felt by those who admit, as Marlow does, that there is "an appeal to me in this fiendish row"; as for others, he continues, "a fool, what with sheer fright and fine sentiments, is always safe." Marlow is implicitly dividing civilised man into three categories: those who respond to savagery and succumb, like Kurtz; those who respond but possess "a deliberate belief" which enables them to resist; and the fools who do not respond at all because they do not notice. This view naturally seems insulting to his comfortable listeners, and one of them is provoked to inarticulate protest. Marlow asks: "Who's that grunting?", and proceeds once again to evade the question of belief by falling back on the defence of work: "You wonder I didn't go ashore for a howl and a dance? Well, no—I didn't." The reason, Marlow affirms, was just that he was too busy navigating the steamboat and keeping an eye on the fireman; these duties, he says, provided enough "surface-truth . . . to save a wiser man."

Surface truths imply deeper truths; and Marlow soon finds himself

needing to posit one which introduces a new dualism. Just below
Kurtz's station, when an attack is imminent, the headman of Marlow's
cannibal crew puts in a claim for any edible enemy carcasses that may
become available. This suddenly makes Marlow realise that, as a result
of the blindness of the trading company to their needs, the crew have
long been on the verge of starvation: their pay—three pieces of brass
wire a week—does not buy the food it is supposed to, mainly because
the villages along the river are deserted or hostile. So the cannibal
crew had every reason to eat the whites on board, and being "thirty to
five" (104), they could easily have done it. The crew had "no earthly
reason for any kind of scruple." "What possible restraint?" then, can
have checked them, Marlow wonders; "Was it superstition, disgust,
patience, fear—or some kind of primitive honour?" He finds no answer, but the overwhelming fact of their restraint remains.

Restraint is tangentially related to the atavism-civilisation duality
because it is a quality which is not usually needed in modern society,
where all necessary sanctions on conduct are supplied externally. As
Marlow puts it to his listeners on the *Nellie:* "Here you all are, each
moored with two good addresses, like a hulk with two anchors, a
butcher round one corner, a policeman round another" (114). This
aside on restraint is given a very specific point by its context: it occurs
during Marlow's long anticipatory parenthesis about Kurtz, which is
itself intercalated between the death of the helmsman during the
attack, and Marlow's ruminations about the helmsman's fate. His
rashness in deserting his post, and opening the shutter through which
the spear entered, came from imitating the hysterical folly of the
white passengers in firing blindly at the unseen enemy in the bush.
Marlow's obituary for the helmsman in effect brackets him with Kurtz
as an example of the destructive effects of first having lost inherited
moral restraints through exposure to another culture, and then being
removed from external restraints by circumstances: "Poor fool! If he
had only left that shutter alone. He had no restraint, no restraint—
just like Kurtz—a tree swayed by the wind" (119).

The thematic opposite to restraint, liberation, is established as soon
as the steamboat arrives off the inner station. The first man Marlow
sees is not Kurtz, but the beckoning figure of the young Russian
sailor, whose patched clothes make him look like a harlequin. His
possession of Towson's *An Inquiry into some Points of Seamanship*—as
neatly mended as his ragged motley—proves him to be endowed with
the right attitude towards work; he has shown courage and unselfish-
ness in nursing Kurtz; and Marlow almost envies him his "absolutely
pure, uncalculating, unpractical spirit of adventure" (126). But he
most emphatically does not envy him "his devotion to Kurtz."

The Russian's youthful innocence is apparent from his "beardless, boyish face" with "smiles and frowns chasing each other over that open countenance like sunshine and shadow" (122); and this betokens both the spontaneity and the self-doubt of youth, a combination which makes him the natural prey of Kurtz's malignant self-assurance. Feeling that he himself has "no great thoughts" (132), the Russian listened enthralled, as Marlow puts it, to Kurtz's "monologues on . . . love, justice, conduct of life—or what not"; and so, despite his knowledge that Kurtz's practice was very different from anything in his monologues, the Russian yielded utterly.

The second part ends on this note. "I tell you," the Russian cries, "this man has enlarged my mind"; and Marlow continues: "He opened his arms wide, staring at me with his little blue eyes that were perfectly round" (125). Romantic individualism had set up the ideal of absolute liberation from religious, social, and ethical norms; and this ideal, later reinforced by many other forces of nineteenth-century history, made the spread of freedom and progress depend on the removal of all "restraints." The Russian harlequin thus represents his century's innocent but fateful surrender to that total Faustian unrestraint which believes that everything is justified if it "enlarges the mind."

The second section of *Heart of Darkness* ends with our attention ironically focussed on the Russian's rapt gratitude to the man who has done him this benefit. In the last section, Marlow at long last meets Kurtz.

Marlow's involvement with Kurtz is of a unique kind both in literature and life. The normal way of thinking about the relationship of two people is based either on set social patterns—parent and child, man and woman, teacher and pupil, master and servant—or on the determining emotions involved—love or hate, admiration or contempt, dominance or dependence: and literature normally uses these set classifications as its basis both for the psychology of the individual characters and for their relationships with others. In *Heart of Darkness*, however, the established emotional and social categories seem almost irrelevant: Marlow and Kurtz are neither friends nor enemies, for instance, and although Marlow learns much from Kurtz, he is decidedly not his pupil. This anomalous situation has led to many divergent interpretations of the psychological ties between the protagonists; and, since the tale says little on the subject, a recapitulation of the literal evidence about the relationship is necessary.

Even before he meets the Russian, Marlow already knows a good deal about Kurtz. From the accountant at the company station he has learned that Kurtz is a "first-class agent" who "sends in as much ivory as all the others put together" (69), and that he will be "a somebody in the Administration before long." At the central station Marlow's curiosity is aroused by the hostility which the pilgrims feel towards Kurtz, and so he questions the brickmaker about him: "He is a prodigy" the brickmaker replies, "an emissary of pity, and science, and progress, and devil knows what else" (79). On the other hand, Marlow receives an unsettling impression from a somewhat more direct contact—a "small sketch in oils" which Kurtz had painted over a year ago. It represents "a woman, draped and blindfolded, carrying a lighted torch"; and by making the classical figure of justice carry not the scales of equity, but a lighted torch, Kurtz was presumably representing colonialism as enlightenment through the two values with which the symbol of a lighted torch is conventionally associated—education and hope for the future. There are, however, two disturbing ironies: Kurtz has portrayed the bearer of these values as blindfolded; and this confusing ambiguity is present elsewhere in the picture: "The background," Marlow reports, "was sombre—almost black. The movement of the woman was stately, and the effect of the torch-light on the face was sinister." We note that the torch has the effect, not of illuminating the darkness, but only of making the lady's face look sinister; and we wonder if Kurtz has inadvertently portrayed the dark perversion of his own professed commitment to civilisation.

Marlow's personal attitude to Kurtz is from the beginning largely dictated by particular external circumstances that make Kurtz seem the lesser of two evils. On his way up, Marlow has felt a growing need to dissociate himself from all the doings of his fellow whites; and at the central station this motive is reinforced when it becomes apparent both that Kurtz is the spearhead of the reform party in the trading company, and that Marlow is regarded as his ally. The obscure machinations of the manager of the central station and his cronies against Kurtz and Marlow remain vestigial as far as the plot is concerned; but they channel Marlow's disgusted bewilderment at everything he has seen into a deeper intellectual and moral identification with his imaginary picture of Kurtz. He believes, for instance, that Kurtz shares his devotion to the work ethic, because he has heard the manager talking about how Kurtz had sent back his last load of ivory with his clerk, and had then paddled back alone to his station, some three hundred miles upriver. On this Marlow comments: "I did not know the motive"; but he imagines that "perhaps [Kurtz] was just simply a fine fellow who stuck to his work for its own sake" (90).

It is, then, a combination of the accidents of circumstance, a reliance on out-of-date reports, and the pressures of personal need,

which give Marlow a vague sense of being captured by Kurtz's mysterious power. During the attack on the steamboat, when Marlow suddenly thinks that Kurtz must have been killed, he immediately feels a
"lonely desolation" which, he says, is as deep as if "I [had] been robbed
of a belief or had missed my destiny in life" (114). But even at this
stage Kurtz's power is a verbal one; as Marlow says: "I made the
strange discovery that I had never imagined him as doing, you know,
but as discoursing. . . . The man presented himself as a voice."

Marlow immediately goes on to anticipate his later talks with Kurtz,
as though to reassure his hearers on the *Nellie* that, in this particular
respect at least, his hopes had not been disappointed: but he adds the
caution that the gift of expression is a dangerously double-edged
weapon: it can be either "the pulsating stream of light, or the deceitful
flow from the heart of an impenetrable darkness." But as soon as the
thematic duality of words and work has been established by the
apposition of Kurtz and the helmsman, Marlow shows his decided
preference for the latter: "I am not prepared to affirm," he tells his
listeners, that Kurtz was "exactly worth the life we lost in getting to
him" (119). The helmsman had, after all, "done something, he had
steered"; he and Marlow shared the "subtle bond" of a common task;
and this had entitled the helmsman, in his last look at Marlow before
he died, to affirm his "claim of distant kinship."

Marlow has no such bond with Kurtz. Their kinship is of a much
more complicated kind: it began in mistaken assumptions; it is in no
sense reciprocal; and it has the curious characteristic that it never
exists as current actuality, but only in prospect before Marlow meets
Kurtz, or as a preempting obligation after his death.

Marlow's first great disillusionment comes when he arrives at the
inner station and learns from the Russian that, as he surmised, the
attack on the steamboat was not really an attack, or at least was only
"undertaken under the stress of desperation, and in its essence was
purely protective" (107). Protective of what? Of Kurtz, Marlow is surprised to discover. And why? Because, the Russian explains, they
adore him, and "they don't want him to go" (124–25). The Russian
further reveals that it was actually "Kurtz who had ordered the attack"
(139). Not only is Kurtz adored; he apparently adores it.

While the Russian is still talking about Kurtz, Marlow accidentally
gets visual confirmation of his tale. Being unable to go ashore, he is
trying to satisfy his curiosity by looking at Kurtz's ruined house, with
its fence now broken down and offering no protection from the wilderness and its denizens. Suddenly, in "a brusque movement" of Marlow's field glasses "one of the remaining posts . . . leaped up"; it bears,
"black, dried, sunken, with closed eyelids,—a head that seemed to

sleep at the top of that pole, and, with the shrunken dry lips showing a narrow white line of the teeth, was smiling, too" (130–31). Marlow discovers that there are other heads on the stakes, and that they are "turned to the house." Their function is clearly not, like those on the palisades of Arab forts, or on Traitor's Gate, to warn beholders against offending the rulers of the land; nor is their function merely aesthetic, like those which one official at Stanley Falls disposed as "a decoration around a flower bed in front of his house."[7] In Kurtz's case the heads, as Marlow puts it, are "not ornamental but symbolic." The Russian, who "had not dared to take these—say, symbols—down" for fear of offending Kurtz, echoes the explanation given of the French bombardment of the African coast, by saying that they are "the heads of rebels" (132). For Marlow, however, their thematic meaning is summed up in saying that "they only showed that Mr. Kurtz lacked restraint in the gratification of his various lusts."

Marlow's horror is soon turned in another direction. Kurtz's long, emaciated body is carried on board; and when Marlow hears the now triumphant manager describe Kurtz's methods as "unsound" because "the time was not ripe for vigorous action" (137), he finds it so vile in its amoral hypocrisy that, despite what he now knows, he "turn[s] mentally to Kurtz for relief." Finding a bitter comfort in the reflection that "it was something to have at least a choice of nightmares," Marlow formally aligns himself with Kurtz by refusing to discuss the matter in the manager's terms. He commits himself only to the ambiguous judgment that "Mr. Kurtz is a remarkable man"; and to appease the Russian's fear that his idol's glory will suffer if he leaves him in enemy hands, Marlow assures him that "I am Mr. Kurtz's friend—in a way," and that "Mr. Kurtz's reputation is safe with me" (139).

That night Marlow is awakened by the sound of native drums and frenzied yells; he happens to glance casually into Kurtz's cabin; it is empty. Earlier, Kurtz's adoring tribesmen had tried to prevent his being taken away from them onto the steamboat; but now it appears that Kurtz's need for his tribesmen is equally imperious. He has gone back on his own. Marlow is "completely unnerved" at "the moral shock . . . as if something altogether monstrous, intolerable to thought and odious to the soul, had been thrust upon me unexpectedly" (141). He quietly goes ashore to bring Kurtz back again; and he finds him crawling "on all-fours" towards the ritual fires, and the nearest black sorcerer with antelope horns on his head. Atavistic re-

---

7. Neal Ascherson, *King Incorporated*, pp. 252–53. Ascherson concludes that "dozens of sources confirm that such things took place," and that Conrad "did not invent the horrors of *Heart of Darkness*."

gression could hardly go further; a man crawling like an animal to be worshipped by followers in the ceremonial guise of animals.

The issue is clear. Marlow must determine whether wilderness and darkness have an invincible power over man's moral being; and so he begins to struggle for Kurtz's soul. Believing that Kurtz could only have been lured back by "the awakening of forgotten and brutal instincts, by the memory of gratified and monstrous passions" (144), Marlow tries to counter them. When he tells Kurtz that unless he comes back "You will be lost . . . utterly lost," it is "a flash of inspiration"—presumably because Kurtz cannot bear to lose the other glories that he imagines he can still win at home; and so, believing that he can still add to his triumphs, Kurtz allows himself to be supported quietly back to the steamboat.

Before considering the moral implications of Kurtz's death on the journey downriver, we should perhaps confront the common objection that Conrad does not show us exactly what Kurtz has done at the inner station.

Actually the scattered evidence makes Kurtz's career at a literal level reasonably clear. When Marlow arrives, Kurtz has been without supplies from downriver for well over a year, and, except for the Russian sailor, completely cut off from "civilisation" for equally long. Despite two severe illnesses, Kurtz's activities expanded. Having run out of trade goods, he used his supply of firearms and cartridges to extort ivory by force; and as he plunged further into the surrounding country, he discovered "lots of villages" and a lake (128). Kurtz then got the tribe by the lake, which was apparently at least a thousand strong, to serve as his private army. Like many other white and Arab traders in Central Africa during the period, he armed his followers and pillaged the countryside for great quantities of ivory on his own account; and at the time of Marlow's arrival, has "only lately" assembled his tribe to prepare for another raiding expedition even further afield (129).

There is nothing inherently improbable in Kurtz's having been accorded sacred, if not actually divine, status. It was commonly accorded African kings and chieftains at the time; and J. G. Frazer had shown in The Golden Bough, whose first edition came out in 1890, that in such cases the illness or impending departure of such a leader as Kurtz would be regarded as calamitous for his people: "In the kingdom of Congo," Frazer wrote, "there was a supreme pontiff . . . and if he were to die a natural death, they thought that the world would perish."[8]

8. J. G. Frazer, The Golden Bough, 2 vols. (London, 1894), vol. 1, p. 113.

Conrad's picture of Kurtz's career at the inner station, then, is sketchy, but not inherently implausible; the way this career is presented, however, is open to somewhat more serious objection. A good many critics[9] have attacked the vague and yet repetitive generality with which Kurtz's relapse into barbarism is presented, and to such clichés as "unspeakable rites" (118), for instance. That there is rhetorical overemphasis and attitudinising in this, as in some of Marlow's other speeches, and indeed in much else of Conrad's writing, cannot be denied, But the objections are not merely stylistic. Human curiosity and modern tastes being what they are, it is as well to admit that we feel cheated at not being given a ringside seat at one of Kurtz's orgies. We probably feel cheated because our attitude towards Kurtz's actions is very different from that which Conrad could presume for his original readers; the various moral and political revolutions of the twentieth century have made us believe that primitive life must be better, or at least more "real," than ours; and we also think that we should refrain from calling the manifestations of another culture "ugly," as Marlow does. There is another important difference. It is now commonly assumed that everyone comes equipped with a heart of darkness; this is surely just as implausible and self-indulgent as the opposite delusion, so widely held in Conrad's day, which attributed to civilised man an inherent moral superiority; but the total reversal of moral attitudes in the intervening decades means that Marlow's moral outrage at Kurtz's participation in human sacrifices is bound to seem exaggerated or false to modern readers who believe not so much, in Henry James's phrase, that "the abysses are all so shallow," [10] as that they do not exist.

In addition to Kurtz's main thematic importance as the supreme exhibit of the dialectic between progress and atavism, he also represents the extreme position in several other dualities. Two have already been taken up: Kurtz stands for liberation as opposed to restraint, and for words as opposed to work. Another polarity, that which opposes belief to hollowness, is perhaps to be regarded as a corollary of the work/words dualism; in any case Kurtz is obviously intended as the climactic example of the inner moral void which Marlow has found in all the representatives of Western progress.

9. F. R. Leavis remains the most forceful of the critics of Conrad's "adjectival insistence." In some parts of *Heart of Darkness*, especially where Kurtz is concerned, he finds a "cheapening" that is "little short of disastrous," and remarks that at times Conrad is "intent on making a virtue out of not knowing what he means" (*The Great Tradition: George Eliot, Henry James, Joseph Conrad* [London, 1948], pp. 179–80).

10. *The Legend of the Master*, comp. Simon Nowell-Smith (London, 1947), p. 122.

Marlow assumes that the wilderness "echoed loudly" in Kurtz "because he was hollow at the core" (131). The hollowness which Kurtz shares with the pilgrims is what led T. S. Eliot to use the savagely contemptuous announcement in pidgin by the manager's servant, "Mistah Kurtz—he dead," as the epigraph to *The Hollow Men*. Eliot's epigraph presents Kurtz as a symbol for the faithless and inner emptiness of the modern world in general. Kurtz's hollowness also defines the nature of his role as the uniquely privileged representative of words; and it is this theme, with its corollary variants not only of hollowness but of the lie, which supplies the main thematic continuity in the last part of *Heart of Darkness*.

During the voyage downstream Marlow discovers that the hopes he had once placed in a dialogue with Kurtz are to be disappointed. Marlow is, indeed, afforded a good deal of the "inestimable privilege of listening to the gifted Kurtz" (114); but Kurtz's verbal virtuosity is reserved for solo performances; as the Russian tells Marlow with "severe exaltation," "You don't talk with that man—you listen to him" (123); and so there is no dialogue. Kurtz is indeed little more than a voice, and that voice, Marlow discovers, issues from a remorseless self-preoccupation "concentrated . . . upon himself with horrible intensity" (144). Kurtz has "kicked himself loose of the earth," and of any feeling or principle which would sufficiently connect him to other human beings to make possible any human reciprocity.

Still, Marlow must try to battle for Kurtz's soul as it "struggl[es] blindly with itself." Kurtz's inner hollowness affords no base from which to resolve the conflict between the two forces—atavism and "progress"—which possess him. Most immediately, there is the mute appeal of the wilderness; his mistress; absolute kingly, even sacred power; and a total liberation from all restraints—Kurtz had once said he would shoot the Russian for his ivory "because he could do so, and had a fancy for it, and there was nothing on earth to prevent him killing whom he jolly well pleased" (128). But Kurtz mentions the wilderness side of his desires only once, when he asks Marlow to close the cabin's shutter: "I can't bear to look at this," he says. Marlow obeys and there follows a silence which is finally broken by Kurtz: " 'Oh, but I will wring your heart yet!' he cried at the invisible wilderness" (148).

Kurtz is essentially one vast indiscriminate appetite, and his greed does not allow him to face the contradiction between the atavistic desires he has appeased in the wilderness and those with which he had set out from Europe—his dreams "of lying fame, of sham distinction, of all the appearances of success and power" (147–48). It is almost entirely of these last—the rewards of civilisation and progress—that Kurtz talks to Marlow, partly because Kurtz regards Marlow as his ally in "the gang of virtue" (135), but mainly because that "gang," at least as Kurtz has learned to exploit it, is essentially verbal. "The wastes of his weary brain," Marlow tells us, "were haunted by shadowy images now—images of wealth and fame revolving obsequiously round his unextinguishable gift of noble and lofty expression" (147). Even in his final twilight Kurtz mouths the moral platitudes of his civilisation like an automaton; but they remain totally unconnected with the realities of his life.

This is not to be seen as hypocrisy; Kurtz might possibly be trying to deceive Marlow when he tells him, "Of course you must take care of the motives—right motives—always"; but it is to himself that, just before the end, Kurtz mutters: "Live rightly, die, die . . . . " The question of sincerity hardly arises, since Kurtz's words really belong to the hollow world of politics and journalism, as Marlow implies when he wonders: "Was he rehearsing some speech in his sleep, or was it a fragment of a phrase from some newspaper article? He had been writing for the papers and meant to do so again, 'for the furthering of my ideas. It's a duty.' "

The total disconnection in Kurtz between words and reality reflects a general tendency in Western culture to place an exorbitant cultural emphasis on the verbal aspects of collective life; and this inevitably involves a disparity between verbal expression and the actual behaviour much deeper than exists in most other societies. The disparity is particularly flagrant in colonisation; it is enacted in the most extreme and climactic way in Kurtz's report for the International Society for the Suppression of Savage Customs. He had penned seventeen pages of a "moving appeal to every altruistic sentiment"; then, much later, he scrawled: "Exterminate all the brutes!" (118). By the time Kurtz comes to confide the report to Marlow, however, he has already forgotten his contradictory postscript, and this has its own kind of larger truth; it exhibits both the progress/regress polarity as it operates in the history and the psychology of colonisation, and, more generally, the ease with which the individual can be unaware of the disjunction between his words and his works in a society which is so widely and deeply fissured by the contradictions between its pretences and its realities.

Marlow naturally decides that Kurtz's is "an impenetrable darkness" (149), but he is proved wrong. One evening he goes into Kurtz's cabin carrying a candle, and notices that Kurtz cannot even see its light. Then, Marlow continues:

> Anything approaching the change that came over his features I have never seen before, and hope never to see again. Oh, I wasn't touched. I was fascinated. It was as though a veil

had been rent. I saw on that ivory face the expression of
sombre pride, of ruthless power, of craven terror—of an intense and hopeless despair. Did he live his life again in every
detail of desire, temptation, and surrender during that supreme moment of complete knowledge? He cried in a
whisper at some image, at some vision—he cried out twice, a
cry that was no more than a breath—
    "The horror! The horror!"

The final gasping anaphora of "The horror! The horror!" strains
rather hard for its effect; but it embodies three effective ironies. First,
that on the only occasion that Kurtz's voice loses its preternatural
resonance, it should also express the truth about his deeds; second,
that Kurtz should so neatly exemplify in this drastic stylistic simplification the utter contradiction between the rhetoric and the reality of
progress; and lastly, that this simplification should also break so completely with the note of consolatory serenity which is traditional for
deathbed utterances in fiction.

Kurtz's last words, however, offer some consolation to Marlow, who
thinks Kurtz "a remarkable man" because: "He had something to say.
He said it" (151). Just what Kurtz was referring to when he said "The
horror," however, is not wholly clear; nor is Marlow's ensuing commentary.

The most usual interpretation is based on Marlow's memory of
Kurtz's "wide and immense stare embracing, condemning, loathing
all the universe" (156). The horror is seen as a verdict on the essential
depravity of man and his civilisation. This interpretation of Kurtz's
final anathema was no doubt that of T. S. Eliot, when he thought of
using the paragraph ending "The horror! The horror!" as his epigraph for The Waste Land on the grounds that it was "somewhat
elucidative."[11]

But the main object of Kurtz's condemnation is surely himself, and
what he has done; his dying whisper pronounces rejection of the
Faustian compact with the wilderness which had "sealed his soul to
its own" (115). His final cry can only be judged, as Marlow judges it,
"an affirmation, a moral victory" (151), if it constitutes an acknowledgment of the horror of his former deeds. Even so, that Kurtz's
"judgment upon the adventures of his soul on this earth" should be
presented by Marlow as a significant moral victory seems a little unconvincing today, and its force largely depends on the intellectual
atmosphere of the late nineteenth century. The question had been

11. The Waste Land: A Facsimile and Transcript of the Original Drafts, ed. Valerie Eliot
(New York, 1971), p. 125. Ezra Pound dissuaded him.

raised, in many forms, whether the universe is, as Dostoevsky's Ivan Karamazov thinks, a fabric of meaningless cruelty in which "everything is lawful."[12] Kurtz's whole career seemed to support this view: he acknowledged no internal or external restraint; but Marlow's worst doubts are set at rest when this "being to whom I could not appeal in the name of anything high or low" (144) makes a final judgment which is "the expression of some sort of belief" (151); and without some ethical belief, Kurtz's judgment would have no logical basis.

The moral trajectory of Kurtz's life embodies a paradox similar to that which had earlier been used by Schopenhauer, when he contrasted Cain with innocents who, somewhat like the Russian harlequin, remain impervious to "the evil inherent in our will": "The first criminal and murderer, Cain, who acquired a knowledge of guilt, and through guilt acquired a knowledge of virtue by repentance, and so came to understand the meaning of life, is a tragical figure more significant, and almost more respectable, than all the innocent fools in the world put together."[13] Marlow makes much the same distinction when he says that "no fool ever made a bargain for his soul with the devil: the fool is too much of a fool, or the devil too much of a devil—I don't know which" (117). But, of course, Kurtz is hardly a real parallel to Schopenhauer's Cain; one momentary expression of horror is hardly enough to make him a tragic figure;[14] and Marlow stops well short of making such a claim. He concedes that Kurtz "was not common" (119), but it is primarily the uncommon scale of his offenses which makes it impossible for Marlow merely to lay him to "rest in the dust-bin of progress."

As to his personal feelings towards Kurtz, whether conscious or unconscious, many critics have taken the view that Marlow identifies himself with Kurtz in the sense that, consciously or unconsciously, he really admires or envies Kurtz, not for what he once was, but for what he has done. Thus Lawrence Graver argues that Kurtz has the attraction of the romantic outlaw who crosses "the boundaries of conventional morality" and explores "the possibilities of living on the other side" (*L G*, 85); Robert F. Haugh takes this interpretation further in seeing Marlow as "a brother to Kurtz . . . impelled by the powerful attraction of the man—or demon—to something in himself";[15] and Lionel Trilling writes that Marlow "accords Kurtz an ad-

12. *The Brothers Karamazov*, trans. Constance Garnett (London, 1913), p. 278.

13. "Parerga," *On Human Nature*, trans. Thomas Bailey Saunders (London, 1913), p. 119.

14. For a view of Kurtz as tragic, see Murray Krieger, *The Tragic Vision* (New York, 1960), pp. 154–65.

15. Robert F. Haugh, *Joseph Conrad: Discovery in Design* (Norman, Okla., 1957), p. 39.

miration and loyalty which amount to homage, and not, it would seem, in spite of his deeds but because of them."[16]

These critics ignore the disavowals which both Marlow and Conrad made of any admiration for Kurtz. Marlow's overt judgments are unremittingly hostile or ironic: "Mr. Kurtz was no idol of mine" (132), he affirms; and in this, as we have seen, Marlow reflects Conrad's intentions. The fact that both Conrad and Marlow overtly dissociate themselves from sharing or admiring Kurtz's satanism is no doubt a major reason why most critics who have assumed that there is some deep identification between Marlow and Kurtz have seen it as unconscious.

Albert Guerard was very influential in, among many other things, making us see Marlow's "spiritual voyage of self-discovery" (G, 38) as the central subject of *Heart of Darkness*. This self-discovery, Guerard argues, occurs when Marlow, having made a "night journey into the unconscious," there discovers an "entity within the self" represented by Kurtz, who is a "double" and who represents "the Freudian id or the Jungian shadow." For Guerard, the "shock Marlow experiences when he discovers that Kurtz's cabin is empty" arises because "his secret sharer is gone; a part of himself has vanished" (G, 41).

Guerard, however, treats the "psychological symbolism" of the tale not as its essential meaning, but only as an illuminating parallel (G, 39). Frederick Crews comes to a much more negative verdict on *Heart of Darkness* because, partly in protest against the excesses of psychological and critical eclecticism, he takes a much less accommodating view of the psychoanalytic theory. In an incisive and diverting commentary Crews begins by presenting Conrad as preeminently a writer in a "quasi-confessional mode," who "indulges our fears of isolation, neglect, and victimization by malign higher powers—the fears of an anxious infant—without locating their source."[17] In this context *Heart of Darkness* is diagnosed as essentially an Oedipal fantasy. The voyage up the snakelike river is Marlow's incestuous incursion into the maternal body; he negotiates a veritable "Freudian obstacle course," and then "symbolically interrupts" his father-figure, Kurtz, who is engaging in the primal scene—the real referent of Kurtz's "unspeakable rites."

The use of psychoanalytic, as of other, categories of understanding, in the criticism of literature, presents three general difficulties. There is the inherent difficulty of demonstrating that the text either proves or disproves the applicability to the literary work of the psychological category in question; there is the problem of whether the categories of

16. *Sincerity and Authenticity*, p. 106.
17. Frederick Crews, "Conrad's Uneasiness—And Ours," in *Out of My System: Psychoanalysis, Ideology, and Critical Method* (New York, 1975), pp. 49; 56.

a particular system actually provide a more "real" interpretation of the evidence than would a literal one; and there is the extent to which the choice of the particular concepts to be applied must be in large part personal—you either believe in night journeys and primal scenes or you don't.

In the present case, the special nature of Conrad's narrative method, combining as it does the impressionist denial of a final and "objective" interpretation by the author with the symbolist multiplication of larger suggested meanings, has tended to authorise the discovery of nonliteral meanings to support whatever conceptual interpretation is being applied. To take one small example, some critics have seen a sense of guilt operating when Marlow hastily takes off his shoes, full of the helmsman's blood: "I flung one shoe overboard, and became aware that that was exactly what I had been looking forward to—a talk with Kurtz" (113). The rapid transition has been seen as linking Marlow's horror at the blood with his unconscious sense of guilty complicity. But the literal meaning is surely rich and convincing enough. What has welled up in Marlow's mind after his jerks on the steam whistle have checked the attack, and all has become silent again, is that there is time now both to take fuller notice of the sensation in his "feet . . . so very warm and wet" (111), and then to do something about it. To a reader unaccustomed to wearing his shoes filled with warm blood it seems perfectly normal that Marlow should be "morbidly anxious" to throw them overboard, even if they are new. The nature of Marlow's sudden transition to the thoughts of Kurtz is equally transparent: the sight of the dead body of the helmsman makes Marlow think of someone else who has also become an immediate part of his mental life, and who—he fears—may have been killed by the same attackers.

The transition in Marlow's mind is certainly evidence that, like much else, his relation to Kurtz is not entirely, nor even mainly, rational and conscious; and Kurtz himself is one of Conrad's closest approaches to the portrayal of the unconscious and irrational pole of human behaviour. But although we may agree that, out of the whole gamut of human behaviour in general, very little, if any, is wholly rational and conscious, our best guide to understanding it must remain the direct evidence; and there is really very little in *Heart of Darkness* which cannot be understood by a literal interpretation of what is said and done.

Such an interpretation must begin by accepting the implications of the fact that most of the evidence is given by Marlow; it is therefore coloured by his own situation and needs; and he reveals quite enough of these to make it clear that his sense of social and moral disorienta-

tion becomes increasingly difficult to control during his journey. Even
before leaving for Africa, Marlow feels that he is "an impostor" (60);
during the voyage out he is completely isolated, and without any
"point of contact" with the others on board; and from then on everything gives an increasing desperateness to his unspoken question:
How can man, and especially civilised man, be and do what he has
seen? This radical unsettling of Marlow's grounds of being, together
with the daily pressure of his solitary responsibility for a steamboat, is
enough to explain his "sheer nervousness" (114) during the attack. We
note that he wrenches the spear out of his dead helmsman "with my
eyes shut tight" (119), and how, when carrying the corpse out of the
cabin, he observes with agonised absorption how its "heels leaped
together over the little door-step."

The most consistent clue to Marlow's psychological state during his
journey up the river is probably the way he often recalls it in terms of
dream and nightmare. The journey surely was, for Marlow as it had
been for Conrad, a nightmare in a common usage of the term: an
experience in which the individual's thoughts and actions are dominated by a terrifying and inexplicable sense of personal helplessness.
Marlow also expresses the main content of his experience in the
traditional terms of a fairy-tale hero's arduous, dangerous, and mysterious quest. "The approach to this Kurtz grubbing for ivory in the
wretched bush," he comments, "was beset by as many dangers as
though he had been an enchanted princess sleeping in a fabulous
castle" (106). The analogies of nightmare and fairy tale suggest two
traditional metaphors for the process whereby Marlow is unconsciously impelled to create a fantasy Kurtz: he needs a magic helper or
at least a secret sharer, in any case a person who will fill the need that
isolated adults as well as solitary children can feel for someone who
will give them unconditional help or total personal reciprocity.

These unspoken hopes are dashed as soon as Marlow arrives at the
inner station. Kurtz has not been able to deal with isolation in the
wilderness; his articulateness and his claims to virtue are shams; and
his behaviour to others has not been better than that of the pilgrims,
but much worse. The "universal genius" has turned into an inflated
version of their greedy and callous egoism. The only problem, then, is
to explain why, despite his total disillusionment, Marlow's "loyalty" to
Kurtz continues until, and beyond, his death.

Outwardly, Marlow's behaviour is still constrained by the fact that
everyone else identifies him with Kurtz; and once he has pledged his
word first to the Russian, and then to the dying man himself, he is
forced to defend Kurtz's memory. His own feelings are no doubt
mixed and unclear even to himself; but the evidence is consistent in

showing that as soon as Marlow has come into contact with Kurtz, his behaviour can reasonably be explained primarily as the result of commitments over which he had little control. Primarily but not entirely; as Marlow remarks: "Perhaps it was an impulse of unconscious loyalty, or the fulfilment of one of these ironic necessities that lurk in the facts of human existence" (155).

The Kurtz-Marlow relationship is certainly anomalous, but it is distinctly less so in the context of Conrad's own characteristics as a novelist. He usually sees relationships between individuals not as essentially personal, but as parts of a larger structure in which—as is surely true of *Heart of Darkness*—chance, occasion, occupational activities, and general attitudes toward the physical and moral world, have enormous determining power, and allow very little autonomy to the wishes of the individual concerned. There is great psychological truth in the way that Conrad shows how the autonomy of one individual's actions can be unexpectedly, involuntarily, and yet imperatively, preempted by the contingencies imposed by the larger forces in which his personal relationships are set. This psychological truth, in turn, reflects Conrad's larger aim, which is to make Marlow enact both the ambiguities and the defeats which attend the individual's effort to build up, live by, and share with others, his vision of good and evil. When Marlow comments that Kurtz "had summed up—he had judged. 'The horror!' " (151), he indicates that they had at least momentarily shared their vision of evil.

(c) *The Lie and the Darkness*

After Kurtz's death, two-thirds of the way through the last section, Marlow's narrative moves very rapidly through his illness, his return to Europe, and the settling of his various affairs concerning Kurtz. Only one episode is given in any detail, that of the lie to Kurtz's Intended. It is very widely agreed that the scene is treated in a rather strained, melodramatic, and repetitive way, with little of the convincing detail which had generated the evocative power of the earlier major scenes; and there has also been a good deal of disagreement about the lie's motives and implications.

The scene with the Intended is actually the last of a series of occasions where Marlow has lied, or at least deceived, on behalf of Kurtz. The first occasion occurs when Marlow's anxiety to hasten the repair of the steamboat, and thus the rescue of Kurtz, leads him "near enough to a lie" (82); he lets the brickmaker "believe anything he liked to imagine as to my influence in Europe . . . simply because I had a notion it somehow would be of help to that Kurtz," even though "at the time" he "was just a word for me." So, disregarding the brickmaker's veiled menaces—"No man—you apprehend me?—no man here bears a charmed life" (84)—Marlow threatens that if the needed rivets are not sent up, his career will suffer. Before relating this, however, Marlow had interjected to his listeners: "You know I hate, detest, and can't bear a lie, not because I am straighter than the rest of us, but simply because it appals me. There is a taint of death, a flavour of mortality in lies—which is exactly what I hate and detest in the world—what I want to forget" (82). Marlow finds the cost of moral choice extortionate, but the hard truth seems to be that to keep our leaky craft afloat we need rivets, and to get rivets we apparently have to tell lies.

When Marlow arrives at the inner station he is forced to make two somewhat more explicit sacrifices of the truth. There is the occasion when Marlow commits himself to suppressing the truth about Kurtz to pacify the Russian; and the other when, to persuade Kurtz to come back on board quietly with him, he uses an ironical form of the lie positive, and tells Kurtz that his "success in Europe is assured" (143).

In these three cases, as in the final one, the normal sense of the word "lie" does not really apply. What happens is that, in order to save the life of Kurtz, and later of the pilgrims, Marlow takes advantage of the subjective delusions of the brickmaker, the Russian, and Kurtz. The particular reason why the need to lie devolves upon Marlow is that he is the only person in *Heart of Darkness* who has an active and disinterested sense of personal responsibility for others. It is a pointed thematic irony that Marlow's vulnerability to the pressures which impel him to lie should be a product of the very same moral sensitivities that make lying so repugnant to him.

Back in Europe, Marlow is immediately engaged in the suppression of the truth about Kurtz's final degradation; for instance, he tears off the damning postscript before offering Kurtz's report to fob off the inquisitive importunacies first of a Company agent and later of a journalist (153). Finally, to terminate his obligations, Marlow sets out to return Kurtz's letters to the Intended, and at last "surrender personally all that remained of him with me to that oblivion which is the last word of our common fate" (155).

Marlow is "not very well" (152), at the time: he has a temperature; his "imagination" wants "soothing"; and his mind is so deeply pervaded by what he has left behind that the ordinary behaviour of the inhabitants of the sepulchral city seem as "offensive" as "the outrageous flauntings of folly in the face of a danger it is unable to comprehend." Marlow's feverish disorientation, it should be remembered, is actually a fairly normal reaction to what he has undergone; for instance, when the grossly insensitive Stanley returned from the

Congo in 1878, his "entire system," he wrote, was "utterly out of order," and he felt "more and more unfit for what my neighbours called civilised society."[18] Marlow's mood when he approaches the apartment of the Intended seems strained and yet torpid; he has "no clear perception of what it was I really wanted" (155). At the door, a vision of Kurtz flashes into his mind, and makes him feel that, once again, he alone will "have to keep back" his awareness of the "conquering darkness" of the wilderness "for the salvation of another soul." Then, when Marlow finally sees the Intended, he senses her "mature capacity for fidelity, for belief, for suffering" (157), and realises once again he is being confronted with a constrained choice.

At first Marlow allows the Intended's praises of Kurtz to run on, with guarded silence or ambiguous assent his only reaction. For instance, when she says, "it was impossible to know him and not to admire him," Marlow merely answers, "unsteadily," that "he was a remarkable man." At one point the Intended's confident and self-flattering delusions about Kurtz anger Marlow, but the feeling soon subsides "before a feeling of infinite pity" (161). Finally, the Intended asks Marlow for "His last word—to live with." There is a pause, in which Marlow hears the whisper of "The horror! the horror!" ringing in his ears; and then he controls himself and slowly gives the Intended a version of Kurtz's last oral performance of the kind she expects: "The last word he pronounced was—your name."[19]

Quite apart from his pledge to the Russian, the pressures on Marlow are obvious and imperative. There is first the tradition embodied in the time-honoured maxim *de mortuis nihil nisi bonum;* it applies with very particular force when dealing with a fiancée or widow, and when the speaker is a total stranger who is only there because he happened to be present at the man's deathbed and has a packet of letters to deliver. There is also the question of kindness; all the Intended has left to live for is her fortifying delusion that Kurtz's words and example will live on, and that, as she tells Marlow, "I am proud to know I understood him better than any one on earth—he told me so himself" (158).

There are, then, all kinds of particular pressures, none of them difficult to explain, which cause Marlow's "lie"; and he can hardly be blamed for it, especially if one considers how universally the world is

---

18. Stanley, *The Congo,* vol. 1, pp. 22; 23.
19. There have been many varying interpretations of the scene with the Intended; they are discussed in recent articles by David M. Martin, "The Function of the Intended in Conrad's *Heart of Darkness,*" *Studies in Short Fiction* 11 (1974): 27–33, and Bruce H. Stark, "Kurtz's Intended: The Heart of *Heart of Darkness,*" *Texas Studies in Literature and Language* 16 (1974): 535–55.

pervaded by customary practices such as Marlow here follows. That they are, incidentally, practices which society has sound reason to exonerate from reprobation, is suggested by the hallowed metaphor—itself highly appropriate to Conrad's main symbolic polarity—of the white lie.

In a 1902 letter to William Blackwood, Conrad used "the last pages of Heart of Darkness" as an illustration of his general "method based on deliberate conviction"; and he went on to explain that "the interview of the man and girl locks in—as it were—the whole 30000 words of narrative description into one suggestive view of a whole phase of life, and makes of that story something quite on another plane than an anecdote of a man who went mad in the Centre of Africa" (B, 154). One of the secondary themes which is "locked in" to the final scene has yet to be mentioned—Marlow's view of women.

At the beginning of the story, Marlow is unable to convince his "excellent aunt" that the company is run for profit. This leads him to interject: "It's queer how out of touch with truth women are," and to add, in terms equally offensive to women and to syntax, "They live in a world of their own, and there had never been anything like it, and never can be" (59). Marlow makes a similar comment when he first mentions the Intended: "Oh, she is out of it—completely. They—the women I mean—are out of it—should be out of it. We must help them to stay in that beautiful world of their own, lest ours gets worse" (115). In the manuscript Conrad made this passage even more explicit, and anticipated Marlow's final scene with the Intended, by adding: "That's a monster-truth with many maws to whom we've got to throw every year—or every day—no matter—no sacrifice is too great—a ransom of pretty, shining lies" (H D N, 49).

Marlow's misogyny may seem a somewhat less disabling prejudice if it is set in the context of his general view of life. Both the remarks quoted clearly refer not to the women in the office of the trading company, for instance, nor to Kurtz's native mistress, but specifically to the well-to-do and leisured class to which Marlow's aunt and the Intended belong. Marlow unquestioningly assumes the Victorian relegation of leisure-class women to a pedestal high above the economic and sexual facts of life; and he also believes that it is only through work—more generally through a direct personal striving to master some external and objective force—that anyone can get "the chance to find yourself. Your own reality" (85). It therefore follows that, merely by allotting women a leisure role, society has in effect excluded them from discovering reality; so it is by no choice or fault of hers that the Intended inhabits an unreal world.

Marlow's opinion of leisured women makes them negative examples of his idea that work is the basis of the individual's sense of reality; but it also makes them positive examples of the complementary idea of the danger of relying on words. Even if the life of the Intended had given her the basis required to understand reality in the experience of work, Marlow could not have conveyed the truth about Kurtz to her, because she is armoured by the invincible credulity produced by the unreality of the public rhetoric.

At one very general level, Marlow's story can be considered as an abortive quest to escape from the breakdown in society's modes of reciprocity. Beginning at the company offices, Marlow experiences a whole series of personal contacts where real communication is blocked by the invisible barriers of egoism, indifference, misunderstanding, insensitivity and suspicion. There are only three people from whose intelligence and disinterestedness Marlow might expect more: the Russian, the Intended, and Kurtz. But in all three cases reciprocal communication proves impossible, and for the same reason: a boundless admiration for Kurtz infects them all.

These characters share one linguistic trait; they are addicted to the idealising abstractions of public discourse, to a language that has very little connection with the realities either of the external world or of their inner selves. Conrad commented on the general prevalence of this disconnection in "An Outpost of Progress": "Everybody shows a respectful deference to certain sounds that he and his fellows can make. But about feelings people really know nothing. We talk with indignation or enthusiasm; we talk about oppression, cruelty, crime, devotion, self-sacrifice, virtue, and we know nothing real beyond the words. Nobody knows what suffering or sacrifice mean—except, perhaps the victims of the mysterious purpose of these illusions" (*T U*, 105–6).

Kurtz's rhetoric has no meaning for Marlow: for him it is merely "one immense jabber" (115) because it has no reference either to the real Kurtz, or to the world Marlow has experienced. There are other people, however, who seem to be predestined victims of Kurtz's high-sounding verbiage, notably the innocents and altruists of either sex, such as the Russian, who should know better, and the Intended, who has no reason to. The illusions of his aunt about the civilising work in Africa, Marlow recalls, came to her because she lived "right in the rush of all that humbug" which had "been . . . let loose in print and talk just about that time" (59); while the illusions of the Intended are, Marlow says, only "the echo of Kurtz's magnificent eloquence" (152). The two women, hypnotised by the self-serving catchwords of the journalistic rhetoricians of progress, are such "thunderingly exalted creature[s] as to be altogether deaf and blind to anything but heavenly sights and sounds" (117); and they unconsciously function as the facade for the operations of the manager and his cronies.

Many other themes of *Heart of Darkness* are also "locked in" to the climactic scene with the Intended. Marlow, for instance, exhibits his much-taxed restraint when he masters his anger at the delusions of the Intended; hollowness is present in the Intended's posture of faithfulness to the memory of a sham whom she never really knew; and the dualism of atavism and progress is very obviously emphasised when memories of Kurtz's savage rites and his native mistress penetrate Marlow's mind while the Intended talks on "as thirsty men drink" (159) about the loss to humanity of Kurtz's "generous mind." In effect, the final scene locks in all the earlier "secondary notions" except that of work, under the large general conception of the lie.

This conception reflects several very pervasive tendencies in late nineteenth-century thought. The most immediate parallel is afforded by Dr. Relling in Ibsen's *The Wild Duck* (1884). A devotee of unpopular and destructive truths, Relling personally much prefers to the "fancy word 'ideals'" the "plain word that's good enough: 'lies'"; nevertheless he knows that "Take the life-lie away from the average man and straight away you take away his happiness."[20] Ibsen was possessed by the nineteenth century's passion for the liberating power of truth; and it led him eventually to defend man's need for the lies which he had so long righteously exposed.

The next two decades saw many similarly sceptical expressions of a disenchantment with truth. In literature, the most telling parallel is perhaps that afforded by the final scenes in the late novels of Henry James, where the most intelligent characters, and most pointedly the protagonists at the end of *The Golden Bowl*, tacitly agree to bury the unpalatable truths about themselves and their pasts, so that the surface of their civilised arrangements can be maintained.[21] Somewhat like them, but in a gloomier vein, Marlow assumes that living on earth demands that we "breathe dead hippo, so to speak"(117) and yet somehow avoid being contaminated. For many reasons, however, very few can avoid contagion, as the fate of Kurtz shows. Those who can, like Marlow, therefore find themselves deeply involved in the uncongenial task of digging "unostentatious holes to bury the stuff in."

Speaking of Ibsen's view of the need for the saving lie, Thomas Mann makes an important distinction: "Clearly there is a vast difference whether one assents to a lie out of sheer hatred of truth and the

20. Act V (trans. J. W. McFarlane [New York, 1961], pp. 226–27).
21. Leon Edel draws attention to the parallels between these "constructive lies" and Marlow's lie, in *Henry James: The Master*, pp. 214–15.

spirit or for the sake of that spirit, in bitter irony and anguished pessimism!"[22] The latter is certainly the spirit of Marlow's lie to the Intended; and it has behind it a sceptical pessimism which is particularly typical of the generation which succeeded Ibsen's. Marlow is not the kind of hero who has ever contemplated a public fight for truth; and in the perspective of intellectual history his whole series of deceptions, equivocations, and silences can be regarded as part of a general trend towards the abandonment of the idea that the truths of philosophy could be applied to any of the practical problems of life.

One form of this trend took the shape of arguing that man cannot do without illusions. In different ways Kant and Schopenhauer had advanced the general position, but it was taken much further by Nietzsche. "Truths," he wrote in 1873, "are illusions about which one has forgotten that this is what they are."[23] Later, in *Beyond Good and Evil* (1886), Nietzsche went further. What really mattered was not whether an opinion was true or false, but rather "how far an opinion is life-furthering," and he argued that "without a recognition of logical fictions, without a comparison of reality with the purely *imagined* world of the absolute and immutable . . . man could not live." We must, in sum, *"recognise untruth as a condition of life."*[24]

Many of Conrad's philosophical contemporaries came to hold very similar versions of these notions. For instance, in their different ways Hans Vaihinger[25] and William James[26] attempted to account for the dependence of society upon a common acceptance of fictions in such areas of thought and belief as religion, ethics, and politics. For Vaihinger, if the idea works it doesn't matter that it is untrue, while William James comes close to saying that an idea should be regarded as true if it works, if it is in harmony with the exigencies of the real world.

Marlow's attitude to illusions is both more absolute and more humble than those of Nietzsche, Vaihinger, James, or Dr. Relling. He lies

22. "Freud and the Future," in *Essays,* trans. H. T. Lowe-Porter (New York, 1957), pp. 308–9. The thematic parallel between *Heart of Darkness* and Mann's *Death in Venice* is presented by Harvey Gross in "Aschenbach and Kurtz: The Cost of Civilization," *Centennial Review* 6 (1962): 131–43.

23. Cited from Walter Kaufman, *The Portable Nietzsche,* p. 47, by Edward W. Said in his illuminating study of "Conrad and Nietzsche" (*Joseph Conrad: A Commemoration. Papers from the 1974 International Conference on Conrad,* ed. Norman Sherry [London, 1976], p. 67).

24. "Prejudices of Philosophers," 4, trans. Helen Zimmern. (*The Philosophy of Nietzsche,* ed. Willard H. Wright [New York, 1954], p. 384).

25. In *The Philosophy of "As If,"* trans. C. K. Ogden (London, 1924); the first German edition appeared in 1911, but was begun as early as 1874.

26. Although the idea found its full statement in *Pragmatism* (1907), it was implicit in James's essays "The Will to Believe" (1897), and especially in "Philosophical Conceptions and Practical Results" (1898).

for many reasons: to honour his commitment to the nightmare of his choice by preserving the decency of Kurtz's memory; to spare the Intended's feelings, and therefore his own; but also because whatever system of belief he may have attained has too dubious and private a status in his own thoughts to be presented as an effective alternative to the illusions of the Intended. Marlow never feels certain that his own truth is not an illusion; and in this he reflects Conrad, who was always prone to refer to most abstract philosophical terms—like truth, ideals, principles, reality—as illusions. He used the term in a rather wide and undefined sense to assert, not so much that they are untrue as that they are unfounded, impermanent, unprovable, or uncertain. This characteristic habit of thought, indeed, was one of Max Beerbohm's targets in his parody of Conrad, "The Feast"; the hero's mosquito-net, we are told, "was itself illusory like everything else, only more so."[27]

Conrad's frequent use of the word illusion is a sign of a philosophical scepticism which would obviously inhibit him from attempting to define the intellectual basis of his own practical human commitments; but this does not undermine, and indeed it may even strengthen, the conviction that although the sceptical mind knows that all ideological structures are really illusions, they may in practice be necessary restraints upon human egoism, laziness, or despair.

Marlow's behaviour in *Heart of Darkness* reflects this dual attitude. His awareness of the fragility and the intellectual hollowness of civilisation inhibits him in his dealings with others; his usual comportment is one of sceptical passivity; even his sympathy is uneasy and reserved, as in the scene with the Intended. Her grandiose illusions about Kurtz gradually force Marlow to go from taut acquiescence to more positive violation of the truth. Thus when the Intended stops her eulogy of Kurtz with "But you have heard him! You know!" (159), Marlow replies, "Yes, I know." Then, "with something like despair in [his] heart," he bows his head before the Intended's "great and saving illusion that shone with an unearthly glow in the darkness, in the triumphant darkness from which I could not have defended her— from which I could not even defend myself."

The lie to the Intended, then, is both an appropriately ironic ending for Marlow's unhappy quest for truth, and a humane recognition of the practical aspects of the problem: we must deal gently with human fictions, as we quietly curse their folly under our breath; since no faith can be had which will move mountains, the faith which ignores them had better be cherished.

27. *Christmas Garland,* p. 130.

At the end of the scene we are left wondering whether it is worse that the ideals of the Intended should continue in all their flagrant untruth, or that Marlow should have been unable to invoke any faith in whose name he could feel able to challenge them. To put the alternatives in terms of the main symbolic polarity of *Heart of Darkness* as a whole: which perspective is more alarming? that people such as the Intended should be so blinded by their certitude of being the bearers of light that they are quite unaware of the darkness that surrounds them? or, on the other hand, that those who, like Marlow, have been initiated into the darkness, should be unable to illumine the blindness of their fellows to its omnipresence?

In the early part of the narrative, the main effect of Conrad's light-dark imagery was to break down many of its associated conventional antitheses in the domain of human values; we move into a world where there are no longer any easy and complacent distinctions between black and white, and there are no longer any simple choices to be based upon them, like a preference for light or dark beer. In the first section, Marlow's European conception of blackness as inferior or evil is undermined when he finds no moral darkness in the black inhabitants of Africa, but is forced to link many of the traditional negative connotations of darkness with the colour white. In *Heart of Darkness* it is the white invaders, for instance, who are, almost without exception, embodiments of blindness, selfishness, and cruelty; and even in the cognitive domain, where such positive phrases as "to enlighten," for instance, are conventionally opposed to negative ones such as "to be in the dark," the traditional expectations are reversed. In Kurtz's painting, as we have seen, "the effect of the torch-light on the face was sinister" (79); the steamboat's final approach to the inner station, which is the goal of Marlow's quest, involves passing through an immobilising "white fog . . . more blinding than the night" (101); and this oxymoron is repeated in the later variant of "the blind whiteness of the fog" (105).

Until Marlow confronts the Intended, the general development of the ramifying symbolic contrasts between light and darkness has been fairly easy to transpose into the terms which define the intellectual perspective that he has acquired as a result of his Congo experience. It can be summarised along the following lines: the physical universe began in darkness, and will end in it; the same holds for the world of human history, which is dark in the sense of being obscure, amoral, and without purpose; and so, essentially, is man. Through some fortuitous and inexplicable development, however, men have occasionally been able to bring light to this darkness in the form of civilisation—a structure of behaviour and belief which can sometimes keep the darkness at bay. But this containing action is highly precarious, because the operations of darkness are much more active, numerous, and omnipresent, both in society and in the individual, than civilised people usually suppose. They must learn that light is not only a lesser force than darkness in power, magnitude, and duration, but is in some way subordinate to it, or included within it; in short, that the darkness which Marlow discovers in the wilderness, in Kurtz and in himself, is the primary and all-encompassing reality of the universe.

Marlow says of his voyage up the river that they "penetrated deeper and deeper into the heart of darkness" (95). There is a very traditional literal basis for this identification of the African wilderness with the "heart of darkness";[28] the wilderness is by definition an extreme example of a place where the light of civilisation has not come; and Africa, for this and other reasons, long figured in European thought as the Dark Continent. But Marlow also gives the wilderness much larger metaphysical connotations. It is an actively malign force; and it is also, Marlow senses, impenetrable to human thought, because it has a primal inclusiveness which confounds the categories which man has constructed as the basis of his civilisation.

Kurtz has internalised the spiritual meaning of the wilderness. Marlow's references to him assume the established equation of darkness with evil, as in such phrases as "a dark deed" for a crime, and "the prince of darkness" for the devil; and Marlow twice applies the term "heart of darkness" to Kurtz. In the first example he merely speaks of "the barren darkness of his heart" (147), but in a later passage he merges Kurtz and the wilderness into a single living presence. The passage occurs when Marlow, on his way to the Intended, suddenly sees his vision of Kurtz: "The vision seemed to enter the house with me—the stretcher, the phantom-bearers, the wild crowd of obedient worshippers, the gloom of the forests, the glitter of the reach between the murky bends, the beat of the drum, regular and muffled like the beating of a heart—the heart of a conquering darkness" (155–56).

There is nothing particularly new in the idea that darkness is the primal reality to which all else in the world is posterior in origin and subordinate in power. In the Judaeo-Christian tradition, for example, the idea is embodied at the cosmic level in the book of Genesis, where "darkness was upon the face of the earth" in the beginning of things. The Western religious tradition as a whole makes light not the rule

28. For the general historical background of European conceptions, see Philip Curtin, *Image of Africa* (Madison, Wisc., 1964), and on the fictional tradition, G. D. Killam, *Africa in English Fiction* (Ibadan, 1968), especially pp. 8–11.

but the exception; it is the result of a beneficent divine intervention, which may be temporary and is certainly not bestowed unconditionally.

This transcendental view of the world is very difficult to embody in narrative, although the general aim was common enough in the nineteenth century, as in Melville's symbolic use of blackness.[29] In *Heart of Darkness* this quasi-transcendental perspective is most obviously apparent in its language: such words as "unspeakable," "inconceivable," "inscrutable," and "nameless" are really an attempt—on the whole unsuccessful—to make us go beyond the limits of ordinary cognition, to transcend what Conrad or anybody else really knows. The ensuing sense of rhetorical strain is particularly marked in the passages dealing with Kurtz, where Marlow uses the language of ethical absolutes, although there is no reason to believe that he accepts any conceptual structure on which they might depend. For instance, Marlow makes the moral judgment that Kurtz was "beguiled . . . beyond the bounds of permitted aspirations" (144), although he has no belief in the existence of anyone empowered to issue or deny such permits.

In the last pages of *Heart of Darkness* there is a final variation on the values associated with whiteness and light. Back in the sepulchral city, the Intended's fireplace has "a cold and monumental whiteness" (156); her "fair hair" and "pale visage" seem "surrounded by an ashy halo"; her eyes "glitter" (159). In the falling dusk, the Intended, all in mourning black, dedicates her soul, "as translucently pure as a cliff of crystal" (152), to the memory of Kurtz; to Marlow her "great and saving illusion" shines with "an unearthly glow" (159); and, although the Intended is illumined by "the unextinguishable light of belief and love," Marlow tells us that "with every word spoken the room was growing darker."

Light has been degraded to a cold and artificial brightness—it can no longer combat darkness; while whiteness has become some diseased albino mutation, capable, no doubt, of producing the cold phosphorescent glow of idealism, but sick and pallid indeed compared with the other tragic and heroic woman whom Kurtz abandoned in the heart of darkness. We seem to have moved from a realisation of the overwhelming power of darkness in the psychological, moral, and spiritual realm, to a larger and intangible change of a metaphysical kind, in which light seems to have a peculiar affinity with unnaturalness, hypocrisy, and delusion, and to be quite as contrary to

29. See Harry Levin, *The Power of Blackness: Hawthorne, Poe, Melville* (New York, 1958).

the positive values of human life as the worst manifestations conventionally attributed to darkness.

How far some such conceptual rendition of the symbolic implications of light and darkness constitutes the main thematic burden in *Heart of Darkness* as a whole depends very largely on how much weight we give to the implications of the imagery, as opposed to other aspects of the novel. If some of the more intangible and abstract of the novel's general concerns are singled out for separate analytic consideration, they certainly tend, in the very process of making its thought seem more consistent than it is, to make its purport more negative. Thus Hillis Miller, only a part of whose complex argument can be touched on here, presents Conrad as unremittingly nihilist in his basic vision of reality: "the heart of darkness is the truth," he writes; it means "the absorption of all forms in the shapeless night from which they have come"; and compared to its power all man's intellectual fabrications, the whole "realm of reason and intention is a lie."[30]

Heart of Darkness is Conrad's most direct expression of his doubts about the foundations of human thought and action, and its mode of narration reflects this. The subjective, questioning, and inconclusive way in which the story is told has led Tzvetan Todorov to move from the implications of "the derisory nature of knowledge" and Marlow's inability to understand Kurtz, to see *Heart of Darkness* as implying the impossibility of expressing the essential reality of human experience in fiction.[31]

But these negative views are surely too absolute: Marlow's tale, and the story as a whole, are not entirely, or even mainly, self-referential—its sepulchral city and its Africa are seen through Marlow's eyes, but they are places full of real horrors. What makes reading *Heart of Darkness* so unforgettable is surely the harrowing power with which Conrad convinces us of the essential reality of everything that Marlow sees and feels at each stage of his journey. Nor can Conrad's social and moral purport be regarded as ultimately nihilist, as Hillis Miller argues; Marlow's positives—work and restraint, for instance—make a less impressive appearance in the narrative than do all the negatives which he discovers; but Marlow's defences are firmly present in the stubborn energy and responsibility of his daily activities. Of course, no very flattering or sanguine view of man's behaviour and prospects emerges from *Heart of Darkness*, and it must have seemed grotesquely pessimistic to its original readers. It surely

---

30. *Poets of Reality*, p. 33. My general reading of "darkness" is indebted to his. See also Royal Roussel, *The Metaphysics of Darkness: A Study in the Unity and Development of Conrad's Fiction* (Baltimore and London, 1971).

31. Tzvetan Todorov, "Connaissance du vide," especially pp. 151, 153–54.

seems a good deal less so eighty years later, except to those who have had a very blinkered view of the century's battlefields. In any case, neither Conrad nor Marlow stands for the position that darkness is irresistible; their attitude, rather, is to enjoin us to defend ourselves in full knowledge of the difficulties to which we have been blinded by the illusions of civilisation.

Marlow had begun his narrative by saying "And this also has been one of the dark places of the earth." His story ends when night has fallen in the sepulchral city, and he stops telling it with his face hidden by the same darkness on the Thames. There is a further formal symmetry when, in the last brief paragraph, the primary narrator reappears.

He sees Marlow in "the pose of a meditating Buddha." A very odd sort of Buddha, to be sure: one who actively applies himself to the practical truths of the secular world, and who, if he still awaits enlightenment, is no more sanguine about its advent than the protagonists of *Waiting for Godot.* But the reference to Buddha is justified in one respect: Marlow's narrative is essentially a self-examining meditation. *Heart of Darkness* is not, like "Youth" or *Lord Jim,* the act of a raconteur; it is the act, rather, of a man who stumbled into the underworld many years ago, and lived to tell its secrets, although not until much later. Then, mysteriously, the right occasion presented itself: a time and a place that supply both the evocative atmosphere, and the stimulus of an audience with whom Marlow has enough identity of language and experience to encourage him to try to come to terms at last with some of his most urgent and unappeased moral perplexities through the act of sharing them.

When Marlow has finished, no one moves. The captain finally breaks the silence on a practical note: "We have lost the first of the ebb." It is a tribute of a sort; Marlow's tale has "arrested, for the space of a breath" the punctual hands of a few yachtsmen. But the turn of the tide is also a reminder of the endless and apparently meaningless circularity of the physical and the human world on every time scale, from that of the daily round to that of evolutionary history. This circularity is finally enacted in the fictional setting and the larger meaning of the tale itself. The river, which had been serenely luminous at the beginning, is now dark; and this becomes the occasion for another tribute. Marlow has not only learned and endured; he has also, it would seem, changed the way that the primary narrator, at least, sees the Thames; for when he raises his head, the narrator's vision, now coloured by the expansive power of Marlow's primary symbol, discovers that "the tranquil waterway . . . seemed to lead into the heart of an immense darkness."

CHAPTER 5

Lord Jim

i. 1898–1900: The Pent and Ford

On 14 January 1899 Conrad received a prize of fifty guineas from *The Academy* for his collection of short stories, *Tales of Unrest;* but he at once felt obliged to send on the cheque to his friend Krieger who was pressing for repayment of an old debt. This prefigures Conrad's life for the next fourteen years: there would be great successes, but the financial rewards were never enough to enable him to escape from the burden of debt, or from the paralysing fear that in deciding to become a writer he had dug himself into a pit from which he would never emerge.

As soon as *Heart of Darkness* was finished, Conrad went back once again to *The Rescue*. Progress, however, proved even slower than before, and at the end of March 1899 he expressed his despair and terror in a letter to Garnett:

> The more I write the less substance do I see in my work. The scales are falling off my eyes. It is tolerably awful. And I face it, I face it but the fright is growing on me. My fortitude is shaken by the view of the monster. It does not move; its eyes are baleful; it is still as death itself—and it will devour me. Its stare has eaten into my soul already deep, deep. I am alone with it in a chasm with perpendicular sides of black basalt. Never were sides so perpendicular and smooth, and high. Above, your anxious head against a bit of sky peers down—in vain—in vain. There's no rope long enough for that rescue.
>
> Why didn't you come? I expected you and fate has sent Hueffer. Let this be written on my tombstone (*E G*, 150–51).

"Hueffer" was the son of Dr. Francis Hueffer who, like a good many of his compatriots, had fled the Germany of Bismarck and settled in London. There he won something of a reputation as a historian, a devotee of Wagner and Schopenhauer, and the music critic of *The Times*. He also married the daughter of the Pre-Raphaelite painter Ford Madox Brown, in whose honor they called their first son, born in 1873, Ford. Ford Hueffer, in turn, continued the tribute to his famous grandfather: he early changed his second baptismal name, Hermann, to Madox; and after the 1914 war, he completed the process of anglicisation by changing his surname also, and thus went down to history under the symmetrical and euphonious appellation of Ford Madox Ford.

It was in the autumn of 1898, and probably at Garnett's, that Conrad first met Ford, as it seems most convenient, though anachronistic, to call him. Ford was then only twenty-four years old; but he had already published some fairy tales, a novel, a volume of poems, and a large-scale authorised life of his grandfather. At their meeting Ford apparently mentioned that his old farmhouse in Kent would soon be available for lease; Conrad, after a last unsuccessful effort to go back to sea, took up the offer; and on 26 October 1898 the Conrads moved in.

The Pent is a substantial brick farmhouse in the green hills of Kent, some five miles inland from Hythe. The house, the landscape, and the neighbourhood were all a distinct improvement on what the Conrads had left in Essex; and they were to live there until 1907—longer than they lived anywhere else. In Essex Conrad had been rather isolated, but now he was within reach of many writers—Henry James lived at Rye, for instance, and H. G. Wells at Sandgate; and since the new house was larger, it was also easier for the Conrads to put up friends—Galsworthy and Cunninghame Graham were among their early guests.

Little in Conrad's life has provoked more confusion as to the facts, and more divergencies about their interpretation, than the association with Ford. It is not even clear whether Conrad moved to the Pent as part of a plan for his literary collaboration with Ford,[1] or whether that idea occurred independently.[2] It is certain, however, that the initial proposal for the collaboration came from Conrad; and it was probably on the basis that Ford had already written the drafts of two novels which Conrad was to help him finish and get published. Joint authorship was a fairly well established practice among the novelists of the period—Stevenson, Walter Besant, Israel Zangwill and Kipling, for instance, all had some experience with collaborators. In the case of Conrad and Ford, however, many of their friends apparently shared Henry James's view that the collaboration was "like a bad dream . . . their traditions and their gifts are so dissimilar" (*J B*, 277).

One reason for this reaction is that Ford and Conrad were such different people, and in many ways; but in fact the most serious difficulty proved to be that Conrad had, as usual, been much too

---

1. As is suggested by Ford Madox Ford's fullest and most recent biographer, Arthur Mizener, in his *The Saddest Story: A Biography of Ford Madox Ford* (New York and Cleveland, 1971), pp. 43–44.

2. See, for instance, Baines (*J B*, 214–22), and Ford's earlier biographer, Frank MacShane (*The Life and Work of Ford Madox Ford* [New York, 1965], pp. 32–39).

sanguine about how quickly he could progress with his own independent work, and had therefore much overestimated how much time he would have left over for their common projects. This became evident shortly after Ford, his wife Elsie Martindale, also a writer, and their young daughter, moved into a nearby cottage at Aldington in November 1898. Work started on Ford's historical novel, then called *Seraphina*, which was the basis of *Romance*, but Conrad was too busy with *Heart of Darkness* to do anything else, and very soon Ford laid the manuscript aside, and started a topical political fantasy called *The Inheritors*.

The "inheritors" are a new race of "Fourth Dimensionists" who are plotting for the control of the whole earth, but who operate, somewhat incongruously, in a world that is otherwise very much the world of 1899—the novel contains a bitter attack on Joseph Chamberlain, who is a Fourth Dimensionist, and numerous portraits of real people, including a very favourable one of Edward Garnett. Although in the later stages Conrad gave much detailed suggestion and criticism, he at most did two thousand words of the actual writing. The novel was finished towards the end of 1899 and published in 1901 as a work of joint authorship. The fiction of collaboration was used mainly because Conrad's name was a help in getting the novel accepted by his publisher, Heinemann; and, of course, there was also the money—as Conrad very disingenuously put it to Ford, "I shall take the money if you make a point of that."[3]

There was, it turned out, very little money to take. Ford and Conrad soon returned to *Romance*, which is much more genuinely a work of collaboration, as well as a far better novel. Though the original draft was Ford's, Conrad did about a third of the writing in the final version, and had a good deal to do with the rest. Conrad regarded it as an experiment in the artistic treatment of a tale of romantic adventure, and it contains some finely presented scenes, although there is little substance in the basic idea. *Romance* was finally published in 1903, but it failed to achieve its primary purpose, to be popular and financially successful. Ford and Conrad planned a further novel together, but in the end their only other collaborative venture was a brief and rather pointless story called *The Nature of a Crime*, which was not published until much later.

The direct literary products of the Ford-Conrad association are its least important consequence. In his brilliant, copious, unreliable, and indispensable reminiscences, Ford, who was notoriously prone to reinvent the past in accord with his current ideal image of himself,

3. MacShane, *Ford*, p. 41.

suggests that they jointly worked out the theory and practice of the impressionist novel (*F M F*, 179–215). When the memoir appeared in 1924, however, Garnett immediately protested against Ford's "fondness for blending himself and Conrad together as a species of literary Siamese twins."[4] Ford's claims are certainly much exaggerated. Conrad's narrative method had been very largely established by 1898; Ford was some sixteen years younger; and in any case his practice as a novelist does not suggest a very full understanding of Conrad's fiction until the appearance of *The Good Soldier* in 1915.

On the other hand, Ford probably played a vital and necessary part in making possible Conrad's greatest works. Conrad had many friends, and possibly valued some of them, notably Garnett and Cunninghame Graham, more deeply than Ford; but they were all very busy men; and in any case, since they were not neighbours, they could not supply two of the things Conrad most needed: a constant alleviation of his loneliness, depression and self-doubt; and an easy and frequent commerce with someone who could help him to become more rapid, correct, and fluent in his use of the English language. From both these points of view Ford was ideal: he was very sociable, never too busy to talk, and quite willing to be Conrad's "thesaurus."[5] Ford's cosmopolitan background and his great admiration of Flaubert and Maupassant also meant that the two men could share their common enthusiasm for French fiction.[6] In these discussions Ford seems to have been mainly the listener and learner, but the chief benefit may nevertheless have been Conrad's. The challenge, under conditions of easy and intimate dialogue, to be articulate about matters which have hitherto been more or less private or unconscious, is perhaps the commonest way in which we clarify our own perceptions and convictions. It is unlikely that Conrad ever arrived at any systematic formulation of a theory of the novel, for if he had, Ford would presumably have reported some of its formulae verbatim, whereas both the language and the ideas in Ford's various published accounts of what purport to be their joint fictional doctrines actually sound very much like his own. However, Ford certainly gave Conrad an informed and devoted companion with whom to discuss particular problems of technique and language whenever they arose; and in general all the works which Conrad wrote after their collaboration had begun show a great advance in the assurance of their language, which is somewhat

4. In his review of *F M F* (*Nation and Athenaeum* 36 [1924]: 366).
5. Ford's phrase (*T S*, 21).
6. Lawrence Thornton points out that even in their use of Flaubert the two were very different ("'Deux Bonshommes Distincts': Conrad, Ford, and the Visual Arts," *C* 8 [1976]: 11).

less influenced by French syntax and vocabulary, and above all are much more fluent in their command of the middle and colloquial styles in English.

The association helped Conrad in many other ways. As far as English society was concerned, both he and Ford were, in different ways, outsiders; but Ford's extensive knowledge of English social and political life must have helped to give Conrad the confidence to turn towards the purely English subjects of such later works as *The Secret Agent, Chance,* and some of the short stories; while Ford's great talent for anecdote—he was never at a loss for the inside story, however false—supplied the basis for several of Conrad's plots, notably those of *The Secret Agent* and the short story "Amy Foster." Ford later claimed to have written parts of *Nostromo* and *The Mirror of the Sea;* and although it is more probable that he mainly acted only as Conrad's amanuensis, as he also did for parts of the *End of the Tether,* there remains the possibility that some fifteen pages of *Nostromo* (comprising most of the present chapter 5 in part 2, which exists in Ford's hand), and a few passages in *The Mirror of the Sea,* may have been written, in whole or in part, by Ford.[7]

The human rewards were perhaps even greater. Ford was a very generous man, and devoted himself to Conrad in many practical ways—including lending him money. After 1898 Conrad's day was less lonely—he had a companion for walks, dominoes, chess, or just talk; and there was also frequent intercourse between the two families—shared pets, toys, festivities, even joint holidays, which somehow survived both Ford's tendency to patronise Jessie, and Jessie's consequent hostility. Until 1906, when Ford moved to London, Conrad had at call an undemanding admirer and helper for whatever he wanted or needed to do.

It was not, by almost any standard, an equitable partnership. Within a year Conrad was writing to Ford that he was sorry "your wife seems to think I've induced you to waste your time"; and he then proceeded to explain, rather offensively, that he "had no idea you had any profitable work to do" (*J B,* 235). Conrad was also very sensitive to the fact that some of his friends thought the association an odd one; and in his letters to them Conrad's references to Ford are often defensive, guarded, or mocking. In at least one case, Conrad is savagely ironic and contemptuous. It is in a letter to Garnett, who had known Ford well since childhood, but who apparently felt a "*physical* antipathy" to

7. Mizener, *Ford,* pp. 88–90, amends Jocelyn Baines's fairly similar account (*J B,* 290–92).

him,[8] and who may also have been somewhat jealous of Conrad's new literary adviser. Conrad is describing their "collaboration" on *The Inheritors:* "And poor *H.* was dead in earnest! Oh Lord. How he worked! . . . I've been fiendish . . . if I've not called him names I've *implied* in my remarks and the course of our discussions the most opprobrious epithets. He wouldn't recognise them. 'Pon my word it was touching."

Conrad dryly added: "You'll have to burn this letter" (*E G,* 169). Instead, Garnett published it, and while Ford was still alive. Ford was rightly indignant. But not with Conrad. For, in his letter of protest to Garnett in 1928, Ford wrote: "My affection for Conrad was so great and remains so unchanged that I have never been able really to believe in his death, and at this moment it is as if he were sitting behind me waiting to read what I have tapped out. You see, we did live together, day in day out, for many years—ten, I daresay and even towards the end he could not really get on without me any more than I could or can get on without him, and I do not shrink from saying that at this moment I cannot see for tears."[9]

Ford's tribute reminds us that although it is not possible to reconstruct how the inequities in the relationship were reconciled in some bookkeeping of the spirit, it is impossible to doubt that some rewarding mutual balance was struck. For Conrad the practical rewards of the intimacy were clear enough; as to the drawbacks, Conrad was probably too old at forty-one to expect an easy and assured reciprocity in all matters, and he no doubt developed his own strategies for avoiding awkward or divisive issues. As for Ford, no friction or disagreement would be very important compared to the fact that, in the only thing for which he most deeply, consistently, and unselfishly cared—writing—he was, and felt he was, immensely Conrad's debtor. When, in a 1920 letter to Herbert Read, Ford surveyed his own career, he affirmed that "I learned all I know of Literature from Conrad."[10]

ii. Composition and Sources

Conrad seems to have had little idea of just how long *Lord Jim* was going to be until it was more than half finished.[1] It may have been

8. Douglas Goldring, *Trained for Genius: The Life and Writings of Ford Madox Ford* (New York, 1949), p. 64.

9. Mizener, *Ford,* p. 55.

10. *Letters of Ford Madox Ford,* ed. R. Ludwig (Princeton, 1965), p. 127.

1. The history of its composition is told in the hundred or so pages devoted to it in

begun as early as 1896;[2] but the first definite evidence comes in a letter
to Meldrum on 3 June 1898. Conrad enclosed the end of "Youth,"
and promised to "send *Jim* along . . . as much as there is of him."
What Conrad sent were "the first 18 pages of *Jim: A sketch*," and he
then expected the story to be worked out in "no less than 20–25
thousand words. Say *two* numbers of 'Maga' " (*B*, 21–22). Conrad
apparently did little more writing on "Jim" for some time; he was busy
trying to finish *The Rescue,* moving into the Pent, and writing *Heart of
Darkness.* When it was finished, Conrad wrote, in February 1899, to say
that if *Lord Jim,* together with "Youth" and *Heart of Darkness,* proved
long enough to make up the volume of short stories he had promised
Blackwood, he would "*try* to get *Jim* finished in April," even if it meant
foregoing the economic rewards of prior magazine publication (*B*,
55). By July, however, the scale of *Lord Jim* had expanded. Conrad
now expected it to be, like *Heart of Darkness,* of near novel length—
"fully 40000 words" (*B*, 59).

In October 1899, serial publication of *Lord Jim* began in *Blackwood's.*
On 25 November, Conrad wrote "the Story will be finished of course
this year" (*B*, 75). Actually it was January 1900 before the seventeenth
chapter was completed, and soon afterwards Conrad was so ill, with
malaria, bronchitis, and gout, that little progress was possible.

Fortunately, Conrad was well ahead of the serial publication; on 12
February 1900 he was revising the proofs of chapter eighteen, and
two more chapters were almost written (*B*, 84). *Blackwood's Magazine,*
meanwhile, had only got to chapters ten and eleven. Even as late as
this Conrad still expected to finish the novel in another two chapters,
which would have made *Lord Jim* end at what is now chapter twenty-
two; and since the Stein interview occurs only two chapters before, it
seems certain that, a full five months after publication had begun,
Conrad was still not thinking of giving the Patusan episode any extensive treatment, let alone the twenty-four chapters it eventually
received.

By 12 April Conrad was beginning to face the length of the book
seriously enough to tell Blackwood that he would cooperate in making
cuts "should you find Jim unconscionably long (for Maga—I mean)"
(*B*, 90). Blackwood and Meldrum must already have been alarmed
about the increasing length of the story, as any magazine editor would

---

Conrad's *Letters to Blackwood's;* it is also available, in abbreviated form, in the fine edition
of *Lord Jim* by Thomas Moser (New York: W. W. Norton, 1968; hereafter cited as
L J N).

2. As is argued in Eloise Knapp Hay's article "*Lord Jim:* From Sketch to Novel,"
Comparative Literature 12 (1960), pp. 289–309.

be, but for a long time no word of their editorial anxieties was passed on to Conrad. In the end, however, William Blackwood had to force Conrad to face the facts. On 15 May 1900, Conrad was told that the plan for volume publication must be changed; "Lord Jim should be made a separate volume," Blackwood wrote, while "Youth" and *Heart of Darkness,* now already set up in type, should be left "until you are able to add one or two more stories which would make up a reasonable crown 8vo volume" (*B*, 93–94). Conrad immediately accepted with good grace, given that, as he wrote on 19 May, *Jim* "will be (it seems incredible) of, apparently, 100000 words or very little short of that."

There remained, however, much more writing to do before Conrad finished the last chapter, the forty-fifth, some two months later. He described that day, the 14th of July 1900, in a brilliantly evocative letter to Galsworthy:

> The end of *L. J.* has been pulled off with a steady drag of 21 hours. I sent wife and child out of the house (to London) and sat down at 9 A.M. with a desperate resolve to be done with it. Now and then I took a walk round the house, out at one door in at the other. Ten-minute meals. A great hush. Cigarette ends growing into a mound similar to a cairn over a dead hero. Moon rose over the barn, looked in at the window and climbed out of sight. Dawn broke, brightened. I put the lamp out and went on, with the morning breeze blowing the sheets of MS. all over the room. Sun rose. I wrote the last word and went into the dining-room. Six o'clock I shared a piece of cold chicken with Escamillo [their dog] (who was very miserable and in want of sympathy, having missed the child dreadfully all day). Felt very well, only sleepy: had a bath at seven and at 1.30 was on my way to London (*L L,* I, 295).

Conrad then went off with his family and the Fords for a holiday in Belgium, having arranged for Blackwood to send him the typed version of the last part of the manuscript, and the proofs for correction. All went rapidly, and the book version was published both in London and in New York in October 1900, a month before the serial in *Blackwood's Magazine* finally came to an end.

Conrad's own attitude to *Lord Jim* is difficult to analyse. Both the novel's first subtitle, "A Sketch," and its later change to "A Tale," suggest a tendency to take it rather lightly. In his later years, Conrad usually disassociated himself from the widespread view that *Lord Jim* was his finest novel, writing on one occasion, "this story which some people think my best—personally I don't."[3] At the time he was work-

3. *The Richard Curle Conrad Collection* (New York, 1927), item 35.

ing on it Conrad's feelings were mixed. There were many expressions
of shame, disgust, and disappointment: "a beggarly tale," he wrote to
Sanderson (*L L*, I, 283), and he told Garnett, "This is the sort of rot I
am writing now," and later, "How bad oh! HOW BAD!" (*E G*, 151; 170).
To others, however, Conrad expressed himself quite differently, saying to Meldrum he was "pleased with it," and that "Jim is very near my
heart" (*B*, 81;89). The balance of Conrad's feelings was probably best
expressed by what he wrote to Blackwood: "Endless discontent; with
remorse thrown in, for the massacre of so many good intentions"
(*B*, 90).

The "massacre" of Conrad's "good intentions" seems to have had
no connection with the conditions of serial publication; Conrad's only
recorded objection to it was about how the breaks between instalments
"destroyed an effect" (*B*, 89); and in any case he found time to make
very heavy revisions of the manuscript for the publication of *Lord Jim*
in book form.[4]

Conrad's later account of the composition of *Lord Jim* is somewhat
unconvincing, and seems influenced by his occasional tendency to
defend himself against charges somewhat different from those that
had, or could have justly, been made. In his Author's Note, written in
1917, he began by admitting that: "When this novel first appeared in
book form a notion got about that I had been bolted away with . . .
that the work starting as a short story had got beyond the writer's
control" (vii). There follows an implausible, and essentially irrelevant,
argument that Marlow could actually have told the whole story in
three hours, before Conrad returns to the charge:

> The truth of the matter is, that my first thought was of a short
> story, concerned only with the pilgrim ship episode; nothing
> more. And that was a legitimate conception. After writing a
> few pages, however, I became for some reason discontented
> and I laid them aside for a time. I didn't take them out of the
> drawer till the late Mr. William Blackwood suggested I should
> give something again to his magazine.
>
> It was only then that I perceived that the pilgrim ship
> episode was a good starting-point for a free and wandering
> tale.

Conrad then goes on to make the surprising assertion: "The few
pages I had laid aside were not without their weight in the choice of
subject. But the whole was rewritten deliberately. When I sat down to
it I knew it would be a long book, though I didn't forsee that it would

4. The manuscript is in the Rosenbach collection; its revisions were first studied by
Gordan (*J D G*, 150–73).

spread itself over thirteen [actually fourteen] numbers of 'Maga'."

Ostensibly to defend *Lord Jim* against the charge of lacking a unified plan, Conrad unwittingly convicts himself not only of having steadily deceived Blackwood—to whom he had originally presented "Jim" as a short tale—but also, through the long drawn-out maintenance of that deception, of having forced upon Blackwood the onus of confronting him with the very evident fact that *Lord Jim* would be much too long to include in a collection of short stories.

Of course, when an author writes to a publisher he is not upon oath; and Conrad was much too proud to use E. M. Forster's defence: "People will not realize . . . how one flounders about."[5] What probably happened is that two genuine but irreconcilable intentions were at play. Unlike Henry James, Conrad did not work from detailed out-lines, or even from notes; and his imagination always ran far ahead of his pen. Thus he wrote very revealingly to Meldrum: "The worst is that while I am thus powerless to produce my imagination is ex-tremely active: whole paragraphs, whole pages, whole chapters pass through my mind. Everything is there: descriptions, dialogue, reflexion—everything—everything but the belief, the conviction, the only thing needed to make me put pen to paper" (*B*, 27). From the spring of 1899 on, Conrad had probably imagined most of what would go into *Lord Jim*, but he continually put off facing how many pages it would actually take to write it all down. This was presumably for two main reasons: he badly wanted to finish it more quickly than was possible; and the longer *Lord Jim* became, the more he was putting himself in a false position not only with Blackwood's, but with all the other editors and publishers to whom he had long ago promised work. Heinemann, McClure, and even Ford would all feel that for Conrad to take time off to write a short story was merely annoying, whereas they would rightly regard his undertaking a long novel as a serious breach of his engagements to them.

The composition of *Lord Jim* is important not only as an example of the extraordinary difficulties under which Conrad worked, but also because it provides some initial clues both to the narrative form and the thematic development of the novel.

The Houghton Library at Harvard owns an elegant album in which Conrad's maternal grandmother copied out twenty-five pages of Polish poems belonging to the early eighteen-twenties; there re-mained many blank pages, and Conrad used twenty-eight of them to write down a heavily corrected and unfinished draft entitled "Tuan

5. "Interview: E. M. Forster, The Art of Fiction," *Paris Review* 1 (1953): 39.

Jim: A Sketch."[6] This draft is the basis, though not the immediate basis, for the first three chapters of the printed version of *Lord Jim*. It ends with the *Patna* steaming towards the entrance of the Red Sea; but there is just enough to enable us to reconstruct with some plausibility what Conrad had in mind when he originally thought the narrative would be worked out in the fifteen or so thousand words needed for two numbers of "Maga."

Like the final version, "Tuan Jim: A Sketch" begins with a visual impression: and this visual impression seems, as with *Almayer's Folly*, to represent Conrad's initial creative impetus.[7] In his Author's Note Conrad recounted: "One sunny morning in the commonplace surroundings of an Eastern roadstead, I saw his form pass by— appealing—significant—under a cloud—perfectly silent." The short story envisaged in the sketch would presumably have passed from the impression of Lord Jim as a water-clerk to an extended flashback of the pilgrim-ship episode; and Jim would probably have ended up, like Almayer and Willems, as a contemptible outcast in a Malay village— the second page of the Harvard manuscript reads: "Afterwards when his perception of the intolerable drove him away from the haunts of white men, the Malays of the village . . . (called) him Tuan Jim—as one would Lord Jim" (*L J N*, 283).

The main difference between the first four chapters of the final version and the rest of *Lord Jim* is suggested by this last sentence. Conrad's original attitude to his hero was distant and ironical; Jim is called "Lord" as a mockingly hyperbolic translation of the honorific "Tuan," a Malay form of address which is actually used in the sense merely of "Sir" or "Master," and is applied to everyone with any claim to authority or status, including that of merely being white.[8] Behind the sketch one can faintly discern a neat structure reminiscent of Daudet or Maupassant, in which a momentary but suggestive glimpse of a local character arouses a narrator's casual interest in how this figure came to be what he now is—a failure; and since the manuscript version contains no suggestion of the "course of light holiday litera-

6. The draft is transcribed, and its significance ably discussed, by Alexander Janta in "A Conrad Family Heirloom at Harvard," *Joseph Conrad: Centennial Essays*, ed. Ludwik Krzyżanowski (New York, 1960), pp. 85–109. A somewhat shorter version is conveniently reprinted in *L J N*.

7. In a 1923 interview Conrad remarked: "I get my hints from a passing face. I saw Lord Jim that way" (Dale B. J. Randall, "Conrad Interviews, No. 6: Louis Weitzenkorn," *C* 4 [1972]: 30).

8. Sir Hugh Clifford, a distinguished Malayan civil servant, and a close friend of Conrad, objected to "Lord" as a mistranslation of "Tuan" (in his Introduction to the Memorial edition of *Lord Jim* [New York, 1925], p. viii). But either "Sir" or "Mr." Jim would sound much too flippant, while "Master Jim" would suggest a boy.

ture" (5) which made Jim want to go to sea, we can assume that in Conrad's original plan Jim was not a romantic.

The mere fact, however, that Conrad could still use much of the early draft suggests that the novel retained one essential quality of the short story; as Conrad wrote to Blackwood after he had finished *Lord Jim*, the novel is "the development of *one* situation, only *one* really from beginning to end" (B, 106). One can see this central unity operating throughout the process of what Conrad called "Jim's expansion" (B, 98); and it probably accounts for Conrad's fear, which he expressed as late as 26 December 1899, that "*Lord Jim* would have hardly the lenght [sic] and certainly has not the substance to stand alone" (B, 79).

The central section—from chapter five to chapter twenty—is essentially an expansion in narrative form of the opening of "Tuan Jim"; instead of merely reporting a rapid generalised impression of how Jim seemed to "all the white men by the waterside and the captains of the ships," the novel in effect multiplies the single observer who narrates the sketch, and gives a long and penetrating series of reports of interviews with people who are either acquainted with Jim or who illuminate his case. This change from a third-person summary, filtered from the gossip of a seaport, to a full and direct presentation is mainly done through Marlow. He does not occur in the sketch (which may date from before Marlow's first appearance in "Youth"), but must have been decided on fairly soon after Conrad began steady work on *Lord Jim*, and certainly before 31 July 1899, when chapter four and the beginning of chapter five were sent to Meldrum (B, 59). It is Marlow's presence which makes *Lord Jim* almost as different from what we would expect from its first four chapters, as *Heart of Darkness* is from "An Outpost of Progress"; Marlow transforms Jim the outcast into "one of us."[9]

The primary source of *Lord Jim* is the history of the pilgrim ship *Jeddah*. She left Singapore on 17 July 1880 with her usual cargo of some 900 pilgrims bound for Jeddah, the seaport for Mecca; and she was abandoned at sea by her white officers on 8 August. The matter attracted worldwide attention because the steamship *Antenor* towed the *Jeddah* into Aden only a day after her officers had arrived there, and, confident that their ship had sunk, told their false story. The event was fully reported in *The Times*, and Conrad, who was in London at the time, probably read about the scandal; later he must have

9. Conrad said nothing about the mode of narration until after finishing *Lord Jim*, and then he merely described it as "personal narrative from a third party" (B, 106).

heard it discussed in nautical circles, especially when he was in Singapore in 1883.

Many of the details given in *Lord Jim* about the *Patna* are based on the actual incident, but Conrad made a number of changes. For instance, he internationalised the cast: the actual captain of the *Jeddah* was English, not German; and the rescuer was in fact not a French but a British officer. Conrad also simplified the events by having only one inquiry, which takes place in an unnamed eastern port, although in fact the original hearing was naturally held at Aden, while the later action for salvage took place at Singapore.[10]

Some of Conrad's other changes have the effect of making Jim's desertion much more difficult to justify. In the novel there is no gale, no breakdown of the boilers, no long period of baling out a gaining sea, no threat of violence from the pilgrims, no lives lost in the rush for the boats; instead there is a mysterious collision on an ominously calm sea with an unexplained something: "She went over whatever it was as easy as a snake crawling over a stick" (28), as Jim picturesquely expresses it. Conrad does not allow our sympathy to be aroused by the many extenuating circumstances of the original story. On the other hand, Jim, unlike the actual first officer of the *Jeddah*, does not recommend abandoning the ship, but goes forward to examine the bulkhead; this emphasises his sense of duty, his superiority to the other officers, and the puzzle of his final jump. We are made to confront the essence of his case in all its starkness: the breakdown of one individual officer's fidelity, under conditions of total moral isolation, as the result of his mistaken but well-founded fear that a catastrophe is imminent which he will be powerless to avert.

Jim's character seems to be derived from at least four sources.

Conrad probably based some aspects of his hero on one Augustine Podmore Williams, the actual chief mate of the *Jeddah*, who was censured by the court of inquiry but did not lose his certificate. Norman Sherry has discovered a good deal about him. Like Jim, Williams was the son of a parson, was indeed the last of the officers to leave the *Jeddah*, did return to Singapore to face the matter out, was often dressed in white, and had blue eyes. The later career of Williams, however, was very different from Jim's in most respects. In 1882 he became first mate of the *Vidar;* Conrad was to be his successor five years later, and he may then have heard accounts of Williams from the other officers. In 1884 Williams served, like Jim, as a ship-

10. The fullest account of the sources of *Lord Jim* is in Norman Sherry, *Conrad's Eastern World* (41–170); the reports of the inquiries are given in somewhat fuller form in his section on the "Sources" in *L J N*.

chandler's water-clerk; later he became a fairly prosperous and respected citizen of Singapore until his death in 1916. Conrad could therefore have met or seen him either when he was in Singapore briefly in the autumn of 1885, or later, in 1887, while he was serving on the *Vidar*. Sherry prints an interesting letter by a Mrs. Viola Allen which denies that the two men met, but adds: "Conrad told me he saw Williams in Singapore and wondered why a man of that—well—class—should be a ship-chandler's clerk." She goes on to relate that Conrad "always wondered why a man like that was doing that sort of job," and that one day she told him the story, which "everyone knew . . . in Singapore" (*S E W*, 85–86).

Some other hints for Jim's character, including his first and only name, probably came from Jim Lingard. Jim Lingard was the son of William Lingard, the Captain Tom Lingard of *Almayer's Folly*. From the age of eighteen onwards he lived at the settlement on the Berau river, and Conrad probably met him there at the same time that he met Olmeijer. Jim Lingard was then about twenty-five, and was probably known as Tuan Jim; apparently he lived with a Sea Dyak woman, and had a devoted servant called Lias; these two may have supplied the basis for Jewel and Tamb' Itam. What other influence Jim Lingard may have had on the novel, apart from his name and his servants, is not known. Sherry surmises that Conrad must have been impressed by "the general inexplicableness of his being at Berau at all."[11] It is a puzzle which occurs whenever one comes across a man living in isolation from all his kind, and the solution that first proposes itself is usually unflattering—the man must be in hiding and for good reason.

The third main source for Jim, and particularly for his exploits in Patusan, are books of travel and historical accounts of the many adventurers who had become rulers of native states. Conrad seems to be mainly indebted to Alfred Wallace's *The Malay Archipelago*, and to a series of memoirs by Henry Keppel, Rodney Mundy, John Templer, and Gertrude Jacobs—all of them largely based on the writings of Sir James Brooke. After an undistinguished earlier career, Brooke had helped the sultan of Borneo's uncle to put down a revolt on the west coast of Borneo, had been made rajah of Sarawak in 1841, and had there founded a dynasty which endured until after the second world war. The analogy with Jim is essentially one not of character but of achievement; and that achievement is merely the most spectacular example of a larger myth. Brooke was himself a confessed imitator of

11. *S E W*, 136. Most of the details about Jim Lingard are given on pp. 80 and 131–38. Sherry supplies a portrait; and there are several of Williams.

Stamford Raffles, who, almost entirely through his individual initia-
tive, conquered Java in 1811 and founded Singapore in 1819; like
Brooke, Raffles also had some temporary success in establishing
Western ideas of order and justice, much as Jim does in Patusan.

A vivid visual impression of someone, possibly Williams, presumably led Conrad to link the scandal of the *Jeddah* with an individual
moral problem; then memories of Jim Lingard and readings about
Rajah Brooke added further suggestions for Jim's Borneo career;[12]
but what gives Jim his peculiar power to engage our imagination and
our affections surely derives from Conrad's own involvement in Jim's
fate; in a somewhat more direct sense than with Almayer, another
major source of Jim is Conrad himself.

The only specific parallel[13] between the lives of the two men is the
course of events which led both of them to yield to the solicitations of
"short passages, good deck-chairs, large native crews, and the distinction of being white" (13). Early in 1887 Conrad had signed on as first
mate of the *Highland Forest,* a barque; in *The Mirror of the Sea* he relates
that in the captain's absence he took charge of loading the cargo at
Amsterdam, and that when the captain learned how the cargo had
been stowed, he commented: "Well, we shall have a lively time of it
this passage, I bet" (*M S,* 53). In fact the *Highland Forest* rolled so badly
that some spars did go, and, as Conrad comments, "it was only poetic
justice that the chief mate who had made a mistake—perhaps a half-
excusable one . . . should pay the penalty." A spar hit Conrad's back;
like Jim, he probably "spent many days stretched on his back, dazed,
battered, hopeless, and tormented as if at the bottom of an abyss of
unrest" (11); and he may even, like Jim, have "felt secretly glad he had
not to go on deck." In any case the passage as a whole has the ring of
personal experience.

This parallel between Jim and Conrad, however, would only apply
to the first part of *Lord Jim;* and in most respects the characters and
experiences of Jim and Conrad are very different indeed. Still, the
existence of an element of identification—including youthful romantic dreams of heroic adventure—would help to explain why Conrad
consistently linked *Lord Jim* to his two autobiographical stories of the
period, "Youth" and *Heart of Darkness.* Thus, even at the end of 1899,
when the novel was very far advanced, Conrad wrote that "the three
tales, each being inspired by a similar moral idea (or is it only one of

12. The name Patusan comes from Sarawak, and Conrad probably picked it up from
Henry Keppel's *Expedition to Borneo* (London, 1846), vol. 2, pp. 76–92; but most of the
topographical and some other details are from Berau, in Eastern Borneo.

13. Though Conrad also confesses that in his days of "youth" and "innocence" his "pen-
sive habits . . . made me sometimes dilatory in my work about the rigging" (*M S,* 122).

my optical delusions?) will make (in that sense) a homogeneous book" (*B,* 79). Here one notices that Conrad admits that he may be wrong in finding a similar moral idea in the three stories; and yet he continued to assert that the three tales belonged together. Even when *Lord Jim* was almost finished he wrote to Blackwood: "It has not been planned to stand alone. *H of D* was meant in my mind as a foil, and *Youth* was supposed to give the note" (*B,* 94). One can surmise that "Youth" was Conrad's Song of Innocence, and that perhaps *Lord Jim,* which Conrad thought "more like *Youth*" than *Heart of Darkness* (*B,* 63), was originally intended to strike the same youthful note, though in a more critical spirit. Then there had intervened the writing of *Heart of Darkness,* Conrad's middle-aged Song of Experience. When he came back to *Lord Jim,* he brought with him a Marlow who had gone through a second and much deeper experience of disillusionment. This may have transformed Conrad's previous conception, and in effect turned *Lord Jim* into a dialogue between the two Marlows, with Jim as the voice of his earlier innocence, and Marlow confronting him with the disenchanted voice of later experience.

iii. The Narrative·Progress and Its Methods

Conrad stands outside the main tradition of the novel of character; or at least his primary interest is not the detailed psychology of the nature, development, and relationships of individual personalities. The special perspective from which Conrad presents his fictional characters is difficult to define; it is broader and yet both more selective and more concentrated than is usual in the novel. The perspective is broader because Conrad's characters are not the centers of a largely autonomous world of personal relationships, but beings whose actions are inextricably connected with the mysterious and yet determining forces of social and natural reality; the perspective is more selective because his scepticism prevents him from telling us many things that we are usually told about characters in novels; and yet the perspective is more concentrated because Conrad's scepticism also leads him to present and explore with exceptional thoroughness whatever pieces of evidence are available, however fragmentary or ambiguous, which may provide clues to understanding what the characters do and are.

Both the immediate effect and the ultimate rationale of the distinctive qualities of Conrad's characterisation are finely suggested by Ramon Fernandez. He wrote in 1924 that Conrad's characters

> become palpable, project themselves on our physical being, react on our souls, and then go on acting, problematic and living, in our imaginations. There is nothing artificial about

their mystery, for it is simply the result of how whatever is immediately experienced by the senses is inaccessible to the process of thought. There are two kinds of mystery: that where things are cleverly hidden from us, and that where we are made to experience things completely. The first is produced through intellectual manipulation; the second through overturning the natural tendency of our minds and immersing us completely into the life which we were previously skimming over.[1]

Conrad overturns the "natural tendency of our minds" very largely through a set of highly idiosyncratic narrative techniques. Many of these techniques were present in *Heart of Darkness,* and have already been discussed, notably the impressionist and symbolist aspects, and the use of Marlow; but in the later and ampler narrative of *Lord Jim,* Conrad develops some of his techniques for immersing us completely "into the lives of the character" a good deal further, and they therefore require separate consideration.

To combine the analysis of these narrative techniques with a connecting summary of the main action and themes of *Lord Jim,* the discussion follows, as far as possible, the order in which the techniques occur in the narrative. This works well enough with two of the techniques, delayed decoding and symbolic deciphering, because they happen to be mainly employed in the first six chapters. The three other technical features, thematic apposition, the use of time, and *progression d'effet,* are not themselves specific to any single part of *Lord Jim* but they are here treated in that order to make possible a continuous account of the story.

(a) *Marlow's Involvement: Delayed Decoding, Symbolic Deciphering*
    and Thematic Apposition

As we have seen, Conrad often used delayed decoding in his earlier works. It served mainly to put the reader in the position of being an immediate witness of each step in the process whereby the semantic gap between the sensations aroused in the individual by an object or event, and their actual cause or meaning, was slowly closed in his consciousness. Since this technique is based on the pretence that the reader's understanding is limited to the consciousness of the fictional observer, it is not surprising that Conrad's use of delayed decoding should reach its climax in the Marlow stories. The explosion on the *Judea* in "Youth," and the four successive examples of delayed decoding when the ship is attacked just below Kurtz's station in *Heart of*

1. "L'Art de Conrad," pp. 733–34.

Darkness, were primarily concerned with the impressionist rendering of surface phenomena. In the early section of *Lord Jim,* which is told by an omniscient observer, there is a fine variant of this visual and objective kind of delayed decoding, but it is characteristic of the novel that it should here be a case of decoding denied.[2] Later, when Marlow takes over the narrative, he so transforms the device for symbolic and moral purposes, that the term delayed decoding applies less well. In a very general way, the passages still enact the subjective process whereby the individual progressively elucidates the meaning of actions or words; but the process of decoding is so much more complex, and the resultant meanings embrace such larger issues, that the term symbolic deciphering seems more descriptive.

The first four chapters of *Lord Jim* are told in a fairly straightforward way, and from a technical point of view their main interest is that they tell the reader many facts about Jim's earlier life, and about the events leading up to his desertion, which Marlow never knows. The voyage of the *Patna* is presented with a controlled intensity whose beauty recalls similar descriptions in *The Nigger of the "Narcissus",* except that the writing is somewhat more economical, and the pervasive atmosphere of ominous serenity is very different. This atmosphere reaches its zenith on the night that the mysterious accident occurs. On the bridge Jim is "penetrated by the great certitude of unbounded safety and peace that could be read on the silent aspect of nature like the certitude of fostering love upon the placid tenderness of a mother's face" (17). In his deluded sense of utter security Jim is merely amused by the vulgar echoes of his own delusions in the drunken engineer's boastful vapourings about his courageous disregard of the dangers of serving on the *Patna;* the plates of her hull, he says, are "like brown paper." Then the crisis grotesquely announces itself:

> ". . . who wouldn't chuck a dratted job like this? 'Tain't safe, s'elp me, it ain't! Only I am one of them fearless fellows. . . ."
>
> He let go the rail and made ample gestures as if demonstrating in the air the shape and extent of his valour; his thin voice darted in prolonged squeaks upon the sea, he tiptoed back and forth for the better emphasis of utterance, and suddenly pitched down head-first as though he had been clubbed from behind. He said "Damn!" as he tumbled; an instant of silence followed upon his screeching: Jim and the skipper staggered forward by common accord, and catching them-

2. For a somewhat fuller treatment of delayed decoding, see my "Pink Toads and Yellow Curs: An Impressionist Narrative Device in *Lord Jim,*" in *Joseph Conrad Colloquy in Poland 5–12 September 1972* (Warsaw: Polish Academy of Sciences, 1975), pp. 11–31.

selves up, stood very stiff and still gazing, amazed, at the
undisturbed level of the sea. Then they looked upwards at the
stars. . . .

The engineer rebounded vertically full length and col-
lapsed again into a vague heap. This heap said "What's that?"
in the muffled accents of profound grief. (26).

Conrad's omniscient narrator here pretends to be strictly limited to
the point of view of an actual observer at the time of the occurrence;
the mystery of the event is made vividly real to us through a sequence
of minutely presented physical sensations, mainly visual but also aural
(the engineer's words) and kinetic (the staggering). In some ways the
passage recalls that in "Youth" about the explosion on board the
Judea, but the partly comic tone soon disappears when the process of
decoding is taken over by a more distant observer whose impassive
deliberation heightens the note of apprehensive expectancy:

A faint noise as of thunder, of thunder infinitely remote, less
than a sound, hardly more than a vibration, passed slowly,
and the ship quivered in response, as if the thunder had
growled deep down in the water. The eyes of the two Malays
at the wheel glittered towards the white men, but their dark
hands remained closed on the spokes. The sharp hull driving
on its way seemed to rise a few inches in succession through its
whole length, as though it had become pliable, and settled
down again rigidly to its work of cleaving the smooth surface
of the sea. Its quivering stopped, and the faint noise of thunder ceased all at once, as though the ship had steamed across a
narrow belt of vibrating water and of humming air (26–27).

The precise notation of sensory images, which are again kinetic
("quivered") and aural ("growled") as well as visual, adds to our picture of the scene; but we are really being given a replay of the event
rather than a chronological continuation; the original passage is
merely duplicated from a different and more comprehensive point of
view; it is really a case of decoding doubly delayed and doubly denied.
This ostentatious denial of our expectation that we will be told just
what unseen physical cause made Jim and the captain stagger, and the
second engineer collapse "into a vague heap," prepares us for the
ultimately inexplicable mystery of how the occurrence affected the
rest of Jim's life.

The passage just quoted ends chapter three, and the third-person
authorial narrative then jumps forward to Jim giving his evidence at
the inquiry a month later. The chapter is very brief; it gives very little
of Jim's testimony; and its main function is to effect the transition to
Marlow's narrative. This transition begins with a simple but charac-

teristically visual impressionist device which Conrad had already used in *Heart of Darkness*. There the Russian "stared" at Marlow "with his little blue eyes," and Marlow in return "looked at him, lost in astonishment" (126). In *Lord Jim* a similarly reciprocal gaze is described at the inquiry: "Jim's eyes," we are told, "wandering in the intervals of his answers, rested upon a white man who sat apart from the others, with his face worn and clouded, but with quiet eyes that glanced straight, interested and clear. . . . He met the eyes of the white man" (32). Jim is much attracted by Marlow's gaze; it shows that one person, at least, is "aware of his hopeless difficulty"; nevertheless, we are told, "Jim looked at him, then turned away resolutely, as after a final parting." In the next paragraph, the unparticularised narrator briefly introduces his successor, and Marlow takes up the tale at the beginning of chapter five with : "Oh yes. I attended the inquiry."

For some time we are left wondering whether this visual exchange may not prove to be Marlow's only direct contact with Jim, since Marlow's narrative begins by taking up various events before the inquiry—first the sight of the four officers of the *Patna* arriving on the quay, then the Captain's grotesquely precipitate flight, and finally Marlow's conversation with the *Patna's* chief engineer. This episode is the first example both of "symbolic deciphering" and "thematic apposition"; it depends on the effect of their combination for its larger meaning.

There happens to be someone in the hospital that Marlow must visit, but once there he discovers to his surprise that both the *Patna's* engineer officers are also patients. Marlow approaches the chief engineer, who is suffering from delirium tremens brought on by a three-day drinking bout. When Marlow casually mentions the *Patna,* the engineer pauses, and finally remarks: "I saw her go down. . . . She was full of reptiles"(51). Soon afterwards the engineer tells Marlow to "Look under the bed"; in an unconscious motor reflex which we later discover is analogous to Jim's when the other officers in the lifeboat tell him to "Jump!"(110). Marlow obeys:

> Of course I stooped instantly. I defy anybody not to have done so. "What can you see?" he asked. "Nothing," I said, feeling awfully ashamed of myself. He scrutinised my face with wild and withering contempt. "Just so," he said, "but if I were to look I could see—there's no eyes like mine, I tell you." Again he clawed, pulling at me downwards in his eagerness to relieve himself by a confidential communication. "Millions of pink toads. . . . It's worse than seeing a ship sink. I could look at sinking ships and smoke my pipe all day long. Why don't they give me back my pipe? I would get a smoke while I watched these toads."

The climax of Marlow's interview comes when the engineer reveals the unconscious displacement which underlies his delusions:

> "The ship was full of them, you know, and we had to clear out on the strict Q.T.," he whispered with extreme rapidity. "All pink. All pink—as big as mastiffs, with an eye on the top of the head and claws all round their ugly mouths. Ough! Ough!" Quick jerks as of galvanic shocks disclosed under the flat coverlet the outlines of meagre and agitated legs; he let go my shoulder and reached after something in the air; his body trembled tensely like a released harp-string; and while I looked down, the spectral horror in him broke through his glassy gaze. Instantly his face of an old soldier, with its noble and calm outlines, became decomposed before my eyes by the corruption of stealthy cunning, of an abominable caution and of desperate fear. He restrained a cry—"Ssh! what are they doing now down there?" he asked, pointing to the floor with fantastic precautions of voice and gesture, whose meaning, borne upon my mind in a lurid flash, made me very sick of my cleverness. "They are all asleep," I answered, watching him narrowly. That was it. That's what he wanted to hear. (53)

There is a gruesome slowness in the process whereby, through interrogating physical movements and expressions as well as words, Marlow gradually leads us towards deciphering the symbolic meaning of the engineer's raw terror of the "pink toads." We are forced to experience every step which leads to the double climax, one physical, the other moral, in which Marlow pacifies the engineer's "spectral horror," and simultaneously proves the correctness of his own gathering conviction that the pink toads are really the engineer's repressed dread of the pursuing vengeance of the pilgrims he deserted.

The episode is told with the same impressionist immediacy as some of the examples of delayed decoding discussed earlier; but here the initial stimulus is verbal—pink toads—and its ultimate cause is inward and subjective. The passage is also puzzling in another, and more fundamental way: even when the reader has seen that he, like Marlow, has deciphered the symbolic meaning of the engineer's delirious language correctly, his puzzlement does not end, but increases. Why is Marlow telling us all this, and with so much emphasis? The answer to this question is not given in the scene itself, which has no manifest relation to the rest of the action. What the relation is can only be surmised by considering what comes immediately before and after.

Before recounting his visit to the hospital, Marlow was wondering aloud to his listeners why he had ever been moved to go "grubbing into the deplorable details" of the *Patna* affair (50). He is now inclined to believe, he says, that perhaps "unconsciously, I hoped I would find . . . some convincing shadow of an excuse" for Jim's actions. But now Marlow sees that it was much more than that: "I see well enough now that I hoped for the impossible—for the laying of what is the most obstinate ghost of man's creation, of the uneasy doubt uprising like a mist, secret and gnawing like a worm, and more chilling than the certitude of death—the doubt of the sovereign power enthroned in a fixed standard of conduct."

Marlow's doubt here about the ultimate basis of the social and moral order is of much the same general nature as in *Heart of Darkness;* unlike Kurtz, however, the engineer makes no explicit moral judgment on what he has done. Still, the passage seems to suggest that Marlow draws some meagre comfort from the engineer's breakdown; and this impression is strengthened when the restoration of the engineer's composure proves very short lived, and he cries out: "They are all awake—millions of them. . . . trampling on me! . . . I'll smash them in heaps like flies" (54), and then collapses completely with a panic-stricken yell of "Help. H-e-elp!"

The nature of the scene's contribution to Marlow's moral comfort becomes a little clearer in its aftermath. On the way out he encounters one of the resident surgeons, who volunteers a comment on the uniqueness of the engineer's case: "There's some sort of method in his raving. I am trying to find out. Most unusual—that thread of logic in such a delirium. Traditionally he ought to see snakes." Marlow makes no effort to tell him why the reptiles which populate the engineer's nightmares are pink and amphibious, but curtly pleads haste and leaves. As he hurries off, however, the surgeon shouts: "I say . . . he can't attend that inquiry. Is his evidence material, you think?" To which, in the last words of the chapter, Marlow laconically replies, "Not in the least." Such evidence as the engineer can provide, then, is not material; and although Marlow does not decode it as spiritual, the emphasis he gives his retort prompts us to look in that direction.

At a fairly literal level the engineer's fear echoes a special feature of Jim's case whose importance is only to be shown much later: how Jim feared that the pilgrims on the *Patna* might panic if the alarm were raised. The engineer's breakdown also points, though more obscurely, to the larger moral preoccupation which was aroused in Marlow when, in the preceding chapter, both Jim and the other officers of the *Patna* seemed completely unmarked by any sign of inward compunction. Now the hospital scene must offer Marlow some slight degree of reassurance, since although the fixed standard of conduct has hardly exhibited a sovereign power, it has, in one instance at least, not been violated with impunity. The engineer cannot be perceived as repentant—he still wants to smash the pilgrims "like flies"; but he is not unmarked by his betrayal. The existence of some form of internal moral control is surely necessary to account for the engineer's saying that for him the sight of the pink toads is "worse than seeing a ship sink." How else could we explain why this case-hardened villain breaks down so many weeks after the event?

The scale and the placing of the hospital episode in the general narrative movement must surely be seen as an indirect and tentative introduction to the novel's main thematic concerns; more specifically, Marlow's first exposure to an inside view of the psychological effect of what happened on the *Patna* discloses some spiritual evidence which begins to allay the worst anxieties which had been aroused by what he first saw and heard about the scandal.

The structure of the episode is intrinsically symbolic in at least three senses: first, that it depends on the symbolic substitution of "pilgrims" for the word actually used, "toads"; second, that this substitution in turn depends upon a variant of the conventional symbolic role of reptiles in alcoholic delirium; and lastly, the structure is symbolic in the larger symbolist sense because it attempts to suggest subjective and indefinable matters which can be presented neither in concrete nor conceptual terms. Mallarmé had described the symbolist method as one whereby the literary object was made to reveal a state of consciousness ("etat d'âme") through a series of "decipherings" ("*déchiffrements*").[3] Here two states of consciousness—Marlow's and the engineer's—are involved; and the meanings of the scene are clearly of a kind that ask, not to be decoded, but to be deciphered: the word decoding suggests a mechanical and systematic process which, once the key is applied, clears up the whole problem; this episode, on the other hand, requires deciphering, because the connotations of that word suggest the much more tenuous and complicated process of making out a message that is inherently difficult to read, and whose meaning is intentionally hidden, or at least ambiguous, mysterious, or unresolved.

The next chapter—six—returns us to the opening of the inquiry, but only for two paragraphs; Marlow then relates a second self-contained episode, which occupies two-thirds of the chapter, and in which another unexpressed motive has to be deciphered.

Big Brierly is one of the two nautical assessors. At the age of thirty-two, Marlow tells us, he has reached the pinnacle of success in his profession as the captain of the crack ship of the Blue Star line. Watching him in court Marlow had imagined that he felt only an "immensity . . . of contempt" for Jim; but he soon learns that Brierly's

3. Mallarmé *Œuvres complètes*, p. 869.

appearance was actually just as deceptive as Jim's. For, although Brierly's apparent "self-satisfaction presented to me and to the world a surface as hard as granite," Marlow adds laconically that in fact, "He committed suicide very soon after" (58). Most of the Brierly episode concerns Marlow's attempt to discover "the secret of the evidence" which Brierly took with him when he "jumped overboard at sea barely a week after the end of the inquiry." The attempt, as with the hospital episode, has two main phases.

The first one taken up in the narrative is the outcome of a chance meeting which, as we discover some four pages later, actually occurred "more than two years afterwards" (64). Marlow runs into an acquaintance called Jones, who was Brierly's chief mate. Jones knows that Brierly's suicide was deliberate, and was indeed planned with meticulous care; but he remains mystified as to what could have brought this paragon to "commit the rash act." At the end of their conversation, however, Marlow remarks to Jones that whatever the cause, "it wasn't anything that would have disturbed much either of us two"; and then, Marlow says: "poor old Jones found a last word of amazing profundity. . . . 'Ay, ay! neither you nor I, sir, had ever thought so much of ourselves.' "

Marlow does not specify where the "amazing profundity" lies; but the fact that their interview ends on Jones's remark, combined with Marlow's emphatic but unexplained signal of its importance, makes us retain some glimmering notion that Brierly's suicide must have been connected with his "belief in his own splendour."

Marlow's narrative abruptly leaves Jones and returns to the court of inquiry. The reason for this inversion of the time sequence is soon made clear: forewarned by our detailed knowledge of Brierly's later suicide, we are alerted to whatever may be diagnostic in his behaviour now.

When Brierly buttonholes Marlow after the first day's hearing has been adjourned, he seems in a state of quite uncharacteristic irritation. The inquiry, Brierly complains, makes him "feel like a fool all the time" (66), and he finally comes out with the defiantly revelatory question: "Why are we tormenting that young chap?" To this challenge Marlow subversively answers, "Hanged if I know, unless it be that he lets you." He is then astonished to see the normally obtuse Brierly "fall into line . . . with that utterance, which ought to have been tolerably cryptic." Brierly confesses that he cannot imagine why Jim should "eat all that dirt," since "Nothing can save him. He's done for." When Marlow points out that Jim may not even have the money to run away, Brierly answers: "Well, then, let him creep twenty feet underground and stay there! By heavens! *I* would." Brierly's "tone" provokes Marlow, and he is moved to defend Jim, and assert: "There is a kind of courage in facing it out as he does."

Marlow's initial diagnosis of Jim as a shameless coward now seems inadequate; and he goes on to explore the larger problems posed by Jim's case. That apparent model of official rectitude, Brierly, certainly proves no reliable defender of the fixed standard of conduct when he suggests that they jointly offer Jim three hundred rupees to leave at once. His reasons are both amoral and personal. Brierly argues that since Jim is "a gentleman if he ain't fit to be touched," he will understand what "infernal publicity" it is to have "all these confounded natives . . . giving evidence that's enough to burn a man to ashes with shame." We know that Brierly must be the highly combustible man Brierly has in mind; and when Marlow refuses to help him end his inward torment by so cavalierly subverting the processes of justice and removing Jim from the scene, Brierly is driven to a fuller expression of outrage: "All you fellows have no sense of dignity; you don't think enough of what you are supposed to be." Jones is right; Brierly thinks too much of what he is supposed to be; and he apparently assumes that this is the universal basis of the code of proper behaviour. Seamen, as a group, Brierly says, "must preserve professional decency" because "the only thing that holds us together is just the name for that kind of decency" (68).

There is something ominous about the words "only" and "name" here. For two reasons. Brierly sees solidarity as something based not on any internal ethical foundation, but entirely as a response to the need to maintain public esteem for the group to which he belongs. His own self-esteem is grounded on equally external and insecure foundations. To base both the fixed standard of conduct, and the individual's sense of his own selfhood, on something as shifting and undependable as public opinion, seems to confirm Marlow's own most troubling fears.

Meanwhile, Brierly continues to undermine any internal and ethical basis for the social and moral order. He confides to Marlow that "such an affair destroys one's confidence," since "a man may go pretty near through his whole sea-life without any call to show a stiff upper lip." Brierly then seems to be about to speculate on how he personally might perform "when the call [came]," but he suddenly breaks off, and returns to his suggestion that Marlow talk Jim into running away. Marlow now becomes "positive" that Jim's facing the inquiry "practically of his own free will" must be viewed as "a redeeming feature." One reason for this is presumably that it demonstrated that Jim's sense of selfhood is, unlike Brierly's, for the most part internally generated.

Brierly goes off in a huff. Marlow is still mystified by Brierly's "state of mind," but his subsequent suicide, and Jones's account of it, do much to decipher the mystery.

In the courtroom, Brierly was clearly, in Marlow's words, "holding silent inquiry into his own case," and Marlow adds that his "verdict must have been one of unmitigated guilt" (58). Jim's desertion had had the effect of starting "into life some thought with which a man unused to such a companionship finds it impossible to live." Brierly's "belief in his own splendour which had almost cheated his life of its legitimate terrors" (64) could not face the slightest test—not even that of being exposed to the thought of someone else's failure. Up to now Brierly had perhaps merely been exceptionally lucky; by the same token perhaps Jim had merely been exceptionally unlucky.

We begin to see why Marlow should make so much of Brierly's suicide, and at this point. In addition to suggesting Jim's courage in living on and trying to be faithful to his internal sense of proper conduct by facing the trial, there are several less direct implications. First, that if Big Brierly cannot face the mere idea of a test in his imagination, Marlow must judge Jim's failure in a real test less severely. Secondly, we are surely invited to compare the blind desperation of Brierly's impulse to obliterate any public manifestation of the vulnerability of the seaman's code, with Jim's steady resolve to stand alone and take his public punishment. Thirdly, the "amazing profundity" of Jones's last remark suggests that a failure of nerve, of which suicide is the most extreme form, is peculiarly liable to affect those who, like Brierly and perhaps Jim, "thought so much of" themselves.

The narrative technique of the Brierly episode is fundamentally similar to that of the hospital scene in three respects: both are structured so as to engage our bewildered participation in a puzzle; the narrative order in both scenes is clearly intended to be interrogative rather than indicative; and this interrogative effect lingers after the episodes themselves have ended.

This sense of a continuing puzzle is an essential part of the difference between both scenes, and those based on delayed decoding. Delayed decoding deals only with external and physical clues; but both the Brierly and the hospital episodes require the deciphering of underlying motives which are largely unconscious, and whose verbal expression is at best partial and ambiguous. The Brierly episode is less obviously symbolic, since its fundamental basis is not an apparently senseless phrase but an act—suicide—whose overt meaning is clear. Still, the episode as a whole is symbolic in the sense that the sum of its surface narrative elements does not compose itself unassisted into an adequate meaning; there remains an insistent semantic gap which

asks the reader to reconstitute all the literal details and the latent
questions they provoke into a larger meaning which has been inti-
mated, but not stated, by Marlow. That process of interrogation and
reconstitution seems to impose itself the more readily because the
formal structure of each scene has an exceptional degree of autonomy. The protagonist exists only for the sake of the episode—we
hear no more of Brierly or the chief engineer; and the episode ends as
soon as—spurred on by Marlow's teasing pressure—we have sufficiently interrogated it for ourselves, and tried to puzzle out how it
helps us to see the general moral issues more clearly.

We have also been encouraged to read the narrative in this inward
and interrogative way by the context. There is, first of all, the way the
official inquiry is treated as more or less irrelevant. After all, there
could hardly be anything more likely than an appearance in the witness box to confirm Jim's (or indeed anybody else's) "opinion that
speech was of no use to him any longer" (33); and the court proceedings are equally pointless as regards Marlow's concerns. "The play of
questions," Marlow comments sardonically, was "as instructive as the
tapping with a hammer on an iron box, were the object to find out
what's inside" (56); the court is inquiring, not into "the fundamental
why, but the superficial how." By so saying, Marlow directs us to look
for "what's inside" Jim's case, for its "fundamental why."

In promoting this search Marlow uses a procedure which takes that
employed in *Heart of Darkness* somewhat further. In both works the
continuity of the narrative is based, not on the chronological sequence
of actions as they occurred, but on the particular stage which Marlow
has reached in his understanding of "the fundamental why" of the
moral puzzles presented by his tale. The sequence of episodes in the
text, therefore, is often purely thematic; but whereas in *Heart of Darkness* these non-chronological interpolations are relatively brief, in *Lord
Jim* many of them are given much more extensive and autonomous
treatment, and leave us much more to do for ourselves in construing
their significance.

The reason why the Brierly episode is told after the hospital scene
has nothing to do with chronology; it is a matter of "thematic apposition." After the first scene of symbolic deciphering has focussed attention on a few particular themes, another scene is laid immediately
alongside it which has no connection with it other than that of continuing and developing the same moral issues. In this case the apposition of the two episodes calls upon us to mediate between two antithetic moral analogies: the engineer has shown that the most unscrupulous
reprobate may not be able to stand up to the unconscious idea of his
guilt; Brierly has shown that the most beribboned pillar of society

may not be able to stand up to the shameful idea of his fear. What, then, is the moral problem, related but presumably not identical to either, which Jim cannot face?

Jim was not mentioned in the scene with the engineer, and although Jim was important to Brierly, he did not know it, and Brierly was nothing to him. Marlow's first two chapters have indirectly prepared us to take a more sympathetic and understanding view of Jim's predicament, and to place it in the context of the novel's general themes. It is only when such themes as courage, the special vulnerability of the imaginative individual, and the relationship of private and public attitudes, have been taken up that the reader is ready for Marlow's first meeting with Jim.

It occurs on the second day of the inquiry, the day Marlow's eyes meet Jim's. Jim's look seems to express either "insolence or despair"; to Marlow it is wholly "discouraging of any intention I might have had to speak to him" (69), and he concludes that he "could be of no use" to Jim. When the inquiry adjourns, Jim walks out alone. Marlow, who is talking to a stranger who has accosted him, follows Jim through the same door. Marlow's narrative continues:

> Whether those villagers had brought the yellow dog with them, I don't know. Anyhow, a dog was there, weaving himself in and out amongst people's legs in that mute stealthy way native dogs have and my companion stumbled over him. The dog leaped away without a sound; the man, raising his voice a little, said with a slow laugh, "Look at the wretched cur," and directly afterwards we became separated by a lot of people pushing in. I stood back for a moment against the wall while the stranger managed to get down the steps and disappeared. I saw Jim spin round. He made a step forward and barred my way. We were alone; he glared at me with an air of stubborn resolution. I became aware I was being held up, so to speak, as if in a wood. The verandah was empty by then, the noise and movement in court had ceased: a great silence fell upon the building, in which, somewhere far within, an oriental voice began to whine abjectly. The dog in the very act of trying to sneak in at the door, sat down hurriedly to hunt for fleas.
>
> "Did you speak to me?" asked Jim very low, and bending forward, not so much towards me but at me, if you know what I mean. I said "No" at once.

The misunderstanding continues for a couple of paragraphs, and then Jim asks:

> "What did you mean by staring at me all the morning?" said

Jim at last. He looked up and looked down again. "Did you expect us all to sit with downcast eyes out of regard for your susceptibilities?" I retorted sharply. I was not going to submit meekly to any of his nonsense. He raised his eyes again, and this time continued to look me straight in the face. "No. That's all right," he pronounced with an air of deliberating with himself upon the truth of this statement—"that's all right. I am going through with that. Only"—and there he spoke a little faster—"I won't let any man call me names outside this court. There was a fellow with you. You spoke to him—oh, yes—I know; 'tis all very fine. You spoke to him, but you meant me to hear. . . ."

I assured him he was under some extraordinary delusion. I had no conception how it came about. "You thought I would be afraid to resent this," he said, with just a faint tinge of bitterness. I was interested enough to discern the slightest shades of expression, but I was not in the least enlightened; yet I don't know what in these words, or perhaps just the intonation of that phrase, induced me suddenly to make all possible allowances for him (71–72).

Marlow has registered that Jim's subjective life is dominated, not, as he thought, by insolence or despair, but by some inward bitterness and resentment; but he cannot resolve its particular cause, and he is meanwhile unable to extricate himself from the mysterious and dangerous impasse, which continues for some time. Finally Jim moves towards Marlow threateningly:

"If you were as big as two men and as strong as six," he said very softly, "I would tell you what I think of you. You . . ." "Stop!" I exclaimed. . . . "Before you tell me what you think of me . . . will you kindly tell me what it is I've said or done?" [After a pause they] spoke almost together. "I will soon show you I am not," he said, in a tone suggestive of a crisis. "I declare I don't know," I protested earnestly at the same time. He tried to crush me by the scorn of his glance. "Now that you see I am not afraid you try to crawl out of it," he said. "Who's a cur now—hey?" Then, at last, I understood.

The reader, however, may not understand, unless he recalls the stranger's casual remark earlier: "Look at that wretched cur" (70). Jim, of course, has no inkling of the truth, and so the agonising suspense continues:

It was, indeed, a hideous mistake; he had given himself away utterly. I can't give you an idea how shocked I was. I suppose he saw some reflection of my feelings in my face, because his expression changed just a little. "Good God!" I stammered,

"you don't think I . . ." "But I am sure I've heard," he per-
sisted, raising his voice for the first time since the beginning of
this deplorable scene. Then with a shade of disdain he added,
"It wasn't you, then? Very well; I'll find the other." "Don't be a
fool," I cried in exasperation; "it wasn't that at all." "I've
heard," he said again with an unshaken and sombre perseverance (73–74).

The intolerable comedy of Jim's deluded obstinacy is finally ended,
but not before Marlow, no doubt impelled by experiences of his own,
has reflected on the general need for the individual to conceal his
inner being:

There may be those who could have laughed at his per-
tinacity. I didn't. Oh, I didn't! There had never been a man so
mercilessly shown up by his own natural impulse. A single
word had stripped him of his discretion—of that discretion
which is more necessary to the decencies of our inner being
than clothing is to the decorum of our body. "Don't be a fool,"
I repeated. "But the other man said it, you don't deny that?"
he pronounced, distinctly, and looking in my face without
flinching. "No, I don't deny," said I, returning his gaze. At last
his eyes followed downwards the direction of my pointing
finger. He appeared at first uncomprehending, then confounded, and at last amazed and scared as though a dog had
been a monster and he had never seen a dog before. "Nobody
dreamt of insulting you," I said.
He contemplated the wretched animal, that moved no
more than an effigy: it sat with ears pricked and its sharp
muzzle pointed into the doorway, and suddenly snapped at a
fly like a piece of mechanism.
I looked at him. The red of his fair sunburnt complexion
deepened suddenly under the down of his cheeks, invaded
his forehead, spread to the roots of his curly hair. His ears
became intensely crimson, and even the clear blue of his eyes
was darkened many shades by the rush of blood to his head.
His lips pouted a little, trembling as though he had been on
the point of bursting into tears.

These long quotations constitute barely half the total scene, which is
by far Conrad's most extended use of symbolic deciphering. It has
some analogies with the hospital episode, but it is far more complex
since both protagonists are separately engaged in parallel acts of deciphering the meanings of the other's words and acts, meanings which
essentially involve their unspoken, and in Jim's case, unspeakable,
inner thoughts.
Marlow at first is utterly mystified; puzzled by Jim's truculence and

quite unaware of what has immediately provoked it, he interrogates every facial expression and every intonation of Jim's voice. This has the effect of intensifying the depth of our participation in the process whereby Marlow decides, long before their misunderstanding has been dispelled, that he has much misjudged Jim, who is both excruciatingly sensitive and yet, far from being a yellow cur, much too like a bulldog for Marlow's comfort.

As in the pink toads episode, Marlow's deciphering of Jim centres on moral self-revelation through a grotesque kind of comedy; and in both passages the words of the symbolic puzzles are themselves misleading. The deciphering process contains at least three elements: first, Jim overhears the words but doesn't see their referent, the dog; secondly, the established symbolic connotation of "cur" affects the transition from the visual to the moral meaning; and thirdly, because these meanings, in turn, are, like the pink toads in the engineer's mind, triggered by the obsessional pressures of Jim's inner self, they offer clues by which Marlow can decipher something of Jim's subjective world.

Something, but not much, and for reasons which are enacted in this first encounter. It is Jim's impulsive inarticulateness that both produces and prolongs the whole imbroglio; it would not have occurred at all if he had merely asked Marlow an explicit question, such as "Did you say, 'Look at that wretched cur?' " As for Marlow, he is normally, of course, far from inarticulate; but it is ironically appropriate that the two men should at last be able to communicate because, for once, words also fail Marlow. After his "hideous mistake" has been exposed, Jim is "incapable of pronouncing a word," and rushes off, making "an inarticulate noise in his throat" (74–75). Marlow pursues him, and it is then that Jim's reserve at last breaks down in the face of Marlow's unwonted incoherence: "I said hurriedly that I couldn't think of leaving him under a false impression of my—of my—I stammered. The stupidity of the phrase appalled me while I was trying to finish it, but the power of sentences has nothing to do with their sense or the logic of their construction. My idiotic mumble seemed to please him."

The yellow cur episode is one of Conrad's finest achievements. Set in the vivid alien surroundings of the courthouse, it is played out in what must have looked to the bystanders like a comic visual pantomime of stiff and aborted physical movements which seem to promise the imminence of fisticuffs. The scene arrestingly prefigures the whole future of the relationship between the two men; Marlow, indeed, begins his narrative by referring to his whole involvement with Jim as "the yellow-dog thing" (34).[4] There is to be a long and intense

---

4. Other aspects of the importance of the scene are the subject of Kenneth B. Newell's

dialogue which largely consists of the dead-ends of their cross-purposes; but the negative direction of their conversations is to be counterpointed by a guarded but ever-increasing mutual concern. That concern is established through a memorable enactment of how a wholly fortuitous misunderstanding ironically reveals the bottomless possibilities of personal humiliation: Jim has inadvertently betrayed those secret inner depths to Marlow, and he eventually has the pain of knowing that he has; as for Marlow, once he has seen all this, it would surely be a worse betrayal of human solidarity for him to abandon Jim than it was for Jim to desert the *Patna*.

In our approach to the central narrative, then, we confront the mysteries of action and character by being made to experience them completely. We pass four signposts, all of which bear different kinds of question marks about the thematic issues in *Lord Jim*. The delayed decoding at the end of chapter three leaves us with an unresolved mystery of a physical kind: what invisible force from under the sea caused the surface manifestations which spelled Jim's ruin? Then there are the two symbolic decipherings which make us wonder how the invisible fears that so agitate the engineer and Brierly may illuminate Jim's case. After that, we are ready for the last signpost, the third and longest scene of symbolic deciphering in which we have the first of our direct "glimpses through the shifting rents in a thick fog" (76), which are all that Jim is to disclose of the mysteries of his interior life. The process by which Jim accidentally reveals his moral essence to Marlow would probably have been much less clear to the reader if he had not previously been taught to interpret dialogue as only the meagre and ambiguous expression of a larger but mainly unconscious and inarticulate confrontation of moral identities. Conrad's narrative technique has also prepared us to appreciate the substance of the fateful encounter between Marlow and Jim; the Brierly episode and that of the engineer have disclosed to Marlow and the reader that both the most despicable and the most admired ship's officers may be even less capable of facing purely imaginary terrors than Jim was on the *Patna*.

Symbolic deciphering is used for the specific purpose of producing an atmosphere of intensely expectant interrogation at the beginning of Marlow's narrative; after this has been done, there are no further scenes primarily based on symbolic deciphering. Thematic apposition, on the other hand, continues throughout *Lord Jim;* it is perhaps the most characteristic feature of Conrad's mature narrative tech-

article, "The Yellow-Dog Incident in Conrad's *Lord Jim*" (*Studies in the Novel* 3 [1971]: 26–33).

nique; and its way of juxtaposing scenes is inextricably connected with Conrad's equally characteristic handling of time.

(b) *Marlow's Inquiry: The Roles of Time and Narrative Impressionism*

From the very beginnings of storytelling there has been a conflict between the impulse to go forwards and the impulse to go back. In most of the shortest and simplest forms—the fairy tale or the ballad, for instance—the words usually follow the presumed chronological sequence of events in the story; one thing happens and then another and then another, and the narrative follows them in that order. But in longer and more complex fictions it is difficult to make the events of the story and the order of their telling in the narrative completely coordinate; the weightier the story's burden of meaning, the greater the tendency towards a disjunction between the original chronological order of the fictional events and the order in which they appear in the narrative. This disjunction is presumably related to the fact that although the mere forward progression of the story may hold the reader's immediate attention through suspense, it cannot satisfy the reflective mind when it comes to ask why an event occurred or what is the moral significance of a character. Neither the why nor the what, however, seem very real questions until after the event or the character concerned have first been presented; but then answering the questions will often involve events that happened long before. The divergent demands of simple story and complex narrative, of action and meaning, were formulated in their simplest terms by E. M. Forster. Conceding that the highest factor common to novels is a story, and that a story is essentially "a narrative of events arranged in their time sequence," Forster adds that good novels are subject to another allegiance: in addition to "life in time," there is also "life by values."[5]

Both for technical and philosophical reasons, the modern novel has been particularly preoccupied with the formal and the substantive problems concerning time. As regards form, the increasing critical sophistication of the genre since Flaubert has required a high degree of consistency in the narrative point of view; and the commonest prescription for this—the principle that everything important in the novel must be shown not told—places a particular obligation on the author's management of time. The main consequence of this obligation has been a tendency towards what may be called the method of the scenic present, towards a narrative form which makes the novel progress as much as possible through a succession of compositional units, where, much as in the scenes of stage drama, the actions,

5. E. M. Forster, *Aspects of the Novel*, 1927 (London, 1949), pp. 29–30.

characters, and meanings of the novel emerge directly from scenes which the reader witnesses going on. The development of the scenic method has proceeded in two main phases. During most of the nineteenth century, the predominant direction was towards contriving a structure of scenes and events which would enable the novel to unfold itself without any need for authorial commentary; in the twentieth-century phase, the novelists tried to face the nature of time itself more directly, and portray the multiplicity and randomness of the individual's immediate experience—most obviously in the stream-of-consciousness novel where, as in Joyce or Virginia Woolf, we are witnesses to a special kind of scene—a scene which is imagined to be taking place inside the minds of the characters.

Both these directions in the use of the scenic method are alike in avoiding two ways whereby much narrative business concerning chronological matters had been done in earlier fiction: authorial intrusion or the extended use of bare historical summary. They also have one advantage in common: the scenic method's combination of the autonomy of the narrative with the fullness with which each scene is described makes the novel seem to be taking place in what can be called the reader's psychological present.

After Flaubert the greatest exemplar of the earlier and more traditional phase of the scenic, or dramatic, method, was probably Henry James, who named it, and was certainly its greatest critical theorist.[6] In James all the important components of his novel's plot, characters, and theme are arranged so that they can be concentrated in certain major scenes with a specific and significant setting in time and place; and the whole structure of the novel, from the bare facts of the plots to their moral and symbolic meaning, is articulated through the forward chronological progression of this sequence of "discriminated occasions."

Flaubert was James's great precursor in this tradition, but he also tentatively initiated one element in the more modern use of the scenic present to portray the internal operations of the consciousness. Until the middle of the nineteenth century, the multifariousness of life had most commonly been suggested through the author's commentary, or merely by multiplying the number of characters, episodes, subplots, or interpolated stories. Neither method was acceptable to Flaubert, but in *Madame Bovary* he experimented with showing a number of diverse thoughts and activities going on simultaneously. In the famous description of the Yonville agricultural fair, the platitudes of the official speeches, the flyblown amorous rhetoric of Rodolphe woo-

6. Especially in the prefaces to *The Awkward Age* and *The Wings of the Dove*.

ing Emma, and the bewilderment of the old farm servant Catherine Leroux, are all juxtaposed in a single montage. Joseph Frank sees this scene as an early example of what he calls spatial form,[7] a form in which the events are arranged, not in linear and causal sequence, but in a succession of moments which are imagined to be synchronic; propinquity in space and in the narrative text becomes an objective way of establishing simultaneous connections or contrasts in the reader's mind. This "spatial" method is analogous to that of T. S. Eliot's *The Waste Land* or Pound's *Cantos,* where events, persons, and thoughts are brought together in such a way that we are obviously not intended to arrange them either in a causal or a temporal order, but according to some intrinsic pattern of moral significance which is inherent in their juxtaposition.

Conrad's handling of the formal problem of time in *Lord Jim* combines a very individual version of the scenic method, as James used it, with other more modern elements: delayed decoding has something in common with how the stream of consciousness puts us inside the perceiving mind; the way thematic apposition brings together multiple viewpoints makes it serve some of the same purposes as what Frank calls spatial form; and Marlow's mode of narrative also shows some affinities with the new attitudes to time which underlie much of modern fiction.[8]

The thought of the past, from Plato and Augustine to Aquinas and Spinoza, had assumed some form of the view that truth was eternal, changeless, and unified, and that therefore the particular experiences of the individual in the temporal world of change were illusory or merely contingent, and certainly gave no reliable access to reality or truth. This dualism of the eternal and the temporal orders was strongly challenged by the empirical and scientific movements associated with the names of Locke and Newton, and as a result man and his world came increasingly to be understood as the results of a temporal process:[9] in their different ways Darwin, Marx, and Freud all suggested that the individual life must be understood in the context of a process of chronological development—biological, economic, or psy-

7. "Spatial Form in Modern Literature," 1945, in *The Widening Gyre* (New Brunswick, N. J., 1963), pp. 3–62.

8. Among the many works on the problem of time in literature, the philosophical background of the modern novel is illuminatingly treated in Hans Meyerhoff, *Time In Literature* (Berkeley and Los Angeles, 1960); a good general survey of the literary problems is provided in A. A. Mendilow, *Time and the Novel* (London, 1952); and John Raleigh acutely describes the transition from the Victorian to the modern novel in "The English Novel and the Three Kinds of Time," in *The Novel: Modern Essays in Criticism,* ed. Robert Murray Davis (Englewood Cliffs, N. J., 1969), pp. 242–52.

9. See especially Jerome Buckley, *The Triumph of Time.*

chic. At the end of the nineteenth century many influential philosophers made time their special study; and two of them are generally
believed to have been important influences on the modern novel:
William James, whose *Principles of Psychology* (1890) described what he
called *"the stream of thought, of consciousness, or of subjective life"*;[10] and
Henri Bergson, whose main aim was to achieve a truer understanding
of temporal duration.

Conrad was not concerned with any particular philosophy of time;
and it is unlikely that he had any knowledge of either William James
or Bergson, except perhaps for some general notions which were a
good deal talked about in the nineties. On the other hand, his novels
express many elements not only of the historicism but of the psychological subjectivism of late nineteenth-century thinking about time. As
we have seen, *Heart of Darkness* presents the individual life as it is
determined by the enveloping pressures of history in its cosmic,
biological, psychological, and political aspects, while Marlow's way of
telling a story also suggests the Symbolist hostility to clock time: crack-
ing a nut is an act in a defined chronological sequence, whereas the
temporal, like the spatial, dimensions of haze or moonshine are much
more indeterminate.

Some of the ways in which *Lord Jim* reflects these larger temporal
perspectives will be illustrated later; but before then it is necessary to
describe in some detail the various roles which time plays in the more
concrete manifestations of its narrative method, and to consider how
far they are adequately analysed in the two main critical accounts of
Conrad's treatment of chronology.

Since Ford's use of the term, Conrad's technique for dealing with
the chronological aspect of narrative has often been called the time
shift.[11] Not altogether happily, because the definite article tends to
confer upon the device a specious definiteness that in Conrad's practice it surely lacks, and the word "shift" has an unduly reductive
meaning, denoting purely technical manipulations for presumably
rather simple narrative purposes. In any case there is no evidence that
Conrad used the term, or even that Ford did during Conrad's
lifetime.

10. William James, *Principles of Psychology* (London, 1902), vol. 1, p. 239. See also Robert
Humphrey, *Stream of Consciousness in the Modern Novel* (Berkeley and Los Angeles, 1954).
11. Ford implies (*The March of Literature* [London, 1939], p. 771) that the use of the time
shift in his novels and those of Conrad infuriated the critics very early in the century. This
may be true, but not under that particular term; Ford does not even use it in his 1924
memoir of Conrad. Joseph J. Martin argues for the prior influence of Edward Garnett
("Edward Garnett and Conrad's Reshaping of Time," *C* 6 [1974]: 89–105), but his evidence
seems most convincing in showing that critical consciousness of the time issue in narrative
was already well advanced.

Ford's *Joseph Conrad: A Personal Remembrance* contains, however, the best single treatment of the general problem. Ford asserts that he and Conrad began by applying the mimetic nature of the novel to its narrative method more radically than anyone had before: "We agreed," he writes, "that the general effect of a novel must be the general effect that life makes on mankind" (*F M F,* 180); and since "we saw that Life did not narrate, but made impressions on our brains" (*F M F,* 182), it followed that "a novel must therefore not be a narration, a report" (*F M F,* 180).

Imitating the impressions made on the brain necessarily required a complete break with previous practice in the narrative ordering of time. In Ford's words: "It became very early evident to us that what was the matter with the Novel, and the British novel in particular, was that it went straight forward, whereas in your gradual making acquaintanceship with your fellows you never do go straight forward" (*F M F,* 129). Later, Ford briskly proposes an example: "Life does not say to you: In 1914 my next door neighbour, Mr. Slack, erected a greenhouse . . . If you think about the matter you will remember, in various unordered pictures, how one day Mr. Slack appeared in his garden and contemplated the wall of his house. You will then try to remember the year of that occurrence and you will fix it as August 1914" (*F M F,* 180–81). The particular association with the outbreak of the war, of course, is in itself quite irrelevant; Ford merely uses it as an illustration of the individual's random way of associating memories from different periods of his life into a larger sense of the biographies and characters of other people. The topic is then embroidered with an abundance of whimsical Fordian detail to enforce the general conclusion that to get a character into "fiction you could not begin at his beginning and work his life chronologically to the end. You must first get him in with a strong impression, and then work backwards and forwards over his past" (*F M F,* 129–30).

Imitating the random and casual multiplicity of the "effect life makes on mankind" also implied a different treatment of the smaller units of narrative composition. Thus Ford asserts that he and Conrad had "one unalterable rule" for conversations—that since in life few people really listen to what other people say, so in fiction "no speech of one character should ever answer the speech that goes before it" (*F M F,* 188). No doubt, Ford concedes, there may arise a few exceptional occasions when characters do "directly answer each other," or where "the necessity to get on" with the novel must have priority over the need to imitate the discontinuities of life; but "on the whole," he affirms, "the indirect, interrupted method of handling interviews is invaluable for giving a sense of the complexity, the tantalisation, the shimmering, the haze, that life is" (*F M F*, 191). The same emphasis on the unpremeditated, the incomplete, and the discontinuous, also applies to other kinds of narrative units; whole scenes, for instance, as well as conversations, must be rendered not in large and autonomous blocks, but in a mosaic composed of the fragments of perceptions, memories, and anticipations which normally pervade the individual consciousness throughout its dealings with others.

Ford's account of the chronological and other discontinuities implied in his version of the impressionist narrative method is very persuasive as far as it goes; it applies fairly well to much that is characteristic of Conrad's narrative technique; and since Conrad himself was uncommunicative on the subject, we have no better guide than Ford, even though the carefree abandon with which he liked to play the genial oracle of the literary mysteries certainly led him both to oversimplify questions of technique and to overlook their connection with the complexity of Conrad's intellectual and moral outlook.

Before considering how far Ford's critical theories about time in narrative apply to Conrad's practice, it may be useful to outline another critic's approach to the particular chronological structure of *Lord Jim*.

In his pioneer study, *The Twentieth-Century Novel*, Joseph Warren Beach proposed his own term, the "chronological looping method," to describe how Conrad first gives a "strong impression" of a character or situation so as to "catch the reader's attention, before bringing the light of retrospection and anticipation to explain and modify the impression."[12] Beach's term has the great advantage of placing the critical emphasis, not on the shift as such, the break which separates chronologically distinct episodes, but on the looping, on the kinds of continuity created by the juxtaposition in the narrative sequence of episodes which would not follow each other if the story were told chronologically. Conrad actually seems to have treated his "time shifts" or temporal junctures as in themselves quite unimportant; in *Lord Jim* he often subordinates them by putting the actual break in the middle of a paragraph, as with the Bob Stanton episode, or by not specifying an episode's chronological register until very late, as with the French lieutenant.

Beach illustrates Conrad's looping effect throughout *Lord Jim* by allotting a letter in alphabetical order to each event according to "the actual chronological order" in which it occurred, and then by indicating the number of the chapter in which it is actually narrated. Thus the letters A to D are allotted to the incidents of Jim's early life, E to

12. New York, 1932, pp. 363–64.

the *Patna* collision, H to the inquiry, K L M to Jim's later life in various
Eastern ports, and so forth all the way to the meeting with Stein (N),
Jim's life on Patusan (P), and Marlow's visit to Jim (Q R), until the end
when Marlow writes his account of Jim's death (Z). On this basis the
novel's first chapter contains the story events denoted by K L M P;
from then on the chronology of the events of the story to the order of
the narrative, as it is structured in the sequence of the chapters, goes
W A(2), E(3), B(4), E(5), E(6), H(7), G D(8), H J(9), F E(10), E(11,12),
F(13,14,15), F K(16), I(17,18), R(19), I(20), K L(21), M N(22), N(23),
and so on, with Z occurring in chapter thirty-nine and the last chapter, forty-eight, devoted to W X Y.

Beach's scheme necessarily omits a good many minor events, such
as the hospital scene; several more alphabets would be needed to
accommodate all the actions in *Lord Jim.* The scheme also fails to take
account of another and more internal kind of chronological complexity: very many different periods are frequently superimposed in what
Beach treats as a single narrative unit. In Beach's system, for example,
chapter eleven is allotted E—the collision; but Jim's account of it is
largely concerned with the lies that the other officers told about it
later; in any case, the whole chapter is based on the conversation of
Jim and Marlow in a hotel room many weeks after that. Conrad's
rendering of a particular event is rarely limited to a single time dimension, and it is therefore virtually impossible to diagram.

Nevertheless the letters help to make Conrad's basic compositional
structure stand out more clearly, and in particular to show how the
"looping" effect can either conjoin many events which were originally
widely separated in time into one chapter, or, on the contrary, disperse the treatment of one single event into several widely separated
chapters. Beach's scheme also reveals the general structural pattern of
Lord Jim. The first chapter gives a kaleidoscopic effect by juxtaposing
many tantalisingly brief pictures of Jim at widely different periods;
then we gradually move to much fuller accounts of single events: the
Patna collision (E), its aftermath (F), and the inquiry (H); and then an
opposite complication of chronological effect occurs, a stereoscopic
concentration in which the same episode is treated in several separate
segments of the narrative sequence. Thus the collision is recounted on
a scale of increasing amplitude in five main scenes: first in one chapter
(3); then in two (5 and 6); then in six (10 to 15); and after that there
are two further brief treatments interspersed with a similarly discontinuous account of the inquiry, which of course concerns the collision
but has a different setting in space and time.

Behind the immediate chronological complexities of the narrative,
then, there is an architectonic arrangement of prefiguring and con-

centrating techniques which is applied to the main events of the story. At the same time, however, the fracturing of the narrative order in which the events occurred coexists with an accurate historical chronology of those events. Most of the main incidents can be dated fairly exactly.[13] Since Stein is said to have been twenty-two when he took part in the abortive German revolution of 1848 (205), and is "threescore" when Marlow goes to consult him about Jim, their interview presumably occurs thirty-eight years later, in 1886 or thereabouts; this in turn places the *Patna* episode three or four years before, in 1882 or 1883, and hence some two or three years after the historical event of the desertion of the *Jeddah* in 1880; while the death of Jim must be placed in 1889 or 1890, and thus a decade or so before Marlow's telling of his story.

As regards the general texture of the narrative there is no doubt that, as Beach's scheme illustrates, the disjunction between the chronological order of the events and the order of their narration is more radical and pervasive in *Lord Jim* than in earlier fiction. This disjunction is evident from the beginning.

One of Conrad's narrative strategies, Ford and Beach agree, is to begin by arresting the reader's attention with "a strong impression," which is taken out of its linear historical sequence, and then subjected to a process of prolonged, though interrupted, qualification and development. This method can be seen operating in the opening words of *Lord Jim:* "He was an inch, perhaps two, under six feet, powerfully built, and he advanced straight at you with a slight stoop of the shoulders, head forward, and a fixed from-under stare which made you think of a charging bull."

Conrad is following the traditional epic principle of beginning *in medias res,* but in a way that embodies the priority of character over plot which is fairly typical of the novel genre; the time of the opening is not that of a specific action but of a phase in the appearance of the protagonist. The emphasis of the opening is primarily on vivid visual impact; and how completely this impressionist aim transforms what might earlier have been treated as a routine piece of authorial expository summary can be seen by comparing Conrad's present opening with his earlier one in the "Tuan Jim" manuscript. It read: "All the white men by the waterside and the captains of the ships in the roadsteads called him Jim. He was over six feet and stared downwards at one with an overbearing watchfulness."

Conrad's earlier version obviously sets out the facts more clearly,

13. See J. E. Tanner, "The Chronology and the Enigmatic End of *Lord Jim,*" *Nineteenth-Century Fiction* 21 (1967): 369–80.

but at the sacrifice of sensory immediacy and therefore of impact on the reader. In the final version we have a "he," not a Jim; and this, combined with the change from "one" to "you," immediately forces the reader into an active role: we are, momentarily, put into a scenic present in which a figure really does "advance on us," and makes us instinctively resolve not to tangle with him, whoever he is. Jim's "slight stoop of the shoulders" and his "fixed from-under stare" suggest a bull; but they also suggest a defeated one, who cannot conceal that he regards the world from a posture whose wary rigidity is both defiant and fearful. These external physical signs of an internal moral dead-lock are given their breadth of symbolic meaning by the lack of specific referent for the first word. Who is this pronominal "he"? How is he defined by the first thing we are told about him—that (having been somewhat reduced from his size in the manuscript) "he was an inch, perhaps two, under six feet"? Would there be any point, we speculate, in mentioning his height and then leaving the matter open, unless it were symbolic in the sense of having a meaning beyond the literal? Are we meant to surmise that the regulation heroic stature has been attempted but missed? And further, does that "perhaps" mean that it is going to be up to us to determine by just how much?

With such issues to occupy our attention, we hardly pause to con-sider the temporal register of the novel's opening. The tenses are past, but of what kind? "He was" is presumably the continuative past tense used for continuing actions or states of being. As for "he ad-vanced," the tense is determined by the pronoun which follows; if the text read "he advanced at *him*," we would know that the novel was going to open with a specific act; but the "you" in "he advanced at *you*" is obviously a generalised one; this defines the action as habitual, and the aspect of the past tense, therefore, as consuetudinal. Jim's "ad-vance" is in some undefined sense plural, and arrests Jim in a per-petual stance of lowering intimidation.

The novel begins, then, by presenting Jim in a timeless and sym-bolic state; and this effect is achieved by applying tenses which de-specify actions that are otherwise presented as highly specific. This feature of Conrad's use of time is not treated either by Ford or Beach; but it is, however, covered in a recent general treatment of the com-plexities of time in fiction, Gérard Genette's "Discours du récit."[14]

Genette uses the term *anachrony* to categorise all the various kinds of chronological difference between the time of the *histoire* and that of the *récit*, between story and its report, between the original historical sequence of events and the order of their telling in the narrative. He

14. Gérard Genette, "Ordre," and "Fréquence," *Figures III* (Paris, 1972), pp. 67–273.

demonstrates the extreme variety of these modes of *anachrony,* notably of the different kinds of retrospection—called analepsis—and
anticipation—called prolepsis. The current term "flashback," and the
neologism "flashforward" for its opposite, both suggest too quick and
definite a change of narrative time; the traditional rhetorical terms,
analepsis and prolepsis, for backward and forward temporal
movements, have the dual advantage of being more neutral and more
inclusive. Genette's terms, therefore, seem worth adopting, as does
anachrony to include both categories, since the word avoids the pejorative connotation of its more current cognate "anachronism"; *anachrony,* therefore, will be used to denote any narrative order which is not
coordinate with that of the occurrence of the events of the story.

Genette treats "frequency" as an independent temporal category in
fiction; and since the repeated or habitual action presented in the first
sentence of *Lord Jim* is by no means an isolated case, the question of
what may be summarily categorised as plural tenses or actions in the
narrative will require further consideration, after the uses of anachrony in the first three chapters have been summarised.

The first chapter of *Lord Jim,* which is largely devoted to filling out
Jim's life as a water-clerk, primarily continues the temporal pattern of
its opening; the action as a whole is proleptic, since it anticipates Jim's
life long after its major crisis is over. The proleptic status of the
narrative, however, is far from quenching our interest in Jim's future;
instead, it fixes our attention more intently on the problem of what
can have occurred earlier to explain his behaviour; and this effect is
intensified by the use of such consuetudinal or iterative forms as
"when the fact broke through the incognito he would leave suddenly"; they are forms of the past tense which emphasise the repetitive and compulsive nature of Jim's actions. It is almost a relief when
we get to an action which only happened once, and are told that
eventually Jim's "keen perception of the Intolerable drove him away
for good" (4–5).

Once our curiosity about this abstract "Intolerable" has been raised
through the mystery of its unexplained persistence, Conrad moves far
back in time to an account of Jim's family, his boyhood, and his life on
the training ship. For this more traditional expository summary, we
get, after the analeptic transition to the earlier period, a fairly regular
linear chronological progression; and in the second chapter Conrad
even assuages the reader's possible impatience at his defiance of
traditional chronology by beginning with a version of the time-
hallowed temporal formula: "After two years of training he went to
sea . . . . " The narrative then moves forward to Jim's earlier career as

a ship's officer, and then to his voyage on the *Patna*. After the end of the third chapter, however, there is a fairly obtrusive prolepsis of about a month: we go from the mysterious collision to the scene where Jim is testifying to the court of inquiry. Very soon the narrative is taken up by Marlow; and, like Jim, he is also introduced in the special chronological status established by using a consuetudinal verbal form.

This proleptic transition is effected at the end of chapter four with the simple words: "And later on, many times, in distant parts of the world, Marlow showed himself willing to remember Jim, to remember him at length, in detail and audibly" (33). This defines Marlow's role as narrator in very different terms from that in "Youth" and *Heart of Darkness;* there we had a single particularised telling, whereas here it is ostensibly consuetudinal. As in the opening sentence of *Lord Jim,* however, a plural action is given a highly specific and dramatic quality: Conrad's primary narrator continues: "Perhaps it would be after dinner, on a verandah draped in motionless foliage and crowned with flowers, in the deep dusk speckled by fiery cigar-ends."

English has no special form of the verb for habitual, consuetudinal, iterative, or frequentative usages; instead, it relies on modal auxiliaries, as in Conrad's "Perhaps it would be." Conrad was no doubt influenced by Polish, which, unlike Latin and the Germanic languages, has a fully developed plural aspect for verbs; and there may have been a residue of this in Conrad's habitual and "slightly unusual use of the word 'would' " on which Ford commented (*F M F,* 84). In any case the consuetudinal nature of Marlow's narration is recalled in occasional later references, as when his actual narrative opens at the beginning of chapter five: "'Oh yes, I attended the inquiry,' he would say" (34). It is difficult to assess how many repetitions are needed to establish a habit, or how seriously we must posit a whole series of recitings of Jim's story; but we must at least retain the suggestion that Marlow's tale should be assigned a vaguely plural status in time and place. This generalised temporal quality of Marlow's narration is reinforced by another consideration. He proves to be the purveyor and interpreter of materials which have come from a great number of sources—notably letters and a host of informers;[15] something like the bard of old, Marlow is the spokesman of diffuse and continuing oral traditions which are current throughout the three-thousand mile circle where, as Jim unhappily discovered in his wanderings, "that scandal of the Eastern seas would not die out" (151).

15. See especially J. Hillis Miller, "The Interpretation of *Lord Jim,*" in *The Interpretation of Narrative: Theory and Practice,* ed. Morton W. Bloomfield (Cambridge, Mass., 1970), pp. 211–28.

The actual version of Marlow's telling of *Lord Jim* that we are read-ing, however, soon turns out to be not hypothetical as the earlier "perhaps it would be" implies, but one given on a particular occasion; an occasion on which the excellent dinner provided by a named host—Charley—has made "a lot of men" feel "too indolent for whist" (94). Nor is this a purely technical matter of tenses; what is told to this particular audience certainly produces the effect on the reader of being a new and intensely committed venture by Marlow at under-standing and conveying the full meaning of Jim's story.

Marlow's oral narrative has hardly begun when the forward chronological progression of the story is abandoned; we go back to various earlier events, such as the captain's discomfiture in the ship-ping office, and the narrative continues to be primarily analeptic until the yellow cur episode at the end of the sixth chapter. The importance of this scene is marked by the fact that it is the first substantial piece of Marlow's narrative where *histoire* and *récit*, the order of events and the order of telling, are wholly coordinate. This synchrony gets a good deal of its effect by contrast with the preceding predominance of its opposite, anachrony. It also functions to initiate the transition not only to the basic forward temporal movement of the largest single narrative block of *Lord Jim*—the conversations between Marlow and Jim at the Malabar House—but to its principal thematic content, in which Jim and Marlow unite to confront, in their own fashions and sometimes mutely, the irremediable meaning of Jim's past act as it projects itself into the blank imponderables of his future.

The account of their first evening extends from chapter seven to chapter thirteen. In Beach's scheme these chapters are categorised as dealing with the *Patna* collision, since that is the main substance of Jim's discourse; but of course their real time dimension is at least dual, and their effectiveness largely depends on the tension between the two periods of time; the reader experiences a narrative present in which the protagonists, with agonising intensity, circle round the intolerable facts of Jim's past. It is mainly this thematic pressure which provokes and justifies the various digressions which are intercalated in the course of Marlow's account of his conversations with Jim.

The most important and the most brilliantly effective of these inter-calations is the proleptic episode of the French lieutenant. The tem-poral juncture occurs at the moment when Jim has told Marlow that if he had seen even the glimmer of a light from the *Patna* he would have swum back to it from the lifeboat (135). Marlow then explains par-enthetically that the issue had been debated at the inquiry, that the lights probably were invisible to Jim, that the abandoned *Patna* was boarded the next day by a French gunboat, and that its two boarding officers were "much struck" to discover the corpse of the third engineer "curled up peacefully on the bridge." Marlow goes on: " *'Fort intrigués par ce cadavre,'* as I was informed a long time after by an elderly French lieutenant whom I came across one afternoon in Sydney, by the merest chance" (137).

In two paragraphs, then, we move backwards or forwards four times: many weeks back to the desertion of the *Patna,* forwards again to Jim now talking at Malabar House, a day or so back to the courtroom discussion, and finally forwards again to the recalled phrase spoken to Marlow "a long time after" during his chance meeting with the French lieutenant in Australia.

The episode is not primarily important for the French lieutenant's firsthand report on the towing of the *Patna,* since the French captain's official account could do that well enough; what matters is that the confrontation of the two ship's officers gives a new moral perspective on Jim's case. As soon as Conrad has established the French lieutenant's realistic and phlegmatic character, culminating in his still-rankling bitterness at the lack of wine on the *Patna,* our attention is turned to the next stage in Marlow's examination of Jim as a puzzle. When the lieutenant comments: "And so that poor young man ran away along with the others" (145), Marlow remarks: "He had made out the point at once. . . . I felt as though I were taking professional opinion on the case. His imperturbable and mature calmness was that of an expert in possession of the facts, and to whom one's perplexities are mere child's-play."

The initiated spokesman of the nautical tradition then goes on to an unembarrassed exposition of the universality of fear—*"L'homme est né poltron"* (147); and at first Marlow is much relieved, believing that he will find even more authoritative support than that inadvertently offered by Brierly for "taking a lenient view" of Jim's apparent cowardice. When Marlow presses further, however, in the hope of finding some basis for a hopeful prognosis about Jim's future, the French lieutenant pricks the bubble with resonant finality:

> The shuffle of his feet under the table interrupted me. He drew up his heavy eyelids. Drew up, I say—no other expression can describe the steady deliberation of the act—and at last was disclosed completely to me. I was confronted by two narrow grey circlets, like two tiny steel rings around the profound blackness of the pupils. The sharp glance, coming from that massive body, gave a notion of extreme efficiency, like a razor-edge on a battle-axe. "Pardon," he said, punctiliously. His right hand went up, and he swayed forward. "Allow me . . . I contended that one may get on knowing very

well that one's courage does not come of itself . . . One truth
the more ought not to make life impossible. . . . But the
honour—the honour, monsieur! . . . The honour . . . that is
real—that is! And what life may be worth when" . . . he got up
on his feet with a ponderous impetuosity, as a startled ox
might scramble up from the grass . . . "when the honour is
gone—*ah ça! par exemple*—I can offer no opinion. . . .
because—monsieur—I know nothing of it."

This episode affords a convenient opportunity for summing up the
characteristic connections between Conrad's narrative method in
general, and his use of time.

From a technical point of view, there is, first of all, the way the
episode finely exemplifies, as do the yellow cur episode and most of
the conversations between Jim and Marlow, Ford's prescription about
the "indirect, interrupted method of handling interviews." The way
that the lieutenant's slow and hesitant enunciation of his limited wisdom is counterpointed by the ruminative generalisations of Marlow at
his most leisurely, makes it an example of what Ford describes as "a
purposed *longueur,* so as to give the idea of the passage of time"
(*F M F*, 183). Ford thought that in his "dramatic working up" of a
scene, "Conrad was matchless" (*F M F*, 191). Here one can observe
how much of the effect comes from Conrad's control of pace; fullness
of detail obviously slows time down; the lieutenant's climactic speech
is presented with an emphatic deliberation whose effect is analogous
to that of cinematic close-up. Close-ups normally accompany some
significant slowing down in the film's tempo; and there is a similar
connection in narrative between space and time: the more the detail,
the longer it takes to tell.

This interdependence between the spatial and temporal dimensions of narrative is one reason why Conrad's frequent changes in the
chronological sequence interfere much less than might logically be
expected with the reader's sense of immediate participation in the
narrative. Marlow's intense visualisation of detail in the scene with the
French lieutenant soon makes us forget that it is technically proleptic;
it seems to be a psychological fact that if we are given sufficient sense-
impressions of a person or an action, we cannot help experiencing it
as if it occurred in the narrative present; if we are there, the time must
be now; presence implies the present.

This is presumably the main reason why the impressionist particularity of Conrad's narrative quickly makes us forget even the most
obtrusive changes in the chronological order. For instance, when we
read how the pilgrims on the *Patna* looked at the French gunboat,
"hundreds of eyes stared, and not a sound was heard when the gun-

boat ranged abreast, as if all that multitude of lips had been sealed by a spell" (137), Marlow's description is so vivid that we forget that he was not himself an eyewitness; the hush and the staring eyes transport us back in time, and momentarily but completely usurp the narrative present.

In general, then, Conrad seems not so much to manipulate chronology, as to make it the wholly plastic instrument of his various purposes. To describe his handling of time, therefore, such terms as flashback or time shift suggest much too gross a calibration of temporal relationships. At the lowest order of magnitude, in the sequence of phrases and sentences in the narrative texture, Conrad's basic pattern is often composed of a series of minute movements forwards and backwards in time. This anachronic oscillation gives an effect of dense impressionist particularity in a fragmented but vivid present. At the middle level of compositional magnitude, in the ordering of scenes and episodes, the basic pattern is set by the development of theme; through thematic apposition, and its subordination of chronological order to thematic continuity, Conrad enacts the priority of meaning over event.

The fundamental aim of Conrad's use of time, then, is not directly mimetic, as Ford implies; Conrad does not use anachrony to be more realistic in representing the discontinuities in the process whereby we ordinarily learn about the lives of others. His aim—the revelation of moral essences—is much more inward than that described by Ford; and so his handling of time is essentially a means of representing a progression of moral understanding. The source of this progression, in *Lord Jim* as in *Heart of Darkness,* is Marlow's probing mind as it tries both to recollect experience and to decipher its meaning. From the traditional point of view about plot, *Lord Jim* is undoubtedly exceptional in the variety and frequency with which the progression of events is interrupted by movements to the past and the future; but once we accept Conrad's moral and internalised definition of what constitutes the main action, the structure of the narrative can be seen as a single forward movement.

This forward progression is in one respect dual. For although anachrony dominates the narrative order as regards the small and medium scales of compositional magnitude, on the largest scale the story and its telling are synchronic; the broad grouping of events in the novel as a whole follows the historical course of Jim's life from his early days to his death; and this conventional biographical progression is loosely superimposed on the thematic progression of Marlow's attempt to understand Jim.

So much for the general structure and function of Conrad's use of

time in *Lord Jim*. A somewhat more intangible connection remains to
be made between the larger effect of Conrad's treatment of chronology upon the temporal status of the novel as a whole, and the already
noted occurrence of verbs denoting repeated action.

To the extent that, except in the largest perspective, our impression
of the narrative is based on an anachronic sequence of elements as
they are shaped through the action of Marlow's understanding, the
basic temporal effect of *Lord Jim* can perhaps be best described, in
Genette's terms, as sylleptic. Syllepsis, the rhetorical term for "taking
together," seems appropriate to denote the way Conrad's complicated
use of anachrony places the main emphasis on linking or bracketing
events, rather than insisting on their original temporal separateness.

Genette makes *syllepse* his third chronological category, and uses it
to cover both the putting together of several actions through the use
of iterative or plural verbal forms, and, more widely, such essentially
atemporal appositions as the interpolated stories in classical fiction,
where the narrative segments are ordered quite independently of the
story's linear time-frame, and are connected only on the basis of some
autonomous identity or similarity of teller or theme.[16]

Marlow is a variant on the classical teller of many stories with similar
themes; and the sylleptic quality of Conrad's narrative is reinforced by
two other factors. There is, first, the suggestion that Marlow frequently "would," rather than on one particular occasion actually
"did," tell the story; secondly, this timeless quality is strengthened by
various suggestions that Marlow, and many other people in the Eastern seas, have not stopped thinking and talking about Lord Jim; his
file has never been closed; perhaps it never can be, because unan-
swered or unanswerable questions are inherently timeless.

Of course, we are given a more structured kind of sylleptic mosaic
than Marlow's remembering mind might be expected to produce if he
were alone; his narrative is spoken to a group of listeners, and this
gives it a marked element of public and intellectual structuring which
differentiates it from the formless flux wholly independent of
chronometric time which typifies Bergson's duration. Nevertheless,
there is enough sense of free retrospection in Marlow's narration to
bring it into partial accord with the views about time in the thought
both of Bergson and James.

In his *Essai sur les données immédiates de la conscience* (1889; translated
as *Time and Free Will*, 1910) and *Matiere et Mémoire* (1896; translated as
Matter and Memory, 1911), Henri Bergson argued that essential reality

16. *Figures III*, p. 121.

should be sought, not in the eternal truths which philosophers had assumed to be beyond the realms of time and the phenomenal world, but in time itself.[17] Bergson developed the not unfamiliar distinction between scientific, objective, calendar, or clock time and the subjective experience of time as duration, which is arrived at through individual introspection. This tells him that the real basis of his sense of identity is what his memory tells him about the continuity of his personal self as it subsists through change; and Bergson insisted that the succession of momentary perceptions in the individual mind was not a discontinuous assemblage of atomised instants, as Hume, for instance, had thought, but a continuity which was in large part effected through the individual memory: in duration "moments permeate each other." William James similarly insisted that in the stream of thought *"the knowledge of some other part of the stream, past or future, near or remote, is always mixed in with our knowledge of the present thing."*[18]

Lord Jim shows how the internal sense of the duration of the self and of others is given a context, shaped, and made real, through memory. The analogy with Bergson is particularly revealing. Bergson had lamented in 1889 that by separating moments of feeling from each other, by spreading "out our feeling in a homogeneous time," the novelists had failed to show the "infinite permeation of a thousand different impressions which [had] already ceased to exist the instant they are named." Nevertheless, Bergson speculated, if "some bold novelist" could tear "aside the cleverly woven curtain of our conventional ego," he might encourage the reader to "put aside for an instant the veil which we interposed between our consciousness and ourselves," and bring "us back into our presence."[19]

Through Marlow, Conrad in part escapes, to use Bergson's words, from the "stable, common, and consequently impersonal element in the impressions of mankind," and from all the fixed notions about time that go with it. Conrad comes considerably closer to expressing the "delicate and fugitive impressions of our individual consciousness" than had the earlier novelists of whom Bergson was complaining; and the formal innovations in the use of time were an important element in the technical basis for what Fernandez described as Conrad's way of projecting his characters on our senses largely by "immersing us completely into the life which we were previously skim-

17. The influence of Bergson on the modern novel has been much discussed; see for instance Shiv K. Kumar, *Bergson and the Stream of Consciousness Novel* (London, 1962).

18. *Principles of Psychology*, vol. 1, p. 606. Freud takes a somewhat similar view, writing of the "importance of optical mnemic residues, when they are of *things*," and adding that "in many people this seems to be the favoured method" for becoming conscious of their thought-processes (*The Ego and the Id*, trans. J. Strachey [New York, 1962], p. 11).

19. *Time and Free Will*, 1889, trans. F. L. Pogson (New York, 1960), pp. 133–34.

ming over." Nowhere more than in *Lord Jim* does Conrad absorb us so deeply in the opacity of the consciousness of his protagonists that we are continually "brought back" into our own presence.

To return to the narrative sequence, after the French lieutenant has declined to speculate on whether it will be possible for Jim to live on despite his lost honour, Marlow rises to his feet; and then, with "infinite politeness," the two seamen face "each other mutely, like two china dogs on a mantel piece" (148). Their comic immobility signifies that the confrontation has ended in total moral deadlock. Marlow makes a last attempt to salvage a fragment of his defensive case for Jim by recurring to the distinction between the personal and the public ethic; he asks the French lieutenant: "Couldn't it reduce itself to not being found out?" But Marlow is quashed with the curt response: "This, monsieur, is too fine for me"; and we are left wondering how the future can ever bring anything to change the lieutenant's dispiriting verdict.

The episode as a whole demonstrates how the anachronic treatment of the order of events makes it easier to connect narrative themes. This thematic linkage continues, for Marlow's narrative does not immediately loop back to his after-dinner talk with Jim. Instead, Marlow explains that before coming to Sydney and the French lieutenant, he had once again seen Jim, then working as a water-clerk at Samarang in Java; and this leads into the next episode, that of young Stanton, which occurred in some undefined past.

Marlow comments to the listeners that nothing could be "more barren of consolation" than being a water-clerk, unless, he immediately qualifies, "it be the business of an insurance canvasser." To escape this dismal fate Stanton had gone to sea and became a first mate; in a shipwreck he went back to rescue a hysterical but doughty lady's maid who refused to leave the ship; he was, however, much too small to be able to overpower her, and they were drowned together. The sardonic contrast between Jim's desertion and this comic, futile, and gallant sacrifice is very clear: we think back to Jim's assertion that he would have gone back to the ship if he could, and think forwards to his present problem as Marlow has seen it in Samarang; will Jim's "adventurous fancy" ever be able to bear the "pangs of starvation" (151) caused by his present thankless occupation? The question gives advance notice that Marlow will have to provide an occupation less deadening for Jim's imagination than being a water-clerk; and we are also warned that Jim's future fate may have been prefigured in the way that, to escape from drudgery, Bob Stanton met his pointless but heroic death at sea.

After these two episodes, Marlow's memories pass rapidly forwards to his talk with Jim at Samarang, and then three years back to the beginnings of his efforts to find Jim a position. After the court has passed its verdict, a significant encounter forces Marlow to act. The unscrupulous adventurer Chester, together with his villainous associate Holy-Terror Robinson, accost Marlow and try to persuade him that Jim's position is so hopeless that he can do no better than assist them in an unsavoury scheme to exploit a guano deposit on a waterless and inaccessible island in the Walpole Reefs. Marlow is forced to see that he alone can save Jim from so squalid a fate. And then, just as the episode of the French lieutenant was succeeded in the narrative order by its comic echo in that of Stanton, so a "fellow fresh from Madagascar" succeeds Chester, and tries to interest Marlow himself in an allegedly "wonderful piece of business" (170). The repetition obviously emphasises the common thematic element—Jim's present vulnerability to unscrupulous adventurers; and the repetition inevitably reduces the importance of the temporal order of the narrative.

There is a similarly sylleptic quality in the account of the three or so years of Jim's career after the inquiry. The chronology of this period is quite indeterminate, and even mildly inconsistent if looked at closely. Four of Jim's particular jobs are specified: the first at a rice-mill, and the others with ship-chandlers—Egström and Blake, probably at Singapore; Yucker Brothers, at Bangkok; and finally De Jongh's, at Samarang. Marlow says that there were "many" other episodes "of the sort, more than I could count on the fingers of my two hands" (197). Six months or more is given as the duration of Jim's jobs with Denver and with Yucker Brothers (187, 198); one would therefore expect this period of Jim's life to have lasted much longer than the "more than three years" (149) which Marlow mentions.

The inconsistency is of no particular importance except that it illustrates how Conrad subordinated chronological consistency to the needs of the narrative. There must be a long series of jobs between the inquiry and Patusan; the doggedness of Jim's character requires that he stay an appreciable time in each; and yet Jim must still be youthful in Patusan—an issue which Conrad emphasised in his revisions (*J D G*, 169–71). Conrad's solution was an ominous series of identical reactions, which could be extended at will; they were compulsive repetitions of a pattern that had been suggested when, after his first evening with Marlow, Jim left the Malabar House; the sound of "the quick crunch-crunch of the gravel under his boots" (155), made Marlow realise that Jim "was running. Absolutely running, with nowhere to go."

(c) *Patusan:* Progression d'effet *and Romantic Distance*

In the first nineteen chapters, Conrad's narrative focus tended to centre our attention on Marlow's discussions with Jim, rather than on Jim himself. These discussions, together with Marlow's various auxiliary confrontations, were powerful and illuminating; but they made it difficult to keep track of Jim, and the story almost seemed to go underground: the protagonists dispersed except for more or less accidental encounters, and the chronology lapsed into an undefined iterative limbo in which Marlow presumably made his usual voyages and Jim emerged only for his sudden disappearances. This changes completely with Stein; events, characters, themes, and narrative devices all converge to propel *Lord Jim* into a single and unchecked forward movement to its end

The interview between Marlow and Stein is narrated in a way very similar to that used for the scene with the French lieutenant, except that the pace is even more deliberate. This emphasis tells us that what is to follow will be much more than a thematic counterpoint to the French lieutenant episode.

The scene with Stein is unique in many ways: thematically, it is more affirmative than any of Marlow's earlier interrogations; as regards the story, it promotes immediate action; chronologically, it is the only scene since Marlow and Jim first met when story and narrative time are fully coordinate; as for character, Stein has the special status of being the first of Marlow's interlocutors since Jim to become a permanent member of the novel's cast.

The substance of the Stein scene must be deferred until later, but one aspect of its technique calls for brief attention here.

In concluding his account of the "formulae for the writing of the novel at which Conrad and the writer had arrived, say in 1902 or so" (*F M F*, 179), Ford has a section headed "Progression d'Effet." It consists of one short paragraph: "In writing a novel we agreed that every word set on paper—*every* word set on paper—must carry the story forward and, that as the story progressed, the story must be carried forward faster and faster and with more and more intensity. That is called *progression d'effet,* words for which there is no English equivalent" (*F M F*, 210).

There is no call to be unduly intimidated by this—or indeed by any other—piece of literary nomenclature merely because it comes bedecked in foreign garb. As doctors most classically exemplify, the devotees of technical jargon find it infinitely to their advantage to claim a much greater exactness of verbal diagnosis than is commonly justified by the phenomena of any particular case. The term *progres-*

sion d'effet had originally been used by Condillac to describe infinite series in mathematics; but it had become an established literary term at least as early as Flaubert.[20] The basic idea behind *progression d'effet* is really very simple: if the novel is a work of conscious and unified literary art, then all its constituent elements must obviously avoid anything repetitive or irrelevant; but the word *effet* places the emphasis on a progression in the effect which the narrative produces on the reader, rather than on the way the action itself develops.

Conrad himself does not seem to have used the term,[21] although he and Ford may have used it in their literary discussions, of which French phrases and examples were a staple feature. In any case, there is little question that Conrad conceived his fiction in terms of a planned sequence of effects on the reader. It is, however, very unlikely that Conrad limited himself to the kind of effects described by Ford, since a mere increase in pace and intensity would be appropriate only in works where the story is the predominant interest, as in *Romance*, the example which Ford used.

The Stein chapters constitute a progression, not only in the content, but in some of the major formal elements in *Lord Jim*. When the scene is over, the narrative does not go back to its earlier pattern; instead, it moves forward more rapidly and eventfully, very much according to Ford's prescription. In addition to this general quickening of the pace, there is also a qualitative change because the narrative method is adjusted to the romantic distance appropriate to the Patusan part of the novel. Some of these qualitative changes are the result of the fact that Marlow becomes more a reporter and less a participant; other qualitative changes follow from the more exciting nature of the events, and their much more remote and picturesque setting. In any case, the moral issues involved are no longer so urgent or problematic.

The handling of time in the last half of *Lord Jim* clearly reflects this reduction in the density of the narrative texture. There are, for instance, only three significant changes from the original chronological order of the events; in chapter twenty-one, Marlow anticipates his own visit to Jim in Patusan long before we have seen Jim set out for there; he also twice anticipates Jim's death, first when he recounts his visit to Stein, and then immediately after, when he describes coming across Brown on his deathbed, just before the full account of the final phase of Jim's life in the last eight chapters. These proleptic episodes, however, are very different in nature from those dealing with Brierly

20. *Correspondence*, vol. 5, p. 69; vol. 8, pp. 223–24.
21. Although the contrary is implied by Robert F. Haugh in "Conrad's *Chance: Progression d'Effet*," *Modern Fiction Studies* 1 (1955): 9.

or the French lieutenant; their main function is not to add new perspectives of moral understanding but merely to explain how Marlow
got firsthand information about matters relating to Jim's story; they
do not materially change the narrative's temporal and spatial focus;
and far from interrupting, they reinforce the reader's sense of a narrowing chronological convergence upon the coming fatality.

Our sense of reduced complexity and rapid confluence of the narrative elements is also influenced by changes in the point of view. In
the first four chapters an omniscient author is the only intermediary
between the reader and Jim. Then when Marlow's narrative begins,
the reader in effect becomes a secondary audience, since there is also
the primary audience of Marlow's actual listeners. The quality of Marlow's relationship to this primary audience changes slightly after the
scene with Stein. In a long paragraph at the end of chapter twenty-
one, where Marlow talks about his own going home, he addresses
himself to his hearers in a more directly personal and specific way, as
when he remarks to them about Jim, "it is only through me that he
exists for you" (224). This more particularised relationship between
Marlow and his audience increases later: and when we are told, for
instance, that "Marlow swung his legs out, got up quickly, and
staggered a little" (320), or that "With these words Marlow ended his
narrative" (337), we lose any lingering sense that Marlow's narrative is
plural.

Later, from chapters thirty-six to the end, there are further changes
in the narrative point of view, especially as regards the implied audience. Marlow began his story with an unlimited series of habitual
tellings to an undefined number of groups of hearers; this was then
reduced to a particular telling to a particular circle of auditors; and
finally the audience shrinks to one. For, after Marlow's auditory has
silently dispersed, the primary narrator returns to tell us "there was
only one man of all these listeners who was ever to hear the last word
of the story. It came to him at home, more than two years later, and it
came contained in a thick packet addressed in Marlow's upright and
angular handwriting" (337).

The packet contains two enclosures: an old letter to Jim from his
father, and a fragment begun by Jim after hearing of Dain's death;
they both have the special pathos which inheres in the relics of any
dead man, particularly when they are so meagre, and here they strike
an eloquently proleptic note of mournful finality. The same note is
echoed in the change of the narrative point of view implied by the
mere presence of this documentary evidence: the novel ends by ringing a last change on Conrad's preoccupation with narrators and informers, and this time it brings the last group of them together,

assembled and concentrated in the form of a posthumous package of writings.

Marlow's written account, which is the main source, is by its very nature both more distant and more rapid than his preceding oral narrative. Conrad himself described his general intentions for the succeeding chapters (forty-one to forty-five) in a letter to William Blackwood written a few days after finishing *Lord Jim*: "The end of Lord Jim in accordance with a meditated resolve is presented in a bare almost bald relation of matters of fact. The situation—the problem if you will—of that sensitive nature has been already commented upon, illustrated and contrasted. It is my opinion that in the working out of the catastrophe psychologic disquisition should have no place" (*B*, 107). Conrad then explains that the reader no longer needs psychological analysis because he "ought to know enough by that time"; and the only exception to the condensed rapidity of the ending concerns Gentleman Brown, who is given relatively full treatment "so as to preserve the sense of verisimilitude and for the sake of final contrast." "All the rest," Conrad concludes, "is nothing but a relation of events—strictly, a narrative."

Conrad's description fits in well enough with what Ford says about *progression d'effet;* but the fact that the changes of method used for these chapters or for the earlier Patusan episode were intentional, does not necessarily mean that they succeed. In the first half of *Lord Jim,* the narrative techniques—the chronological complexities, the thematic appositions, and so on—all enact a process of prolonged moral and psychological probing; but such probing is impossible when we get to the "other" world (408) of Patusan; such events as Jim's triumph over Sherif Ali, for instance, would be revealed for the romantic schoolboy adventures that they essentially are if they were subjected to the extended and rigorous cross-examination which is applied to Jim's desertion of the *Patna.* In the second part of *Lord Jim,* Conrad is not dealing with realities that can stand up to three-dimensional scrutiny; he is trapped in an intractable contradiction between the basic terms of his previous, and his present, narrative assumptions; it is somewhat as if, in the end, Almayer had found gold up the river.

Conrad was aware of this disparity in the structure of *Lord Jim,* calling "the division of the book into two parts" a "plague spot" (*E G*, 172). Garnett, indeed, reported to Galsworthy that as soon as he had pointed it out, Conrad went "too far in acceptance."[22] Conrad's al-

22. *Letters From John Galsworthy: 1900–1932*, ed. Edward Garnett (London, 1934), p. 24.

ready quoted letter about his narrative method for the ending of *Lord Jim* seems itself to have been a response to some intimation of disappointment at the ending voiced by Blackwood. In his letter to Edward Garnett, Conrad gave a somewhat similar explanation: he had "wanted to obtain a sort of lurid light out [of] the very events."

Conrad's metaphor for the last stage of the *progression d'effet* in *Lord Jim* seems apt; after the brilliant spotlights playing starkly on every detail of human inadequacy and weakness in the first part, the lighting changes, and Patusan appears in a soft pink glow behind a gauze curtain; and then for the catastrophe there is a sudden wrenching change to a spotlight of a more livid hue, which illuminates the dying Jim in the stark contours of melodrama.

Quite apart from the particular difficulties raised by the incommensurate nature of the content of the two parts of *Lord Jim*, there is a more general problem of narrative form. Changing the nature of a novel's technique as it proceeds is a very different matter from changing the stage lighting during a play, since it violates the assumption of a transparent and consistent reflecting medium for the reader's viewing of the action. Such a change is certainly contrary to Henry James's notion of a unifying mode of fictional point of view, or to Mark Schorer's argument that the novelist's narrative technique is his main avenue to discovering the realities of his subject.[23]

Conrad's progressive series of changes in narrative technique for the last half of *Lord Jim* have the effect, and perhaps the intention, of avoiding any such discovery. But, as Conrad very well knew, the novel is "in the end a matter of convention" (*F M F*, 187); and if we are willing to waive the somewhat theoretical demand for formal consistency, we can find much to admire in the technical skill with which Conrad adjusts his narrative method from the closeness and intensity of the first part of the novel to the romantic distance of the second. The combination is so perfectly engineered that we are hardly aware of the changes as we read; and when we look back we can see how deftly, out of what may seem the obdurately contradictory materials of the two parts, Conrad has achieved a remarkable *progression d'effet*.

In the few paragraphs after Jim's death, for instance, we come to a full close in which the form finely enacts its content. By means of an inconspicuous modulation of tone, which comes naturally enough at the end of a long letter to a friend on so sad a matter, we are momentarily returned to the sound of Marlow's living and troubled voice as he bids farewell to Stein and Jim. Stein, we are told, "waves his hand sadly at his butterflies" (417); as for Jim, "He passes away under

23. "Technique as Discovery," 1948, *The World We Imagine*, pp. 3–23.

a cloud, inscrutable at heart, forgotten, unforgiven, and excessively
romantic." The novel began in the past tense—"He was . . ."; it ends
in the present tense, and with Marlow asking a question which finely
gathers together the essential timelessness of romantic quest, the persistently inconclusive and interrogative note on which the narrative
opened, and elegy's traditional compensatory promotion of the dead
hero to immortality: "Is he satisfied—quite, now, I wonder?"

iv. Jim and Marlow

Much has been written about *Lord Jim,* and what follows is mainly
centered either on a few matters where little has been said, such as the
personal and ideological relationship between Jim and Marlow, or on
other matters where there is considerable disagreement, such as the
interpretation of Stein's famous speech or the question of what final
judgment on Jim is implied by Conrad's ending. First, however, something must be said about the central situation, and its meaning for us
and for Conrad; at the same time, some aspects of the story which
have not yet been touched on must be briefly noted.

As was early recognised, *Lord Jim* deals with a situation of universal
appeal: the results of a single irreparable act. O. Henry, for instance,
who went to prison for alleged embezzlement in 1898, said later: "I
am like Lord Jim because we both made one fateful mistake at the
supreme crisis of our lives, a mistake from which we could not recover."[1] Jim's error is also a dramatic form of a much more general
psychological problem; in the words of Albert Guerard, "nearly
everyone has jumped off some *Patna* and most of us have been com-
pelled to live on . . . reconciling what we are with what we would like
to be" (*G,* 127).

The intractable consequences of an unwitting error provide one of
the classic themes of tragedy, as witness Oedipus; but no one could be
the protagonist of a classical tragedy if he were deficient in the
traditional heroic quality of ready courage; to portray an attempt to
recover from an act of cowardice belongs to a much later and less
heroic phase of literature. Such had been the theme of Stephen
Crane's *The Red Badge of Courage* (1895), whose hero, Henry Fleming,
runs away in unthinking panic at his first exposure to battle, but then
recovers and carries his regimental colours in a victorious charge.

Jim's initial error does not allow us to expect any such triumphant
resolution, because his failure is not a momentary lapse, but the outcome of a conflict rooted in his own personality. Thus, when Jim's first

1. C. Alphonso Smith, *O. Henry Biography* (New York, 1916), p. 145.

opportunity for heroism occurs on the training ship, he is too slow to take his place on the cutter because he is immobilized by his sense that the "fierce purpose in the gale . . . seemed directed at him" (7). As soon as all is over, however, Jim rationalises naively that "he was rather glad he had not gone into the cutter, since a lower achievement had served the turn" (9). When the captain predictably comments, "This will teach you to be smart," we are less sanguine; it seems unlikely that Jim will ever learn from experience while his rationalisations so assiduously protect his innate certitude that he is a "man destined to shine in the midst of dangers" (6). Later, on the *Patna*, and even at the inquiry, Jim continues to shield himself from the truth; he is sure that he only failed because "a directing spirit of perdition" had singled him out (31).

In some form, alas, these psychological traits are universal; youth's song of innocence is largely concerned with mentally rehearsing the fine figure it will cut in later life; and in that heroic drama any failure must be written off as the result of the world's pursuing malice. These general attitudes had probably been present in the youthful Conrad, and some of them, perhaps, even in the specific form they take in Jim. Conrad had himself been inspired to become a seaman, not exactly "after a course of light holiday literature" like Jim (5), but by the sea stories of Fenimore Cooper and Captain Marryat; he wrote of them in 1898 that they "shaped . . . the life of the writer," and that he had "never regretted his surrender" (*N L L*, 56–57). More generally, Conrad no doubt spoke for himself when he wrote in *Chance* that "we are the creatures of our light literature much more than is generally suspected" (288); and we can surely assume that Conrad did not think it altogether a bad thing. We do not know of any closer parallel to Jim's failure in Conrad's own life, but we can at least be sure that it contained a good deal that he wished forgotten, and very little that belonged to the domain of light literature.

(a) *The Rescue*

When Marlow takes up the narrative, his most overt and articulate attitude to Jim is that to be expected from his vocation and his audience: Marlow is merely the devoted sea captain talking after dinner to some acquaintances about the as yet unfinished adventures of a rather notorious third party. Thus neither the immediate circumstances of his tale, nor the attitudes to be presumed in his audience, encourage Marlow to go into the ultimate grounds of his personal involvement with Jim. Instead, Marlow assumes an ironical impatience with the "familiar devil" who, in this case as in others, causes him "to run up against men with soft spots . . . and loosens their tongues at the sight of me for their infernal confidences" (34). Behind the bluff manner, however, we gradually come to see that although Marlow's initial involvement with Jim was accidental and involuntary, his present commitment is both complicated and profound.

The most obvious difficulty arises from the dilemma which Jim creates for Marlow's social and moral allegiances. In itself Jim's violation of the code would hardly have become an enduring problem were it not that, as Marlow says, "he came from the right place; he was one of us" (43). In the ten or so places where the term "one of us" occurs in *Lord Jim,* its usage is roughly consistent. It denotes a member of the social, vocational, and, in some unexamined sense, moral, elite; to belong it is necessary to be a gentleman—both Brierly and the second engineer agree that Jim is that (67, 190); and it is also necessary to work, but in a managerial capacity, or, to put it somewhat more concretely, to be a member in good standing of the group which comprises the members of the professions, such as Marlow, and the colonial planters and business men who are his auditors. Marlow does not "care a rap" (41) about the other officers from the *Patna,* since their appearance and manners make it clear that they are "no-account chaps" (46); but Jim, who is obviously and proudly "not one of them" (80), has now forfeited his moral claim to be "one of us" because he has betrayed "the one great secret of the craft" (45), by which Marlow presumably means something like the Nelsonian injunction that every man shall do his duty.

When Marlow first sees Jim he looks so "clean-limbed, clean-faced, firm on his feet" (40), that it seems impossible to believe that he has done what he has; and Marlow's shock is increased by Jim's apparent unconcern. With his hands in his pockets, and an "air of a man about to go for a walk as soon as his friend is ready" (42), Jim seems either "silly" or "callous"; in either case Marlow wants to see him "overwhelmed, confounded, pierced through and through, squirming like an impaled beetle." This vindictiveness is mainly as Marlow says, "for the honour of the craft" (46); but there are more personal reasons. Like Brierly, Marlow finds the thought that even someone of "this sort can go wrong like that" (40) deeply disturbing; it means that "not one of us is safe" (43). Inescapably confronted with the exposed vulnerability of the moral guarantee of his whole way of life, Marlow finds all kinds of latent doubts arising about "the sovereign power" of the established code; and, as we see in the hospital scene, he fears that his doubt can only be dispelled by a "miracle," a miracle which, Marlow surmises, he really desires not for the survival of society but "for my own sake" (51).

By the time the two men actually meet, then, the reader knows that

Jim arouses a highly complicated and unstable assortment of personal and moral problems for Marlow; and this puts the reader in a position to appreciate the tensions and hostilities in Marlow's subsequent behaviour. These tensions are most obviously expressed in his testy and ironic impatience with Jim's egocentricity, which comes out in the yellow cur scene; and Jim becomes the object of the same barely controlled aggression whenever he indulges his characteristic weaknesses in Marlow's presence. For instance, when Jim, instead of seeing his desertion as a crime, exclaims "What a chance missed!", Marlow interjects, "If you had stuck to the ship, you mean!" (83–84). Marlow is particularly exasperated by the obstinate consistency of Jim's passionately maintained fine distinctions. Thus when Jim argues that there was not "a hair's-breadth" of difference between jumping off the *Patna* when he did, and jumping shortly after, which he would certainly have done when she sank, Marlow comments, "a little viciously": "It is difficult to see a hair at midnight" (131). To defend "the solidarity of the craft," Marlow continually tries to halt Jim's extenuating rationalisations, but Jim's persistence is too much for him. For instance, when Marlow goes on to comment: "And so you cleared out—at once," he reports that Jim immediately "corrected me incisively" with "Jumped."

Marlow slowly learns that when Jim jumped it was not out of mere selfishness or cowardice; it was, rather, the outcome of an unfortunate combination of two basic components of his character: duty, and imagination. A sense of duty led Jim, alone among the officers of the *Patna,* to face the danger of going below to examine the rusty bulkheads; he thus knew better than anyone else the probability of disaster, and it was this which stimulated his overactive imagination to visualise the panic that would ensue if he attempted to waken the sleeping pilgrims and herd them into the seven lifeboats, which could not have held more than a third of them. As for the jump itself, it can most plausibly be explained as an unconscious reflex action—the word "unconscious" had already come into vogue, and the term "reflex action" dates from 1877 (*O E D*); the jump is certainly an involuntary action of which Jim has retained no memory: "I had jumped . . . It seems" (111), Jim says, and adds: "I knew nothing about it till I looked up." Marlow certainly accepts Jim's view of this, commenting: "That's possible, too. . . . He didn't know."

Jim does recall feeling the *Patna* move under him at the first swell of the approaching squall, and it is surely in the bewildered curiosity of good faith that he challenges Marlow: "What would you do if you felt now—this minute—the house here move, just move a little under your chair" (106). Marlow admits that he does estimate how long his jump to safety would have to be, but he refuses to "be drawn into a fatal admission about myself which would have had some bearing on the case." The risk of such an admission, he explains, was that Jim was really "too much like one of us not to be dangerous"; the danger, presumably, being that if Marlow admitted that he, too, might have jumped, he would fatally compromise the absolute distinction between right and wrong on which the code of solidarity depends.

Marlow's early attitude to Jim, then, might seem gratuitously harsh if it were not in part motivated by his personal anxieties about the larger bearing of Jim's case; but Marlow's curt needlings have the further function of establishing his persona in the eyes of his listeners and readers as that of a crusty moralist turned sour and impatient by his long exposure to human egotism and irresponsibility. This posture is an important part of Conrad's narrative strategy for dealing with the most obvious difficulty in presenting the Marlow-Jim relationship—the danger of sentimentality. There are various other ways in which Conrad keeps his presentation of the Jim-Marlow relationship aseptic. For instance, we can often observe Marlow's comic underplaying of the gentler side of his character; thus, when Jim tries to master his silent agony on the evening after the court's verdict, Marlow wryly tells us that when it was time to light a candle, his solicitude for Jim made him proceed "with the greatest economy of movement and as much prudence as though it were an illegal proceeding" (172).

Marlow's self-deprecating irony prepares us to understand what the reader has already surmised from his "worn and cloudy face": he is not what he seems; the complicated internal conflicts between his public and his private attitudes have produced a personality whose breadth of silent sympathy and impatience with conventional morality are uneasily at variance with the uncompromising rigidity of attitude which dominates what he says to Jim. In his past life, Marlow confesses, he often found the "want of moral . . . posture" in the bad company he kept both "instructive" and "amusing"(41). Instructive, no doubt, because such frequentations opened his eyes to the diversity of moral attitudes by which different individuals justify themselves; and Marlow found it difficult to attribute any absolute validity to any one of these attitudes. His exposure to such broadening experiences has left him sceptical and ironic; and so he naturally finds Jim's inward struggles both "solemn, and a little ridiculous" (81). The struggle is ridiculous because, as the sceptical side of Marlow knows, the standards involved are, after all, only a "convention, only one of the rules of the game, nothing more"; but the struggle is solemn because the convention is "all the same so terribly effective by its assumption of unlimited power over natural instincts, by the awful penalties of its failure."

So it is not only public adherence to the seaman's code which drives Marlow to resist Jim's claims; his flexible and imaginative side makes him afraid of being pushed into "taking a definite part in a dispute impossible of decision if one had to be fair to all the phantoms in possession—to the reputable that had its claims and to the disreputable that had its exigencies" (93). Marlow cannot disclose his sceptical side to Jim, or even reveal his own initiated understanding of Jim's moral conflict, if only because Jim would only accept what suited him, and use it in argument to defend himself. Jim thinks that he only wants to be understood: "I don't want to excuse myself; but I would like to explain—I would like somebody to understand—somebody—one person at least!" (81); but, of course, what Jim unconsciously wants is "an ally, a helper, an accomplice" (93), someone who can grant him the absolution that is supposed to follow confession.

Marlow is lacerated to see Jim "[burrow] deep, deep in the hope of my absolution" (97), because "this was one of those cases which no solemn deception can palliate," and whatever Marlow said "would have been of no good to him." In any case, as Marlow realises, Jim is involved in "a dispute with . . . another possessor of his soul" (93), and, very humanly, cannot accept what he knows to be true—that one of the possessors of his soul has disgraced the other. Jim's early relationship with Marlow, then, is dominated by unacknowledged and impossible hopes: he clings unconsciously to the not uncommon delusion that others have the power to make us become the person we would have liked, but are no longer able, to be.

Jim forces Marlow to confront his fears about "the convention that lurks in all truth and . . . the essential sincerity of falsehood." So, although the attitudes which compose Jim's internal conflicts are by no means the same as Marlow's, they find a responsive echo in both sides of Marlow: in that which recognises Jim as a lost colleague, and in that which once shared his secret dreams. Jim, Marlow says, "appealed to all sides at once—to the side turned perpetually to the light of day, and to that side of us which, like the other hemisphere of the moon, exists stealthily in perpetual darkness, with only a fearful ashy light falling at times on the edge." No wonder that, as Marlow says, Jim "swayed me." Marlow recognises, as Jim does not, the kinship which exists between those who, in the stealthy and penumbral sides of their being, are deeply aware of their isolation from their fellows.

The fear that he may not be able to help Jim after the inquiry, and that his efforts may even be "an obstacle to some mysterious, inexplicable, impalpable striving of his wounded spirit" (182), impels Marlow

to an eloquent expression of the difficulties of achieving human reciprocity: "It is when we try to grapple with another man's intimate
need that we perceive how incomprehensible, wavering, and misty are
the beings that share with us the sight of the stars and the warmth of
the sun. It is as if loneliness were a hard and absolute condition of
existence; the envelope of flesh and blood on which our eyes are fixed
melts before the outstretched hand, and there remains only the capricious, unconsolable, and elusive spirit that no eye can follow, no hand
can grasp" (179–80). The melancholy urgency of the prose convinces
us that it mourns not only for Jim but for the Marlow who, while
marching loyally in the ranks, knows very well that this means living
with the "good, stupid kind" of people (44), people who are not "disturbed by the vagaries of intelligence and the perversions of–of
nerves, let us say."

To the further vision of Marlow, as of Conrad, the phrase "one of
us" must have had overtones of complex and self-divided irony. The
members of the tribe to which he publicly belonged were boring;
worse than that, they could only secure their survival through various
unacknowledged mechanisms for hiding or falsifying whatever might
disturb their complacent rectitude. Thus after the court announces its
cancellation of Jim's certificate, Marlow reflects: "To bury him would
have been such an easy kindness! It would have been so much in
accordance with . . . all that makes against our efficiency—the memory of our failures, the hints of our undying fears, the bodies of our
dead friends" (174). During the whole period of the inquiry, only
Marlow seems to see Jim as a human being; and the reason is surely
that, as in *Heart of Darkness*, while Marlow wants to act as a loyal
member of the group, he is not willing to let this group loyalty blind
him to what the private being sees and feels. The more deeply Marlow
responds to Jim's plight, the more his internal self becomes conscious
of its separateness from the group's established patterns and loyalties.
This was made particularly clear in a passage in the Rosenbach typescript which was entirely omitted in the published versions. Just before the court's verdict is read, Marlow remarks about all the people
in the courtroom: "I don't know what was the matter with me that
morning but . . . they all seemed to me strange, foreign, *as if* belonging to some order of beings I had no connection with. It was only
when my eyes turned towards Jim that I had a sense of not being
alone of my kind, as if we two had wandered in there from some
distant regions, from a different world. I turned to him for fellowship. He alone seemed to look natural."[2]

2. *J D G*, 153–54. The passage came immediately before the present paragraph in
Lord Jim beginning "By Jove!" on p. 158.

Conrad probably cancelled the passage because he felt that it was better to keep Marlow's spiritual kinship with Jim much less explicit, especially at this early stage. But the deeply unsettling effect of Jim's unconscious challenge to Marlow's customary ways of thought is made very clear; it keeps Marlow's feelings in an increasingly painful oscillation between sympathy and resentment. For instance, after the court's verdict, the apparent hopelessness of the burden he has assumed leads Marlow to say that Jim's suffering "sank to the bottom of my soul like lead into the water, and made it so heavy that for a second I wished heartily that the only course left open for me were to pay for his funeral" (174).

It is the Pharisee, not the Good Samaritan, who talks about his virtue. This is one explanation of why Marlow makes light of his efforts on Jim's behalf; another is the social decorum which Marlow and his auditors presumably share—the special reticence of the anglo-saxon masculine code. It must be that code's notion of good form, for example, which we see operating when Jim thanks Marlow for his help: Marlow says that he felt "humiliated," and rightly punished, as a "sneaking humbug" (183–84). To be "one of us" also involves maintaining the tenderness taboo inviolate; and this repression of feeling leads to unconscious aggression. In their first evening together, Marlow goes so far in expressing his feelings as to tell Jim that he knows how "bitter" the inquiry must be "for a man of your kind" (153). Jim whispers "It is, it is," and blushes deeply; whereupon Marlow comments to his auditors: "Believe me or not, I say it was outrageously heart-rending." But he also reports his immediate and Brierly-like response at the time: "It provoked me to brutality. 'Yes,' I said, 'and allow me to confess that I am totally unable to imagine what advantage you can expect from this licking of the dregs.' "

The irreconcilable conflict between the group code and inner feeling also operates in Jim, although in a different way. The ostentatious unconcern which at first disgusts Marlow, is probably Jim's habitual posture of compliance to the code of good form; as "one of us," Jim knows that, in Leslie Stephen's words, "sensitive" is generally regarded as "a polite word for morbid."[3] Throughout his public ordeal, and even with Marlow, Jim feels he must maintain that stiff upper-lip for which the Victorian gentleman was celebrated. Given Jim's actual circumstances, it is a strenuous and unnatural psychological posture; and so when he is challenged, his precarious surface calm turns rapidly into the suspicious and taciturn belligerence which so disconcerts Marlow at their first meeting.

3. Noel Annan, *Leslie Stephen* (London, 1951), p. 226.

Jim's sensitivity, however, does not seem to extend to any internalised awareness of the intrinsic moral basis of solidarity. He does
not even seem to be aware that he has committed a crime, whose "real
significance," Marlow explains, lies "in its being a breach of faith with
the community of mankind" (157). In other respects, however, Jim's
personal moral code is stricter than Marlow's: Jim is egocentric, but
his ego sets the highest possible standards for its dealings with others;
for instance, he shrinks with horror at the mere thought of touching
the wages due to him from the *Patna*. Marlow is ironic about Jim's
"exquisite sensibilities" in handling his "delicate position" (200), but
the mockery is based on purely prudential considerations; and this is a
reminder that one of the many reasons why the relationship of Jim
and Marlow is so beset by friction, crosspurposes, and latent hostility,
lies in the difference between their ages. Chronologically, Jim is
twenty years younger (236), and psychologically much more; he is,
Marlow later tells Stein, "the youngest human being now in existence"
(219). This disparity in age is very important for each of them, though
in different ways.

When Jim turned down Marlow's suggestion that he leave before
the court rendered its preordained verdict, Marlow says that he did
not contest the point because he "felt that in argument his youth
would tell against me heavily: he believed where I had already ceased
to doubt" (153). The worldly wisdom of age knows that "it is not the
haunted soul but the hungry body that makes an outcast" (197); but it
does not necessarily rejoice in its possession of that information. So
when Jim continually throws up his various jobs, Marlow understands
his behaviour, and even concedes that "to fling away your daily bread
so as to get your hands free for a grapple with a ghost may be an act of
prosaic heroism," even though, as is the case with Jim, the grapple
happens to be absurd because "it is impossible to lay the ghost of a
fact." But even in the caution and fatigue of his maturity, Marlow can
understand and even admire Jim's youthful intransigence; and this
complementary relationship constitutes an important element in the
universality of the situation in *Lord Jim*.

Many of the qualities in Jim which first infuriated Marlow were
essentially youthful. There was, for instance, the discrepancy between
Jim's flagrant guilt and his "conviction of innate blamelessness" (79); a
good many years of life have to elapse before anyone gives up believing that the past can be wiped out and that tomorrow will be a wholly
new day. Jim combines youth's intense need to be understood with a
number of attitudes which in fact make this understanding very difficult to establish. Jim typically rebuffs, as often as he welcomes, Mar-

low's offers of help; his self-absorption leaves no room for any curiosity about Marlow's motives; and while he in effect asks for the deepest kind of sympathy, he is offensively reluctant to accept the human implications of such a demand. For instance, even after their first long evening together, Jim is so afraid of exposing himself to possible humiliation that, Marlow reports, he takes it "into his fanciful head that I was likely to make some difficulty as to shaking hands" (155); and the next evening Jim is so touchily independent that he announces that he can't come to dinner again, although Marlow hasn't even mentioned it. Youth's emerging sense of selfhood some- times requires to be fortified by sympathy, and sometimes by hostility.

But if Jim's youth makes him such difficult company, it also ac- counts for the special intensity of Marlow's sympathy. "The secret motive of my prying," Marlow early surmises, was that Jim's "appear- ance alone added a touch of personal concern to the thoughts sug- gested by the knowledge of his weakness—made it a thing of mystery and terror—like a hint of a destructive fate ready for us all whose youth—in its day—had resembled his youth" (51). What Marlow orig- inally saw behind Jim's shoulder were the unrealised aspirations, the foolish intransigencies, and the luckily surmounted perils, of his own earlier years; and so there is an autumnal nostalgia in Marlow's awareness that he no longer has Jim's energy of expectation—"that faculty of beholding at a hint the face of his desire and the shape of his dream, without which the earth would know no lover and no adventurer" (175). It is easy, therefore, to understand why, when they part after the inquiry, Marlow, despite everything, feels envious of Jim: "I was no longer young enough to behold at every turn the magnificence that besets our insignificant footsteps in good and in evil. I smiled to think that, after all, it was yet he, of us two, who had the light" (185–86).

Lord Jim, then, deals with more than one archetypal situation: there is the irreparable error; there is the trying to live it down; and there is also the complex communion of youth and age. Jim's error under- mines the whole basis of solidarity; but in the course of probing the internal sanctions that underlie the fixed standard of conduct, Mar- low encounters another continuing basis for solidarity in the personal bonds formed between one generation and another.

In Marlow's case this is an extension of his role as a seasoned ship's officer. Even before meeting Jim, he has reminisced about the "youngsters" he has "turned out . . . for the service of the Red Rag" (44); and he confesses that he has "glowed all day long and gone to

bed feeling less lonely in the world" when one of his protégés has
greeted him long afterwards, no longer a sea-puppy but a fine chief
mate.[4] In the public context Marlow must see Jim as a traitor to the
succession of generations which have ensured the continuing tradition of solidarity; but in the private context he can find some consolation. After all, Marlow is not the first teacher who has been forced to
discover that although his pupil happens not to be interested in what
he is accustomed to provide, he can make himself useful in other
ways.

Jim is too concerned with his inner dreams to be much interested in
the code of solidarity as it concerns collective action and public attitudes to it; but he both needs and evokes in Marlow some of the
other elements of solidarity which Conrad wrote about in the preface
to the *Nigger of the "Narcissus"*, notably the "conviction of solidarity
that knits together the loneliness of innumerable hearts." Jim makes
this bond explicit when he thanks Marlow for listening to him: "You
don't know what it is for a fellow in my position to be believed—make
a clean breast of it to an elder man" (128). Marlow is feeling very old at
the time, and "uselessly wise"; but his glimpse of Jim—which "was not
the last of that kind"—brings to life in him "the fellowship of these
illusions you had thought gone out, extinct, cold, and which, as if
rekindled at the approach of another flame, give a flutter deep, deep
down somewhere, give a flutter of light . . . of heat!" Jim, in Marlow's
words, has "reached the secret sensibility of my egoism" (152); and
part of this sensibility is surely Marlow's sense of that kind of solidarity
which "binds men to each other . . . in aspirations, in illusions." Jim's
disgrace brings him and Marlow together in a tacit community of
defeated expectation. That their defeats were so dissimilar, and that
they cannot share them completely, only gives their relationship a
more universal meaning. Marlow expresses this recognition to his
hearers in the words: "What wonder that when some heavy prod gets
home the bond is found to be close; that besides the fellowship of the
craft there is felt the strength of a wider feeling—the feeling that
binds a man to a child" (129).

The relationship between Marlow and Jim, then, slowly develops
into the most universal of the intergenerational solidarities—that of
parent and child. Jim knows that he "can never face" his real father:
"I could never explain. He wouldn't understand" (79). Marlow,
though never explicitly, slowly accepts his paternal role. He speaks at
least once of his responsibility as that towards a "very young brother"

4. Conrad seems to have been like Marlow in his devotion to those under his
command. One of his young apprentices wrote thirty years later: "I have loved you
more than any man I ever knew except my own father" (*L L*, vol. 1, 156).

(223), but more often his terms are paternal. When Jim is in agony after the verdict, Marlow comments that "my compassion for him took the shape of the thought that I wouldn't have liked his people to see him at that moment" (173); elsewhere he speaks of Jim as "a dear good boy in trouble" (180), or "manageable as a little child" (170). Nor is Marlow unlike a parent in wishing that his charge had not got into trouble in the first place, or that, having done so, he would at least have the grace to say he's sorry in exactly the terms Marlow thinks appropriate.

After the verdict Marlow writes a letter to a friend who may be able to give Jim a new start, and recommends him "in terms that one only ventures to use when speaking of an intimate friend" (183). A few minutes before Jim had been ruminating aloud that he was "no better than a vagabond now . . . without a single—single." Jim then stopped, because if he had brought out the word he presumably had in mind, "friend," (179) he might have seemed to be imposing on Marlow a reciprocal avowal. However, when Jim realises what is implied by Marlow's making himself "unreservedly responsible" for him after they have, after all, only known each other for two days, Jim gasps out: "Jove! . . . It is noble of you!" (183).

Nobody, one imagines, has been called noble to his face within living memory, even in a novel; one can hardly wonder that Marlow professes to suspect mockery. But, of course, the old-fashioned epithet is only an extreme example of Jim's touching inarticulateness; and the comedy of his gaucheness continues when Marlow's impressionist eye catches his immediate reflex of gratitude in the very moment that it is inhibited by his fear of offending against decorum. Jim, Marlow says, "snatched my hand as though he had just then seen it for the first time, and dropped it at once" (184).

Marlow pretends that Jim is exaggerating the "definitely small thing" he has done for him; he finds it quite as awkward as Jim to handle the emotional ties that are being formed. The reader, however, should not take Marlow's reticence at face value: it is a protective superficial cover for a more than ordinary sensitiveness. "Greater love," it has been said, "hath no man than hearing his friend out patiently"; and Marlow has heard Jim out.

Later, Marlow is rather slow in seeing the full implications of Jim's throwing up job after job; but that, too, is normal enough. Fathers, friends, and counsellors are alike prone to define the problems of others in terms sufficiently simple to be easily amenable to practical solutions. The only problems to which we will readily concede the dignity of raising complex metaphysical issues are our own. Still, Marlow eventually discovers what the problem is. Jim is working at De Jongh's, and drops the remark "This is killing work" (201). Marlow

suggests that he go further afield—try California perhaps. With defeated honesty Jim asks "What difference would it make?"; and then
at last Marlow seems "to perceive dimly that what he wanted, what he
was, as it were, waiting for, was something not easy to define—
something in the nature of an opportunity." Man does not live by
bread alone; Marlow must do more; and so, although he suspects that
Jim, like many another, is probably "waiting . . . for the impossible,"
Marlow goes to see Stein.

(b) *At Stein's*

Stein is the only interlocutor whom Marlow seeks out. He is an old
friend, and, like the French lieutenant, wins the admiration of that
side of Marlow which belongs to the daylight world of action. But
Marlow also reveres him with the more inward and sceptical side of
his personality because Stein is deeply reflective, and even an avowed
intellectual.

Marlow describes his human specimen, Jim, and when he has finished, Stein's classification is immediate and categorical: "I understand very well. He is romantic" (212). Marlow says he was "quite
startled to find how simple" the problem was. We need not, however,
assume that he felt unduly humiliated by this miracle of taxonomic
clairvoyance, for he had in fact anticipated Stein's diagnosis much
earlier, when, observing Jim's "ecstatic smile" at the thought of the
heroic achievement that could have been his had he stayed on the
Patna, he realised how deeply Jim desired "the impossible world of
romantic achievements" (83). But whereas Marlow used the label
"romantic" to consign Jim to the ranks of self-deluding egotists, Stein
gives quite another meaning to the term: and it assigns Jim to the first
rank among the specimens of humankind's most distinguishing
hunger.

As a prominent entomologist, Stein expresses the main impact of
his century's biological thought: man's position in the universe is
anomalous. The beetles and butterflies Stein studies are examples of
perfected evolutionary life; the rare butterfly on his desk, for instance, is a masterpiece: "Look! the beauty—but that is nothing—look
at the accuracy, the harmony. And so fragile! And so strong! And so
exact! This is Nature—the balance of colossal forces. Every star is
so—and every blade of grass stands *so*—and the mighty Kosmos in
perfect equilibrium produces—this. This wonder; this masterpiece of
Nature—the great artist" (208). The perfection of each natural
specimen, Stein explains later, is duplicated in its external relationships; there is a total harmony between the creature and the role,
between the individual specimen and its environment.

With human creatures it is sadly otherwise. "Man is amazing, but he is not a masterpiece," Stein comments. In the Rosenbach manuscript, Conrad originally made the point much more crudely: "Man is a freak" (p. 417). He is a freak in the sense that, as Stein believes, "Man is come where he is not wanted, where there is no place for him." Stein then makes the application of this to Jim somewhat more explicit: "We want in so many different ways to be. . . . This magnificent butterfly finds a little heap of dirt and sits still on it; but man he will never on his heap of mud keep still. He want to be so, and again he want to be so. . . . He wants to be a saint, and he wants to be a devil— and every time he shuts his eyes he sees himself as a very fine fellow—so fine as he can never be. . . . In a dream" (213).

So fine as he can never be. The memorable metaphysical eloquence which Conrad generates from this dislocation of English idiom reminds us of how deeply representative Stein is of German romantic idealism. There is the twin enthusiasm for geographical exploration and scientific discovery which such men as Alexander von Humboldt (1769–1859) had bequeathed to the nineteenth century; there is the fact that Stein, "rich in generous enthusiasms" (217), is also an exile from the 1848 revolution, and thus a representative of German political liberalism; and there are his poetic quotations, which make him the spokesman of German Romantic literature.

Today, Romantic idealism may seem somewhat simpleminded; but it was the dominant cultural and literary force when Conrad grew up. He no doubt learned something about the two German authors he cites in Lord Jim—Novalis and Goethe—from the German element in his Cracow schooling; and in any case, one can hardly do justice to Lord Jim without coming to terms with the romantic outlook.

The matter is too vast and diffuse for more than the most summary treatment here.[5] Both in Conrad generally and in Lord Jim, the meaning of the word "romantic" swings between two main centres of reference. There is the common usage of romantic to denote the adventurous content of "romances," the modern popular form of which had impelled Jim and Conrad to become seamen; but behind this sense there are also the loftier aspirations of the Romantic movement, aspirations which had later done much to form the nineteenth-century ideal of the individual self. Stein embodies both the adventurous and the idealising aspects; and Conrad himself consistently expressed both the strong appeal which the romantic attitude had for him, and his awareness of its dangers. In 1920 he affirmed this dual

5. See especially the fine discussions of Romance, Lord Jim, and of Conrad's autobiographical writings in David Thorburn's Conrad's Romanticism.

allegiance in terms which seem particularly appropriate to *Lord Jim.*
"The romantic feeling of reality was in me an inborn faculty," Conrad
wrote in the Author's Note to *Within The Tides,* and added: "This in
itself may be a curse but when disciplined by a sense of personal
responsibility and a recognition of the hard facts of existence shared
with the rest of mankind becomes but a point of view from which the
very shadows of life appear endowed with an internal glow" (*W T T,*
v–vi).

One of the main residual legacies of the Romantic movement was a
disheartened awareness of the discrepancy which the individual imagination is continually discovering between the self as it is and the self
as it would like to be. As Stein puts it: "Because you not always can
keep your eyes shut there comes the real trouble—the heart pain—
the world pain" (213). Here Stein is translating the German
Weltschmerz, "world suffering," a well-known Romantic catchword:[6]
and he goes on to place Jim's suffering in this context: "I tell you, my
friend, it is not good for you to find you cannot make your dream
come true, for the reason that you not strong enough are, or not
clever enough."

Jim still believes that, to use another phrase from Novalis, "our life
is no dream, but it should and perhaps will become one."[7] Marlow and
Stein no longer share his hope, but they are both vividly aware of the
particular tensions in the individual self which André Malraux
thought typical of Western man in general: we all retain, Malraux
writes, "a sense of latent power . . . as if we lacked only the opportunity to carry out in the real world the exploits of our dreams; we
retain the confused impression, not of having accomplished them, but
of having been capable of accomplishing them." Malraux concludes
his characterisation of the Romantic and post-Romantic consciousness
in terms which both Marlow and Stein would have recognised as a
picture of Jim: "We are, in our own eyes, creatures in whom is dor-
mant an unsophisticated and jumbled procession of the possibilities of
act and dream."[8]

The universality of this way of thought is best known, perhaps,
through its parody in James Thurber's *Walter Mitty;* the particular
poignancy of Jim's case arises from the youthful vigour with which he
unsuccessfully attempts to transcend man's unhappy place in Stein's
post-Romantic biological scheme, and thus exemplifies the suffering

---

6. Coined by Jean Paul in 1823 (*Deutsches Wörterbuch,* J. and W. Grimm, s.v.).
7. No. 237, *Das Allgemeine Brouillon* (*Schriften,* vol. 2, p. 281).
8. *The Temptation of the West* (1926), trans. Robert Hollander (New York, 1961),
p. 52.

which follows from man's consciousness of his failure to be a master-piece.

The practical strategies enjoined by that inevitable failure are the subject of the most celebrated of Stein's pronouncements:

> Yes! Very funny this terrible thing is. A man that is born falls into a dream like a man who falls into the sea. If he tries to climb out into the air as inexperienced people endeavour to do, he drowns—*nicht wa[h]r?* . . . No! I tell you! The way is to the destructive element submit yourself, and with the exertions of your hands and feet in the water make the deep, deep sea keep you up. (214)

We can readily participate in the literal meaning of the simile's first phase—if you fall into the sea don't panic and try to climb out. But Stein's advice fails to commend itself to the practical mind: we cannot easily imagine ourselves wanting to go on treading water forever if there is no prospect of rescue. In any case, why should dreams be destructive? And if Stein thinks they are, isn't he recommending self-destruction in adjuring us to "follow the dream"?

It seems to be a universal principle in criticism that the more interpretation a passage has had, the more it shall be given. The principle will be honoured here, although only to the extent that the interpretation of Stein's parable seems interesting in itself, or helpful in furthering our understanding of *Lord Jim*.

Each of the last five decades has discovered in the passage an image of its own characteristic preoccupations. Thus in the twenties, I. A. Richards used the passage to summarise the spiritual desolation which he took to be the message of *The Waste Land*.[9] Stephen Spender spoke for the political thirties in his critical study, *The Destructive Element* (1935), when, following Richards, he interpreted his title phrase to denote "the experience of an all-pervading Present, which is a world without belief," although he applied it to the literary effects of the social and political breakdown of modern civilisation.[10] Neither of these uses of the term had much to do with Conrad, and Edward Crankshaw protested in 1936 that Richards and Spender were in fact giving an interpretation which was "at odds with all we know of Conrad," because they used it to denote some form of the "surrender of individuality when, surely, precisely the opposite meaning was intended."[11]

9. *Science and Poetry* (London, 1926), p. 71.
10. *The Destructive Element* (London, 1935), p. 14.
11. *Some Aspects of the Art of the Novel*, p. 62n.

The first reasonably close analysis of the meaning of the passage was given in the forties by Morton Dauwen Zabel, a pioneer interpreter of the moral relevance of Conrad to the postwar world. He agreed with Crankshaw that Stein "was not talking about the loss or surrender of personality," but about its "salvation . . . by the test of experience and the necessary recognition of selfhood"; and he further saw the scene as affirming "the means of redemption" for modern man to rescue himself from "the moral nihilism to which the world encourages him to surrender himself."[12] Zabel's equation of the sea with the "moral nihilism" of the external world is surely contrary to the literal meaning of Stein's words; and to suggest that Stein implies a "means of redemption" is surely to introduce a note of unsupported optimism.

The fifties also tended to give Stein's words a similarly affirmative interpretation. Its most detailed, eloquent, and influential voice was undoubtedly that of Robert Penn Warren in 1951:

> It is man's fate to be born into the "dream"—the fate of all men. By the dream Conrad here means nothing more or less than man's necessity to justify himself by the "idea," to idealize himself and his actions into moral significance of some order, to find sanctions. But why is the dream like the sea, a "destructive element"? Because man, in one sense, is purely a creature of nature, an animal of black egotism and savage impulses. He should, to follow the metaphor, walk on the dry land of "nature," the real, naturalistic world, and not be dropped into the waters he is so ill-equipped to survive in. Those men who take the purely "natural" view, who try to climb out of the sea, who deny the dream and man's necessity to submit to the idea, to create values that are, quite literally, "super-natural" and therefore human, are destroyed by the dream. They drown in it, and their agony is the agony of their frustrated humanity. Their failure is the failure to understand what is specifically human. They are the Kurtzes, the Browns, in so far as they are villains, but they are also all those isolated ones who are isolated because they have feared to take the full risk of humanity. To conclude the reading of the passage, man, as a natural creature, is not born to swim in the dream, with gills and fins, but if he submits in his own imperfect, "natural" way he can learn to swim and keep himself up, however painfully, in the destructive element. To surrender to the incorrigible and ironical necessity of the "idea," that is man's fate and his only triumph.[13]

12. "Conrad in his Age," *Craft and Character in Modern Fiction* (London, 1957), p. 221. The passage was originally part of a short essay which appeared in 1941.

13. Introduction, *Nostromo*, Modern Library Edition (New York, 1951), pp. xxii–xxiii.

Warren was writing an introduction to *Nostromo,* and his interpretation must therefore be primarily judged as a general view of Conrad's thought rather than as an explication of the Stein passage in its context. Even in these terms, however, Warren's interpretation seems to take a more constructive view of Stein's—and Conrad's—ethical perspective than a literal reading of the passage allows.

One can agree that Jim feels the need "to justify himself by the idea," for instance; but Conrad stands outside the traditional ethical and religious view that people are wicked because they have failed to understand the good. For him, all men, whether good or bad, may have an "idea" behind the way they act, so that, contrary to Warren's interpretation, it is probable that Conrad thought of Gentleman Brown and Kurtz as individuals who, in their different ways, had also "surrendered to the incorrigible and ironical necessity of the 'idea.' " Of Brown's massacre of Dain Waris and his men, for instance, Marlow comments: "Notice that even in this awful outbreak there is a superiority as of a man who carries right—the abstract thing" (404). Such men as Brown are by no means "creatures of nature," but dedicated ideological villains who have decided: "Evil, be thou my good."

Warren assumes that there is something "specifically human" in man which is opposite to the "black egotism" of the "creature of nature." Here Conrad and Stein would probably disagree, though on different grounds. Conrad would have no particular quarrel with Warren's low view of "natural" man; he wrote to Cunninghame Graham that "L'homme est un animal méchant," and added that his "mechanceté doit être organisée" (*C G,* 117). For Conrad, one had to rely on organised solidarity, on the values that men have jointly constructed over the centuries; there was no question of relying on some innate knowledge of what is truly human. For Stein, and for romanticism in general, on the other hand, what is most truly human is the individual dream and its struggle with reality. Warren finds a basis for his position by setting up an ontological dualism between the natural and the human, and arguing that such men as Brown suffer agony and drowning because they have "feared to take the full risk of humanity." It would be nice if it were true; but evidence of their agony or their fear is lacking, at least in Conrad, and in the text of *Lord Jim.* In fact, Stein's parable makes no ethical distinction between kinds of men; they all fall into the sea; those that drown do so out of an inexperience which has got nothing to do with their human adequacy or otherwise.

The main reason why Stein's parable resists any consensus of interpretation is the patent asymmetry of its basic metaphor: there is nothing that can stand as a satisfactory opposite to the sea, and thus give some measure of concreteness both to the individual's struggle in the water, and to its different outcomes. This has been the main stumbling-block in most interpretations of "in the destructive element immerse." Warren takes Stein literally, and therefore equates the sea with the dream; but he is then confronted with the need to perform the delicate manoeuvre of supplying some solid ground on which to base man's animal egotism, although Stein happens not to mention land. Most critics, on the other hand, have equated the sea not with the dream but with the forces of reality which destroy it. Zabel, for instance, described it as "a realm of elemental nature in which the conscious personality and egotism of man dissolve on encountering a force unbroken to the reason and assertive will of civilised life. . . . It symbolises for Conrad the anti-human—cleansing, purging, primitive, but destructive too."[14] This view of the sea as hostile to man seems in general to have been shared by Conrad; the fear of drowning, and the endless struggle to avoid it, certainly informs the whole Stein passage—even the kinetic suggestion of "make the deep, deep sea keep you up" is that of the non-swimmer, which Conrad apparently was.[15] On the other hand, the only contrary realm which Stein mentions is the air; and here again the passage violates our metaphorical habits. We normally think of dreams and ideals not as visible, tangible, and destructive, but as invisible, intangible, and life-giving; we place them not down in the sea but up there in the sky; and very few people have ever entertained the idea of "climbing into the air."

By a no doubt inevitable reaction, the less grandiose ambitions of literary criticism in the sixties fostered a closer attention to the literal difficulties in the text; and this usually meant finding the passage opaque or illogical. Here the lead was given by Albert Guerard's suggestion, advanced as early as 1958, that "Conrad produced without much effort a logically imperfect multiple metaphor, liked the sound of it, and let matters go at that" (G, 166).

Perhaps the oddest feature of the situation is that so many other people have liked the metaphor too; the main reason may be the imperative resonance of the phrase "In the destructive element immerse," combined with its accommodating openness to almost any meaning. What can be more universally acceptable than a saying which announces that its user has survived his ritual immersion in life's destructive traumas and has now emerged into the maturity of tragic acceptance?

If it is impossible to resolve the contradictions in the Stein passage satisfactorily, it is at least fairly easy to explain how they arose. The

14. *Craft and Character*, p. 182.
15. Interview, John Conrad, 15 November 1955.

Rosenbach manuscript of *Lord Jim* shows that Conrad's original version began: "A man that is born is like a man who falls into the sea."[16]
It was only later that he substituted the words "falls into a dream" in
the place of the second "is." Without this mention of "the dream," the
parable therefore merely continued Stein's earlier theme of how man
feels out of his element in the world he is born into. The original
version would therefore have meant something like: "Of course you
don't like being thrown into the sea, that is, into the reality where you
find yourself; but if you try and escape into the air, into unreality, you
will merely drown; so your only chance of survival is to force yourself
to accept the reality which surrounds you, and use it to keep your
head above water and go on living."

It is ironical that the manuscript version of Stein's parable should in
effect have anticipated the later tendency of critics to equate the sea
with the threats and denials by which reality destroys the individual's
hopes. When Conrad later added "falls into a dream," he made the
connection with Stein's earlier statements more explicit, but in so
doing he equated the sea with the dream, rather than with the realities
of the world into which man is born; and the logic of his sea metaphor
then led to the confusing notion that man should "follow the dream,"
by trying to keep out of it, but not too hard.

There remains the question of how far whatever meaning we attribute to Stein's parable is to be regarded as a reliable diagnosis of Jim's
character. The beginning of the passage—"a man that is born"—is
usually taken to mean that the parable applies to "all men." But
neither "a man" in English, nor Stein's presumed German equivalent,
Mann, without an article, need have quite so definite a meaning: in
either case the generality may be of the kind also expressed by the use
of "one"; and to say "one is born into a dream" is to make an appeal
for general assent rather than to assert a universally valid proposition.
This makes better sense for the context of the passage, since Stein
could hardly have thought that to say "He is romantic" was in any
sense a diagnosis of Jim if everyone else is too, which would logically
follow if "all men" without distinction are born into a dream. Stein
presumably means that Jim, like many other, though not necessarily
all other, men, ought not to renounce his romantic dreams (that is, try
to climb out of the sea), but rather use them to support himself.

On the other hand, we must also take due note of the doubts raised
when Stein returns to Marlow's practical question: "If you ask

16. A facsimile of the manuscript page concerned is reproduced in Kenneth B.
Newell, "The Destructive Element and Related 'Dream' Passages in the *Lord Jim* Manuscript," *Journal of Modern Literature* 1 (1970): 30.

me—how to be? . . . I will tell you!" (214), Stein says, in a strong voice which sounds to Marlow "as though away there in the dusk he had been inspired by some whisper of knowledge." But when Stein approaches the bright circle of the lamp to make his pronouncement on the "only one way" to be, Marlow reports that "his twitching lips uttered no word, and the austere exaltation of a certitude seen in the dusk vanished from his face." Once again, as with the French lieutenant, the clinching statement that might resolve Marlow's doubts is withheld; Conrad characteristically uses the scene's climax to dramatise the waning of certainty, the fading of vision, the absence of final truth.

After that anticlimax, Stein nevertheless returns, though "in a subdued tone," to his previous assertion: "And yet it is true—it is true. In the destructive element immerse." But by the time Stein has said goodnight to Marlow and returned to his butterflies, we realise that although, as an intellectual, Stein loves generalising, he has essentially been talking with his own experience of life in mind.[17]

Marlow admires Stein for his resolution in pursuing an adventurous life rich "in all the exalted elements of romance" (217), but he fears there may be a danger in the way Stein's romantic idealism throws the "charming and deceptive light" of its "impalpable poesy . . . over pitfalls—over graves." Marlow also remains uneasy about Stein's view of Jim's fate. When Stein first said Jim was a romantic, Marlow had found it "natural to ask—'What's good for it?' " (212). Stein replied: "One thing alone can us from being ourselves cure!"; and Marlow reflects: "The case which he had made to look so simple before became if possible still simpler—and altogether hopeless." The two friends jointly pause at the presage of death as the only permanent solution for Jim; they then agree to defer the problem of what is to be done for Jim until the morning; but, meanwhile, Stein adds to his earlier diagnosis of Jim a disquietingly ambiguous comment: "He is romantic—romantic . . . And that is very bad—very bad. . . . Very good, too" (216).

Marlow's need to "dispose of" Jim had become particularly pressing because he was planning to go home for a while; and this brought reflections which increased the pathos of Jim's situation:

"For each of us," Marlow says, "going home must be like going to render an account"; even those who are most "bereft of ties . . . have to meet the spirit that dwells within the land, under its sky, in its air, in its valleys, and on its rises, in its fields"; and to "face its truth, one must

17. Kenneth B. Newell argues this in his article, "The Destructive Element," pp. 40–43.

return with a clear consciousness" (221–22). Marlow then goes on, assuming a voice which might be Conrad's evoking his feelings for Poland: "It is the lonely . . . those who return not to a dwelling but to the land itself, to meet its disembodied, eternal, and unchangeable spirit—it is those who understand best its severity, its saving power, the grace of its secular right to our fidelity, to our obedience."

As far as Marlow is concerned, "those who do not feel" that spiritual allegiance to the homeland "do not count." Jim counts. "I don't know how much Jim understood," Marlow comments, "but I know he felt, he felt confusedly but powerfully, the demand of some such truth or some such illusion—I don't care how you call it, there is so little difference, and the difference means so little." Jim is oppressed by the "unbearable" thought that he "would never go home now"; and for Marlow, Jim's sense that he cannot face the spirit of his land "with a clear consciousness" is evidence that in one respect at least Jim's suffering comes from having betrayed, not the dedication to the romantic dream which Stein espouses, but the code of solidarity. As Marlow puts it, "We exist only in so far as we hang together. He had straggled in a way; he had not hung on; but he was aware of it with an intensity that made him touching" (223).

This is not a problem which concerns Stein; and it is not the only matter in which Marlow remains unsatisfied. The effect of the Stein consultation turns out to be very like that of his earlier confrontations. Jim's hope that "age and wisdom can find a remedy against the pain of truth" (129) seems baseless; Stein has not resolved either the internal contradictions between Marlow's diverse allegiances, or his puzzlement about Jim; and so in the end Marlow falls back on the code of solidarity to express his final and rather petulant judgment of the interview: "Even Stein could say no more than that he was romantic. I only knew he was one of us. And what business had he to be romantic?" (224).

(c) *The Friendship*

The next day Marlow tells Jim about the plan that he should go out to take over Stein's trading post in the remote and dangerous settlement of Patusan, where no one can possibly have heard of the *Patna*. When Jim tries to thank him, "his gratitude" causes Marlow "inexplicable pain" (230), and he brusquely cuts him short with the self-disparaging evasion that he "had done no more than to mention his name" to Stein. Jim is quite unabashed and goes on to promise that he will justify the trust that has been placed in him; at this Marlow, like a stern father, insists that it is purely Jim's affair; he and Stein have merely offered him the opportunity he asked for. Marlow puts this in the most pitiless way: "He had shown a desire, I continued inflexibly, to go out and shut the door after him." Jim interrupts Marlow, "in a strange access of gloom that seemed to envelop him from head to foot like the shadow of a passing cloud," and comments bitterly: "Did I? . . . You can't say I made much noise about it."

Jim naturally hates to be reminded that it was his decision to cut himself off from his own world forever; but when he comes back from his visit to Stein he is once again full of enthusiasm, and his "elated rattle" (234) jars badly on Marlow's nerves. When Jim tries to tell him how good it is to have a friend, Marlow makes a "disclaiming gesture," but Jim still refuses to have his ardour damped: "I'm ready for any confounded thing. . . . I've been dreaming of it . . . You wait." Marlow's impatience mounts, and, forgetting earlier occasions, he tells his auditors that "for the first and last time in our acquaintance I perceived myself unexpectedly to be thoroughly sick of him." Marlow warns Jim that his unreal exaltation is not a proper frame of mind to approach any serious undertaking; Jim demurs "with a smile," in which Marlow detects "something insolent" (236). Marlow comments: "But then I am twenty years his senior. Youth *is* insolent; it is its right—its necessity; it has got to assert itself."

Jim typically assumes that Marlow is still thinking of the *Patna,* and reproaches Marlow that "even I remembered—remembered—against him—what—what had happened." At this, Marlow's exasperation explodes: "It is not I or the world who remember . . . It is you—you, who remember." Jim takes the rebuke very well, promises to "forget everything, everybody, everybody," and then irrepressibly adds in a low voice, "But you." Jim's qualification obviously invites some reciprocal acknowledgment; but Marlow rebuffs Jim with: "Yes—me, too—if it would help." Jim then assures him that it will be "easy enough to remain" in Patusan; but Marlow, refusing to let the matter drop, insists on the lesson taught by his longer experience of life: "If you only live long enough you will want to come back." To this poor Jim, looking at the clock on the wall, can only answer absently, "Come back to what?"

It is an inauspicious beginning for Jim's adventure, and a lacerating valediction for them both. Fortunately its gloom is relieved by the eternal comedies of the youth's preparations for departure. Jim does not start his packing until the last moment, and the consequent confusion turns out, ironically enough, to be providential. He forgets the two boxes of cartridges which Marlow has given him as a going-away present, together with his revolver; so Marlow has to go out with the cartridges to the brigantine that is to take Jim to Patusan. On board there at least occurs, "a moment of real and profound intimacy, unexpected and short-lived like a glimpse of some everlasting, of some saving truth" (241). Marlow recalls that "My heart was freed from that dull resentment which had existed side by side with interest in his fate"; and he continues that "the sort of formality that had been always present in our intercourse vanished from our speech." During this farewell, Marlow recalls with a consciously ironic underplaying of his feelings: "I believe I called him 'dear boy,' and he tacked on the words 'old man' to some half-uttered expression of gratitude, as though his risk set off against my years made us more equal in age and in feeling." There are, it appears, occasional rewards in the process whereby one generation succeeds another; and Marlow reports that, in silent acknowledgment of the transition, Jim dutifully "exerted himself to soothe me as though he had been the more mature of the two. . . . 'I promise to take care of myself. . . . Don't you worry.' "

Some two years later, combining, he says, friendship and business, Marlow goes to Patusan (309). There he discovers that Jim has apparently achieved that dream self which he had so long despaired of attaining. Jim is now "loved, trusted, admired, with a legend of strength and prowess forming round his name as though he had been the stuff of a hero" (175). He has won himself a high place in the human hierarchy as the revered and indispensable ruler; he has also found another father in Doramin, a mother as well as a wife in Jewel, a devoted friend of his own age in Dain Waris, and even the hero's traditional faithful retainer in Tamb' Itam.

Yet the bitter aftertaste of failure remains to haunt Jim's spectacular triumph. Jewel complains that "there is something he can never forget" (314); to which Marlow emphatically retorts: "So much the better for you." Marlow comes to the "sober conviction" that Jewel "went through agonies of apprehension" during his long talks with Jim (308); for Jewel, Marlow represents that unknown outside world which disturbs Jim's thoughts and threatens to steal him away from her; and to relieve this anxiety Marlow finds himself driven to promise her that "I shall never come again" (317).

Jim accompanies Marlow on the first stage of his "journey back to the world he had renounced" (331), and their separation acquires a deeper poignancy now that the contradictions of circumstance have doomed it to be final. "When we spoke," Marlow comments, "it was with an effort, as if to force our low voices across a vast and increasing distance." Later, when they walk together on the white beach, Jim tries once again to explain how "sometimes I wish . . . ," but he breaks off with "Can't expect anything more" (333). He must, Jim says, "go on, go on for ever holding up my end" because the trust of the people of Patusan makes him "feel safe"; and he adds that there is another reason for him to be faithful to the obligations of solidarity; it will serve as a way of prolonging his spiritual bond with Marlow; it will be, Jim says, a means " 'to keep in touch with' . . . his voice sank suddenly to a murmur . . . 'with those whom, perhaps, I shall never see any more. With—with—you, for instance.' "

Marlow is "profoundly humbled by his words," and comments: "I felt a gratitude, an affection, for that straggler whose eyes had singled me out." The remark carries us back to their first meeting, and we realise what a long, intense, and difficult journey it has been. Now it is at an end. Once again Jim allows himself to wonder "When shall we meet next?", but Marlow firmly answers "Never—unless you come out" (335); and this time it is Marlow who avoids Jim's glance.

They shake hands, and Marlow boards the small boat that is to take him to the waiting schooner. Jim makes one last effort at sending a message back to the "outside world": " 'Tell them . . . ' he began." Marlow signs to the men to cease rowing, and waits "in wonder. Tell who?". Jim gives up: "No—nothing." Marlow is rowed out to his schooner, and from its deck sees Jim alone standing on the beach. The ship gathers headway, and Marlow sees Jim with "the stronghold of the night at his back, the sea at his feet, the opportunity by his side—still veiled."

Marlow then asks his auditors, "What do you say? Was it still veiled?" As for himself, Marlow says, "I don't know." Having placed this unresolved question in the forefront of the minds of the audience, Marlow's eyes watch Jim slowly fade out of sight: "The twilight was ebbing fast from the sky above his head, the strip of sand had sunk already under his feet, and he himself appeared no bigger than a child—then only a speck, a tiny white speck, that seemed to catch all the light left in a darkened world. . . . And, suddenly, I lost him."

In their early meetings Jim was naturally very unsure of where he stood with Marlow, and remained shy in his presence throughout; still, by the time of their last farewell there had been a number of occasions when Jim had managed to express his gratitude and affection in his own inarticulate way. Marlow, on the other hand, never really expressed his affection to Jim. This is partly because of the role Marlow has to play in their relationship; he must be the dull voice of the reality-principle and conventional morality; but there are other reasons. For one thing, as Thoreau said, "It is impossible to say all that we think, even to our truest Friend";[18] for another, there is Marlow's character to be taken account of. He usually gives the impression of being difficult, impatient, impersonal, and emotionally very reticent, even when he has no cause to be reserved. To the auditors of his narrative, for instance, all the explanations Marlow gives underplay the real feelings in his association with Jim: it is the result of mere chance, of curiosity, of a momentary emotional impulse, of his sense of responsibility, or of pity. "There was nothing but myself between him and the dark ocean. I had a sense of responsibility" (174) he says on one occasion; and on another: "I happened to be handy, and I happened to be touched. That's all there is to it" (223).

It is curious that our strongest sense of the depth of Marlow's feelings for Jim comes from the tone of many of his more general reflective passages, passages where Marlow seems so oblivious of his hearers that the writing produces an effect of soliloquy. There is, for instance, the peroration about going home, where Marlow imagines "the spirit of the land uprising above the white cliffs of Dover, to ask me what I—returning with no bones broken, so to speak—had done with my very young brother." The same tendency to be most direct about his feelings when he is thinking aloud is found in Marlow's final letter to the privileged friend about Jim's death: "At times it seems as though he must come in presently and tell the story in his own words. . . . It's difficult to believe he will never come. I shall never hear his voice again, nor shall I see his smooth tan-and-pink face with a white line on the forehead, and the youthful eyes darkened by excitement to a profound, unfathomable blue" (343).

The friendship of Jim and Marlow is not based on any particular mutuality of understanding or belief. Marlow never tells Jim that his interest in him began largely as a rather abstract moral puzzle; and he never persuades Jim to view his failure as a betrayal, not of himself but of human solidarity. The relationship in general very largely lacks the intellectual closeness or the other elements which are usually thought to constitute the basis of friendship. Marlow and Jim are neither soulmates like David and Jonathan, nor heroic comrades in arms like Roland and Oliver; and there is no question of one offering to sacrifice his life for the other, like Damon and Pythias or Orestes and Pylades. Many of the other standard features of friendship are also absent: there is no equality of age or status; and Marlow and Jim, far from being lifelong friends, do not spend a total of much more than a few weeks in each other's company.

Conrad's novel could hardly have been called "Charlie and Jim," but it is nevertheless the tale of a friendship. That friendship, how-

18. Henry David Thoreau, *A Week on the Concord and Merrimack Rivers* (New York, 1921), p. 209.

ever, is dominated by elements of separateness, incompleteness, and misunderstanding which are reflections not only of the personal idiosyncrasies of Jim and Marlow but of some of the characteristic social and intellectual divisions of the modern world.

The world of *Lord Jim* is a far cry from that of the much smaller, closer, and more leisurely societies which produced the classical patterns of heroic friendship in Greek epic and the Old Testament. In such warrior societies friendship is essentially a companionship between men who are the preeminent exponents of such virtues as courage, loyalty, and military prowess, which are the common ideals of the community as a whole. Jim and Marlow belong to a society whose scale and diversity are of a vastly greater magnitude, and where personal relations therefore tend to a much greater individual autonomy, and have very little continuity with the activities and values of the social order in general. It is true that the friendship of Marlow and Jim grows out of what are perhaps the two strongest and most universal forms of solidarity which remain in modern society: that of the occupational group, and that of the hierarchy of generations within it. But the depth of their friendship, as we have seen, largely depends on how each feels an internal conflict between his role as a member of a group and his inner self. In this their friendship is really a special case of a very general tendency in modern society for personal relations to begin on the basis of educational and occupational likeness, but to be transformed into a private intimacy which functions as an escape, an alternative, or even as a counterforce, to the public attitudes of their own group, and of society in general.

For Conrad, the question of how to live, in the simplest and most immediate occupational sense, was overwhelmingly important; at the same time, however, his consciousness of its demands sharpened his sense of individual separateness. Conrad's successive exposure to two national and two occupational allegiances had given a very special prominence to this contradiction between the public and the private; if he felt a deeper and more conscious commitment to solidarity, he also felt a deeper and more conscious resentment of its obligations. This contradiction is no doubt reflected in Marlow's continual and uneasy oscillations about his attitude to Jim, and in his somewhat surprising remark that "there is never time to say . . . the last word of our love, of our desire, faith, remorse, submission, revolt" (225). The same contradiction is found in what is most distinctive about Conrad's treatment of his characters and their personal relationships. The characters are intensely individual, but their consciousness is very largely determined by what they do in the world of work, and both their internal conflicts and their relationships with others are deeply and continually subject to the external and internal conditions imposed by collective human activities.

The friendship of Jim and Marlow is representative in this kind of way; it is not an intensification of the usual social or occupational relationships and values, but a private and even collusive alternative to them: to use Durkheim's terms, it is based not on individual likeness but on complementary needs; isolation, separateness, and conflict are the essential bases of its development, its intensity, and its meaning.

The closest literary analogy to the Marlow-Jim relationship is perhaps that portrayed in the oldest of surviving epics, the story of how a more than half divine Sumerian king, Gilgamesh, and a more than half animal man, Enkidu, become close friends. The initial differences between Marlow and Jim are much less, of course, but the development of their friendship is almost as surprising. Some of Marlow's narrative recalls Gilgamesh's threnody when Enkidu dies;[19] and if Jim does not, like Enkidu, come back from the underworld, he lives again and endures as an active presence in Marlow's imagination.

It is probably the sense of mutual need between two such disparate people which gives *Lord Jim* its special appeal. Among Conrad's novels, it is unique in having at its center so rewarding and touching a personal relationship; and this undertone of emotional warmth goes far to qualify the sadness of Jim's life and the gloom of Marlow's meditations. In many of his other works, Conrad's psychological and intellectual distance from the characters prevents us from feeling very deeply for them; our hearts do not go out very fully to Almayer, James Wait, or Kurtz, and if they do to Singleton or some of Conrad's later characters, it is with admiration rather than intimate emotional identification. In *Lord Jim* there is a more direct pattern of sympathy, both between Marlow and Jim, and between them and the reader. We see how a friendship can subsist despite great differences of age, temperament, and outlook; how there may be no deeper bond than the silent reciprocities of loneliness; how it doesn't matter that Jim has a "commonplace hand" (340) or a schoolboy banality of diction; and how the closest human communion may exist most intensely in no more than "the sound of a faint sigh that passed between us like the flight of a bird in the night" (130).

Yet another of the universal themes in *Lord Jim*, then, is that of the unequal and difficult friendship: and it is made very real because the vividness of Conrad's impressionist presentation of Jim and Marlow

19. See Alexander Heidel, *The Gilgamesh Epic and Old Testament Parallels* (Chicago, 1949), especially pp. 78–79.

has made us participate so deeply in its existential realities, realities
which are so distinctively representative of the difficulties and doubts
of the modern world; under some conditions, apparently even the
mysterious barriers to human understanding can strengthen personal
ties; as Marlow puts it: "The less I understood the more I was bound
to him in the name of that doubt which is the inseparable part of our
knowledge" (221).

It is perhaps the scepticism of Montaigne which gets nearest to
expressing the nature of the relationship between Marlow and Jim.
Montaigne confesses that, if pressed to explain his friendship with
Etienne de la Boétie, he can only reply: "Par ce que c'estoit luy; par ce
que c'estoit moy."[20] Because it was him; because it was me. In enacting
how Jim is Jim and Marlow Marlow, Conrad portrays a friendship
much closer to ordinary experience in the modern world than is to be
found in earlier fictional treatments of friendship; and this goes far to
explain why *Lord Jim* has become the cherished and enduring work it is.

v. The Ending

Critical discussion of the Patusan episode has largely concentrated
on Jim's state of mind in three periods of the narrative: during Marlow's visit; at the time of his dealings with Gentleman Brown; and
when the final catastrophe occurs. In all three cases Conrad's intentions have often been obscured by modern preconceptions.

Marlow's account of his month or so in Patusan is dominated by an
atmosphere of foreboding. The enclosing jungle, the Stygian river,
the general prevalence of dusk, obscurity, and shadow, compose a
dark backdrop against which Jim, "white from head to foot," (336)
stands out in "total and utter isolation" (272). Even Jim's three years
of fame, Marlow says, took their "tone from the stillness and gloom of
the land without a past, where his word was the one truth of every
passing day."

Jim's own consciousness also has its sombre undercurrents; although he tells Marlow that he is "satisfied . . . nearly" (306), he still
yearns to "frame a message to the impeccable world" (339). To some
extent, therefore, one must agree with the judgment of many of the
novel's best critics that Jim has not achieved "redemption"[1] or
"atonement"[2] in Patusan, nor "transcended the world of the *Patna*."[3]

20. "De L'Amitié," *Œuvres complètes* (Paris, 1962), p. 187.

1. Guerard writes that "the novel . . . asks us to decide whether Jim . . . is truly
redeemed" (*G*, 129).

2. The term is used by Robert E. Kuehn, in his introduction to *Twentieth-Century
Interpretations of Lord Jim: A Collection of Critical Essays* (Englewood Cliffs, N. J., 1969),
p. 12.

3. Tony Tanner, in his fine study *Conrad: Lord Jim* (London, 1963), p. 48.

But it is surely playing with loaded dice to apply such terms to *Lord Jim*. Neither the terms nor the assumptions underlying them would have been accepted as appropriate by Conrad, who firmly rejected the optimistic religious or transcendental assumptions which they imply. Conrad, like Marlow, is willing to settle for more relative and modest gains; and neither would expect much more than what has happened: that courage, work, and self-discipline have led Jim, not to apotheosis, but to feel "I am all right" (247).

It is in any case far from clear what "atonement" or "redemption" might mean in the secular world of *Lord Jim*. There is no one to whom Jim can make reparation for his desertion of the *Patna*, and he himself was, and remains, its chief victim. It is true that Jim, very humanly, had earlier hoped that he might begin again "with a clean slate" (185), but this was obviously unrealistic; as Marlow put it in the manuscript, "Once some potent event evokes before your eyes the invisible thing there is no way to make yourself blind again" (395). On Patusan Jim faces the truth that none of his triumphs can ever wipe the slate clean; there is always, he says, "the bally thing at the back of my head" (306). "The world outside," Jim confesses, "is enough to give me a fright . . . because I have not forgotten why I came here. Not yet!"

This inability to forget the *Patna*, however, will not seem to Jim's discredit to anyone who believes that the moral life depends, among other things, on treating our actions as in some sense permanent for ourselves and others. In any case, to wish otherwise would be to require Jim to accept the kind of celestial illusion on which the Intended relies in *Heart of Darkness*, and which, indeed, would have been needed to exorcise Jewel's continual terror that one day the outside world would rob her of Jim. Marlow knows very well that to kill such fears "you require . . . an enchanted and poisoned shaft dipped in a lie too subtle to be found on earth" (316); and to find that kind of deliverance, Marlow comments scornfully to his listeners, would be "An enterprise for a dream, my masters!"

The same ancient hunger for a magical transformation of reality has been at work in much of the psychological criticism of *Lord Jim;* it animates, for instance, such objections as that Jim fails to achieve full self-knowledge, that he is still "an outcast from himself . . . unable to recognize his own identity,"[4] or that he continues to exist in the "mist of self-deception" (*G*, 141). Here again there is evidence to support the charges; Marlow certainly says that Jim "was not clear to himself" (177); but he concedes that "I did not know so much more about myself" (221), and also makes the wider judgment that "no man

4. Dorothy Van Ghent, *The English Novel: Form and Function* (New York, 1953), p. 236.

ever understands quite his own artful dodges to escape from the grim shadow of self-knowledge" (80). Conrad's austere scepticism would probably have echoed Marlow's denials that complete self-knowledge is possible in this vale of tears; and the question therefore arises whether Jim, or indeed anyone, should be judged and found wanting by standards derived from the unsupported modern dogmas that full self-knowledge is possible and that it can deliver us from the ig-nominious fate of being what we are.

In general Conrad's novels suggest that he thought character was impervious to full comprehension; it was also nearly as intractable as circumstance, and equally unlikely to be transformed in accordance with our wishes. *Lord Jim* is not a *Bildungsroman*,[5] and it treats charac-ter from two resolutely sceptical points of view. Conrad's presentation of Jim is sceptical in the impressionist way, because he is portrayed almost entirely through Marlow, who has no privileged knowledge of the "real" person such as an omniscient author might have claimed. Secondly, Conrad's portrayal is sceptical morally, because it does not show any large transformation of Jim's character. Jim, like everyone else, no doubt dreams of salvation, but he must settle for being seasoned.

At that more modest level of improvement, Marlow has cause to be delighted; but Jim's essential nature is unchanged: his way of thought, his naïve romanticism, his ingenuous and boy-scoutish devotion to the importance of his role, his moody self-preoccupation—all these com-ponents of the old Jim are still there on Patusan; all that has changed is that they are no longer disabling; all that has been transformed, as Marlow nicely puts it, is that now "there was a high seriousness in his stammerings" (248).

For similar reasons it is surely a mistake to make too much of how Jim has lost his freedom and is in effect "possessed by this land of his dreams."[6] Jim has made his choice, and every choice has a price. All that can fairly be asked of him is that he should be clearsighted about the price; and this he surely is—taking his chance of drinking the rajah's coffee, which may be poisoned, making a fuss over disputes about turtles' eggs, and accepting all the other trivial annoyances of his daily routines. And in fact he is more than just satisfied with the result of his choice. "Now and then," Marlow reports, "a word, a sentence, would escape him that showed how deeply, how solemnly, he felt about that work which had given him the certitude of rehabili-

5. See Jerome Hamilton Buckley, *Season of Youth: The Bildungsroman from Dickens to Golding* (Cambridge, Mass., 1974), p. 18.

6. Tanner, *Lord Jim*, p. 47.

tation" (248). Earlier, as a seaman, "the perfect love of the work," had "eluded him" (10); Jim has now found a form of this love: Marlow reports that "he seemed to love the land and the people," although he adds the qualification that he loved it "with a sort of fierce egoism, with a contemptuous tenderness" (248).

The question is how seriously one must assess such reservations. Much has been made, for instance, of the damaging implications of Marlow's observation that "all his conquests, the trust, the fame, the friendships, the love—all these things that made him master had made him a captive, too." But this is not really a sign of Jim's failure; in the real world, such a captivity is surely an unanticipated but in practice inevitable result of assuming almost any responsibility—even that of literary criticism—seriously: the subjects are what they are, and make their own demands.

Many of the critics who take a severe view of Jim's failure to transform himself have centered their argument on his dealings with Gentleman Brown, the piratical ruffian who turns up in desperate straits and attempts to plunder Patusan. It has often been maintained that Jim is still psychologically crippled by an enduring sense of guilt, which leads him to identify unconsciously with Brown, and that this is why he lets Brown escape, thus bringing disaster upon himself and Patusan.[7] The various versions of this view, first put forward by Gustav Morf, and widely accepted—by Albert Guerard, for instance— argue that Jim's error is due to the "paralyzing" and "immobilizing bond" brought about by his unconscious identification with Brown (G, 150), that he "simply cannot resist the evil *because the evil is within himself.*"[8]

Marlow certainly stresses the moral intensity of their confrontation. On Brown's side the motives are conscious and very obvious. Brown, we are told, "hated Jim at first sight" (380), because he "seemed to belong to things he had in the very shaping of his life contemned and flouted." Jim provokes the ideological hatred of Brown, the lawless and cruel adventurer, because on Patusan Jim represents the established moral and social code; and on his deathbed Brown still exults in the thought that he had "paid out the stuck-up beggar" (344). When he first meets Jim, Brown tries to establish that they are equals, not only as English seamen but as criminals; he assumes that they both had to escape from civilisation for discreditable reasons, and that they are both in Patusan only in quest of "pretty pickings" (383).

As to Jim, he is certainly shaken when Brown implies that no one

7. By Bernard Meyer, for instance (*B C M*, 159–62).
8. Gustav Morf, *The Polish Heritage of Joseph Conrad*, pp. 157–58.

would immure himself in so isolated a spot unless he had something
to hide, and he completely loses his self-possession when Brown asserts that if "it came to saving one's life in the dark, one didn't care
who else went" (386). So Jim's consciousness of his own failure may
well have strengthened his wish to spare Brown's life; and he may
even have identified with Brown to the extent that he thought that,
like himself, Brown ought to be given another chance. Nevertheless,
the weight of the evidence is far from supporting the view that Jim
acted as he did out of guilt, whether conscious or unconscious, or that
any other decision was possible.

When Gentleman Brown arrives with fourteen of his armed followers in a longboat, he is able to gain a foothold in Patusan only because
Jim is absent, and the Rajah, Doramin, Dain Waris, and Jewel are
unable to act in concert. They decide to await Jim's return, and by
then only two choices remain: to give Brown "a clear road or else a
clear fight" (388). In a fight, Brown and his men would sell their lives
dearly—they have already inflicted six casualties; and so Jim, who
feels "responsible for every life in the land" (394), decides to let
Brown go. Realpolitik and local custom would no doubt dictate a
more ruthless policy; but—quite apart from the fact that Brown is his
countryman—everything that Jim stands for makes this alternative
impossible: the extermination in cold blood of any human being—
whatever their colour—would be morally offensive to anyone raised
in the Western and Christian tradition, even if he were not, like Jim,
the son of a parson; the decision, as Marlow sees it, ultimately involves
Jim's "truth" as against the "creed" of Patusan (393). There is also a
more idiosyncratic psychological reason: Jim has already shown that
he prefers to take great risks rather than shed blood—as when he
spared the three assassins who had been sent to kill him. In practical,
in moral, and in psychological terms, then, Jim had no real alternative
but to let Brown go, and whatever he may—consciously or
unconsciously—have thought or felt about Brown could hardly have
changed this.

Of course, Jim must take the blame, as anyone in charge must be
blamed, when things turn out badly; it is quite normal for him to be
criticised after the event. In objective terms, however, Jim was not
even seriously imprudent. It is true that the catastrophe would not
have occurred if Brown and his men had been disarmed; but Jim had
originally made this stipulation, and gave it up only when Brown
made it clear he would fight rather than surrender his arms. What
finally happened, the massacre of Dain Waris and his men, could not
have been predicted; no one could have foreseen the combination of
what Marlow calls Brown's "almost inconceivable egotism" (394),

which impels him to an otherwise pointless act of murderous revenge, with the "intense hate" (344) of Cornelius, who guides Brown to the backwater so that he can revenge himself indirectly against Jim, the man who has ousted him as Stein's representative.

There is, then, no reason to believe that Jim must have let Brown go out of guilt; but the question of guilt has a larger importance in the interpretation of Jim's character and fate. From the very beginning Jim puzzles and annoys Marlow largely because he apparently feels no guilt at having transgressed the mariner's code; what really matters to Jim is his personal failure to live up to his ego-ideal; and what he cannot bear is to face those who think that his real character is defined by his desertion of the *Patna*. Against such people Jim has only two reactions: to fight, or to blush. We see both reactions succeeding each other on his first meeting with Marlow: when Jim realises his mistake about the yellow cur, he is foiled of his unconscious need to relieve his feelings by giving Marlow "that hammering he was going to give me for rehabilitation" (74–75); instead, he blushes, and so deeply that "his ears became intensely crimson." Similarly, at the thoughts provoked by Brown's first question—"What made you come here?"—Jim gets "very red in the face" (381).

In both cases Jim's blushing is surely a sign not of guilt, but of shame. The nature of the distinction remains moderately obscure, partly because the word "guilt" is used in so many different ways; but it is usually agreed that shame is much more directly connected than guilt with the individual's failure to live up to his own ideal conception of himself. As Gerhart Piers puts it in his psychoanalytic treatment of the distinction: "Whereas guilt is generated whenever a boundary (set by the Super-Ego) is touched or transgressed, shame occurs when a goal (presented by the Ego-Ideal) is not being reached. It thus indicates a real 'shortcoming.' Guilt anxiety accompanies transgression; shame, failure."[9] Marlow characteristically judges Jim on the basis of guilt: "The idea obtrudes itself," Marlow comments, "that he made so much of his disgrace while it is the guilt alone that matters" (177). The case of Brierly establishes the contrast. Brierly characteristically sees Jim primarily as a "disgrace" because his basic standards of judgment for himself and others are based on shame; and it is the thought of possibly falling short of his own ideal, not of transgression as such, which drives him to suicide.

The wider psychological implications of shame have been suggested

9. Gerhart Piers and Milton B. Singer, *Shame and Guilt: A Psychoanalytic and a Cultural Study* (Springfield, Ill., 1953), p. 11. The second chapter of Helen Merrell Lynd's *On Shame and the Search for Identity* (New York, 1958) surveys literary as well as psychological views of shame.

by Max Scheler in terms which recall Stein's diagnosis of Jim. Scheler sees the origin of shame in the discrepancy between the individual's inward conception of himself and how his appearance and acts seem to others. As the most famous example of this disparity between man as a conscious spiritual being and man as an unreflective animal, Scheler cites the shame of Adam and Eve after the fall.[10] For Jim the equivalent crisis of self-knowledge presumably came after his jump from the *Patna;* and his intense suffering, as Stein saw, arose from his realisation of the disjunction between essence and existence, between his dreams and his act.

To return to Jim's motives with Gentleman Brown, it should be pointed out that Marlow does not see guilt as an explanation. When he emphasises Brown's "sickening suggestion of common guilt" (387), he is clearly referring to guilt in its sense of culpability for crime;[11] and in any case Marlow emphasises that Brown didn't as he thought, "turn Jim's soul inside out," because it was, Marlow affirms, "so utterly out of his reach" (385).

If we seek to explain the causes of the widespread assumption that Jim's decision to let Brown go, and therefore his death, were the product of his guilty identification with Brown, we must surely find them, not in the text, but in that strange Freudian mutation of the doctrine of original sin, which has now established as an *a priori* postulate that all errors are the result of unconscious guilt. This convenient moral melodrama enables us to retain two comforting beliefs: that the world is just; and that despite all contrary appearances people who suffer have only themselves to blame. These doctrines give us the pleasurable duty, as soon as we see Jim make a fateful error, to discover discreditable unconscious motives which prove that Jim deserved to be punished. Dorothy Van Ghent, for instance, compares the fates of Jim and Oedipus, and asks the question, "Is one guilty for circumstances?"[12] Through the privileged immunity to the complexities of other people's circumstances which is granted by a modern psychology, we can return the unhesitating verdict of "Guilty."

On hearing that Brown has massacred Dain Waris and his follow-

10. Max Scheler, *La Pudeur,* trans. M. Dupuy (Paris, 1952), pp. 10–12. It is interesting that in the manuscript Marlow assumes that in his original diagnosis Stein "generously refus(ed) to fasten upon the obvious guilt" as the immediate cause of Jim's troubles after the *Patna,* and chose instead to speak about the "as it were, abstract cause of suffering" (p. 426). By deleting the passage Conrad detached Stein from any connection with the idea that Jim was driven by guilt.

11. This is the only meaning of the nine uses of "guilt" and "guilty" listed in James W. Parins et. al., *A Concordance to Conrad's "Lord Jim"* (New York, 1976).

12. Van Ghent, *English Novel,* p. 239.

ers, Jim's first thought is to avenge their death: but when Tamb' Itam says that the people of Patusan have turned against him, Jim realises that this is out of the question. Three possible courses of action remain. If Jim is to keep Jewel and his followers with him, he must, like Brown, either fight or run. Both are hazardous; neither would benefit Patusan; fighting would cause much bloodshed; and escape might be a repetition of *Patna*. Jim's few, and rather oracular, answers to Jewel and Tamb' Itam make it clear that he does not choose to fight because "I have no life," and so "There is nothing to fight for" (412). As for escape, Marlow thinks that Jim soon resolved that "the dark powers should not rob him twice of his peace" (409).

The third possible course of action is to go to Doramin, and Marlow assumes that Jim decided on this almost at once; he would "defy the disaster in the only way it occurred to him such a disaster could be defied," and "conquer the fatal destiny itself." In making his choice Jim must have known that Doramin would want a life for a life—Jim's blood for that of his son, Dain Waris; and so Jim is in effect choosing a form of suicide. The mood in which Jim silently makes up his mind certainly suggests a defeated apathy somewhat similar to that which immobilised him on the *Patna*, and Marlow's comment on Jim's frame of mind then seems equally appropriate now: "The desire of peace waxes stronger as hope declines, till at last it conquers the very desire of life" (88). In the lifeboat Jim had wished for death partly out of revulsion from the defiling contact of the three other officers; and Cornelius and Brown are very like them in that they take the lowest possible view of life as egotistical survival. They represent what Tony Tanner has called the beetle view of the world; on this analogy, Jim's final choice is that of a butterfly who wants to fly above the earth-bound corruption which once again has fouled his life.[13]

Conrad, however, knew very well that a particular action could be psychologically complex and yet inevitable: Marlow's lie to the Intended is an example. Jim's mood of defeated self-withdrawal during his last hours need not in itself, therefore, invalidate the view that he really had very little choice except to go to Doramin; and it is surely Marlow's—and Conrad's—intention to make us feel that Jim's decision was inevitable. After all, it conforms to Jim's most explicit obligation, his formal promise to the people of Patusan that "he was ready to answer with his life for any harm that should come to them if the white men with beards were allowed to retire" (392). Great harm has come, and what Marlow calls "the sheer truthfulness of his last three years of life," that same truthfulness which had swayed Jim's people

13. *Lord Jim*, pp. 47–56.

when he argued them into letting Brown go, now demands that Jim should be ready to keep. his word and thus affirm his solidarity with those who had trusted him.

On the basis of its first four chapters, we would expect *Lord Jim* to be about the follies and the dangers of the simple human impulse to daydream about flattering romantic adventures. In his youth Conrad had shared the dream; but he began his career as a writer under something like the standard modern prescription—when fearful of self-exposure, take cover in irony: and so *Lord Jim* opens with a critical and sardonic view of its hero and his self-indulgent dreams. This negative attitude is increasingly qualified by sympathy during Marlow's narrative, but it does not wholly disappear until the Stein episode. There Jim is elevated to an unexpected metaphysical dignity; to have failed as an adventure-story hero is to become a symbol of the romantic world-view. On Patusan a paradoxical reversal occurs, and Jim becomes a genuine hero of romance. It is as though, having demonstrated that he knew the case against adventurous aspirations, Conrad had decided to try out a new fictional hypothesis. In the apt terms of Jean-Jacques Mayoux, "A romantic finds his bearings again in a romantic situation; a devotee of unreality is at least at ease in an unreal and fabulous world where his imaginings precede and create the events instead of being surprised by them."[14]

Conrad's reversal of his original fictional assumptions no doubt reflects a continuing personal irresolution. If *Lord Jim* is the most romantic of Conrad's works, it may be because he began it as a sad and affectionate farewell to an earlier self, but then discovered that the parting would be too painful unless he first granted that romantic self some of the satisfactions it had dreamed of long ago. This changed aim may have helped to impel the last part of *Lord Jim* towards other formal literary models, and in particular towards the very different traditions of romance and tragedy; both had been intermittently suggested earlier, but in Patusan romance becomes the dominant spirit until that of tragedy partly displaces it at the end.

Much of the action, the setting, the characters and the symbolism of Patusan suggest fable, fairy tale, and especially medieval romance. In Patusan, where "Romance had singled Jim for its own" (282), the land and its people "exist as if under an enchanter's wand" (330). Like a wandering knight, Jim arrives in an enchanted kingdom and there triumphs over incredible odds to deliver the people from their oppressors, notably Sherif Ali and his "infernal crew" (264). In addition,

14. *Vivants piliers*, p. 127.

just as his mentor Stein had been rewarded for his "innumerable exploits" with the hand of a princess, so Jim wins the hand of a persecuted maiden, Jewel; they come together, we are told, "under the shadow of a life's disaster, like knight and maiden meeting to exchange vows amongst haunted ruins" (312).

It can hardly be denied that such conventional elements of romance necessarily involve a marked falling off from the moral and dramatic intensity of the first part of *Lord Jim;* and this led F. R. Leavis to place *Lord Jim* among Conrad's minor works on the ground that "the romance that follows" the *Patna* episodes, "though plausibly offered as a continued exhibition of Jim's case, has no inevitability as that."[15] The continuity between Jim of the *Patna* and Tuan Jim of Patusan is certainly not one of complete inevitability. On the other hand, Conrad is remarkably successful in adjusting the formulae of romance to his very different fictional premises. This is evident, for instance, in the ingenuity with which the silver ring is used to bring about an ironic variation on the folk-tale motif of the poisoned gift, and thus to symbolise the transition from Jim's moment of glory to his fatal destiny.

The ring was given to Stein by Doramin, his old "war-comrade," as a token of "eternal friendship" (233). Stein gives it to Jim as his introduction to Doramin; and soon after his arrival in Patusan, when Jim is being pursued by his enemies, the ring becomes the magic emblem which causes Doramin to save his life and set him on the road of triumph. After that, however, the ring plays a less auspicious role. Jim sends it by messenger to Dain to vouch for his order that Brown be allowed safe-passage to the sea; it is then returned to Doramin with Dain's corpse; and the cycle of friendship and trust comes to an end when, as he rises to shoot Jim, the ring falls from Doramin's lap and rolls against Jim's foot. The talisman which had, first "opened . . . the door of fame, love, and success" (415) to Jim, now closes it forever.

This symbolic reversal is complemented by another. Doramin owns a pair of huge ebony and silver flintlock pistols which Stein gave him long ago in return for the ring. Stein, in turn, had received the pistols from his early benefactor in the Celebes, a Scot called Alexander M'Neil; and it is out of gratitude to him that Stein plans the reciprocal gesture of adopting a Briton, if not a Scot, and decides to make Jim his heir. The continuity of this cycle of trust and friendship is also broken when Doramin avenges the death of his only son; he does it by shooting Stein's adopted son with the gift his old friend had given him to seal their friendship.

15. *The Great Tradition*, p. 190.

Jim's romantic imagination has made him what he is; it has brought him to Patusan; and there his destiny is consummated with something of the spare and sudden brevity of Greek tragedy. This destiny, however, has been foreshadowed throughout the novel. The conflict between Jim and the world can never be appeased or resolved; and the unyielding determination with which he confronts it gives Jim something of the moral grandeur of the tragic hero. As Marlow puts it, Jim becomes an "individual in the forefront of his kind," because his problem is one where "the obscure truth involved" seems "momentous enough to affect mankind's conception of itself" (93).

In this respect also Patusan constitutes, not a new departure, but a concluding thematic variation. Jim thinks that he can at last be wholly isolated from the past; but in fact the *Patna* not only robs him of any inner peace, but also separates him from Patusan. No one there can understand Jim: neither his adoptive family—Doramin and his wife—nor his friend, Dain Waris, knows his secret; and when Jim tells Jewel the story of the *Patna*, "she did not believe him" (320). Jewel can only see the determining event of Jim's life as "an inexplicable and incomprehensible conspiracy to keep her for ever in the dark"; and when she asks him—"Has it got a face and a voice—this calamity?" (315), Marlow finally realises that, despite the touching closeness of Jim and Jewel, their unhappy pasts will always keep them apart, and that therefore "their two benighted lives" must be irremediably "tragic."

Jim cannot possibly reconcile all the just claims upon him. It is this intractability of moral circumstance which goes far to justify Robert B. Heilman's claim that "Jim is that rare creature in English fiction—the tragic hero."[16] Several other critics, including Dorothy Van Ghent, have also considered him in this light, although usually to arrive at a qualified dissent.

The problem of whether we should see *Lord Jim* as tragedy is largely a matter of what we understand by the term. If, following the common critical view, we take as our main criterion for tragedy the hero's achievement of self-knowledge, Jim does not qualify. Heilman, it is true, speaks of Jim's having to go through "the tragic course of knowing himself and thus learning the way to salvation"; but convincing evidence of Jim's final moral maturity is surely far to seek. Marlow comments during his Patusan visit that "It's extraordinary how very few signs of wear he showed" (269); and what continues to make Jim attractive is largely his youthful surface of imperviousness to fortune's frown. In any case, Marlow's most explicit judgment on the issue of

16. Introduction, Rinehart edition of *Lord Jim* (New York, 1957), p. xxiii.

Jim's self-knowledge runs completely counter to Heilman's view: Jim, Marlow says, "was overwhelmed by his own personality—the gift of that destiny which he had done his best to master" (341).

To postulate self-knowledge as a criterion of tragedy, however, may be yet another of the modern secularised versions of the consolations which religion offers in the face of suffering, waste, and evil. Certainly Heilman's assumption that self-knowledge leads to "salvation" might be taken as confirmation of this, and so might Dorothy Van Ghent's argument that what distinguishes Jim's death from the "atonement" of the exile of Orestes or Oedipus is that the expiation of Jim's blood-guilt brings about not the "restoration" but the "destruction" of "community health."[17] Much could be said in general against the Hegelian theory that tragedy is socially reconstructive; but even if it were true of Greek tragedy, it is surely evident that both the form and the substance of Lord Jim take a very different view of the relation between society and the individual. To adopt Van Ghent's terminology, Lord Jim, like the modern novel in general, assumes "the disintegration" of those very "moral bonds between men," which in classical tragedy are assumed to be the world's normative order.

In any case all the evidence suggests that the various Christian, Hegelian or Marxist theoretical systems which present suffering, conflict, or death as necessary parts of some promised transcendental recompense or dialectical reconciliation were, or would have been, completely alien to Conrad's way of looking at the world. That at one moment Marlow sees a "terrifying logic" (342) in the operation of Jim's destiny does not mean he sees it as part of an ultimately just or moral process; on the contrary, as Marlow suggests in connection with the Patna episode, Jim's fate may be as meaningless, accidental, and "devoid of importance as the flooding of an ant-heap" (93). Such a bleak perspective would not necessarily discount the view that Lord Jim is much closer to tragedy than most novels; but it would have to be tragic in other meanings of the term.

Another more archaic and less moralistic view of tragedy sees it primarily as the expression of humanity's awed astonishment at the works of fate, and more especially at its remorseless dealings with individuals who are far above the common run, not only in their position and achievements, but in the resolution with which they confront suffering and death. Such a reaction is expressed by one of the men of Patusan at the fate of Dain Waris: he is "struck with a great awe and wonder at the 'suddenness of men's fate, which hangs over their heads like a cloud charged with thunder' " (411). This feeling is

17. *English Novel*, pp. 232–33.

surely the essence of Marlow's own reaction to Jim's destiny; and
Conrad probably intended Jim's last act to leave the reader with a
sense not of pity but of a half-comprehending yet dazzled admiration
very similar to the awe which the death of the tragic hero inspires.

Many other views of tragedy see it not as the resolution but as the
culmination of conflict. Schopenhauer, for instance, saw the "purpose" of tragedy as "the description of the terrible side of
life . . . the wretchedness and misery of mankind, the triumph of
wickedness, the scornful mastery of chance, and the irretrievable fall
of the just and the innocent." Jim's state of mind before going to
Doramin is consistent with Schopenhauer's view of the tragic protagonist who eventually refuses to be deceived by "the phenomenon,
the veil of Maya," and whose "complete knowledge of the real nature
of the world, acting as a *quieter* of the will, produces resignation, the
giving up not merely of life, but of the whole will-to-live itself."
Schopenhauer also dismissed the "demand for so-called poetic justice" as "a dull, insipid, optimistic, Protestant-rationalistic, or really
Jewish view of the world." Jim's death would be tragic, in
Schopenhauer's view, not because it is just but because it is not; it
exemplifies "the guilt of existence itself," on which Schopenhauer
quotes the famous lines from Calderon's *La Vida es Sueño,* which Conrad also used, *"Pues el delito mayor / Del hombre es haber nacido"* ["For
man's greatest offence / Is that he has been born"].[18]

A somewhat similar, but much more general, view of tragic conflict
is that of Conrad's contemporary, Miguel de Unamuno, and it applies
to the central theme of *Lord Jim* as a whole. The moral perspective of
the three chief characters, Jim, Marlow, and Stein, is dominated by a
sense of inexorable contradiction: for Jim it is his preoccupation with
the intolerable discrepancy between what he has done and what he
would like to have done; for Marlow it is the distance between his faith
in solidarity and the apparently random and amoral meaninglessness
of the physical and social world; for Stein it is the radical disjunction
between the individual's ego-ideals and the world he struggles to
realise them in. All three of these irremediable disjunctions exemplify
what Unamuno called the tragic sense of life;[19] and Jim's struggles can

18. *World as Will and Representation*, vol. 1, pp. 252–54. Conrad used the couplet as
the epigraph of *An Outcast of the Islands.*

19. There are, of course, several differences between Unamuno's sense of the tragic
and Conrad's in *Lord Jim;* but there are also a good many similarities, beginning with
the general idea of a specifically Catholic kind of "transcendental pessimism" in the face
of the conflict, exemplified in Don Quixote, between reason and nature on the one
hand, and feeling and imagination on the other. The conclusion of Unamuno's first
formulation of the tragic sense of life recalls both Stein's view of Jim, and the frequent
burden of Conrad's own letters: "Man, by the very fact of . . . possessing consciousness,

be seen as embodying Unamuno's affirmation that, despite his awareness of foredoomed defeat, the individual should nevertheless, like
Don Quixote, live as though his faith were more real than any of
the negations by which reason and experience alike demonstrate its
futility.

Marlow exhibits a different, and later, phase of the same conflict.
The pathos of Jim's presence sends Marlow's memory back to the
defeated aspirations of his own youth; and this continual reminder is
complemented by Marlow's increasingly bitter awareness that the
code of solidarity is usually supported on grounds that are complacent or prudential, if they are not actually hypocritical; solidarity may
be only the code of those whom experience has brought into an un-
protesting conformity with the attitudes of their group. "The wisdom
of life," Marlow remarks ironically, "consists in putting out of sight all
the reminders of our folly, of our weakness, of our mortality" (174).
But Patusan exposes the triviality of such wisdom; there, Marlow
discovers, "the haggard utilitarian lies of our civilisation wither and
die" (282), and in their place is revealed to Marlow a world "that
seemed to wear a vast and dismal aspect of disorder" (313). Of course,
a more sheltered vision, Marlow sardonically reassures his com-
fortably established hearers, presents "in truth, thanks to our un-
wearied efforts . . . as sunny an arrangement of small conveniences as
the mind of man can conceive."

His desolate irony at modern Western civilisation as a system of
"small conveniences," is an indication not only of Marlow's tragic
sense of life in general, but of how his way of seeing Jim has been
transformed. The nature of this change is suggested in Marlow's letter to his privileged friend. The friend had argued that "we must fight
in the ranks or our lives don't count" (339), and that Jim's "kind of
thing" in Patusan could only be "endurable and enduring when based
on a firm conviction in the truth of ideas racially our own, in whose
name are established the order, the morality of an ethical progress."
Marlow replies that on this general position he can "affirm nothing,"
but that Jim's death forces him to wonder whether Jim, who "of all
mankind . . . had no dealings but with himself . . . at the last . . . had
not confessed to a faith mightier than the laws of order and progress."

Marlow does not name Jim's faith, but the immediate context makes
it clear that it belongs to a different and older phase of civilisation
than that of modern "order and progress." The only such faith that
has been mentioned in connection with Jim is Stein's diagnosis of him

---

is . . . a diseased animal. Consciousness is a disease" (Unamuno, *The Tragic Sense of Life*,
trans. Crawford Flitch [London, 1921], pp. 17–18. See also pp. 130–131, 294).

as romantic; but Marlow has earlier tended to equate "romantic" with
an unrealistic, irresponsible and self-indulgent placing of the individual self above social norms. This equation, however, hardly does justice to Jim on Patusan, as Marlow realises. When Jim repeats his
promise, "I shall be faithful," at their last parting, Marlow recalls
Stein's romantic injunction "To follow the dream, and again to follow
the dream—and so—always—*usque ad finem;*" and this leads Marlow
to conclude of Jim that "He was romantic, but none the less true"
(334).

If we seek to find an ancient ideal of individual behaviour which can
be called romantic, but which emphasises the obligation of being
"true" and "faithful," it is surely to be found in medieval romance,
which established both the word romantic and, long before, Europe's
most distinctive and enduring ideal of personal conduct. That ideal
has already been named, and given a kind of transcendental status, by
the French Lieutenant: "The honour . . . that is real—that is!" (148).

Honour is primarily associated, both in the chivalric romances and
in common parlance, with the fame earned by exceptional exploits.
Here Jim, who has filled Patusan "with the fame of his virtues" (243),
obviously qualifies. Serious doubts about his courage were raised by
the *Patna* episode; but Jim's going to face Doramin constitutes the
most dramatic refutation of the charge that on the *Patna* he had put
his life above his honour; and it is surely this which makes Marlow
believe that Jim's final act may have been "that supreme opportunity,
that last and satisfying test for which I had always suspected him to be
waiting" (339). Jim may once have jumped, but when the last test
comes he doesn't run away.

Jim's final act also gives him a supreme opportunity to embody two
of the other key values of knightly honour: friendship and keeping
faith. Jim's death is, in its way, an act of friendship for Dain Waris:
Roland must not survive his comrade-in-arms Oliver. In obeying his
pledge to Doramin, Jim is also implicitly keeping faith with Stein,
Doramin's sworn comrade. Of course, to keep faith with Dain Waris,
Doramin, and Stein, must entail betraying Jewel. Hers is the "jealous
love" which Marlow must have in mind when he gives his final verdict
on Jim: "We can see him, an obscure conqueror of fame, tearing
himself out of the arms of a jealous love at the sign, at the call of his
exalted egoism" (416). The "sign" and the "call" refer back to Jewel's
question about the nature of the mysterious power that would rob her
of Jim: "Will it be a sign—a call?" (315), she had asked Marlow. But
after Jim's death, when Jewel asserts that Jim "was false," Stein protests. "Not false! True! true! true!" (350).

The contradiction reflects how, although the code of honour, like that of solidarity, is based on approved social values, its more peremptory claims on the individual tend to convert it into a personal absolute, and thereby exalt it above all other obligations, whether public or private. It is their attitude to the claims of honour which makes Jewel and Stein see Jim's final choice differently. The depth of Jim's feeling for Jewel is not an issue: he "love[s] her dearly," and finds being "absolutely necessary" to her "wonderful" (304); the determining force, as Stein well understands, is the absolute nature of Jim's pledge. Jim obviously has this in mind when he says to Jewel that, if he were to respond to her appeal and flee Patusan, "I should not be worth having" (412). The argument is a commonplace in the literature of honour; as Richard Lovelace put it in "To Lucasta, Going to the Wars": "I could not love thee (Dear) so much / Loved I not honour more."

When Marlow refers to Jim's faith as "exalted egoism," he is in effect repeating the common Stoic and Christian objection to the code of honour, an objection repeated in such later political and ethical philosophies as those of Montesquieu, Rousseau, and Kant.[20] The basis of their objections is essentially that suggested by Marlow's statement that Jim "had no dealings but with himself": honour encourages a personal pride and self-sufficiency which leads the individual to put his primary trust in himself, instead of relying on divine grace, moral virtue, civic duty, or personal feeling.

That such charges can fairly be made against Jim, and against the code of honour in general, is incontestable; on the other hand, the gravity of the charges is not indisputable. It can be argued that contradictions arise when any theoretical system of behaviour is brought to the test of practice, and that, in "trying to save from the fire his idea of what his moral identity should be" (81), Jim is trying to save an identity which has clearly incorporated a loyalty to the Western ethical tradition. This is made clear in Jim's dealings with Brown. For instance, when Brown says "even a trapped rat can give a bite," Jim immediately answers, "Not if you don't go near the trap till the rat is dead" (381). It is clear that he knows very well what the safest course would be, but Jim would betray himself if he acted accordingly; the code of chivalric honour requires that an enemy should be treated with charity and as a human equal. So Jim asks "Will you promise to leave the coast?" (387). When Brown agrees, and then breaks his word, it is not Jim who is dishonoured, as he would have been had he gone against his conscience.

20. There is a schematic historical summary of philosophical attitudes to honour in L. Jeudon, *La Morale de l'honneur* (Paris, 1911), pp. 5–72.

His fatal generosity towards Brown is the climactic example of how, on Patusan, both Jim's romantic idealism and his rigid sense of personal honour have been shown to have a strong social and ethical component; and it is this component, rather than the "egoism and pride" of which Guerard speaks (*G*, 144), which is primarily responsible for the catastrophe. Jim's personal allegiance to the heroic ideal is only involved to the extent that, when all else is lost he prefers to die rather than to live on with the sense that he has broken his troth and thus—and this time consciously—betrayed his conception of himself.

When Marlow speaks of Jim's "pitiless wedding with a shadowy ideal of conduct" (416), the words "pitiless" and "shadowy" suggest that he has considerable reservations about the code of honour. In this Marlow reflects the whole modern intellectual and psychological outlook, which tends to see the code of honour as rigid, inhumane and retrograde; it suggests the stuffy and hypocritical moralism of the Victorian public school, as we are incidentally reminded in Jim's only use of the word—the old schoolboy oath of fidelity, "Honour bright" (269). Many features of Jim's character no doubt exemplify Hannah Arendt's view that the psychological effect of the British colonial system tended to "a certain conservation, or perhaps petrification, of boyhood *noblesse* which preserved *and* infantilized Western moral standards."[21] Conrad, however, would probably have regarded a degree of intellectual callowness as a price well worth paying in exchange for fixed principles of honour; and all the evidence suggests that he saw Jim's character in this perspective. In his preface to *The Red Badge of Courage,* for instance, Conrad discussed its hero in a way which applies quite closely to Jim's shame after the *Patna.* Crane's Young Soldier, Conrad writes, is "the symbol of all untried men"; his fear does not make "him a morbid case" because "the lot of the mass of mankind is to know fear"; and Conrad then specifies that he means "the decent fear of disgrace" (*L E*, 123). The fear of disgrace, in a somewhat different form, is also defended in the Author's Note to *Lord Jim.* There Conrad mentions that a lady had once objected to the novel as "morbid," and to this he retorts huffily that "no Latin temperament would have perceived anything morbid in the acute consciousness of lost honour" (ix). The ideal of honour, as Conrad here implies, tends to be Latin,[22] Catholic and communal, rather than Germanic, Protestant and individual; it is also distinctively masculine, noble and secular; all these are values to which Conrad had been predisposed by his national and family traditions. It can, indeed, be

---

21. *Origins of Totalitarianism,* p. 211.
22. See *Honour and Shame: The Values of a Mediterranean Society,* ed. J. G. Peristiany (London, 1966).

argued that Conrad's emphasis on solidarity essentially derives from a chivalric tradition of honour which had continued to animate the Polish nobility long after it had been replaced or transformed elsewhere.[23]

Lord Jim, indeed, reflects this by presenting a continuous confrontation between the exalted ideal of personal honour on the one hand, and the more modern, more widely applicable, but much more prosaic collective values of the code of solidarity on the other. In that conflict Conrad found himself siding more and more with his ancestral inheritance, and its ideal of individual honour; though possibly fated to isolation and failure in the modern world, it nevertheless possessed an unmediated directness of personal application, and a nostalgic heroic resonance, which Marlow's conception of solidarity was found to lack.

Lord Jim was André Gide's favourite among Conrad's novels, and it was its "despairing nobility" that he singled out for admiration. This gives a particular significance to a letter in which Gide told Conrad that if he were ever to write an article about him it would be to Alfred de Vigny and "to him alone, that I would wish to establish your kinship."[24] Like Conrad, Alfred de Vigny was a nobleman, a stoic, and a disillusioned romantic; both men combined deeply isolated natures with an emphasis on a collective ethic which had its roots in their careers of professional service—although in Vigny's case as an officer of the infantry rather than of the merchant navy. In the peroration of his *Souvenirs de servitude et grandeur militaire* (1835), Vigny wrote that honour was the only lamp still left "which keeps its vigil in us like the last lamp in a devastated temple."[25] The devastation was that caused by modern unbelief; but being a "purely human virtue that seems born from the earth," honour had outlasted all other creeds.

In some form, honour, and its corresponding human and artistic style, nobility, are timeless and indispensable values; and they continue to find exemplars or admirers even in the most relativist and sceptical climates of thought. Wallace Stevens once observed that "there is no element more conspicuously absent from contemporary poetry than nobility."[26] If the statement were extended to modern

23. See Najder, "Conrad and the Idea of Honor," in *Joseph Conrad: Theory and World Fiction* (Lubbock, Texas, 1974), pp. 103–14.

24. Ivo Vidan, "Thirteen Letters of André Gide to Joseph Conrad," *Studia Romanica et Anglica Zagrabiensia* 24 (1967): 163. The friendship of Conrad and Gide is analysed in Frederick Karl's "Conrad and Gide: A Relationship and a Correspondence," *Comparative Literature* 29 (1977): 148–71.

25. *Œuvres complètes* (Paris, 1948), vol. 2, p. 677.

26. "The Noble Rider and the Sound of Words," in *The Necessary Angel: Essays on Reality and the Imagination* (New York, 1951), p. 35.

fiction, Conrad, and especially *Lord Jim,* would be conspicuous exceptions. Jim does something which no other hero of a great twentieth-
century novel has done: he dies for his honour. His action embodies
Stein's dispiriting truth that "one thing alone can us from being ourselves cure!" (212); still, in his style of being cured, Jim implicitly
confirms Stein's view that although, unlike the creatures of nature,
man is not a masterpiece, by refusing to settle for less he can be
amazing.

Epilogue

By the time of his forty-third birthday on 3 December 1900, Conrad had cause for deep satisfaction. *Lord Jim* was selling well—after the first impression of 2,100 in October, a second, of 1,050, had already been called for (*B*, 116 n. 1); Conrad had also begun another novel, *Typhoon*, which was progressing so rapidly that it would be completed in the following month; and so if he looked back on the past few years, he must have seen that his life, surprisingly, was turning into a success story.

Conrad's career as a writer had started very late, when he was already thirty-eight years old; but his maturity of experience had rapidly found its expressive complement in a new and highly original kind of narrative technique. The subjects of his later works would continually change, and there would be countless variations in his fictional methods, but the essential nature of Conrad's literary and moral repertoire had been firmly established.

For instance, although the literary devices of symbolic deciphering and delayed decoding were never again used on the same scale as in *Lord Jim*, the impressionist and symbolic directions of his writing continued in other forms; Conrad's fiction was to remain dense with concrete images that impelled the reader's imagination to look for larger meanings. Conrad also continued to use his very idiosyncratic chronological method for a great variety of purposes. Its break with linear temporal progression in the order of the narrative ultimately reflects Conrad's sense of the fragmentary and elusive quality of individual experience. In its objective and externalised form, this sense controls much of the action in the later works; the random and the incomplete figures as largely in the plots of *Nostromo*, *The Secret Agent*, *Under Western Eyes*, *Chance*, and *Victory* as of *Lord Jim*. On the other hand, Conrad did not continue to develop the subjective aspect of the disjunction between the individual consciousness and everything outside it; or at least it was in the phase of intense experimentation which began in 1896 and ended in 1900 that Conrad was most deeply involved in presenting the obdurate incompatibility of the self and the world in which it exists.

This may be because the five novels which Conrad wrote in the nineteenth century are those which are most directly and recognisably concerned with his own personal experience. *The Nigger of the "Narcis-*

sus" is a distillation both of a particular voyage and of his whole life at sea; and the protagonists of Conrad's other early novels are either, like Marlow, fairly obvious embodiments of their creator, or at least are driven, like Almayer, Willems, and Jim, by some of his most pressing fears and aspirations. Of course, many of the characters, situations, and themes of the later novels are also projections of Conrad's spiritual biography: but the projections are normally much less direct, and play a less dominating part in the work as a whole. One very general biographical reason for the less personal nature of Conrad's fiction after 1900 may be surmised: it was in the early works that Conrad had drawn most directly upon his own experiences of disillusionment, isolation, and suffering; and after he had once painfully discovered his own ways of coming to imaginative terms with these experiences, there was no longer the need, and there could hardly be the wish, to do it again.

Still, the general nature of Conrad's moral outlook remained recognisably the same. It centres on how the individual's actions determine his character and his fate: on the one hand, a positive personal engagement in the common life can bring with it the development and the stability of the individual self; but there is also the negative form of the process where, as in the cases of Almayer or Kurtz, the individual's failure to move out of a self-enclosed egoism into some kind of larger commitment brings about his destruction. In the preface to *The Nigger of the "Narcissus"* Conrad had called this theme solidarity; subsequently he tended to use such terms as "fidelity" or "faithfulness," which allowed for a much wider range of private and individual commitments; nevertheless, the later novels reveal a continuing absorption in the imperative necessity, and the insoluble difficulty, of personal and social commitment.

Both the necessity and the difficulty surely reflect the combined effects of Conrad's national and family heritage and his own personal experience as an orphan and an exile. The great and difficult battle of Conrad's early maturity had been to escape the fate which Marlow had feared lay in wait for Jim: "Woe to the stragglers!" (223). Conrad had decided that "we exist only in so far as we hang together"; and the intensity of his preoccupation with solidarity, like his tendency to romanticise his life at sea, is surely the hunger of "a straggler yearning inconsolably for his humble place in the ranks." But, of course, it was not only that; like Stein, Conrad also knew that his sense of loss was not merely familial, social, and national; alienation was a much more universal condition, and one with deep roots in the romantic imagination, and all the echoing dissonances of his civilisation.

It is largely Conrad's tragic awareness of the reciprocal but conflicting demands of the individual and of society which makes his fiction seem so modern today. But his modernity has other, and more purely literary, reasons. It has been argued that the idea of an artistic *avant garde* only established itself in the last quarter of the nineteenth century.[1] These were Conrad's formative years, and in some sense Conrad was a member of that first *avant garde:* he was a friend or acquaintance of many of its English members, notably Ford and Arthur Symons; he knew the work of the French *avant garde* writers, from Baudelaire and Flaubert on; and both in his own eyes and those of his contemporary critics his subjects and methods were distinctively modern.

But Conrad's literary modernity is just as idiosyncratic and divided as his moral vision. Conrad belonged to no coterie; he seems to have had no interest in experiment for its own sake; and in his fiction, far from flaunting his differences in taste and attitude from mankind at large, he often attempted to appear more affirmative and conformist than he really was. There were, no doubt, many motives underlying this attempt, including Conrad's economic need to widen his circle of readers; and the wish to be popular certainly had some adverse effects on Conrad's writing. At the same time, it was precisely because he attempted to write for a larger audience, and steadily kept his distance from the *avant garde* in its hot pursuit of literary, social, and ethical innovation, that Conrad was able to express the problems of his own time and of ours with a much more inclusive and penetrating understanding than his contemporaries.

Conrad's modernity is most evident in *Heart of Darkness* and *Lord Jim,* the works which have received the most critical attention in the last few decades. That the works which Conrad wrote during the reign of Queen Victoria should have been his most modern is a paradox which can be explained on various grounds; but the decisive factor, it may be hazarded, was that he was closer to the personal experiences which had formed his view of the world. Conrad may be said to have inherited much of his modernity—perhaps his post-modernity—from his Polish past. It had given him a vision of life which was to remain relatively uncommon for writers in the West until much later; in a solitude that was not merely exile Conrad had extracted from his inheritance of loss and alienation a deep understanding of the need for moral resistance and affirmation, a need whose subsequent topicality neither he nor his contemporaries could possibly have imagined.

1. By Renato Poggioli, *The Theory of the Avant-Garde,* trans. Gerald Fitzgerald (Cambridge, Mass., 1968), p. 17.

Index